reasons
{for Faith}

reasons
{for Faith}

Philosophy IN THE SERVICE OF Theology

K. SCOTT OLIPHINT

P U B L I S H I N G

P.O. BOX 817 • PHILLIPSBURG • NEW JERSEY 08865-0817

Page design and typesetting by Lakeside Design Plus

Printed in the United States of America

Library of Congress Cataloging-in-Publication Data
Oliphint, K. Scott, 1955–
    Reasons for faith : philosophy in the service of theology / K. Scott Oliphint.
      p. cm.
    Includes bibliographical references (p.   ) and index.
    ISBN-10: 0-87552-645-4 (paper)
    ISBN-13: 978-0-87552-645-4 (paper)
    1. Apologetics. 2. Christianity—Philosophy. I. Title.

BT1103.O46 2006
261.5'1—dc22

                                           2006041566

To

Arthur Johnson,
Christian philosopher

Contents

Contents

Preface

This book has a number of goals in view. It is, first and foremost, an apologetic. As such it seeks to set forth and commend a Christian approach to thinking philosophically. There are, it seems to me, two general aspects involved in any apologetic. The first aspect is the defensive one; it involves "destroy[ing] strongholds . . . and every lofty opinion raised against the knowledge of God" (2 Cor. 10:5). This book will not concentrate on this first aspect primarily because, as we will see, there is no significant body of knowledge that is taken to be universally true with respect to the subject matter of philosophy. Surely the fact that a discipline such as philosophy has had a few millennia to define itself, and has thus far not been successful, is reason enough to set forth a positive commendation for another approach to the discipline itself. So, the defensive aspect of apologetics will have less emphasis here.

It should be noted here—*and this is all-important*—that there are glaring exceptions in the history of philosophy, and currently, to the philosophical trends critiqued herein. It is surely *not the case* that philosophy is always or intrinsically opposed to biblical Christianity. One of the reasons for setting forth the position in the coming pages is the supposition that philosophy and Christianity can, *and do*, in some cases, happily and consistently coexist, each informing and helping the other.

ix

The other aspect of apologetics is the offensive one. With this aspect the emphasis is on commending the Christian position (in the context of the failure of other positions) not simply as a plausible alternative, but as the consistent, cogent, and altogether reasonable position that is able to offer solutions to the problems posed. It is not simply consistent, cogent, and reasonable *for Christians*, but because Christianity is true—and true in its affirmations of God and the world—it is the only consistent, cogent, and reasonable position to hold.[1] Thus, the apologetic approach of Cornelius Van Til is between every line of the pages that follow.

Citations and references to the work of Van Til, however, are few. Nevertheless, his fingerprint is on every page. I could not have written anything here had his influence not been profoundly present in my wrestling with the issues that follow. They are issues, nevertheless, that Van Til himself, for perfectly good reasons, never worked through in any detail. The attempt here, therefore, is to bring Van Til's Reformed thinking into contemporary discussions in philosophy and philosophy of religion. Since apologetics has always had to reckon with natural theology (which is just the old term for philosophy of religion), this work is meant to stand firmly in that tradition.

One of the more encouraging developments in Reformed theology in the last few decades, in large part thanks to the work of Richard Muller, is the revival of interest in the Protestant scholasticism of the seventeenth century. Thought in the past (by Karl Barth and others) to be rationalistic and contrary to Calvin and the "spirit" of the Reformation, the Reformed scholastics, in the main, were carrying on—while deepening and enriching—that same theology which was so instrumental in marking the Reformation of the sixteenth century, as Muller and others have demonstrated convincingly.

While the substance of the following material was developed independently, the reader will notice at strategic points references

---

1. As we will see later, to be reasonable is to be in conformity to, as well as subservient to, God's revelation. Any position lacking such conformity and subservience is, *ipso facto*, unreasonable.

to such scholastic material for purposes of support. Happily, the methodological and epistemological consistency of a Reformed apologetic was applied and demonstrated in much, if not most, of the concerns and responses of the Reformed orthodox in the seventeenth century. The reader may also notice that such material is monumentally useful for dealing with present-day concerns and problems in philosophy of religion. In citing the Protestant scholastics, we are attempting to point out a large and substantial tradition in Protestant theological history, disagreement with which places the burden of proof squarely on the one disagreeing, and not on that tradition. Given the sheer intellectual weight of their work, no disagreement with them should be taken seriously that does not at the same time provide direct refutation of the exegesis and, following on that, the theology that is the sum and substance of that work.[2]

My hope is also that Christians who are philosophers, or who are aspiring to be, will be convinced that their endeavors philosophical can be conducted only on the basis of the *principia* of Reformed orthodoxy. Francis Turretin's warning is as relevant now as it was then:[3] we must not allow our great love of philosophy so to captivate us that we become all too ready to abandon our theology for the sake of philosophical acumen or academic respectability.

That said, it will be obvious to the reader that there are other major influences in the material set forth here. The genius of Thomas Aquinas, though not always friendly to Reformed orthodoxy, is at times employed in significant ways. This is as it should be. Surely a theologian of his caliber, who himself was interested in setting forth a Christian philosophy, cannot be overlooked simply because some of what he said is hostile to Reformed theology. Our hope in this regard is that the dirty bath water has been discarded, but that the baby remains securely in place.

2. A question left unanswered here is to what extent the *methodological* and *episte-mological* concerns of Old Princeton were in line with that of the seventeenth-century Reformed. It may be that, because of fundamental philosophical influences at Old Princeton, the *principia* of Protestant scholasticism—and, as I would argue, of Van Til—were eclipsed.

3. See the discussion below for Turretin's analysis.

There is in the chapters that follow significant discussion of and interaction with Alvin Plantinga and his ideas. The influence of Plantinga in philosophy and philosophy of religion is enormous. In 1980, *Time* magazine called Alvin Plantinga "America's leading orthodox Protestant philosopher of God." Philosophy in the previous generation was dominated almost exclusively by atheists and agnostics. This was in large measure due to the influence of positivism on the philosophical terrain. Plantinga himself notes, "When I left graduate school in 1957 there were few Christian philosophers in the United States, and even fewer Christian philosophers willing to identify themselves as such." Why was that the case? Primarily because positivism with its "Verifiability Criterion of Meaning" had hegemonic influence. And, as most who look back on that period note, Christians were by and large either jumping on the positivistic bandwagon or fearful of positivism's conclusions.

We can learn something from history here. One of the questions that I occasionally get from some students who have either studied philosophy or read a bit in it is, "What will Christianity do in the postmodern era?" or "How can we be relevant; how can we even be 'players' in the game, now that postmodernism has gained ascendancy?" The answer is twofold.

First, Scripture seems clear that whatever false philosophy is currently in vogue, it is, nevertheless, decidedly *not* the central position in its adherent's heart and mind. It is, as a matter of fact, a secondary, deceptive, subservient, subordinate, and altogether unsatisfactory position (the genesis of which, as we will see, is the suppression of the truth known). We should remember that.

The second thing follows from the first. Since it is a dependent and altogether unsatisfactory philosophy, it will soon be eliminated and replaced by yet another unsatisfactory philosophy, like all the rest historically. So postmodernism may be all the rage now, but it will so quickly become passé (even as it already has in some quarters) that it will be as irrelevant in a few years as positivism is to us today.

It seems that such was the case through the sixties and most of the seventies. Philosophy's skepticism toward religion generally and Christianity specifically had won the day. Plantinga, however, was instrumental in changing that. Kelly Clark lists two watershed events that contributed to that change, and Plantinga is front and center in both of them. First is the formation of the Society of Christian Philosophers in 1978. Begun by Plantinga, together with George Mavrodes, Arthur Holmes, William Alston, and Robert and Marilyn Adams, this society became, as Clark puts it, "the largest single interest group among American philosophers" and has well over twelve hundred members.

Notable also is the presentation of Plantinga's inaugural address as the John O'Brien Professor of Philosophy in 1983, entitled "Advice to Christian Philosophers." This address has perhaps had more influence on Christians' doing philosophy than any other in the latter part of the last century. Plantinga begins:

> My aim, in this talk, is to give some advice to philosophers who are Christians. And although my advice is directed specifically to Christian philosophers, it is relevant to all philosophers who believe in God, whether Christian, Jewish or Moslem. I propose to give some advice to the Christian or theistic philosophical community: some advice relevant to the situation in which in fact we find ourselves. "Who are you," you say, "to give the rest of us advice?" That's a good question to which one doesn't know the answer: I shall ignore it. My counsel can be summed up on two connected suggestions, along with a codicil. First, Christian philosophers and Christian intellectuals generally must display more autonomy—more independence of the rest of the philosophical world. Second, Christian philosophers must display more integrity—integrity in the sense of integral wholeness, or oneness, or unity, being all of one piece. Perhaps "integrality" would be the better word here. And necessary to these two is a third: Christian courage, or boldness, or strength, or perhaps Christian self-confidence. We Christian philosophers must display more faith, more trust in the Lord; we must put on the whole armor of God.[4]

This is good—one could even say *essential*—advice for Christian philosophers. Plantinga continues:

4. Alvin Plantinga, *The Analytic Theist: A Collection of Alvin Plantinga's Work in Philosophy of Religion*, ed. James F. Sennett (Grand Rapids, MI: Eerdmans, 1998), 297.

Christian philosophers . . . are the philosophers of the Christian community; and it is part of their task as *Christian* philosophers to serve the Christian community. But the Christian community has its own questions, its own concerns, its own topics for investigation, its own agenda and its own research program. Christian philosophers ought not merely take their inspiration from what's going on at Princeton or Berkeley or Harvard, attractive and scintillating as that may be; for perhaps those questions and topics are not the ones, or not the only ones, they should be thinking about as the philosophers of the Christian community. There are other philosophical topics the Christian community must work at, and other topics the Christian community must work at philosophically. And obviously, Christian philosophers are the ones who must do the philosophical work involved. If they devote their best efforts to the topics fashionable to the non-Christian philosophical world, they will neglect a crucial and central part of their task as Christian philosophers. What is needed here is more independence, more autonomy with respect to the projects and concerns of the non-theistic philosophical world.[5]

It is for this reason, at least, that Plantinga deserves the credit and attention that he currently enjoys in philosophical circles generally, and in philosophy of religion circles more specifically. Our interaction with Plantinga will be both appreciative and critical. Any critique, however, should not in any way undermine or obfuscate his plea given above. To state what should be obvious, Christian philosophers must be about the task of *Christian* philosophy.

Thus my goals are (1) to set forth a theological structure, for epistemology and metaphysics, that shows the relevance of Reformed thought, centrally set forth in Van Til's works, to current discussions in philosophy and philosophy of religion (natural theology); (2) to demonstrate that Reformed thought has already broached virtually every discussion now in play in philosophy of religion; and (3) to interact with (at least some of) the main proponents in philosophy of religion.

5. Ibid., 298.

There is another goal in view as well. I hope to advance the discussion with respect to philosophy and philosophy of religion. I will try to show that, given what we know of God (through his revelation), there is a *Christian* way to approach the topics in such philosophy. A Christian approach will have Christ as its central and essential element. Thus, bare theism will inevitably be off the mark with respect to a Christian approach to philosophy.

A couple of personal remarks before we begin: First, special thanks to Allan Fisher and to P&R Publishing Company. There are certain ideas, concepts, and proposals that have been ruled out of bounds by many, if not most, evangelical publishers. I would be remiss if I did not recognize the ministry P&R has had in this regard. Their history has modeled what a Christian publishing house should be.

Second, I tend to wince when I read authors who routinely refer readers to their own works. In that regard, I'll likely wince when I read this work. To clarify, however, this work is meant to be a kind of "third step" in apologetics. It is meant to build on *The Battle Belongs to the Lord* and *Revelation and Reason*.[6] The ideas and concepts in those works are foundational to what is written in this one. Thus, I do reference those works on occasion, and others where relevant, rather than repeat what was said in them. I hope those references do not read like crass self-promotion.

Thanks to my colleagues Bill Edgar, Dick Gaffin, and Lane Tipton for their helpful comments on this manuscript. Thanks also to Oliver Crisp, Bill Davis, Paul Helseth, Esther Meek, David Reiter, and R. T. de Velde for constructive analysis, most of which I have attempted to address. Thanks finally to Cynthia Nielsen and Jared Oliphint for helpful suggestions along the way.

---

6. *The Battle Belongs to the Lord: The Power of Scripture for Defending Our Faith* (Phillipsburg, NJ: P&R, 2003); K. Scott Oliphint and Lane G. Tipton, eds., *Revelation and Reason: New Essays in Reformed Apologetics* (Phillipsburg, NJ: P&R, forthcoming).

Introduction and Survey

Reasons of Faith

*The Scriptural teaching concerning God's infinite and spiri-
tual essence ought to be enough, not only to banish popular
delusions, but also to refute the subtleties of secular philosophy.*
—JOHN CALVIN

R easons of Faith"—the two terms themselves (so far, "of" has
remained relatively free from the fires of controversy) spark
passions and debates, from past to present, that cause contenders
quickly to choose sides and to profess allegiances.[1] The reaction
is due, in part, to the subject matter under scrutiny when these
words appear together.

Just what do we mean when we use the terms *faith* and *reason*
together? The literature is not abundantly clear, and there remains
some confusion regarding the answer to that question. One promi-

1. For the best collection of historical material on the faith/reason debate, see Paul
Helm, *Faith and Reason*, Oxford Readers (Oxford: Oxford University Press, 1999).

nent description of the relationship between the two is the following (we'll call it *FR*):[2]

> [FR] The major theistic traditions draw a distinction between religious truths that can be discovered and even known by unaided human reason and those to which humans have access only through a special divine disclosure or revelation. According to Aquinas, e.g., the existence of God and some things about the divine nature can be proved by unaided human reason, but such distinctively Christian doctrines as the Trinity and Incarnation cannot be thus proved and are known to humans only because God has revealed them.[3]

Perhaps *FR* will suffice for now as a general description of the relationship of faith and reason. When discussing *faith*, what we primarily refer to is any truth, or belief in a truth, that is beyond the ability of reason to prove. When we use the term *reason*, we refer to any truth, or belief in a truth, that is or can be known without the aid of any source external to it. As noted, *FR* itself finds its focus in the genius of Thomas Aquinas.

For example, according to Thomas, "there are some truths [about God] which the natural reason . . . is able to reach."[4] If that is the case, then it is assumed that natural reason can infer certain truths about the true God without the aid of faith and outside the context of regeneration. In this case, a universal use and application of reason is available to all without discrimination, by which we can prove God's existence and perhaps some aspects of his character.

What role, then, does faith play in such a construal? As indicated in *FR*, faith is the means by which we believe truths (of Christianity) that are beyond reason's pale. "Some truths about God exceed

2. To simplify, from here on, *FR* will include the notion that there are religious truths known by unaided reason and other religious truths known only by revelation.

3. Robert Audi, *The Cambridge Dictionary of Philosophy* (Cambridge: Cambridge University Press, 1995), 607.

4. Thomas Aquinas, *Summa Contra Gentiles*, trans. Anton C. Pegis (Notre Dame, IN: Notre Dame University Press, 1957), 1:63.

all the ability of the human reason. Such is the truth that God is triune."[5]

It is this general structure, a structure articulated in *FR* above, that has formed one of the primary (perhaps even the predominant) contexts in which the terms *faith* and *reason* have been discussed.[6] In order to see more clearly the tension between the two, we need first to review a little history.

Reforming Reason

The view of *FR*, historically speaking, ought not be seen as the only approach to the debate between faith and reason. It is certainly the case, as noted above, that Thomas Aquinas set out the general parameters of *FR*. Thus there are a few centuries of historical precedent for its tenets. But we should not think that we can draw a straight line from Thomas's view to present discussions, as if there has been historical uniformity with regard to the debate. The fly in the ointment of continuity between Thomas and present discussions is the intervention of Reformed thought. The Reformation brought with it, not only a reform in theological thinking per se, but a reform in the way in which theology relates to philosophy, and thus in the way in which we think about the relationship of faith to reason.

In his *Institutes*, Calvin sets up for us, and for theology since his time, a framework in which to discuss theology—the so-called *duplex cognitio Dei*, or the twofold knowledge of God: knowledge of God the Creator and knowledge of God the Redeemer. Within this *duplex*, Calvin discusses some of the ways in which we have knowledge of God the Creator. For example, Calvin begins book

---

5. Ibid.

6. This is not exactly true. The faith/reason discussion, in the context of Christianity, goes all the way back to the ancient church and is prominent in such figures as Justin Martyr, Tertullian, and especially Augustine. It also plays a key role in the theology and philosophy of Anselm. In order to avoid the entire history of the discussion, however, we begin with Thomas because it was in him that the debate seems to have its historical epicenter.

1, chapter 3 of the *Institutes* with a consideration of the *sensus divinitatis*. He begins:

> There is within the human mind, and indeed by natural instinct, an awareness of divinity [*divinitatis sensum*]. This we take to be beyond controversy. To prevent anyone from taking refuge in the pretense of ignorance, God himself has implanted in all men a certain understanding of his divine majesty. Ever renewing its memory, he repeatedly sheds fresh drops.[7]

Further on he says:

> Men of sound judgment will always be sure that a sense of divinity which can never be effaced is engraved upon men's minds. Indeed the perversity of the impious, who though they struggle furiously are unable to extricate themselves from the fear of God, is abundant testimony that this conviction, namely, that there is some God, is naturally inborn in all, and is fixed deep within, as it were in the very marrow. . . . I only say that though the stupid hardness in their minds, which the impious eagerly conjure up to reject God, wastes away, yet the sense of divinity, which they greatly wished to have extinguished, thrives and presently burgeons. From this we conclude that it is not a doctrine that must first be learned in school, but one of which each of us is master from his mother's womb and which nature itself permits no one to forget, although many strive with every nerve to this end.[8]

Consistent with this discussion in Calvin, Peter Martyr Vermigli (1500–1565) produced the most extended treatment and explanation of natural theology (which, as we will see, is now called philosophy of religion) during the Reformation period. Though Vermigli was trained in the Thomistic tradition (e.g., one of his teachers was Juan Valdes of Spain), in his *Loci Communes* (posthumously published in 1563) his theological focus is more Reformed than

7. John Calvin, *Institutes of the Christian Religion*, ed. John T. McNeill, trans. Ford Lewis Battles, Library of Christian Classics (London: SCM, 1960), 1.3.1.

8. Ibid., 1.3.3. More on the *sensus divinitatis* and its relationship to epistemology later.

Roman. He denies, for example, Thomas's *analogia entis*, in which Thomas sought to show that there was a metaphysical coincidence between the being of God and the being of everything else. Vermigli held that God was "other than men" in the nature of his simplicity, goodness, righteousness, wisdom, and so forth.[9] Because of this view of God, Vermigli did not think it possible to understand who God is simply by applying the tools of the mind. God was of a different order of being than anything else. So, the only way truly to learn of him and of his creation was by way of God's revelation. Thus, a true natural theology could only be constructed within the context and confines of faith, which alone is able to understand and grasp God's revelation.

For Vermigli, then, natural theology had significant theological limits. This is, as we will see, important with respect to the doctrine of God per se, as well as for apologetics. Regarding the doctrine of God, Vermigli notes that the purely philosophical doctrine of God as Creator is at best marginally useful since to know God rightly one must have faith.

Vermigli went on to develop an important distinction in the context of the discussions of natural theology, a distinction that follows Calvin's discussions. There were, according to Vermigli, two kinds of knowledge of God that rightly belong under the rubric of natural theology. There is, first of all, what we might call the *implanted* knowledge of God—what theologians called the *cognitio insita*. This was knowledge that God himself *implanted* or *inserted* into each creature made in his image. The second kind of knowledge of God was called the *cognitio acquisita*, the acquired knowledge of God.[10]

9. Richard A. Muller, *Post-Reformation Reformed Dogmatics: Prolegomena to Theology* (Grand Rapids, MI: Baker, 1987), 172.

10. Francis Turretin (1623–87) was very obviously dependent on Vermigli at this point. He notes as well that there are two aspects to natural theology: "The orthodox, on the contrary, uniformly teach that there is a natural theology, partly innate (derived from the book of conscience by means of common notions) and partly acquired (drawn from the book of creatures discursively)." Francis Turretin, *Institutes of Elenctic Theology*, ed. James T. Dennison Jr., trans. George Musgrave Giger, 3 vols. (Phillipsburg, NJ: P&R, 1992–97), 1:6.

It is important to understand in this regard that, with respect to the *cognitio insita*, Vermigli, Turretin, and others wanted to distance themselves from the standard philosophical notions of "innate knowledge," on the one hand, and a kind of *tabula rasa*, on the other. Philosophically speaking, the idea of "innate" knowledge, particularly after Descartes, carried with it a notion of autonomy. That which was innate was thought to be ours simply by nature, without regard to any Author of nature who might have given such a knowledge to us. At the same time, a *tabula rasa* understanding of our minds would render men with an excuse in their standing before God. That would be in direct conflict with what Paul says in Romans 1 and 2.[11]

The emphasis among most of the Reformed during the sixteenth and into the seventeenth centuries was that this *cognitio insita* was present in us because of who *God* is, and what *he* had done.[12] It was not defined as in any way autonomous (though some would call it innate); it was only there because God had given it. As given, it was knowledge that was intuitive, immediate, non-ratiocinative in its apprehension of God.

We should realize, however, that this Reformed distinction, as explicated in Calvin and others, has been obscured by the forces of the Enlightenment,[13] which began to change the terms of this discussion altogether. The change of terms with regard to natural theology was brought about because of the Enlightenment's insistence on autonomous reason.

11. Note Turretin: "The mind of man is a *tabula rasa* not absolutely, but relatively as to discursion and dianoetical knowledge (which is acquired necessarily by inferring one thing from another); but not as to apprehensive and intuitive knowledge. For even according to Paul, the work of the law is in such a manner written in the hearts of the Gentiles that they do by nature the things contained in the law." Ibid., 1:9.

12. For a modern, clear presentation of the distinction between implanted and acquired knowledge of God, see Herman Bavinck, *Reformed Dogmatics: God and Creation*, ed. John Bolt, trans. John Vriend (Grand Rapids, MI: Baker, 2004), 59–91.

13. By "the" Enlightenment here, I simply mean to include what some have called the "Age of Reason," beginning roughly around the eighteenth century, and having many precursors and many contours. The primary aspect of the Enlightenment—its focus and emphasis on the power and magisterial place of reason—is the central aspect of any of its permutations and is our primary concern here. See Jonathan Irvine Israel, *Radical Enlightenment: Philosophy and the Making of Modernity, 1650–1750* (Oxford: Oxford University Press, 2001).

According to Richard Muller, from the mid-eighteenth century on, with the influence of Christian Wolff (1679–1754) and others, reason, even among some in the Reformed orthodox tradition, was thought to be the *principium cognoscendi theologiae*—or the foundation of knowledge for theology—such that natural theology and related notions began to be defined differently than they were just a few decades earlier. Under the influence of Enlightenment thinking:

> Natural theology could be viewed as the basic theology upon which a system could be built and to which certain revealed but rationally explicable data could be added. This idea of reason as the foundation of theology becomes the normative view of [some] eighteenth-century Reformed writers. . . . The presence of this rationalistic perspective in eighteenth-century theology, therefore, marks the end of genuine Reformed orthodoxy, at least in those systems that adopt it as the basic perspective for theological formulation.[14]

It was the influence of rationalism, which has its focus in the Enlightenment, that served to undermine Reformed orthodoxy generally and to change the categories of the debates on faith and reason. The Enlightenment, therefore, resulted in a loss, not an advance, of orthodox theology.

Though the focus of the debate about natural theology prior to the Enlightenment centered on the relationship of the *cognitio insita* and the *cognitio acquisita*, part of the problem with the debate since the Enlightenment is that there has been some confusion about the meaning of natural theology itself.

The Enlightenment influence has caused some to reformulate the terms of natural theology. It has caused some to understand that, while there may be a *cognitio insita*, in which we all have some inkling of a divine Creator, there is also and more importantly (for natural theology) a *cognitio acquisita*, which employs natural reason

---

14. Richard A. Muller, *Post-Reformation Reformed Dogmatics: The Rise and Development of Reformed Orthodoxy, Ca. 1520 to Ca. 1725: The Divine Essence and Attributes*, 2nd ed. (Grand Rapids, MI: Baker, 2002), 192–93.

to ascertain the existence and perhaps something of the character of a god. Thus, *FR* above, as well as apologetics since the mid-eighteenth century, and, as we will see, the concerns of philosophy of religion, have their focus in an Enlightenment reinterpretation of the *cognitio acquisita*, a reinterpretation that seeks to ground such knowledge, not in revelation, but in reason alone.

Because of that focus, it has been tempting for some to read Calvin's discussion in book 1 of the *Institutes* (on the knowledge of God the Creator) as making a clear distinction between the *cognitio insita* and the *cognitio acquisita*. Some have been tempted to think that the *cognitio insita*, whatever its use, plays a minimal role in natural theology, while the *cognitio acquisita* becomes the focus and content of developing a theology—based on reason—from nature alone, without the aid of special revelation. Specifically, just to use one example, Edward Dowey in his work *The Knowledge of God in Calvin's Theology* reads Calvin as developing a distinction between the *sensus divinitatis*, on the one hand, and our experience of the world, on the other, a distinction that corresponds to the two different kinds of knowledge, *insita* and *acquisita*, respectively.

Thus, although the *sensus divinitatis* may be implanted within us, our experience of the world is that "on the basis of which," says Dowey, "the mind of man says 'therefore' with respect to God."[15] A post-Enlightenment read of Calvin, therefore, would want to see, for example, Calvin's *Institutes* 1.3 (and 1.4) as dealing specifically with the *cognitio insita* and 1.5 as dealing with the *cognitio acquisita*. It seems, however, that this reading of Calvin is suspect.

In the quotations from Calvin above, in which he discusses the *sensus divinitatis*, Calvin is treating the knowledge of God as *implanted* in us. Some would conclude that this is his *only* concern in this chapter. Some would say that Calvin has clearly in his mind at this point *only* the *cognitio insita*. But, in this same context and chapter, he says this: "Since, therefore, men one and all perceive that there is a God and that he is their Maker, they are condemned

---

15. Edward A. Dowey, *The Knowledge of God in Calvin's Theology*, expended ed. (Grand Rapids, MI: Eerdmans, 1994), 74.

by their own testimony because they have failed to honor him and to consecrate their lives to his will."[16] This notion of a "perception of God" is typically reserved for discussions of the *cognitio acquisita*. So, for Calvin to interject it here would be unnatural if what he had in mind were a clear distinction between the *implanted* knowledge of God, on the one hand, and the *acquired* knowledge of God, on the other.

In chapter 5, he does make a distinction between the *kinds* of knowledge of God: "Lest anyone . . . be excluded from access to happiness, he not only sowed in men's minds that seed of religion of which we have spoken but revealed himself and daily discloses himself in the whole workmanship of the universe. As a consequence, men cannot open their eyes without being compelled to see him."[17]

It might be thought, as Dowey implies, that since Calvin makes a distinction here between that which God implants and that which he reveals through his works, then the way to God through the revelation *in his works* is by the right use of reason. The way to discover God in his works is by using reason properly. So the task of natural theology (or philosophy of religion), as well as the task of apologetics, is in using those works to reason toward a *cognitio acquisita*.

It is instructive, however, to notice again Calvin's language in the *Institutes* 1.5. Speaking of the revelation of God through his works, he says, "Upon his individual works he has engraved unmistakable marks of his glory, so clear and so prominent that even unlettered and stupid folk cannot plead the excuse of ignorance."[18] And later he says:

> There are innumerable evidences both in heaven and on earth that declare his wonderful wisdom; not only those more recondite matters for the closer observation of which astronomy, medicine, and all natural science are intended, but also those which thrust themselves upon the sight of even the most untutored and

16. Calvin, *Institutes*, 1.3.1.
17. Ibid., 1.5.1.
18. Ibid.

ignorant persons, *so that they cannot open their eyes without being compelled to witness them.*[19]

This sounds more like a kind of immediate awareness than a process of discursive reasoning. Calvin adds, "How detestable, I ask you, is this madness: that man, finding God in his body and soul a hundred times, on this very pretense of excellence denies that there is a God?"[20]

There seems to be no way legitimately to distinguish between God's revelation implanted in us and that revelation that comes through our experience of the world. In both cases, the knowledge of God is given to us by God, and it is given to us in such a way that it is clearly seen, understood, and thus it renders us without excuse before him.

It seems altogether likely, therefore, as we compare *FR* above with our glance at Reformed theological discussions on these matters, that current contexts of debate on the place of faith and reason have been wide of the mark since the Enlightenment. There has been, since roughly the eighteenth century, an underlying assumption of reason's capability to know God on its own ("unaided reason"), an assumption that is at odds with Reformed orthodoxy.

It is the categories of Reformed orthodoxy prior to the Enlightenment, therefore, that give us better clarity in our discussion of faith and reason. Given those pre-Enlightenment categories, both the *cognitio insita* and the *cognitio acquisita* were elements of natural theology, but—and this is all-important—natural theology itself was defined in terms of its relationship to faith.

In other words, a distinction developed after (and based on) Calvin with respect to natural theology between two *kinds* of natural theology—a distinction that was obscured and virtually erased after the Enlightenment. The distinction was between a *theologia vera* (true theology) and a *theologia falsa* (false theology). The former, *theologia vera*, was also referred to as *theologia naturalis regenetorum* (natural theology on the basis of regeneration). That

19. Ibid., 1.5.2, my emphasis.
20. Ibid., 1.5.4.

is, natural theology could *only* be true theology if developed by and in the context of the regenerate (faith), since only then would it be based on God's revelation in Scripture.[21]

Unbelievers, on the other hand, must inevitably develop a *theologia falsa* since they will always and by nature twist and pervert the knowledge of God given both within them and without them. This is the case because reason does not have the ability in and of itself to ascertain truth with respect to God and his existence. It must be governed by faith. So, says Calvin, "Hence it appears that if men were taught only by nature, they would hold to nothing certain or solid or clear-cut, but would be so tied to confused principles as to worship an unknown god."[22]

From Theology to Philosophy

In our now "enlightened" context, the terms *faith* and *reason*, when discussed together, fall under the rubric of philosophy of religion. As was mentioned, this is terminology used to designate an old, old task, that of *natural theology*. So, with respect to the tasks philosophy sets for itself, *philosophy of religion* is fairly new terminology. That is, it is a subset of philosophy, coined toward the end of the eighteenth century as a substitute phrase for what used to be called natural theology.[23]

21. See Muller, *The Divine Essence and Attributes*, 180ff.

22. Calvin, *Institutes*, 1.5.12. Note also Calvin's comments on Acts 17:28: "And though so soon as they begin to think upon God, they vanish away in wicked inventions, and so pure seed doth degenerate into corruptions; yet the first general knowledge of God doth nevertheless remain still in them. After this sort, no man of a sound mind can doubt to apply that unto the true God which we read in Virgil touching the reigned and false joy, that All things are full of Jove. Yea, when Virgil meant to express the power of God, through error he put in a wrong name." John Calvin, *The Comprehensive John Calvin Collection*, CD-ROM (The Ages Digital Library System, 2002). As we will see later, Paul's use of pagan poets is not because those poets got it right, for surely Aratus's reference to Jupiter renders the statement false, but rather was because Paul knew the statement to be a product of the suppression of the truth.

23. We should note here that, generally speaking, natural theology reaches all the way back from the pagan gods of Old Testament times through to the present pagan religions. In the West, natural theology can be seen as far back as the fourth century BC, during which time philosophers began to speculate on the unifying principle of the universe,

During the beginning stages of these philosophical investigations in the West, the more common term initially used was *natural philosophy* (since there was no categorical distinction made, as is the case now, between matter and spirit). Natural philosophy sought to discover, through nature and the use of reason, the one unifying principle of life and of everything else. Later on, philosophers and theologians of the medieval period labeled this kind of endeavor, *metaphysics*, or *wisdom*, or *holy teaching*, or just *theology*.

The fact of the matter is that philosophy of religion, as a subfield of philosophy, became established as an academic specialty because philosophy as a whole was no longer engaged with questions about God or about religious beliefs about God. Though the actual discussion of the issues with which philosophy of religion deals—issues such as the existence and nature of God, faith and reason, miracles, death and immortality, and so on—has in the last few decades moved more to the center of philosophical debate, particularly in the analytic tradition of philosophy, the "subset" mentality still persists and is likely here to stay.

By the late eighteenth century, philosophy of religion was thought to consist of a set of questions, inquiries, theories, or truths that were both accessible to philosophy and helpful to or even needful for Christianity. The phrase itself was popularized in part by John Caird (1820–98), in his book *An Introduction to the Philosophy of Religion* (1880).[24] To help us understand the concerns of philosophy of religion we may look briefly at Caird.

Caird hoped to use absolute idealism to defend Christianity. Absolute idealism, in its various forms, sought to transcend the experiential world to some "thing" that would make sense of those experiences. Caird's book, which was influenced to a great extent by Hegel, in many ways clarified the agenda of philosophy of religion to the present day. Caird begins:

---

ascribing to that principle attributes of immutability, indivisibility, unity, transcendence, goodness, and so on.

24. Caird was one of the proponents of absolute idealism, a view on which Cornelius Van Til was a renowned expert and which he sought, from the time of his dissertation onwards, to refute.

A Philosophy of Religion starts with the presupposition that religion and religious ideas can be taken out of the domain of feeling or practical experience and made objects of scientific reflection. It implies that, whilst religion and philosophy have the same objects, the attitude of the human spirit towards these objects is, in each case, different. In the one they are present to it in an immediate way as objects of devotion or spiritual enjoyment; they come before it at most only in the form of outward fact or of figurative representation. In the other, they become the objects of reflection or intellectual apprehension, and are finally elevated to the form of pure or speculative thought.[25]

Caird goes on to argue that, while "feeling" is a kind of knowledge, any knowledge worthy of the name must pass out of the immediacy of the sensible world and enter "that colder yet loftier region in which reason opposes itself to its object, breaks up the natural harmony wherein no contradiction of thought has yet betrayed itself, and advances to the search after a deeper and indissoluble unity."[26]

In a statement that seems to identify philosophy with religion, Caird goes on to assert that "the peculiar domain of philosophy is absolute truth."[27] One of the interesting points about Caird's contention for a philosophy of religion is his understanding of the nature of philosophy with respect to religion: "According to this view, then, there is no province of human experience, there is nothing in the whole realm of reality, which lies beyond the domain of philosophy, or to which philosophical investigation does not extend."[28] Then Caird asks:

> But can this high claim of philosophy be justified? Before we yield ourselves up to its guidance, must not philosophy be asked

25. John Caird, *An Introduction to the Philosophy of Religion*, The Croall Lectures; 1878–79 (Glasgow: J. Maclehose, 1880), 1.

26. Ibid., 2. One will notice similarities here to Dooyeweerd's *Gegenstand* relation. See Herman Dooyeweerd, *A New Critique of Theoretical Thought*, ed. William S. Young, trans. David H. Freeman (Nutley, NJ: Presbyterian and Reformed, 1969).

27. Caird, *Philosophy of Religion*, 3.

28. Ibid., 5.

15

to prove that there is nothing presumptuous in this assertion of its universal authority? Before we admit the pretensions of reason to treat thus of all things in heaven and earth, to regard nothing as too high or sacred to be subjected to its inquiries, must we not, as a preliminary condition, ask it to give us satisfactory proof of its capacity to deal with them?

It may be answered, in general, that the only way in which philosophy *can* prove its rights is by philosophising. The capacity or incapacity of reason to deal with any object or class of objects cannot be determined by a preliminary inquiry, for this, if for no other reason, that the inquiry could only be conducted by the faculty which is impugned. *If the incapacity is asserted on external authority, it is only reason itself that can judge of that authority and pronounce on its claims.*[29]

This, of course, brings up the age-old question of the relationship of philosophy to theology, a question to which we will turn shortly. It should be noted for our purposes here, however, that, according to Caird, it is the province and domain of reason to pronounce on its own capacity to judge authoritatively. This, as we will see, is in part what brings discussions of faith and reason to fever pitch. Before we ask about the truth of Caird's bold statement, let me attempt to clarify.

How does *FR* relate to Caird's pronouncement that it is up to reason to judge of its own legitimacy and of faith's? To put Caird's comment above in its best light, Caird seems to be thinking of reason simply as a faculty, a tool that is used in any and all thinking, conceiving, and similar acts. As a faculty, then, reason is a *sine qua non* of *all* thinking, even thinking about faith and reason. *FR*, however, seems not to be referring to such all-inclusive categories, but rather sees reason as a mode of truth- and/or belief-acquisition.[30]

So which is it? Is reason simply the faculty that pervades every conscious moment, or is it more specifically a mode of acquiring truth? For our purposes, it is best to see the terms of the faith/reason

29. Ibid., 4, emphasis mine.
30. From here on, we'll use notions of truth and belief as synonyms, recognizing that the two are quite distinct in reality.

debate as best described in *FR*, though Caird's analysis cannot be far from the center of the discussion either. Suffice it to say, at this point, that *FR* is and remains, generally speaking, the common view among philosophers of religion (and whatever natural theologians there might be) today.

The Contemporary Context

Perhaps an example or two from the contemporary scene will help set the agenda for our discussion in chapters to come. The current controversy over faith versus reason could be summarized in one word—*evidence*. Whatever position one takes or has taken with regard to the relationship of faith to reason will be determined, centrally, by the way in which one thinks about evidence generally and, more specifically, the way in which one thinks about evidence relative to faith.

For example, the history of the controversy surrounding natural theology has to do primarily with the way in which one thinks about evidence for the existence of God. The question is *not*, we should note, whether one thinks there are, or are not, evidences for God's existence. It is, rather, just exactly how one construes the notion of evidence itself with respect to God's existence.

Before setting those options out, they should both be seen against the backdrop of what has been called the "evidential objection to belief in God." This objection claims, in its milder forms, that it is irrational or somehow unacceptable to believe in God except on the basis of evidence of some kind. In its stronger form, the objection claims that, given that there is no evidence for belief in God, to hold such a belief is to embrace a falsehood. How might one respond to this objection? Generally speaking, there seem to be two options available.

In response to the evidential objection, one view would attempt to demonstrate by way of syllogistic or evidential proof that the existence of God is properly concluded from evidential premises that we all can accept. So, for example, Thomas Aquinas's famous "five ways" seeks to prove the existence of God, as well as his unity, from universally accepted or acceptable premises—premises such as, "Everything moved is moved by another."[31] This is a premise, surely, that anyone with eyes to see and a mind to think should have no trouble affirming.

But there is another side to the current debate (a helpful thing to have in debates). There is a side that seeks to answer the evidential objection, not on the basis of universally accepted premises, but on the basis of what might be called an "acceptability thesis." An acceptability thesis obtains when any position seeks to argue for the rationality of (in this case) belief in God on the basis of something other than universally acknowledged premises. One can readily see how this latter view would be more at home in a postmodern world and culture. An acceptability thesis, by definition, argues for the acceptability of a belief, not because such a belief has attached to it any kind of universal obligation, as if all *ought* to believe, but because, given something peculiar to one's own situation, or context, or personal story, it is perfectly proper to believe such a thing. Because, in part, of its conducive character to the current culture, the acceptability thesis has become the most predominant response to the evidential objection.[32]

The acceptability thesis comes in two main varieties. The first variety is sometimes called "Wittgensteinian fideism," owing to its dependence on Wittgenstein's notion of "language games." For example, in his essay, "The Groundlessness of Belief,"[33] Norman Malcolm argues that one's belief in God, because it is embedded in religion, which is its own "form of life," needs no more justification than does science, which itself is another form of life. This does not, of course, mean that *if* one believes in God, then God does in fact exist. It only means that one's belief in God, since it needs no ground, is perfectly acceptable within its own context. Says Malcolm, "The obsessive concern with the proofs reveals the

---

31. This is one way that Thomas seeks to prove God's existence. See Aquinas, *Summa Contra Gentiles*, 1:85f.

32. It is probably more accurate to say that the wide *acceptability* of the acceptability thesis is due in part to the culture in which it is presented. It is certainly not the case that many offering such a thesis are doing so because of the culture.

33. Norman Malcolm, "The Groundlessness of Belief," in *Philosophy of Religion: An Anthology.* 4th ed., ed. Louis P. Pojman (Belmont, CA: Wadsworth, 2003), 391–99.

assumption that in order for religious belief to be intellectually respectable it *ought* to have a rational justification [evidence]. *That* is the misunderstanding. It is like the idea that we are not justified in relying on memory until memory has been proved reliable."[34] Our belief in God, therefore, to put it in Wittgensteinian terminology, is just one part of our religious "language game" and thus is justified by virtue of what it is.

Alvin Plantinga has taken similar tenets of Wittgenstein's and Malcolm's but has situated them differently in order to argue for the same conclusion. The response to the evidential objection is not (or at least need not be) to answer the objection on its own terms. Rather, we may respond by reminding the evidential objector that, contrary to his own basic tenet, we all hold other beliefs that are not in need of evidence in order to be deemed rational or justified. In other words, the evidential objector has, and must have, beliefs that are assumed to be rational and (in that sense) justified even though there has yet to be a good argument for them—beliefs such as "I had an orange for breakfast this morning," or "I did not begin to exist just five minutes ago," or "I, like you, am a person." Surely, if we all have beliefs for which there are no evidential arguments, and if we can have and hold those beliefs rationally, then a belief in the existence of God is perfectly acceptable (though there may be no evidence available for such a belief) if I so choose to believe such a thing.[35]

In the first response to the evidential objection, it is assumed that reason is not in need of faith in order to make its case against that objection. In the second response, it is assumed that belief (or faith) carries, in some way, its own warrant-conditions with it; it is acceptable because of what it, itself, *is* in the context of its own peculiar function.

So, the discussion concerning faith and reason, in its current context, has to do with arguments of acceptability with regard to

34. Ibid., 397.

35. This has been the primary thrust of Plantinga's epistemological development (of which more later) since the late sixties. See Alvin Plantinga, *God and Other Minds: A Study of the Rational Justification of Belief in God* (Ithaca, NY: Cornell University Press, 1972).

beliefs or truths that are either beyond (in Malcolm's case) or, perhaps, beside (in Plantinga's case) other beliefs or truths we might accept or believe to be rationally acceptable. The relationship of faith to reason, then, is determined according to the status of "faith-truths" rather than, as in times past, according to the status of reason and its inherent abilities.

2

Reason Reformed

Ectypal theology is the wisdom of divine things given concep-
tual form by God, on the basis of the archetypal image of him-
self through the communication of Grace for his own glory.
—Junius

But how *should* Christians think about this relationship of faith
to reason? What is faith's role with respect to standard rules
of thinking? How might we think about reason and its abilities?
And how would that affect the way we think about the philosophy
of religion? To the first question first.

Reason within Faith

If we think of reason as a necessary and necessarily useful tool
for all of our thinking, the natural question is, What is its proper
use with respect to our knowledge? Just as a hammer, though well
fitted for its proper use, is ill-equipped to tighten a screw, so also

reason is ill-equipped to perform any function for which it is not intended. What, then, is the proper use of reason in reference to faith, that is, to the truth given in Christianity?[1]

First, it is reason's task to judge the consistency and coherence of biblical truth. Not only so, but reason is to function as a judge of what is contradictory and what is not. Having said that, I should clarify that our reason is only able to function in this capacity after it has been restored and renewed by the grace of God. "Thus the judgment of contradiction as to a perfectly blind reason is dangerous when the judgment is formed from corrupt principles," wrote Turretin. "But we speak of enlightened reason giving its decisions from the word."[2]

This does not mean that reason is the final arbiter of what is possible and what is impossible—a point to be remembered in coming chapters. This seems to have been Cornelius Van Til's primary concern with respect to the law of contradiction:

> It is therefore pointless for Christians to tell non-Christians that Christianity is "in accord with the law of contradiction" unless they explain what they mean by this. For the non-Christian will take this statement to mean something entirely different from what the Christian ought to mean by it. The non-Christian does not believe in creation. Therefore, for him the law of contradiction is, like all other laws, something that does not find its ultimate source in the creative activity of God. Accordingly, the non-Christian will seek to do by means of the law of contradiction what the Christian has done for him by God. For the Christian, God legislates as to what is possible and what is impossible for man. For the non-Christian, man determines this for himself. Either positively or negatively the non-Christian will determine the field of possibility and therewith the stream of history by means of the law of contradiction.[3]

1. We will follow Turretin's discussion on the proper use of reason in theology. See Francis Turretin, *Institutes of Elenctic Theology*, ed. James T. Dennison Jr., trans. George Musgrave Giger, 3 vols. (Phillipsburg, NJ: P&R, 1992–97), 1:32ff.

2. Ibid., 1:33.

3. Cornelius Van Til, *The Works of Cornelius Van Til*, CD-ROM (New York: Labels Army Co., 1997). The more than eight hundred references to the law of contradiction in

This means, second, (as was affirmed in Reformed orthodoxy) that reason always functions as a servant, never as a master, to theology. Its proper place with respect to theology is to provide whatever tools might be helpful for theology to carry out its own task.[4] It also means that the law of contradiction, and the use of that law, can never finally determine whether or not a particular Christian doctrine is true. *That* determination is left to revelation. What reason can do is help theology to organize, articulate, and expand its truths in such a way as to clarify their meaning. Turretin explains:

> Although the judgment of contradiction is allowed to reason in matters of faith, it does not follow that the human intellect becomes the rule of divine power (as if God could not do more things than human reason can conceive). God's being able to do something above nature and human conception (which is said with truth in Eph. 3:20) is different from his being able to do something contrary to nature and the principles of natural religion (which is most false).[5]

Van Til's works show the overwhelming consensus of his thought to be simply that such a law must be grounded in God's creative activity and is justified on the basis of that activity alone. So overwhelming is this point in Van Til that I found only one quotation in which he seems to undermine the role of logic. Note: "Faith abhors the really contradictory; to maintain the really contradictory is to deny God. Faith adores the apparently contradictory; to adore the apparently contradictory is to adore God as one's creator and final interpreter." Here Van Til is not using the notion of "contradictory" in a formal and technical sense, but rather—as the context from which this quotation is taken suggests (i.e., the will of God in his decree)—he is thinking more broadly of compatibility.

Furthermore, Van Til does not argue that those outside the faith are, *ipso facto*, illogical. He is concerned to make the apologetic point that one can ask an unbeliever as to the possibility of logic itself, given that an unbeliever's own view of the world will serve to refute any notion of law and consistency altogether. Note also Turretin: "Nor is the power of God in this manner limited by the rule of our intellect, but our mind judges from the word what (according to the nature of a thing established by God) may be called possible or impossible." Turretin, *Institutes*, 1:34.

4. For more on this relationship, see chapter 5.

5. Turretin, *Institutes*, 1:34. It may be that Turretin gave a bit too much away when attempting to assign to reason its proper place. Thus, an argument could be made that Turretin may have paved the way for some of the errors of the Enlightenment with regard to the faith/reason debates. His central point, however, that reason must submit itself to revelation, is without question the driving force of his exposition. See Richard A. Muller,

Third, and following on the point just made, the law of contradiction's service to theology is *not* in matters of interpretation per se, but rather in the organization and articulation of our interpretations. As Turretin notes, given the Reformation principle of *sola Scriptura*, interpretation of Scripture is given to us by way of other Scriptures. We do not need another external source in order to compare and bring together the truth as God has given it to us in his Word.

> The judgment of contradiction belongs to reason . . . with conformity to Scripture itself which clearly interprets itself and requires no other interpreter to establish its sense. Thus reason enlightened by the Holy Spirit through the word is able to consider and to judge from the word (according to the rules of good and necessary consequence) how the parts of a doctrine cohere, and what may or may not follow from them.[6]

Given these truths—that (regenerate) reason is to judge of the consistency of doctrine, that reason is never to take a magisterial role with respect to theology, and that reason is to help articulate and organize our interpretations of Scripture—the next question has to do with the relationship, not of *reason* to theology, but, more specifically, of *philosophy* to theology.

Philosophy as Minister

So how do we go about understanding the relationship of philosophy to theology? One way to go about it would be to set out the general *subject matter* of each discipline. What is the subject matter of theology? The primary subject matter of theology is God's revelation, both in creation and in his Word.

What, then, is the subject matter of philosophy? Most philosophers would hold that anything and everything is the subject matter

---

Post-Reformation Reformed Dogmatics: The Rise and Development of Reformed Orthodoxy, Ca. 1520 to Ca. 1725: The Divine Essence and Attributes, 2nd ed. (Grand Rapids, MI: Baker, 2002), 192f.

6. Turretin, *Institutes*, 1:33.

of philosophy. From the minutest particle to the nature of being itself, philosophy sees its domain as extending universally.

So it may be best to think of theology and philosophy in terms of the historical notion of *principia*. The word *principium*, at least historically, is the Latin translation of the Greek word *archē*, which means "source," or "cause," or "foundation." It is that which gives something its *reason* to be, or its justification for existence. Under this rubric distinctions have been made between a *principium essendi* and a *principium cognoscendi*.[7] There are essential principles, reasons, or sources; and there are epistemological principles, reasons, or sources.

The question as to the differences between philosophy and theology will revolve around the answers to the questions of philosophy's and theology's *principia*. What is philosophy's *principium cognoscendi* (principle of knowledge)? That, of course, depends on whom you ask. Someone may say that philosophy's *principium cognoscendi* is reason itself. Without reason's asking and answering questions there could be no philosophy at all. This was Caird's understanding, as we saw in chapter 1, and would likely be the understanding of most of philosophy in one form or another.

To answer this question is also to answer the question of authority. The reason or cause or source of a discipline, in this sense, gives it its justification as well; it points to its boundaries and its rules or laws. If reason is the *principium cognoscendi* of philosophy, then philosophy's boundaries are determined by reason, its authority lies in reason, and its rules and laws are the rules and laws of reason. Not only so, but it seems that the *principium essendi* (essential principle) has been made identical to the *principium cognoscendi*. This, it would seem, creates numerous problems.

One problem lies in the area of authority. Those who would tout reason as the *principium cognoscendi* of philosophy would simply say that philosophy's authority is only as strong as the laws of logic, or the force of a sound argument, or something like that. In that way, one accepts philosophy's conclusions as one accepts

7. We will further develop and make application of these ideas in the chapters that follow.

these laws and forces. But nagging questions still remain. Whence come these laws and what kind of laws are they? Are they eternal, unchangeable laws? Conventions of society? So intuitive that no one can disagree and thus consent-compelling? These questions need to be addressed by those who want to hold to a magisterial use of reason and thus of philosophy.

The standard view in theology is that its *principium essendi* is God himself. He alone provides what is needed for us to understand him and his revelation to us. The *principium cognoscendi* is revelation itself. In the Christian sense, the *principium cognoscendi externum* (external principle of knowledge) is God's special revelation in his Word, and the *principium cognoscendi internum* (internal principle of knowledge) is regenerate reason and the Holy Spirit.

Now, the question in this context is just what should a *Christian* believe the relationship of philosophy to theology to be? That question, too, depends on one's theology. Caird and others would think that the relationship of philosophy to theology should be one in which philosophy dictates to theology what it should think about certain things. He is far from alone in that sentiment. That is because philosophy's *principium cognoscendi* is *reason*. So, to put it rather crassly, philosophy (including as it does philosophy of religion) is for the intelligent folk who should then tell the plain and simple theologians how they ought to think about God and his relationship to the world.

Those who were participants in or are students of the Reformation and its theology have had a different view of things. Reformed theology teaches us that God is the *principium essendi* of *all* disciplines, since it is from God alone that any and every discipline derives all that it is and has. On this view, the *principium cognoscendi* is the revelation of God, both natural and special. If that is the case, then *every* discipline is related directly to these two *principia*. The only way properly to understand God's revelation is through God's own revealed Word, which is the *principium cognoscendi* of theology. Thus, it is theology that ought to set the parameters, the rules, and the laws for the other disciplines. Hendrik Stoker notes:

The distinction between *theology* and *philosophy* does not, according to my opinion, coincide with that between the revelation of God in his *Word* on the one hand and the *cosmos* (or created universe) on the other. This is the case, because on the one hand theology also deals with God's revelation in *creation*, the *cosmos*, viewed in the light of his Word-revelation, whereas the Scriptures on the other hand disclose not only who God is and what his relation to all "things" is, but also matters concerning the created universe (or the *cosmos*) as such. (God's Word even makes assertions on matters relating to the field of some particular science or other, for instance that the labor*er* [note: not labor] is worthy of his [not of its] reward.) Because to the field of theology belong the ultimate problems, it may be called the *"scientia prima inter pares."*[8]

Turretin notes four primary uses of philosophy in theology, once it is established that philosophy's role is as a handmaid, not a mistress. There is, first, a specifically *apologetic* thrust to the use of philosophy in theology. In this sense, theologians should be quick to use philosophy and its tools when and where they can in order to demonstrate something of Christianity's own truth. According to Turretin one of the primary uses of philosophy for theology is that

> it serves as a means of convincing the Gentiles and preparing them for the Christian faith. . . . So God wishes us to apply all the truths of the lower sciences to theology and after rescuing them from the Gentiles (as holders of a bad faith) to take and appropriate them to Christ who is the truth, for the building of the mystic temple; as formerly Moses enriched and adorned the tabernacle with the Egyptian gold, and Solomon procured the assistance of the Sidonians and Syrians in building the temple.[9]

8. Hendrik G. Stoker, "Reconnoitering the Theory of Knowledge of Professor Dr. Cornelius Van Til," in *Jerusalem and Athens: Critical Discussions on the Theology and Apologetics of Cornelius Van Til*, ed. E. R. Geehan (Nutley, NJ: Presbyterian and Reformed, 1971), 39.

9. Turretin, *Institutes*, 1:45ff. All four points will be taken from here.

An example from Scripture might help to illuminate this point: As Paul waits in Athens for Silas and Timothy, he is moved and provoked because of the abundance of idolatry that is present, and explicitly so, throughout this center of intellectual activity. So he sets out to defend the Christian faith, both in the synagogues and in the marketplace. In the course of his defense, some Epicurean and Stoic philosophers become curious (or perhaps agitated) because of Paul's strange teaching that One who walked the earth also rose from the dead. This would be abhorrent to a Greek mind, since the overwhelming consensus of the time is that there is a cyclical pattern to the universe. For one to rise from the dead would mean, rather, that there is a continuity between death and "after death" that would give the lie to a Greek view of history. So, they want Paul's teaching to be evaluated by the intellectuals in Athens. The Hill of Aries was so designed that just such evaluations can take place. So Paul goes before the philosophers and other Athenians in order to defend the Christian faith.

Without going into the details of Paul's encounter, there are a couple of specific passages that help us understand something of the ministerial use of philosophy for theology. Paul begins his address, not by attempting to "prove" to the philosophers that the Christian God exists. That is, he is not concerned to set forth syllogisms that conclude for the existence of the triune God. Rather, Paul begins by telling his audience just what kind of God the Christian God is. Though the philosophers at Athens have concluded that there is some god who could not be known at all, Paul begins by proclaiming to them just what kind of God this is that they think is unknown.

After this description of God, Paul does something that is fascinating, and that points us in a particular direction with respect to our topic. He quotes from two separate Greek philosopher-poets. Why does Paul do this? Is he affirming the Greeks in what they have thus far concluded with respect to God? Is Paul attempting simply to add to their otherwise coherent (though incomplete) knowledge of the true God?

It doesn't seem so, and for the following reasons. First, notice Paul's quotations:

. . . for

"In him we live and move and have our being";

as even some of your own poets have said,

"For we are indeed his offspring." (Acts 17:28)[10]

We might first ask, is it true that "in him we live and move and have our being"? In other words, is Paul using these quotations because the poets have accurately described the true God, albeit incompletely?

The answer depends on at least a couple of factors. Without engaging the entire debate concerning propositions, let's agree for our purposes that propositions are bearers of truth-value; they can be either true or false. Let's also agree that propositions are expressed in sentences or clauses like, "In him we live and move and have our being."

In that case, what we have in Paul's quotations are propositions, expressed in clauses, whose meaning depends, not simply on the linguistic meaning of the clauses themselves, but on the references of the indexical elements of the clauses themselves. For example, when Paul says to those on Mars Hill, "*In him* you live . . . ," to whom is Paul referring? He is obviously referring to the true God, the God whom he has just described to his listeners, the triune God who "made the world and everything in it," who is "Lord of heaven and earth," who "does not live in temples made by man," who is not "served by human hands, as though he needed anything," who "gives to all mankind life and breath and everything," who "made from one man every nation of mankind to live on all the face of the earth," and who "determined allotted periods and the boundaries of their dwelling place." In other words, there is no question to whom Paul is referring when he borrows the quotations from Epimenides and Aratus. Given that Paul's references are to the

10. The first quotation (Ἐν αὐτῷ γὰρ ζῶμεν καὶ κινούμεθα καὶ ἐσμέν) is likely from Epimenides of Crete, the latter (Τοῦ γὰρ καὶ γένος ἐσμέν) from Aratus's poem, "Phainomena."

29

true God, the propositions are true; they express the truth of the matter as it really is.

Worth noting, however, is that when Epimenides and Aratus wrote these words, the propositions themselves were utterly false. The "him" to which the both referred was not the triune God, but rather a false god (likely Zeus). Thus, the reference of the indexical elements of the propositions as uttered by Paul is the true God, whereas the reference of the indexical elements of the same propositions when uttered by the Greek poets was an idol.[11]

So, why does Paul use the very poets who have, in the context of Paul's listeners, promoted not Christianity or true religion but idolatry? In part, the answer is "persuasion."[12] Paul knows that the reason idolatry exists is not ignorance on the part of the idolaters, but an attempt at complete suppression of the truth as it is found in God's general revelation. But since that revelation cannot be fully and completely suppressed, since, as Paul says, the suppression is worked out in terms of an exchange of the truth revealed for a lie, an exchange that results in the worship and service of *some* false god or gods (Rom. 1:23–25), Paul is able to take those statements and transplant them back into their proper, biblical, context and thus to move them from false and idolatrous expressions to expressions of the truth. In doing that, he takes something with which his audi-

11. Or, could it be that the propositions were neither true nor false? This is the case if Frege is correct. "Names such as 'Romulus' or 'Odysseus,' and phrases such as 'the least rapidly converging series' or 'the present King of France' express senses, insofar as they lay out criteria that things would have to satisfy if they were to be the references of these expressions. However, there are no things which do in fact satisfy these criteria. Therefore, these expressions are meaningful, but do not have references. Because the sense of a whole proposition is determined by the senses of the parts, and the reference of a whole proposition is determined by the parts, Frege claims that propositions in which such expressions appear are able to express thoughts, but are neither true nor false, because no references are determined for them." Kevin C. Klement, *Gottlob Frege (1848–1925)*, The Internet Encyclopedia of Philosophy, www.iep.utm.edu. For an application to the ontological argument of the Frege/Meinong discussion see Nicholas Wolterstorff, "In Defense of Guanilo's Defense of the Fool," in *Christian Perspectives on Religious Knowledge*, ed. C. Stephen Evans and Merold Westphal (Grand Rapids, MI: Eerdmans, 1993), 87–111.

12. For a fuller exposition of the persuasive value of Paul's address, see Oliphint, *The Battle Belongs to the Lord: The Power of Scripture for Defending Our Faith* (Phillipsburg, NJ: P&R, 2003), 143ff.

ence is familiar and "recontextualizes" it, changing its truth-value and its meaning, so that what is familiar to them becomes also what communicates the truth to them, truth that they all know, but are seeking to suppress (Rom. 1:18). There is value, therefore, in using the language of the philosophers, poets, and others to show them just how the truth of Christianity fulfills the aspirations expressed in that language.

Philosophy might also serve theology as a "testimony of consent in things known by nature." Here Turretin has in mind the fact that to the extent that philosophy has its focus in natural revelation, it can be used to better confirm things that are revealed by God, things that are true and certain in themselves.[13] This is because natural and special revelation both reveal God, and the truth of God, all of which is brought together as one truth. This can perhaps be seen in the way, for example, that notions of design present in philosophical discussions today serve to "better confirm" the truth of God's creating and controlling activity.[14]

Philosophy can help theology in its ability properly to distinguish and to clarify the truth as it is found in Scripture, and in God's revelation generally. Turretin explains, "For although reason receives the principles of religion from the light of faith, yet (this light preceding) it ought to judge from these principles how the parts of the heavenly doctrine cohere and mutually establish each other; what is consistent with and what is contrary to them."[15]

We should note in this regard that, contrary to a steady stream of criticism since the nineteenth century, the categories and terms that philosophy has given to theology to aid in the latter's expression of the truth of Scripture, though not always completely per-

13. The central truths of theology, according to Turretin, "are founded upon certain and indubitable principles and truths known per se." There is, therefore, no necessary connection between philosophy's task and theology's task. Rather, philosophy, given its subservient status, *may* help clarify what is otherwise known. Turretin, *Institutes*, 1:47.

14. This "confirmation" does not address the stickier problem of the *use* of design *arguments* for apologetic purposes. Those arguments can of course be used, just so long as one's approach neither sacrifices nor undermines the *principia* of theology, that is, just so long as one's *principium cognoscendi* (Scripture), as grounded in the *principium essendi* (the triune God), are not compromised in the method used to set forth such arguments.

15. Turretin, *Institutes*, 1:45.

31

spicuous, have been immensely helpful in warding off heresy and in helping the church to confess and confirm what is given to her in Holy Scripture. Railing against such terms as *hypostasis* or *ousia* or *persona* has done nothing to help the church better express her truth.[16] It has only fed a (now) postmodern mind-set that assumes newer to be better and older to be dead. This mind-set not only is forced to ignore the depth and breadth of scholarship that has been handed down to us, but it also is intent on setting the focus of one's work strictly on oneself. Thus, it remains both historically uninformed and almost irrationally self-absorbed. This way of thinking will never serve the church. The need of the hour is not for the new and the different divorced from the past, but for a deeper, fuller, elucidation and application of what God has taught the church for two millennia. Philosophy can be extremely useful in that regard.

Finally, notes Turretin, "the mind may be furnished and prepared by these inferior systems for the reception and management of a higher science." Here another warning is in order. Until and unless one is grounded resolutely in the *principia* of theology, the danger can be almost overwhelming for anyone who studies philosophy and, perhaps especially, philosophy of religion.

As will be mentioned in the chapters to follow, one has to search far and wide for a philosophy of religion that takes seriously its place as a handmaid to theology. Conversely, one need hardly search at all for an article or essay in philosophy or philosophy of religion wherein the historic truths of Christianity are under attack. Not only so, but philosophy, because of its subject matter and its general methodology, has an allure to many that is Sirenically seductive in its force. So, says Turretin, "This [use of philosophy] must however be done so carefully that a too great love of philosophy may not

16. Note, for example, this kind of criticism given in N. T. Wright, "Jesus' Self-Understanding," in *The Incarnation*, ed. Stephen T. Davis, Daniel Kendall, and Gerald O'Collins (Oxford: Oxford University Press, 2002), 53. Interestingly, given what seems to be significant confusion on Wright's part with regard to the incarnation, the essay itself is better read as an apology for the *use* of established, historic terms, than as an argument for their abandonment.

captivate us and that we may not regard it as a mistress, but as a handmaid."

Turretin goes on to outline the differences in the respective domains of philosophy and theology. Perhaps many of the errors in thinking about the relationship of these two disciplines lie in a failure to grasp the boundaries of each. In that light, Turretin mentions four errors explicitly.

The first error has to do with an illegitimate transfer of principle from philosophy to theology. We will notice this error in the chapters to come. Specifically, Turretin notes errors maintained, such as that virgins cannot be mothers, in spite of what God's revelation teaches. Though philosophy is correct in its general affirmations, we dare not allow those affirmations to rule out the plain truth of God's Word.

Second, and like the first error, we must not let false teachings of philosophy be introduced into theology such that it denies Scripture. For example, Aristotle's belief that the world is eternal must not be imported into theology or defended as a theological truth, given that it serves to undermine the teaching of Scripture with regard to creation.

The third error, according to Turretin, is "when philosophy assumes to itself the office of a master in articles of faith, not content with that of a servant (as was done by the Scholastics who placed Aristotle upon the throne; and by the Socinians who would not admit the doctrines of the Trinity, of the incarnation, etc. because they did not seem to be in accordance with the principles of philosophy)." We have mentioned this above, and will mention it again in chapter 5. Turretin also mentions it more than once. One can hardly overstate the seriousness of this error. It may be the reason, as we will see, that philosophy of religion that purports to be Christian is loathe to include in its analysis any notion of the incarnation.

Fourth, Turretin warns against introducing more new phrases or concepts than are necessary into theology "under which . . . new and dangerous errors lie concealed." In order to avoid this error, one must be acutely aware of the concepts, principles, and presuppositions that accompany philosophical language and concepts in order either to reconfigure them or to keep from borrowing them altogether.

For example, Cornelius Van Til's apologetic method has been described, by him and others, as a "transcendental" method.[17] The terminology itself is used by Immanuel Kant and others. In Kant's context, a transcendental method presupposes Kant's own construction of the nature of reality, of the phenomenal and noumenal, of distinctions made by Hume regarding analytic and synthetic propositions, and so on. Is it advisable to borrow such a term for one's apologetic method? Here Stoker is of some help. In a "letter" to Van Til, he notes concerning Van Til's use of philosophical language:

> No one may deny you the right of giving new meanings to distinctive old terms as long as you clearly define them. And that you do. But there is a deeper issue at stake. The distinctive old terms concerned may have been formed in answer to (and they thus may presuppose in some way or other) *false problems*. For instance, the interesting and complicated history of the term *universal* (from Socrates up to the modern absolute idealists) presupposes the (according to my view, false) problem whether and to what extent reality can or may be grasped in terms of general concepts of thought, *thereby implying* (in some way or other) that reality should conform to the "nature" of general concepts of human thought; and the terms "rational," "rationality," and "rationalism" presuppose a (according to my views, wrong) special stress on reason (*Vernunft*) as distinct from understanding (*Verstand*). To what extent is it possible, by giving Christian meanings to such distinctive technical old terms used in non-Christian philosophy, based as they may be on non-Christian and accordingly false problems, wholly to avoid the predilective or preferential slant which the false problems gave these terms?[18]

This is a fair question, and fair warning for any who want to commandeer philosophy's concepts and terms for the sake of clarification in theology. Sometimes such commandeering may not be

17. For an analysis of this method, see K. Scott Oliphint, "The Consistency of Van Til's Methodology," *Westminster Theological Journal* 52, no. 2 (Spring 1990): 27–49.
18. Stoker, "Reconnoitering," 53–54.

possible; sometimes, though possible, not wise; sometimes, both possible and wise, but clearly in need of elaboration and explanation within the (new) context of orthodox theology.

The question of the relationship of theology to philosophy will be, in one sense, the underlying assumption behind everything that we discuss in the pages that follow. As we attempt to set forth a Christian approach to philosophy generally, and philosophy of religion (natural theology) more specifically, we will also borrow terms, methods, and procedures from philosophy's own domain in order to clarify how such things might be both consistent with orthodox Reformed theology and useful, given that theology, to philosophy. If the errors and dangers mentioned above, however, have not been avoided, then to that extent we must go back to the drawing board. If they have been avoided, then it may just be that, to that extent, there is a road ahead for natural theology, philosophy of religion, and philosophy to do their work and accomplish their tasks within the deep and rich context and confines of biblically Reformed theology.

Reason's finest hour can be realized only as it is nurtured and caused to grow and produced within the warmth of Reformed orthodoxy. *Reasons of faith*, then, are philosophical categories—categories, specifically, of metaphysics and epistemology—that are meant to flourish when they take their rightful place. They can develop, and develop deeply, only when the faith of Reformed theology gives them their *raison d'etre*.

3

Somewhere out There

A small error at the outset can lead to great errors in the final conclusions. —THOMAS AQUINAS

There is no more important subject for philosophical theology and philosophy of religion than the delineation of the relationship of God to his creation. The discussions of that subject that have historically taken place in those disciplines, however, have been altogether turbid, murky, opaque, not to mention simply fallacious. In order to get a clearer picture of the problem and to suggest a way ahead, we should delve into some of the fundamentals of the discussion, and (some of) the key implications and applications of those fundamentals, so that we can begin to try to clarify the discussion itself.

A Philosophical Primer

We should have some idea of the nature of reality in order to have some idea of the nature and scope of our knowledge of it. Or, conversely, we should have some idea of the nature and scope of our knowledge in order to have some idea of the nature of reality. These two statements sum up the task of Western philosophy—or at least the better part of it.[1] This is not a task that is easy to flesh out; neither is it a task on which the experts are much help. As we will see, a perusal of the historical debates in these matters does more than provide fuel for skepticism. The experts in matters philosophical have not been able to give us something readily acceptable by the philosophical masses. As a matter of fact, part of the problem here *is* the experts. But, problems provide opportunities, of which we hope to take full advantage.

Peter van Inwagen in his book *Metaphysics* boldly states that there is no one metaphysical theory that has won the philosophical day. He contrasts metaphysical theories with the body of knowledge presently available in geology, just to use one example, and he notes:

> In the end we must confess that we have no idea why there is no established body of metaphysical results. It cannot be denied that this is a fact, however, and the beginning student of metaphysics should keep this fact and its implications in mind. One of its implications is that the author of this book . . . is [not] in a position in relation to you that is like the position of the author of [a] text . . . in geology. . . . All of these people will be the masters of a certain body of knowledge, and, on many matters, if you disagree with them you will simply be wrong. In metaphysics, however, you are perfectly free to disagree with anything the acknowledged experts say—other than their assertions about what philosophers have said in the past or are saying at present.[2]

Without arguing the case, we will simply take for granted that van Inwagen is right (he did, after all, write *the* book on metaphysics). We will therefore take for granted that we are "perfectly free to

1. We will not be dealing here with the other major task of philosophy, ethics.

2. Peter van Inwagen, *Metaphysics*, 2nd ed. Dimensions of Philosophy Series (Boulder, CO: Westview, 2002), 12. Even with respect to "their assertions," van Inwagen notes that the best that can be done is to get the actual words right, and then pick the best argument as to the interpretation of those words.

disagree with anything the acknowledged experts say" with regard to metaphysics, and we will exercise our freedom to disagree with (at least a large number of) the experts (though not *just* for the sake of disagreement).

We should dwell for just a minute on the impact of van Inwagen's frank admission. For the Christian, this is philosophical good news. It is not that philosophy has given us a slim but adequate account of the nature of all that is. It is not even that philosophy has decorously defined the parameters within which all metaphysicians must operate. The state of the union with regard to metaphysics, he is telling us, is that there is no union after all. It is rather a kind of philosophical free-for-all when it comes to metaphysical discussion and presumption. This is good news indeed.

We should therefore be ready to enter the contest without fear of disqualification. We should shake off ideas of irrelevance and enter the fray with confidence—confidence that the playing field is, if perhaps chaotic, at least level.[3]

Simply because there is no received metaphysical tradition does not, however, mean that the discipline is without constructive content or completely devoid of experts in the field. It only means that *whatever* the content of a particular position or postulation, and *whoever* the expert, there is as of yet no good reason to give one view priority or to let any view go unchallenged. As in any free-for-all, participation in metaphysical discussion and postulation is free for *all*, including any whose views might at first glance appear to be radically different from others that have been proffered. As a matter of fact, it might just be that a little radical difference is the need of the moment.

Before joining the free-for-all, however, it might be beneficial to get some idea of the playing field. Though no one idea or position has gained ascendancy, there are certain universes of discourse that seem to fit most comfortably in metaphysical (and epistemological) discussions. This does not preclude what

3. We would be naive to think that the playing field is *completely* level, but the point to be made here is that it is level with regard to any "received tradition" in metaphysics since, as a matter of fact, there is no such tradition.

was said above about a lack of consensus; any subject will have a particular subject *matter*, regardless of the consensus, or lack thereof, in the details.

Furthermore, the fact that there *is* no consensus does not entail that there are no experts in the field. It only entails the fact that, for whatever reason or reasons, the experts in the field are unclear or otherwise confused about the particulars of the field itself. So we can stick with a kind of standard idea of just what the "field" is and then notice certain significant attempts to further define its particulars. Or, to put it another way, we can stick with the subject and notice the different ways in which the subject *matter* has been discussed by the experts.

Expert Opinion

But just who are these experts? No doubt even the experts would disagree here as well, but hardly any expert would disagree that Plato and Aristotle were among *the* experts in things metaphysical.[4] It should help us define the problem if we look briefly at their proposed solutions.

Plato

For Plato, the answer to the question of the nature of ultimate reality was in his doctrine of the forms. The forms, known only in and by the mind, are those eternal, unchangeable, abstract entities that exist as foundational to the world in which we live. These forms were not discovered or discoverable by any of our five senses, but were postulated as necessary for an (at least partial) explanation of the nature of a "thing" in this world and the way in which we know it. How, for example, can we make sense of two different things, both of which we think are beautiful? What are we to think of an abstract quality like beauty, which seems to inhere in two different things? Plato thought of it this way:

4. The experts may not *agree* with Plato and Aristotle, but they would be hard pressed not to include them in their peer group.

I think that if anything is beautiful it is beautiful for no other reason than because it partakes of absolute beauty; and this applies to everything. . . . If anyone tells me that what makes a thing beautiful is its lovely colour, or its shape or anything else of the sort, I let all that go, for all those things confuse me, and I hold simply and plainly and perhaps foolishly to this, that nothing else makes it beautiful but the presence or communion (call it which you please) of absolute beauty, however it may have been gained; about the way in which it happens, I make no positive statement as yet, but I do insist that beautiful things are made beautiful by beauty. For I think this is the safest answer I can give to myself or to others and if I cleave fast to this, I think I shall never be overthrown, and I believe it is safe for me or anyone else to give this answer, that beautiful things are beautiful through beauty.[5]

For Plato, the *beauty* of a flower and the *beauty* of a painting are (is?) explained by relating the two "beauties" to "beautiful," which is an eternal, unchangeable abstract form. It is because these two things participate in "beautiful" (as form) that we can know the nature of the beauty in them both. Without this form, there would be, according to Plato, no adequate way to postulate or to understand the two different instances of "beautiful."[6] Plato sought to explain notions of equality, justice, goodness, and so on in the same way.

It is important to note here that Plato was attempting to make sense of something that he knew to "be," and to be related. That is, while it is true that Plato's notion of the forms originated, as it were, totally in the abstract, from principles generated by his mind, it is certainly *not* the case that Plato's doctrine of the forms was formulated to *account for* problems that are abstract. He posited the forms as an attempt to make sense of what the senses reported. That is, the forms are necessary to account for aspects of things in this world, things that he knew. In other words, in answer to the question, "What made Plato posit the world of the forms?" we

5. Plato, *Euthyphro, Apology, Crito, Phaedo, Phaedrus,* The Loeb Classical Library, trans. H. N. Fowler (New York: Macmillan, 1913), 345.

6. See also, for example, Plato's *Timaeus* for more of his teaching on the forms.

could answer, "The facts, just the facts." At least two things should be highlighted in this regard.

First, Plato's metaphysical notion was set forth in part as an explanation for what he already knew to be the case, that is, what he took for granted. In fact, it was in the *Phaedo* (where we first meet his doctrine of the forms) that Plato attempted to work out his theory of reminiscence in answer to the question of how we know. There was in Plato's philosophy a close connection between how we know and the metaphysical nature of the thing known. Metaphysics and epistemology are always inextricably intertwined.

This should not surprise us. There will always be, in any discussion of the nature of knowledge, the question of the nature of the thing known lurking somewhere in the background, *and vice versa*. It was in the context of his "interaction" with the world around him that Plato developed his notion of the forms. It was not as though Plato was sitting in his ivory tower, isolated from the world, with no apparent problems, asking what ultimate reality must be. Rather he was aware of a relationship between things in the world, a relationship in which there are both differences and similarities, and he was attempting to account for the knowledge of things and their qualities, things he already took for granted *as known* by him. So we can see in the early days of metaphysical formulation that there was a close connection between metaphysics and epistemology. To be more specific, there was a kind of dependence of one on the other, a dependence that smacks of a certain circularity.

Second, Plato's formulation of the forms was designed to provide an account or a grounding for that which he knew to be true. Plato was attempting to frame his knowledge of beautiful things, and equal things and just things within a context that would explain how these different "things" can have some kind of connection, how they can relate and still remain what they appear to be. Perhaps a quick look at Plato's philosophical predecessors will help us elaborate this point.

The problem that Plato's predecessors set for themselves was whether or not (and if so how) the things of this world can be related or connected to each other. This problem seems to be most clearly illustrated in the pre-Socratic school commonly called the Eleat-

41

ics. Heraclitus (c.540–c.475 BC) attempted to explain the nature of different things by affirming their difference, to the neglect of any (or almost any) unifying element or concept. "One never steps into the same river twice," he asserted. The immediate problem (to oversimplify a complex point) is that if the "river" (and here, I take it, the "river" represents all things in this world) is always and everywhere changing, then even the notion of the river changing changes, and there is no notion, principle, or concept that does not, at the moment of being thought, change into something that it was not at that moment.

Parmenides (b. 515 BC) tried to rescue the Heraclitean skeptic by arguing that whatever is, remains what it is. What "is" is being; everything else simply "is not." Parmenides tried to show that, only that which "is" is; and since the only other thing that some "thing" (which "is") *could* be would be something that it "is not"—in which case it would not be that thing—it seems likely that it is what it is. Better yet, it seems likely that only "is" is, and that anything that would not be "is" would be "is not," which, of course, is not.

But what about all the other things that are not "is"? To ask such a question, according to Parmenides, is to walk along the "common way" and not the "way of persuasion." The "way of persuasion" assures us that only "is" is, and there *is* nothing else.

Though we seem to have lost Heraclitus's flowing river in Parmenides' static ocean, we seem also to have lost Heraclitus, and Parmenides, and the differences that forced the theories in the first place.

It was into this philosophical panoply that Plato's dialogues about the nature of things entered. Plato had the failures of Heraclitus and Parmenides in mind when he attempted to posit *both* different, changing things *and* unifying, unchanging things. So the world of the forms seemed to take the best of Parmenides, while the "beauties," "justices," "equalities" and so on of this world tip the hat to Heraclitus. With Plato (at least so he thought) the metaphysical cake could *both* be had in Heraclitus *and* eaten in Parmenides. What more could a philosopher want?

Notice that in the metaphysical examples so far discussed, there are similar concerns. Whether in Heraclitus's river or in Parmenides' "common way" or in Plato's flower, the way in which the world presents itself plays a leading role in the discussion. This is obvious in Heraclitus and in Plato, but perhaps not as obvious in Parmenides, since, against all that he "sensed," he posited the notion of pure abstract being. But Aristotle's critique of Parmenides is to the point here:

> For, claiming that, besides the existent, nothing non-existent exists, he thinks that of necessity one thing exists, viz. the existent and nothing else . . . , but being forced to follow the observed facts, and supposing the existence of that which is one in definition, but more than one according to our sensations, he now posits two causes and two principles . . .[7]

There are, according to Aristotle, two isolated and autonomous areas in the philosophy of Parmenides, which cannot be brought into any fruitful or meaningful relationship, *given Parmenides' own philosophy*. There is the existent, which is discovered by way of reason, leading Parmenides to posit a single, unifying, all-encompassing being, and there are the observed facts, the way of the senses, which gives us a diversity of things. There is, however, no way of relating these two areas. While Parmenides gives us some idea of the characteristics of each realm, he cannot say how the two relate to each other; or better, he can only say that they cannot relate at all. To relate the two would be to acknowledge something besides being, an acknowledgment that the philosophy of Parmenides cannot abide.

Note that all of our metaphysical options up to this point (we're only *up to* the third century BC) have taken seriously the relation between that which is ultimate and the state of affairs of the world in which we live. Even in his attempt to exclude such a world from his philosophy, Parmenides still had to include it in order to try to argue for its exclusion in his philosophy. This is no mean point and should become even "less mean" when we discuss a Christian response to this problem.

7. *Metaphysics* 986b 27–33, in Aristotle, *The Basic Works of Aristotle*, ed. Richard McKeon (New York: Random House, 1968), 699–70.

Aristotle

Aristotle, Plato's most famous student, began the time-honored tradition of rejecting his teacher's best insights in order to set forth his own. Aristotle began his book *Metaphysics*[8] by stating, "All men, by nature, desire to know."[9] This statement is both metaphysically and epistemologically packed. In it Aristotle asserted something about knowledge and about the nature of people. There is something about my nature, as a person, according to Aristotle, and that "something" is that I desire to know. Essential to a person is that desire.[10] But there is something, too, to be said about knowledge, according to Aristotle. Knowledge is that which is the goal of my essential desire.

Why would Aristotle want this to be the first statement read in a discussion on metaphysics? Perhaps it was his attempt to cut off any questions of epistemic apathy from his peripatetic students, questions like, "But Master, who cares?" Perhaps Aristotle was just stating at the outset that it is an essential part of who we are to want to know about things in general, including the nature of reality. More likely, though, it was his attempt to give account of what he had observed obviously to be the case. So given that we want to know, what can we know about the nature of that which is?

Though the *Metaphysics* begins with a proposition about knowledge, or knowing, it is not knowledge that occupies the subject matter of the book. The desire (which we have by nature) to know includes our innate desire to know the nature of reality. And though Aristotle gave us comparatively little material on the subject of metaphysics per se, he nevertheless set the agenda for discussions of metaphysics even to the present day.[11]

8. Though it was most likely a student of Aristotle's that put together his *Metaphysics*, there is no reason to doubt that what is there is what Aristotle actually taught.

9. I take it here that Aristotle had a less-than-technical notion of "know" in mind when he made this statement. He was not saying that it is the nature of all people to desire to justify every belief that they have, but rather he was thinking of the necessity to relate our thinking to the world, a relating that includes some kind of cognitive content.

10. And whenever we ascribe an essential quality to something we are in the general neighborhood of metaphysics. See chapter 10.

11. This is *more or less* true historically; Aristotle's influence was relatively small until the twelfth and thirteenth centuries, and his works were even condemned by the Roman

For Aristotle, metaphysics was the study of "being *qua* being." Given that subject matter, Aristotle began to think about the relationship of "being" to the rest of what is. In his discussion of nature, in the *Physics* and elsewhere, Aristotle supposed that all things have existence, or being, in common, but that it is the essence of a particular thing that both limited being in that thing and provided for the difference, the individuation, of the thing. So, while being itself was an inherently unlimited notion, it was limited in particular things by the essence of each thing.

This was Aristotle's answer to the dilemma that was illustrated in Parmenides and Heraclitus above. How can we affirm that there is some kind of commonality in the different things that we experience? Is there anything that ties these different entities together without destroying the difference itself? Heraclitus's answer to the latter question was (at least a qualified) no. Parmenides' answer was yes, but only as long as we ignore the information that we have from the senses and allow reason to dictate the nature of reality without recourse to empirical data.

Aristotle takes something of Parmenides' solution, in that he affirms the centrality of "being" in his metaphysical construction, but not to the exclusion of those things we experience. As in Heraclitus, Aristotle affirms that the things we experience are real things, drawn together by their participation in being, though different by virtue of what they are essentially.

But this metaphysical structure could hardly account for the nature of ultimate reality. When trying to apply this notion to a supreme being, Aristotle was stumped. He could never quite resolve how many gods there were, 55 or 47, but no matter what the number, there had to be something that was higher than everything else.[12]

Because of the way in which the Greeks tended to view material stuff (matter), as inherently evil, whatever was "above" everything

---

church in 1277. In the big historical picture, however, particularly in discussions of metaphysics, it was Aristotle's insistence on "being" as *the* subject matter of metaphysics that holds considerable sway. More on that below.

12. This notion of "higher" is only a metaphorical way of speaking. It is typically meant, in this context, to describe something or someone that, because of the attributes ascribed to it or him, transcends everything else.

else could not partake of anything material. In trying to articulate the nature of ultimate reality, then, Aristotle needed to divorce its nature from anything material. For him, the ultimate thing that was essentially immaterial must be *thought itself*. He had learned from his master, Plato, that thought is limited only by the material that contains it. So for the soul, in which thought resides, to be released from the material (thus inherently evil) body would be the ultimate goal. Whatever attributes the highest thing must have, therefore, it must first be essentially thought.

But what is it that this thought is thinking? A thought with no content is no thought, so it must be thinking some*thing*. But what thing can the highest thought think? Or, to paraphrase an old question, what kind of thought could a highest thought think if a highest thought could think a thought? Aristotle was convinced that the highest thought could think of nothing other than itself because to do so would imply, if not outright entail, a dependence of thought on the thing. And a dependent thought is automatically disqualified from the status of "highest" since it would be in need of something lower than itself to define what it is. There can be no other solution, therefore, than that this thought can only think itself. In this way its aseity is guarded, both in the origin of the thing thought, as well as its content. As Aristotle says, "so throughout eternity is the thought which has itself for its object."[13]

Now this may be a handy construction if one is looking for a perfect, abstract something that can have no relation to the world and its particulars. It at least allows one to posit an ultimate something, a thing, presumably, than which no higher can be posited. But it is not so handy if one is seeking an explanation of the meaning or cause or rationale of things that exist in this world. Of course, Aristotle said more than this about metaphysics. More particularly, he creatively noted four different causes, which are useful when attempting to discover why a thing is what it is, and why it is the way it is. He also set firmly into metaphysical concrete the notion of substance.

13. *Metaphysics* 1075a 10, in Aristotle, *Basic Works of Aristotle*, 885.

We need not detail those areas here. More important to our discussion is to note that, in developing a notion of the ultimate as a part of his metaphysical position, Aristotle posited something that by its very nature can have no relationship to anything else that exists. And he did this in the context of his discussion of being, which is the only proper subject matter for metaphysics, according to him.

There are two primary ideas here that will serve to define and delimit much of our discussion later. First, both Plato and Aristotle were searching for something—something clearly and necessarily beyond the changing world—that would provide a rationale for things that we experience here. Second, both were concerned that whatever the relationship of the ultimate "Thing" to this world, it could not be adversely affected by the changes that we experience here. They, therefore, sought a unifying principle that would provide an understanding of the world as we know and experience it.

This is, in sum, what philosophy has been busy doing for a few thousand years. More specifically, philosophy of religion (natural philosophy/theology) has been attempting to understand just how theism can be articulated, given what we know of the world. This, as we shall see, has not been a very encouraging development.

For the sake of economy, then, it will serve us best to keep in mind the overriding notion of being that has occupied metaphysics in the tradition generally since Parmenides, through Plato to Aristotle, and then in the Christian tradition at least since Anselm (discussed below), reaching its apex in the thought of Thomas Aquinas.

Aquinas

The influence of Thomas Aquinas on Christian thought generally, and philosophical theology more specifically, can hardly be overstated. Aquinas is the Bill Gates of philosophical theology—one may love him or one may not like him or anything he stands for, but his influence cannot be avoided. We will want to say much more about Aquinas later, but for now we will concentrate on his genius in areas metaphysical.

One of the most radical innovations brought about by Aquinas was the shift in thinking—of those who were thinking—from the general direction in metaphysics set forth by Plato and his followers, to a different emphasis and construction of Christian metaphysics (primarily) à la Aristotle. At least since Augustine, in the Western Christian tradition, Plato's notion of abstract ideas, or forms, thought to be originals or archetypal of the derivative, ectypal things of our experience, was common metaphysical fare for Christian thinkers, thinkers like Anselm of Canterbury. Most Christian Platonists would identify Plato's forms with ideas in the mind of God, thus "Christianizing" an otherwise secular metaphysic. With his superior knowledge of and interest in Aristotle, Thomas Aquinas changed all that.[14]

For Thomas, it was not "the good" that was to be thought of as primary, but "being."[15] Being was primary because everything that exists participates in it, including the good.[16] As Aquinas says it:

> On the other hand the *Book of Causes* says that *existence is the first thing created*. Existing is a more fundamental idea than being good. For the idea expressed in a word is something the intellect conceives from things and expresses in speech. A more fundamental idea then is one met with earlier in this process of intellectual conception. Now the first idea met with in intellectual conception is that of an existent, for as Aristotle says in order to be known a

14. It's not that the transition from a more or less Platonic way of thinking to a more Aristotelian context was simple and smooth; there were ripples both before and after Aquinas. Before Aquinas, Boethius had translated two of Aristotle's works in the sixth century AD. More significantly, Arabic philosophy began to incorporate Aristotle's works into its own philosophy in the tenth century. After Aquinas, in 1277 to be exact, the Roman church condemned Aristotle's works, and by implication at least caused suspicion to be drawn to some of Aquinas's works, fearing them to be harmful to the faithful. In spite of these and other ripples, however, Thomas's influence has grown almost exponentially since his death, and, much like Augustine's influence, continues today both in Protestant and in Roman Catholic circles.

15. Without detailing the discussion, it was Platonists who attempted to set forth "the good" as the supreme idea or form or person. There are nuances here that don't need to detain us. For example, Thomas affirmed that the good was primary in the context of the final cause. Metaphysically, however, he shifts the discussion from the primacy of the good to the primacy of being.

16. See, for example, Thomas Aquinas, *Summa Theologiae: Latin Text, English Translation, Introduction, Notes, Appendices and Glossary*, ed. Thomas Gilby (London and New York: Eyre & Spottiswoode and McGraw-Hill, 1964), 1.5.1.

thing must actually be. This is why existent being is the primary
and distinctive object of intellect, just as sound is the primary
object of hearing. Existing therefore is a more fundamental idea
than being good (. . . *prius est ens quam bonum*).[17]

This constitutes a change of direction in the metaphysical thinking of the West. Given this shift, Thomas begins to apply his inter-
ests to an understanding of God and of his world. With being as
primary, how should we think about God?

The Arabic philosopher Avicenna (980–1030), himself no mean
Aristotelian, attempted to apply the notion of the primacy of being
to God by asserting that God was Existence itself, without essence.
While Aquinas wanted to agree with Avicenna's distinction between
existence and essence, he could not follow that understanding of
God. But perhaps a foray into the existence/essence distinction
itself will help us understand the debate.

As we have seen, Aristotle dissented from his master's metaphysics in wanting to see the forms, not as residing in some world
somewhere, but as existing in individual things themselves. Every
material thing, therefore, consisted of both form and matter. In
order to know what a material thing is, one must mentally abstract
the form of the thing from the matter, since it is impossible to have
the matter of the thing in the mind itself. In the realm of physics,
then, according to Aristotle, there is both form and matter.

Along with this hylomorphic (form/matter) theory, Aristotle contended that what makes things different from one another (what we
sometimes call the principle of individuation) is what a thing particularly is, rather than the nature of its existence. In this, Aristotle
paved the way for what would come to be a significant distinction
in Thomistic metaphysics, that between essence and existence.

Aristotle was saying that the essence of a thing (and here we can
define essence generally as that without which a thing would not
be what it is) is what distinguishes it from other things, and that
existence is the actualization of the thing. A thing could be essentially different but only potentially (not actually) exist. So it cannot

17. Ibid., 1.5.2.

be that existence is the distinguishing factor of a thing. Distinction must be located, according to Thomas, in a thing's essence.

Thomas took this distinction of essence and existence and raised it to metaphysical status. Whereas Avicenna wanted to keep the distinction but maintain that it could not apply to God, Aquinas asserted that God is one, the only one as it happens, in whom essence and existence are identical. That is, in God, essence and existence cannot be separated or in any substantial way distinct.[18]

This is not to say that God *has* no essence (only existence); it is rather to say that it is of the essence of God, unlike anything else, to exist. Existence is essential to what and who God is. So, in a way not thought of by Aristotle, Aquinas moved from essence as the principle of individuation, and therefore not applicable to God, to essence as existence in God, who himself is *ipsum esse subsistens* (subsistent being itself).[19]

For Aquinas, then, being was "act" in distinction from essence, which was potential existence or potency. Being, by definition, was pure actuality. Thus, Aquinas saw existence as at the root of the real.[20] It is the one attribute or characteristic that is common to all things and thus is, in Aquinas's system, a transcendental notion: it transcends the limitations and perfections of any and every thing. Aquinas's metaphysics, then, begins with the primacy of existence over essence. In this, it has been called an "existential," in distinction from an "essentialistic," metaphysic, the latter of which would be more in line with Aristotle.

It is existence that confers on an essence its act of existing. Aquinas seeks to delineate this, very simply, by asserting that we

18. In this application, it should be said here, Aquinas combines ideas from both Plato and from Aristotle.

19. Aquinas could not attribute pure form to God because, in the hylomorphic theory, form implies some kind of limit. Angels, for example, were separated substances, nonmaterial intelligences, in whom there is form but no matter. Such could not be the case for God, because he must partake of an inherently unlimited notion, which being is and form is not. It should also be noted here that Aquinas thought Ex. 3:14, wherein God reveals himself as "I AM WHO I AM," is best understood in this Aristotelian context. This will be central to our discussion later.

20. See Etienne Gilson, *The Christian Philosophy of St. Thomas Aquinas. With a Catalog of St. Thomas's Works* (New York: Random House, 1956), 34.

can know what a thing is without asserting its actual existence.[21] Because we can conceptualize, for example, a unicorn without asserting its actual existence, there must be a distinction between a thing's essence, in this case a unicorn, and its existence.

Given Aquinas's distinction between existence and essence, he seeks to show that every thing participates in its received act of to be to the extent that its respective essence permits. This is the Aristotelian potency-limiting-act principle in natural philosophy translated by Aquinas into the science of metaphysics. In Thomas's metaphysics, potentiality limits actuality. That is to say, essence is potential existence. It is not in itself existence and therefore does not have existence in itself as essence. When the perfection of being, which is inherently unlimited, confers existence on an essence, that which is unlimited and transcendental (i.e., being) becomes limited and actual only to the degree that a thing's essence will allow.

We must remember in this discussion that Aquinas always maintained that our knowledge comes to us by sense experience. It is because we experience through our senses certain things as both existing and yet different that we can postulate this metaphysical theory. Being as inherently unlimited and as the act of to be, is limited and actualized through essences. There can be nothing that is more existent than being or more perfect than being. For Aquinas, the relationship of being and essence could be called a transcendental relation in that it must transcend any other lesser relationship.[22]

More could be said about Thomas, and more will be, but we can rest for now in the knowledge of Aquinas's metaphysical distinction between essence and existence. There can be no doubt that Thomas has changed the metaphysical landscape from questions of *bonum* (the good) to questions of *esse* (being). This change has brought about considerable discussion, even to the present day. And since there's no time like the present, this might be a good time to

21. See Thomas Aquinas, "On Being and Essence," in *Selected Writings of St. Thomas Aquinas*, trans. Robert P. Goodwin (New York: Bobbs, 1965), 54.

22. For an example of the synthetic relationship, as in the composition of body and soul, see Thomas Aquinas, *Summa Contra Gentiles*, trans. Anton C. Pegis (Notre Dame, IN: Notre Dame University Press, 1957), 3:80.

move (albeit slowly) from the somber metaphysical monastery of medievalism to current considerations.

Being, a Problem

It might prove helpful at this point to illustrate just how the problem of "being" has moved full speed ahead to the present day. Thus, the discussion below will provide an illustration of how some philosophers of religion today are trying to negotiate the metaphysical terrain. Other examples could easily have been chosen. This example, however, is particularly helpful in that it seeks to interact with much of the medieval tradition, while at the same time bringing current philosophical concerns to the fore.

It is in the context of discussions of being as a transcendental notion that modern and contemporary philosophers have begun to wonder if it is proper and accurate to speak of God in terms of "being." But the problem has not just surfaced in contemporary discussions. As a matter of fact, Thomas had barely left the quodlibetic quadrants of his monastery before his successor at the University of Paris, Meister Eckhart (c.1260–c.1328), began to question the coherence of Thomas's existential metaphysic. So perhaps we should peer into the medieval university one more time and approach the contemporary discussion through Eckhart.

In Eckhart's sermon on Matthew 5:3, "Blessed are the poor in spirit, for theirs is the kingdom of heaven," we can see something of the heart of the problem that Aquinas left to philosophical and ecclesiastical posterity. Whether or not Eckhart was a good metaphysician, there can be no doubt that he was a homiletician (though, by modern standards, as will be seen, not a very good one); his sermon on Matthew 5:3 had three points. He focused his sermon on a poverty of the soul, which he called a "stilling." His first point is that there must be a stilling of the will if we are to be poor in spirit. His second point is that there must be a stilling of the intellect, so that our goal would be to have no conceptual knowledge of God at all. And in attempting to make that point, he says:

Why I pray God to rid me of God is because conditionless being is above God and above distinction: it was therein I was myself, therein I willed myself and knew myself to make this man and in this sense I am my own cause, both of my nature which is eternal and of my nature which is temporal. For this am I born, and as to my birth which is eternal I can never die. In my eternal mode of birth I have always been, am now, and shall eternally remain. That which I am in time shall die and come to naught, for it is of the day and passes with the day. In my birth all things were born, and I was the cause of mine own self and all things, and had I willed it I had never been, nor any thing, and if I had not been then God had not been either. To understand this is not necessary.[23]

What could Eckhart be saying here? One can only imagine the discussion over pot roast that Sunday afternoon. Leaving aside the question of whether Eckhart's congregation understood anything of what he said, we can see something of what he is attempting to do, given our previous discussion.

At least this much is clear in the sermon: while wanting to tip the metaphysical hat to *some* notion of being, Eckhart is attempting to move away from his predecessor's metaphysical ideas. In discussing being, he wants to maintain that there is being above which God himself is.[24] Just what that being *is* Eckhart is not concerned to say (no doubt to the delight of his congregation). His point is to separate the notion of being currently discussed—Thomas's notion—from the "being" of God.

This seems to be an admirable goal and one with which we can initially agree, at least on the surface of it. But Eckhart then goes further to note that he himself "was" wherever this "being above being" was, and that, because he was there, he is the cause of himself. Not only so, but he maintains that he himself is the cause of the fact that God is God. Now this would perhaps keep his listeners awake, but it would not seem to be something that would

23. Meister Eckhart, *Meister Eckhart*, trans. C. de B. Evans (London: John M. Watkins, 1924), 220.

24. This notion was not new to Eckhart, but goes at least as far back as the early church.

gain much of a hearing at the Annual Minister's Conference. That we are the cause of God's "God-ness" is a strange, if not heretical, belief indeed.

It appears, however, that Eckhart is wrestling with the Thomistic doctrine of being as a transcendental notion, especially as the implications of such a notion would apply to the Christian doctrine of God. And in his wrestling, he seems to revert to a kind of Neoplatonic idea of God.

Since (at least) Augustine, segments of the Christian church took Plato's notion of the forms and trans-formed it to make it more palatable to Christianity. So the forms, which Plato thought to be perfect originals of the imperfect and derivative things of this world, were interpreted by Augustine as ideas in the mind of God. It was thought, then, that Plato had gotten hold of some metaphysical truth, but that his notion of the good, as the *summum* of all that is, was not able properly to incorporate those truths.

With a Christian understanding of God, however, we can try to put Plato's forms into a different context. Because Christians believe that God has no beginning and no end, that he is simple in that he is identical with all that he is (more on this later), and because Christians believe that God created everything (including time), it must be the case that the things of the world exist(ed) in the mind of God all along. But then those things were actually created, which, whatever else it did, placed those things which are in the mind of God into the context (and the *mode*) of creation as well.

Putting the best possible light on Eckhart's sermon (not always an easy thing to do with sermons), we can see Eckhart as wanting to move from an Aristotelian-Thomistic understanding of the notion of being, back to a Platonic notion. When he says, for example, "If I did not exist, God would also not exist," he is attempting to maintain the simplicity of God, as well as his aseity. That is, Eckhart is saying that, because and to the extent that he exists and has always existed in the mind of God, which mind has never not existed, and given that God is what he thinks (which is a part of what the doctrine of simplicity wants to assert), his (Eckhart's) existence is inextricably linked with God's. If there were no Eckhart, there would be no God.[25]

Now it might have been some comfort to Eckhart's congregation when he concluded this second point in his sermon with the phrase, "to understand this is not necessary." Those less philosophical types in his congregation may have wiped their brows with relief, thinking themselves to be off the hook if sermonic questions were discussed over Sunday lunch that day. It seems, though, that what Eckhart wanted to communicate is that the best way to apply his sermon is by not understanding it, by somehow bringing it about that the ideas he expressed remain beyond whatever the mind would naturally want to do with them. We can begin to see, therefore, the mysticism that was Eckhart's ecclesiastical downfall.

Eckhart's concern, we should note here, will become our own in chapters to come. Just how *do* we think about God's relationship to "being," and how do we think about God's ideas of creation, relative to the actual creating. What is the relationship of creation as it exists in the mind of God to creation as it exists *as created*? These are knotty questions, and we should see Eckhart's burden as, at least in part, an admirable one.

25. Perhaps we could call this the morphological proof for the existence of God; since Eckhart exists in the mind of God as form, and since God's thinking and being are one, Eckhart (and anything else that exists) is proof of God's existence. On the other hand, perhaps not.

4

Can God Be?

[Jehovah] implies that being, or really to be, is in the strict sense applicable to God alone; for although unbelievers may attempt to tear his glory to pieces, he continues perfect and unchanged.
—JOHN CALVIN

We have seen how problems can result when an attempt is made to have the common philosophical notion of "being" relate to God. There is no need to trace this development through history, but it might be instructive to see how Eckhart's attempt has had some influence even into the (post)modern period.

Back to the Future

No less a philosopher than Martin Heidegger (1889–1976) has expressed similar Eckhartian concerns, though perhaps for different reasons. Heidegger was once asked if it was proper to posit being and God as identical, to which he responded:

Being and God are not identical and I would never attempt to think the essence of God by means of Being. Some among you perhaps know that I come from theology, that I still guard an old love for it and that I am not without a certain understanding of it. If I were yet to write a theology—to which sometimes I feel inclined—then the word Being would not occur in it. . . . This is what Luther understood. Even within his own church this seems to be forgotten. One could not be more reserved than I before every attempt to employ Being to think theologically in what way God is God.[1]

Eckhart and Heidegger[2] have something in common with respect to the relationship of metaphysical discussions to discussions about God. They have surveyed the metaphysical "received tradition," especially theistic metaphysical theories, and have found them wanting with respect to an adequate characterization of God. They are both wary of the notion of being when discussing a theistic answer to the question of the nature of ultimate reality. There is something demeaning or otherwise insufficient in (at least one of the main) common metaphysical theistic formulations. Being doesn't seem adequate as a concept to designate God and then further to attempt to show his relationship to the world. Something else must be added to, or perhaps substituted for, the notion of being if a theistic metaphysic is adduced. And Heidegger is not alone in this concern.

There is also a recent curious development afoot, one that is more recent even than Heidegger, which attempts to distance the metaphysical notion of being from God altogether. Jean-Luc Marion, the Roman Catholic philosopher, has attempted to show that the (at least, ecclesiastical) historical notion of being has been either unduly imposed on the thinking of significant church leaders, as in the case of Anselm, or utilized in such a way as to do an injustice

1. Quoted in Jean-Luc Marion, *God without Being: Hors-Texte*, trans. Thomas A. Carlson (Chicago: University of Chicago Press, 1991), 61–62.

2. And others. Emmanuel Lévinas, to add just one other, could be included here as well. See Emmanuel Lévinas and Seán Hand, *The Levinas Reader* (New York: B. Blackwell, 1989).

to what we think about God. A note of explanation on each might help clarify.

In order to understand Marion's first concern noted above, that of an undue imposition of metaphysical notions on theology proper, we need a quick review of the eleventh-century Archbishop of Canterbury, Anselm (c. 1033–1109).[3]

Anselm, so it is said, wanted to use the notion of being to prove the existence of God. There seems to be no doubt that Anselm's chief commitment was to Christianity. However, it was not Christianity that he sought to prove in his famous argument for God's existence, but rather the greatest conceivable being, or, more particularly, a being than which no greater could be conceived. It seems that Anselm's concern was to offer a conceptual argument for the actual existence of God. That is, he wanted to follow the implication(s) of a certain idea in order, in the end, to conclude that at least one idea is incoherent unless it is matched by the objective existence of that which the idea itself represents. And the general idea that he wanted to posit was none other than being, with certain necessary qualifications. His argument went something like this.[4]

The fool, says Anselm quoting Psalm 53:1, says in his heart, "There is no God." Now it must be the case that, for all his foolishness, the fool at least knows what it is that he thinks there is not. The fool must have, in order to deny the existence of God, some idea as to just what kind of God he assumes there isn't. He need not attach much by way of content to this notion of the nonexistent God; as a matter of fact, all he really needs in order to deny God's existence is an understanding that this God who does not exist, if he did exist, would be the greatest possible being.

3. Anselm is a major figure in the history of theology and philosophical theology. Our summary will not do him justice, and is not intended to. We introduce a segment of his thought here because of its relevance to discussions of "being" in some (primarily continental) philosophical contexts.

4. His argument has been construed, misconstrued, and re-construed since its initial development. From Descartes to Kant to Malcolm to Plantinga, differing versions of the argument are offered. We will attempt here to keep it as simple as an ontological argument can be.

So, says Anselm, since the fool must have an idea that this God who is thought not to exist would, at the very least, be the greatest, it must be the case that the fool has a concept of this being such that to conceive of one greater would be impossible. The fool understands the idea of a being so great that nothing greater than it can be conceived.

Anselm then insists that if this being exists in the mind of the fool, then it does at least somewhere, exist. The problem however is that it cannot be what it is and just pitch its existential tent in the fool's mind—it must exist in the objective world as well. If it did not exist in the objective world, then it would still exist, but only in the fool's mind. But how can something so great that nothing greater can be conceived exist only in the mind and maintain its maximally great status? According to Anselm, it cannot. It must, therefore, by virtue of its existence in the fool's mind, exist objectively.

There are really only two points, then, that Anselm needs to assert in order to set forth his proof. The first is that God is one than which nothing greater can be conceived, and the second is that this same God exists in the mind of the fool. If those two points are conceded, then Anselm sees his conclusion as compelling.

A number of concerns have been raised regarding this "proof," concerns that we will not review, particularly since they have been painstakingly played out elsewhere. Our point here is that Anselm's argument relies on a metaphysical notion of the greatest being, a notion that appears to have no further immediate content, except that inherent in it is the impossibility of conceiving of anything greater. Anselm does not say that we can conceive of this being; he only says that we understand that it can brook no rival or superior conceptions. Whatever we decide to think of this being, we cannot think of anything greater, or it would not be the being of which we are thinking.

Whatever one wants to think of Anselm's argument, there is no doubt as to its intuitive appeal. Its appeal does not lie in a general proposition that whatever great thing we can think of must exist; that charge was laid at Anselm's feet by Guanilo. Rather, the appeal lies in the fact that one can scarcely utter the word *God* without thinking of a maximally great being.

While it is true that both Plato and Aristotle had "gods," there was nevertheless, even in their philosophies, something than which nothing greater could be conceived and which was thought to exist objectively, somehow, somewhere. So Anselm is in good metaphysical company in employing such an idea. Even if Anselm is right, however, problems remain as to just what this being would be like. Would it be like Aristotle's Thought Thinking Itself? Or Plato's good? Or maybe Plotinus's One? In any case, it might be difficult to reconcile with the Christian God.

Whatever the case, Marion wants to call into question the entire supposition that the "ontological argument" has much to do with ontology.[5] According to Marion, the argument from Anselm relies, not on a concept, but on a non-concept. Marion rightly notes that Anselm himself never referred to his argument as "ontological"; that designation was the invention of Immanuel Kant. It is entirely possible, then, according to Marion, that Anselm's argument has little to do with the notion of being. Without doing justice to Marion's brilliant article, at least part of his point centers on a linguistic shift within Anselm's *Proslogion*, a shift from *majus* (greater) to *melius* (better) when referring to this being. That is, as Marion puts it, "does the '*id quo majus cogitari nequit*' [that than which no *greater* can be conceived] admit to being interpreted . . . in terms of the question of being or ousia?"[6] Marion's answer is no, and he supports his answer with Anselm's further designation of the argument, taken from Proslogion, 14, wherein Anselm uses the formula, "*[id] quo nihil melius cogitari potest*" (that than which no *better* can be conceived).

This, according to Marion, specifies further what Anselm meant more generally in the earlier (*majus*, greater) formula. That is, it is not the case simply that Anselm was concerned to argue from the standpoint of the greatest being, but rather his chief concern was that this being be defined as the best, or (referring back to Plato),

5. Jean-Luc Marion, "Is the Ontological Argument Ontological: The Argument according to Anselm and Its Metaphysical Interpretation according to Kant," *Journal of the History of Philosophy* 30, no. 2 (April 1992): 201–18.

6. Ibid., 213.

the *summum bonum*. Or, as Marion puts it, "to be greater means to be better."[7]

Without going into further detail here, Marion's argument carries at least some exegetical weight. It is surely true that Anselm's terminology changes in the context of his argument. Not only so, but Marion refers us both to Augustine and to Boethius as support for his position from the church fathers.[8] This is significant since both were heavily influenced by Plato and thus would have been more comfortable with God as *summum bonum* rather than as *ipsum esse subsistens*. So the argument that the ontological argument is not, after all, ontological carries some support, whether or not it is true.

The interesting point here is that Marion seems concerned in this article to place the understanding of God more in an Eckhartian framework than in a Thomistic (and Aristotelian) one. His exegetical point is that Anselm's argument leans more on Plato than on Aristotle. This point could easily be conceded, particularly given the fact that Anselm saw himself as Augustinian, and Augustine was decidedly dependent on Plato for much of what he thought. Marion's interpretation of Anselm's argument is "that God's transcendence has to be termed a transcendence of the good and not a mere maximum of entities."[9] This is Marion's Platonic rendition of what has characteristically been an Aristotelian interpretation of Anselm's ontological argument.

But Marion's further concern—the Eckhartian twist we might call it—is that Anselm's argument commits us to a non-understanding of God. As he puts it: "God exists *in re* in a very special way—not because he is in understanding, but despite the fact that he is not. Further: he is in reality because he is not in understanding. And this is the last and highest degree of being."[10] We can hear echoes here of Eckhart's last line: when it comes to God, "to understand this is not necessary."

---

7. Ibid., 214.
8. Ibid., 216.
9. Ibid., 217.
10. Ibid., 212. Note that being still plays a role in the discussion, but it is being that transcends being.

It was Marion's book, *God without Being*,[11] however, that more clearly set forth his agenda for a kind of Christian philosophical theology, a theology against what Heidegger liked to call "onto-theologic." In that book, Marion suggests that our understanding of God, to be proper, should move outside of the tradition of Thomistic metaphysics. The metaphysical notion of being, as we have it handed down to us from Aquinas, cannot adequately express the Christian notion of God as we have it from biblical revelation. Thus, it is time, says Marion, to move beyond being, beyond Aquinas, to something that transcends the being of medieval metaphysics.

Marion is attempting an answer to the question he poses at the beginning of the book: "Can the conceptual thought of God . . . be developed outside of the doctrine of Being (in the metaphysical sense, or even in the non-metaphysical sense)? Does God give himself to be known according to the horizon of Being or according to a more radical horizon?"[12] Marion's answer is the latter: God gives himself to be known, he says, according to the gift, which is itself *agape*. Any other notion ascribed to God is an idol, including the Thomistic metaphysical notion of being.[13]

One can begin to see again the inextricable link, in Marion, between epistemology and metaphysics. Since the historical notion of being has failed us, we must construe another context in which God can be known. That context, for Marion, is the gift.[14]

The point to be made in this and the previous discussions is that the relationship of God to reality, to the world, to being has been and remains a knotty problem in philosophical theology. It could be argued (and without arguing it here I will affirm) that this relationship has been *the* central problem in the philosophy of religion, and in any other discipline (philosophical or otherwise) that

11. Originally published as *Dieu sans l'etre: Hors-texte*, librarie Arthéme Fayard, 1982. See also Jean-Luc Marion, "Metaphysics and Phenomenology: A Theological Reader," in *The Postmodern God*, ed. Graham Ward (Malden, MA: Blackwell, 1997), 279–96.

12. Marion, *God without Being*, xxiv.

13. Marion has a somewhat technical idea of an idol, distinguishing it from an icon. Without going into the technicalities of it, however, it seems to include the negative connotation of that which takes the place of the true God.

14. For developments in this discussion see Calvin O. Schrag, *God Otherwise than Being* (Evanston, IL: Northwestern University Press, 2002).

attempts to make sense of God, his character, and his relationship to his creation.[15] This is the problem that will occupy our attention throughout; it will occupy our attention, not simply with respect to being (metaphysics), but also with respect to how we can know about this relationship in the first place (epistemology).

The focus of this problem in the modern period is set forth with almost incalculable influence in the thought of Immanuel Kant.

No Immanuel

Perhaps the most obvious interrelationship between metaphysics and epistemology occurs in the thought of the eighteenth-century philosopher Immanuel Kant. It can fairly be said that nothing has been the same since Kant wrote. Nothing has been the same for philosophy or, more importantly, for philosophical theology (and theology generally). We need, therefore, to have an understanding of Kant's general concerns.

There is a sense in which metaphysics was a delightful playground for philosophy until Immanuel Kant (1724–1804) published his *Critique of Pure Reason* in the late eighteenth century. Of course, there were vigorous debates about things metaphysical prior to Kant; the playground was rarely peaceful. But it was a playground nevertheless—a place where certain things were taken for granted, where one could count on a particular kind of activity and where anyone who entered could feel relatively secure about certain ideas and concepts. Kant changed all that. Whether his arguments are true or false is still a matter of debate. Just *what he said* is still a matter of debate. What is not a matter of debate, however, is whether what he said significantly impacted the discussion and study of metaphysics and epistemology. It did, in spades.

Some background on Kant may be needful at this point. He is, by most accounts, the most influential philosopher of the modern period and is surpassed in his influence on philosophy and

15. It should be noted here that there is a significant rise in discussions and publications that want to work out the relationship of God to everything else. This is, at least on the surface, a positive step. On the other hand, because so many of these discussions go dangerously wrong at crucial points along the way, the end result may be disastrous.

philosophical discussion only perhaps by Plato and Aristotle. Kant's philosophy is sometimes called critical philosophy.

Descartes (1596–1650) may be considered the forerunner of critical philosophy, but Kant was certainly the one who developed and institutionalized it. Critical philosophy is so named because it attempts to "critique" or to analyze or ask about certain aspects of knowing and being, typically aspects that we might take for granted. It is an attempt to avoid both dogmatism, on the one hand, and skepticism, on the other. So, for example, Descartes began to ask just what he could know clearly and distinctly, that is, without doubt. He did not want dogmatically to hold what his predecessors held to be true, but neither did he want to conclude that nothing whatsoever could be known. He was "critical" of everything that most of us take for granted in order to establish something that was indubitable, something that was absolutely certain. In this radical critique Descartes concluded with his now famous, *cogito ergo sum*, "I think, therefore I am."

After Descartes, others (namely Leibniz and Spinoza) attempted to work out a philosophy based on ideas, concepts, and principles that were assumed to be innate in the mind. When those attempts were found still to be wanting, a group of empiricists emerged, among whom the most radical was David Hume (1711–76). Rather than approach philosophy critically, Hume surmised that knowledge could only be founded and grounded on an empirical basis. So the development of his radical form of empiricism included arguments that denied certain things that we all tend to take for granted.

Hume argued, for example, that there can be no way to establish the notion, just to use the most popular example, of cause and effect simply by way of empirical categories. Since it is empirical categories that give us knowledge, it follows that there is no way that we can know anything about cause and effect. We may use those terms, and we do use them. But we do simply out of habit and custom, not as categories that have any sound basis in reality.

Kant said that it was David Hume who woke him from his dogmatic slumbers. He agreed with Hume that such things as cause and effect could not be ascertained on a strictly empirical basis, but he disagreed with Hume that we therefore cannot know that such processes apply to reality. So Kant developed what he called his transcendental method. Why call this method transcendental?

Kant designated his approach as transcendental in order to stress that, while certain crucial and important elements *of* experience are *in* experience, they nevertheless transcend the thing experienced, the matter, that is seen or touched or heard. The source is different; so is the status. Kant begins his *Critique of Pure Reason* this way:

> There can be no doubt that all our knowledge begins with experience. For how should our faculty of knowledge be awakened into action did not objects affecting our senses partly of themselves produce representations, partly arouse the activity of our understanding to compare these representations, and, by combining or separating them, work up the raw material of the sensible impressions into that knowledge of objects which is entitled experience? In the order of time, therefore, we have no knowledge antecedent to experience, and with experience all our knowledge begins. *But though all our knowledge begins with experience, it does not follow that it all arises out of experience.*[16]

That is, the source of much of what we know and its status transcend experience. In the first section of his *Critique*, for example, the section entitled the "Transcendental Aesthetic," Kant tries to show that space and time, while being empirically real because they are present in actual experience, are at the same time, transcendentally ideal, since they are forms imposed on reality by the mind. Kant seeks to show that these forms, and the categories that he develops in the second section of the *Critique* (the "Transcendental Logic"), are valid *in* experience because they are necessary conditions *of* experience. He then goes on to argue in the third section of his *Critique* (the "Transcendental Dialectic") that there are other things, things outside our experience, to which we cannot apply these categories and forms. Those things are (1) God, (2) the self and (3) the things in themselves. These three categories transcend experience altogether, and so the categories of

16. Immanuel Kant, *Critique of Pure Reason*, trans. Norman Kemp Smith (New York: St. Martin's, 1958), 41, my emphasis.

experience cannot be applied to them. But just what is Kant's concern here? Why begin to delve into such detail with respect to the way reality is structured, as well as our knowledge and the ways of the world?

In order to understand Kant's project, we must look again for a moment at Hume. For Hume, there are three, and only three, kinds of propositions. Propositions are either analytic, synthetic, or nonsense. In his *Enquiries*, Hume put it this way:

> When we run over libraries, persuaded of these principles, what havoc must we make? If we take in our hand any volume; of divinity or school metaphysics, for instance; let us ask, *Does it contain any abstract reasoning concerning quantity or number?* No. *Does it contain any experimental reasoning concerning matter of fact and existence?* No. Commit it then to the flames: For it can contain nothing but sophistry and illusion.[17]

An analytical statement, for Hume, is any statement whose negative entails a self-contradiction. So, "All bachelors are unmarried," negatively stated is "All bachelors are married," which is self-contradictory. Therefore it is an analytic statement. Furthermore, according to Hume, analytic statements are true with regard to the meaning and relations of *words*, not with regard to the *world*.

Synthetic statements, on the other hand, are explained by Hume this way:

> On the contrary, all impressions, that is, all sensations, either outward or inward, are strong and vivid: The limits between them are more exactly determined: Nor is it easy to fall into any error or mistake with regard to them. When we entertain, therefore, any suspicion that a philosophical term is employed without any meaning or idea (as is but too frequent), we need but enquire, *from what impression is that supposed idea derived?* And if it be impossible to assign any, this will serve to confirm our suspicion.[18]

17. David Hume, *Enquiries Concerning the Human Understanding and Concerning the Principles of Morals*, 2nd ed. (Oxford: Clarendon Press, 1902), 165.
18. Ibid., 22.

All synthetic propositions, therefore, are such only if their source is in sense data. Aside from these two, any proposition not traceable to sense data, and not analytic, is nonsense. These distinctions, you may have surmised, have some serious implications with respect to the questions of epistemology, of metaphysics, and specifically of God's existence.

Consider the proposition, "God exists." If we stay with Hume's distinctions for a moment, we would ask first of all whether that statement is analytic, synthetic, or nonsense. One way to ascertain the answer to that question is, first, to put it in the negative and ask if it is self-contradictory; is "God does not exist" self-contradictory? Hume would say it is not (this, of course, is highly questionable and loaded with presuppositions that cannot here be explored). Hume's point is that if it were an analytic statement, it would be redundant, such that existence would be identical with God. Also, Hume points out that to say, "A necessary being necessarily exists" does not tell us whether there *is* such a being.

So, "God exists" is not an analytic statement. The next Humean question is, is it synthetic? In order to be synthetic one would have to have an impression, or observation, of God (because, remember, Hume is a radical empiricist); the proposition would have to be loaded with the content of sense data. Since ideas can reach no further than our experience, according to Hume, an idea of God seems unreachable. Remember how Hume stated it in the *Dialogues Concerning Natural Religion*, part 2:

> In reality, Cleanthes, . . . there is no need of having recourse to that affected skepticism so displeasing to you, in order to come at this determination. Our ideas reach no further than our experience. We have no experience of divine attributes and operations. I need not conclude my syllogism. You can draw the inference yourself.[19]

Hume's "inference" is not, at least in this dialogue, that statements about God are meaningless. Philo (whether or not the Philo

---

19. J. C. A. Gaskin, *Dialogues and Natural History of Religion* (New York: Oxford University Press, 1993), 44–45.

of the *Dialogues* is the Hume of Edinburgh is an open question) concludes that "just reasoning and sound piety here concur in the same conclusion, and both of them establish the adorably mysterious and incomprehensible nature of the Supreme Being."[20] The fact of the matter remains, however, that statements about the existence of God, given Hume's philosophy, are highly suspect at best. It would appear that the only category left, given Hume's analysis, is that the proposition, "God exists," is a nonsense statement.

From this "ontological" critique (because dealing with talk about God's "being"), Hume moves to a cosmological critique, particularly with regard to causality. Suppose we assert that God (x) causes the universe (y). The first Humean question to consider is whether "x causes y" is analytic? Again, we can think of its negative. Is the statement, "x does not cause y" self-contradictory? Hume says no. We can think, to use his example, of a billiard ball striking another and the second one not moving. There is no contradiction in such a notion. Or to put it another way, in order for the statement to be analytic, y must be contained in x. The universe must be contained in God in the same way that "unmarried" is contained in "bachelor." So, "God caused the universe" is not an analytic statement.

Is "x causes y" synthetic? Hume answers no, because he can see no *necessary connection* between x and y. For Hume it is impossible for the mind to find an effect in a cause. He is convinced that an effect is totally different from a cause, and consequently one cannot discover the former in the latter.[21] It would appear that what we are left with, again, is a nonsense statement with respect to God. So much for Hume.

It was these discussions, among others, that provided the fodder for Kant's genius. Kant's intent in *The Critique of Pure Reason* was (in part) to answer the radical empiricism of Hume. Kant had previously been enamored with Christian Wolff's attempts to systematize Leibniz's philosophy—until he read Hume. Kant accepted Hume's analytic/synthetic distinction with respect to propositions. He agreed that all analytic statements are *a priori* and that all *a*

20. Ibid., 45.
21. See, for example, Hume, *Enquiries*, sections 7 and 8.

posteriori propositions are synthetic, but he did not agree with Hume's argument that all synthetic propositions are *a posteriori* and that all *a priori* propositions are analytic.

Kant argues in his *Critique* that there are, contra Hume, "synthetic *a priori*" propositions—propositions whose truth is known independently of observation (thus, *a priori*), and in which the predicate is not contained in the subject (thus, synthetic). Or, to put it in terms of a question, Kant attempts to show that the question, "Are synthetic *a priori* judgments possible?" could be answered in the affirmative. This is the only way Kant could see to refute Hume—the knowledge that Hume denied must be shown to be synthetic *a priori* knowledge.

Kant begins by attempting both to incorporate and revise Hume's (and the empiricists' generally) notion that "space" and "time" are not perceived. He does this by developing his notion of *intuition*. In transcendental fashion, Kant asks as to the possibility of perception itself. Notice that he begins with the fact of perception (against skepticism) and then asks as to its possibility (which is the hallmark of critical philosophy). Kant is convinced that we do, in spite of what the empiricists tell us, perceive objects in space. One can perceive, for example, that "I am sitting at my desk."

In perceiving such a thing, we must of necessity have what could only be called a "spatial" perception (i.e., a perception involving my existence at some spatial location—"at my desk"). How do we perceive such a thing if, as radical empiricism wants to argue, we never perceive space? Kant maintains that an *a posteriori* (synthetic) statement like, "I am sitting at my desk," presupposes the notion that "things exist in space."

Moreover, because we *know* the first sentence ("I am sitting at my desk"), the precondition for that knowledge must be the second (Things exist in space").[22] But this latter statement, which is the precondition for the former, according to Kant, is neither *a posteriori* (he agrees with Hume that space and time were not sense data) nor analytic. It must therefore be a synthetic *a priori* judgment, a precondition for other things that we take for granted.

---

22. Notice again the interrelationship between epistemology and metaphysics.

In this development, remember, Kant agrees with the empiricists, but only so far. Remember how he begins his *Critique* with the statement, "There can be no doubt that all our knowledge begins with experience," but then continues ". . . though all our knowledge begins with experience, it does not follow that it all arises out of experience." That is, the source of knowledge, in some way, transcends experience, while being embedded in it. In this, Kant would be closer to the rationalists than to the empiricists. Thus, Kant's method of "Transcendental Deduction" attempts to transcend, or get behind, observation, in order to grasp the conditions behind it.

Space and time, then, for Kant, are structures of the mind. They are the "goggles" through which we see everything else. So, Kant thinks that he has taken the best and thrown out the worst of both rationalism and empiricism. Thus, his famous dictum, "Thoughts without content are empty [contra rationalists], intuitions without concepts are blind [contra empiricists]."[23] Space and time, then, relate to the faculty of intuition.

Kant then turns to the faculty of understanding. Again against the skeptic, he asks, not whether we know anything, but, given that we do, how is knowledge possible? At this point, he introduces us to the synthetic *a priori* categories of the understanding. Kant imagines that we have four such categories, each with subcategories. These are all categories of the understanding that the mind imposes on its observations in order to know something. So, again to counter Hume, the notion that "every event is caused," which Hume said was neither empirically true nor analytic, is a synthetic *a priori* judgment of the understanding. These categories are not innate *ideas*, but rules of thought (i.e., not Cartesian).

Believe it or not, this all has relevance for our coming discussions of metaphysics and epistemology. Like Hume in this respect, Kant argues that we can only know that which has passed through the mind, through the grid of space and time, and through the categories of the understanding. While synthetic *a priori* judgments

23. Kant, *Critique of Pure Reason*, 93: "Gedanken ohne Inhalt sind leer, Anschauungen ohne Begriffe sind blind."

are possible, they must nevertheless be propositions that have their foundation and basis in experience itself. Whatever does not have its foundation in experience cannot be known at all.

All claims to knowledge must be claims about the world of sense data, the world of the phenomena. Thus, while there may be metaphysical realities, we have no access to them and therefore no way of positing their existence. This does not bode well for the three entities that Kant argues are outside of our experience—God, the self, and things in themselves. The Kantian bomb has exploded onto the playground of traditional metaphysics, and traditional metaphysics has been devastated.

In order to make sure the playground is thoroughly demolished, Kant goes on to analyze the faculty of reason. This is the faculty that produces the higher, purer, concepts such as God and the soul. The problem, however, is that there is and can be no synthetic *a priori* with regard to the concepts of reason. Why not, according to Kant?

Traditional metaphysics has erroneously applied notions of space, time, causality, and so on to a world that is not, and cannot be, experienced—the noumenal world. That world, by definition, has no observable phenomena. If there are no observable phenomena, then there is nothing to which our categories can be applied; there is nothing there to "synthesize." There is, therefore, with respect to our faculty of reason, no synthetic *a priori*; thus knowledge of the noumenal world is impossible. Ideas of God exceed the limits of knowledge.

This helps us see the explanation and the magnanimous impact of Kant's other famous dictum: "I have therefore found it necessary to deny knowledge in order to make room for faith."[24] In this latter statement from Kant lies the metaphysical and epistemological tension that is with us even to the present.[25]

24. Ibid., 29 "Ich mußte also das Wissen aufheben, um zum Glauben Platz."
25. The view presented here of Kant is of necessity general and could easily be, and perhaps ought to be, expanded and elaborated. However, to avoid the bog of philosophical detail, the reader might best reference a helpful summary of matters Kantian in Alvin Plantinga, *Warranted Christian Belief* (Oxford: Oxford University Press, 2000), 9–30.

Kant's Legacy

Kant denied knowledge, at least a particular kind of knowledge, in order, as he says, to make a place for faith. It is not altogether clear just why it was, when Kant wrote, that faith was needing such a place. Most likely, it was the empirical philosophy of David Hume primarily that had given way to skepticism, and skepticism is never tolerant of religious faith. So, in Kant's mind, he was doing religion a service. Though, in agreement with Hume, Kant concluded that there was no room in the metaphysical "inn" for faith, he nevertheless made room for faith in the "manger" of religion. And that "manger" was associated with what Kant called the "practical reason," with its primary focus on the ethical.

There can be no question that Kant's analysis had and continues to have almost hegemonic influence over (post)modern thought, particularly (post)modern philosophical theology. Friedrich Schleiermacher (1768–1834), called by some the father of modern theology, devoted much of his academic career to the study of Kant. His own initial religious "awakening" was an experience that, like Kant's awakening from his dogmatic slumbers, carried him through the "storms of skepticism."[26] It is no wonder, then, that Schleiermacher resonated with the Kantian system of philosophy—the way out of skepticism in religion is through the practical, the ethical. It is not by doctrine or knowledge that one is religious. Rather, according to Schleiermacher, it is by a "feeling of absolute dependence." While arguments have been proposed that Schleiermacher's intent was not purely subjective, it is highly questionable whether he was able to extricate himself from subjectivism. The focus of religion for Schleiermacher, against the Christian tradition before him and in line with Kant's philosophy, was on the experience of the believing community, not on the revelation of a self-existent God.

Albrecht Ritschl (1822–89), not to be outdone by Schleiermacher, attempted to make Christianity even more Kantian than Kant. For him, religion's focus is to be entirely upon the ethical;

---

26. Friedrich Schleiermacher and Frederica Rowan, *The Life of Schleiermacher as Unfolded in His Autobiography and Letters* (London: Smith Elder and Co., 1860), 1:283.

the metaphysical is dead. Knowledge is a hindrance to religion; experience is its key. So, says Ritschl,

> Christianity is the monotheistic, completely spiritual and ethical religion, which, on the basis of the life of its Founder as redeeming and establishing the kingdom of God, consists in the freedom of the children of God, includes the impulse to conduct from the motive of love, the intention of which is the moral organization of mankind. . . .[27]

Since reams have been written about the relationship, teaching, and influence of Kant, Schleiermacher, and Ritschl, it might be best to move to a current-day example in order to show just how far Kant's anti-metaphysical influence has taken us.

Cupitt's Conundrum

The current conundrum is just this: " 'I can't live with it and I can't live without it.' Such is the verdict of many people upon traditional religious belief. They find it especially difficult to accept the objective or metaphysical side of religion, the side that postulates and describes various supernatural beings, powers and events."[28] Cupitt's conundrum is that people simply can't live with the old, old story of supernatural beings, but they can't live without them either. The solution, in a post-Kantian world, like the conundrum itself, has two sides.

First of all, argues Cupitt, it should be recognized that the attempt to do away with religion altogether, to secularize it, was all too hasty. It assumed a notion of religion as *dependence*, a notion that was clearly at odds with our modern ways of thinking, and was, as well, according to Cupitt, refuted by Buddhism (a religion that does *not* have dependence as one of its corollaries). So, the solution must not take the tactic of attempting to do away with

27. Albrecht Ritschl, H. R. Mackintosh, and A. B. Macaulay, *The Christian Doctrine of Justification and Reconciliation: The Positive Development of the Doctrine* (Edinburgh: T.&T. Clark, 1900), 3, 13.

28. Don Cupitt, *Taking Leave of God* (New York: Crossroad, 1981), 1.

religion; it must find a way, alternatively, of doing away with this notion of dependence.

Doing away with dependence is as simple as redefining terms. Whereas the old, old story used to speak of gods and demons "out there," all we need do now, in speaking of such beings, is make sure that we do not mean that they are in any way "out there," but that they "come up from below. We no longer receive them; we have to create them."[29] This Cupitt calls internalization.

Second, we may still speak of sin. But the sin of which we now speak is the sin, not of rebellion as it was during those dark and dreary days of the old, old story, but of obedience. Obedience implies dependence, but (post)moderns like Cupitt will have none of that. What we must now realize is that autonomy is the (post)modern condition, and it is religion's task to respond to it.

So how does religion respond to the (post)modern, post-Kantian condition? By affirming at least the following: first "it seems doubtful whether there is any immense cosmic or supra-cosmic Creator-Mind."[30] Second, what matters is not objective theism, the belief that there really *is* such a person as God. "What matters is spirituality. The highest and central principle of spirituality. . . . is the one that commands us to become spirit, that is, precisely to attain the highest degree of autonomous self-knowledge and self-transcendence."[31] This does not of course mean that there is no God; it simply (you guessed it) redefines him (or it):

> God is a unifying symbol that eloquently personifies and represents to us everything that spirituality requires of us. The requirement is the will of God, the divine attributes represent to us various aspects of the spiritual life, and God's nature as spirit represents the goal we are to attain. Thus the whole of the spiritual life revolves around God and is summed up in God. God is the religious concern, reified.[32]

29. Ibid., 3.
30. Ibid., 8.
31. Ibid., 9.
32. Ibid.

This may come as a surprise to those of us who want to hold
onto the Christian tradition, but Cupitt has a solution for that as
well. In speaking of the notion of reductionism, Cupitt grants that
our knowledge, by necessity, comes to us through our experience.
All talk, therefore, "about the world of physical objects is talk about
them as they are in and for our experience, and we cannot pretend
to be able to talk about physical objects as they are absolutely and
quite apart from our experience."[33] This is Cupitt following Kant
like a bird follows bread crumbs. Kant has convinced Cupitt that the
best we can do is maintain the truth of what we know subjectively.
As expected, this Kantian notion has significant implications for
our Christian beliefs as well.

What about the resurrection of Christ? Is that, too, only "in
and for our experience"? Cupitt says yes, and necessarily so. If the
resurrection were an objective fact, then it would cease to be religious altogether. If it were an objective fact, it would be the kind
of thing that would be testable, repeatable, subject to falsification.
But to hold to the resurrection in that way is to destroy its *religious*
element. So how do we think about the resurrection of Christ?
Cupitt thinks that we should think about the resurrection in the
same way that (he thinks) Paul did.

> The resurrection is a state of the self and a way of living for and from
> God by the power of God. St. Paul, for example, shows no interest
> either in the mechanics of Jesus' rising or in the empty tomb, which
> he never even mentions. His thought about the resurrection is in-
> tensely communal, participatory and existential. . . . Preoccupation
> with Jesus' resurrection as a historical problem (whose evidence
> are in fact pathetically weak) is ludicrously disproportionate to
> the world-filling present reality of the resurrection as a power of
> demand and grace that presently transforms my life.[34]

As a matter of fact, thinks Cupitt, if the resurrection were thought
of as an objective fact, it would not have the power to change my
life at all. We just don't think that way anymore.

33. Ibid., 38.
34. Ibid.

It is this Kantian "religious reality" that Cupitt wants us to embrace. It is this Kantian "religious reality" that Cupitt says we *must* embrace. "Compared with this tremendous religious reality, 'historical' claims about walking corpses and empty tombs are foolish and irrelevant."[35]

These are strong words, particularly strong for those of us who still foolishly and irrelevantly talk of empty tombs and atonements. With such strong words, we would expect Cupitt to have equally strong arguments. Surprisingly, he does not. Two examples will suffice.

Cupitt sets out to dismantle any suggestion that the Christian doctrine of creation is anything objective in which we might believe. His discussion (note, not *argument*) seems to run along two lines. The first way toward a refutation of the millennia-held doctrine of creation, is to point out that there are other creation myths. "The first line of argument starts from the recognition that there are two fundamentally different accounts of creation"[36] It is difficult to assess just why the fact that there is another account of something would shatter one's own account of that thing. I may believe strongly that Neal Armstrong landed on the moon in 1969, and may be able to give a fairly accurate account of the flight: the time of liftoff, the landing on the moon, the touchdown, and so forth. You may, however, believe that the entire "flight" of Apollo 11 was played out as a Hollywood movie. You may be able to name the director of the movie and explain how they replicated the moon, weightlessness, and the rest. It is difficult to see, however, at least *prima facie*, how such an account as yours would compel me to recant of my view.

Cupitt's answer is that the language that I use to describe my theology, though historically the popular view, is now outdated, thanks to Rudolph Bultmann and others. For, according to Cupitt, "what has happened in modern times is that the development of the scientific world-picture has annihilated the mythological way of seeing the world as creation, exposing its ideas of causality, of

35. Ibid., 45.
36. Ibid., 47.

76

degrees of being and so forth as absurd."[37] In other words, to use my example again, we are now more used to thinking in terms of "movies" than of real "facts" when it comes to things of religion. Science has now determined that the old, old story is not only old, but so old it has finally died.

Second, Cupitt tells us that the notions of prayer and providence give us reasons to give up on any traditional idea of God and of his creating the world. In the case of prayer, the matter is easily dismissed: "It would be impious and foolish to suppose that I had the power to manipulate God or to coerce God, or that God needs information, or waits for encouragement from me before he acts."[38] Prayer, therefore, is impious and absurd.

Providence is a bit more complicated, according to Cupitt, but he still attempts to dismantle it in a page and a half. His conclusion?

> If faith in divine providence were the empirical belief that at least the great majority of good people have happy endings, and at least the great majority of bad people come to sticky ends, then one can only say that such a belief is too absurd for anyone to hold and too absurd for anyone to think it worth checking by systematic counting. Faith in divine providence is not a factual belief from which we can deduce predictions about the future course of human history. On past form there seems little profit in claiming that God will not permit mass starvation or the use of nuclear weapons, for example.[39]

So, the crux of Cupitt's argument against the old, old story of Christianity is that it is absurd. It is absurd because science has told us it is (just *which* science has told us, or which *scientists*, Cupitt neglects to say). It is absurd because we can't quite get to the bottom (rationally speaking) of the nature of prayer and providence. It is absurd, when all is said and done, simply because Cupitt says so.

37. Ibid., 52.
38. Ibid., 53.
39. Ibid., 55.

Of course, Cupitt is not alone in telling us of the absurdity of traditional Christianity. The main reason we have chosen to look at Cupitt is the recognized influence of Immanuel Kant on his thinking. Cupitt gives credit as well to Rudolph Bultmann, Ninian Smart, and other pillars of the (post)modern world. But in the end, Cupitt asks us to believe him, to surrender to the notion that Christianity in its traditional form is absurd, and to *internalize* it, making it *autonomous*. At least this much can be said for Cupitt's modern view of Christianity—it itself is fully internalized (since it seems to have its source in Cupitt), and it is autonomous (since it seems to be accountable only to Cupitt's own law). In that, he is consistent.

Just how *should* we think of God's relationship to creation? Is a Christianized Platonism correct, that God has eternal forms in his own mind, out of which comes creation? Is Aquinas right, that the identity of God's existence and essence gives us a foundation from which to posit other essences? Is Kant right that God transcends our experience altogether? Is Marion right that God is not thought, but simply given? These are serious questions—questions that have occupied and will continue to occupy philosophers of religion and theologians for years to come. How should we begin to think about these things?

Conclusion

Plato's forms lead to Aristotle's essences; Aristotle's essences lead to Thomas Aquinas's being; Thomas's being leads to Marion's "God without Being." And Marion's God without being has dangerous affinities to Kant's unknown (because noumenal) god, and to Cupitt's internalized god.

From Plato to Marion, Kant to Cupitt, we have at least seen something of the wisdom of van Inwagen's admission: there is no real consensus when it comes to the nature of ultimate reality. We have also seen that discussions about the nature and existence of God, as attempts to come to grips with the nature of ultimate reality, have themselves offered a good bit of diversity, even contradiction.

78

There is most likely no resolution to this, at least this side of heaven, but that should be no reason to avoid the matter altogether.

Given the concerns that we have highlighted above, there may be a very good alternative to these (and other) notions of God, of being, and of God's relationship to everything else. There may, as well, be a good alternative to the Kantian conclusion. It may be that we can offer an alternative way of thinking about the nature of ultimate reality, an alternative that would address some of Marion's concerns, as well as an alternative to the way in which the discussions should begin. Perhaps there is another way to begin to think about God and his relationship to the nature of all that is.

Epistemology

5

Knowing God's Knowing

. . . as the Scripture is the first Instrument of every healthful knowledge concerning God: so God is the first, and supreme Principle of the being of those things which serve this knowledge, on whom all things immediately depend. —TRELCATIUS

Just how do we go about knowing the nature of ultimate reality? What method do we use, what sources do we consult in order to know how to bring certain things together? How do we know not only *what* is ultimate, but *how* what is ultimate relates to what is not?

In chapter 3, we noted Plato's and Aristotle's attempts to find the unifying "ultimate" that would help us understand and "systematize" our experience and our lives. Plato, and we should not underestimate his genius and influence, worked with philosophical discussions of the past and with his own reasoning tools in order to postulate an ultimate and its relationship to everything else. Aristotle continued in that tradition, yet capitalized on new ways of seeing the world and new elements of concern. Anselm and Aquinas took what they knew of philosophy's past and attempted to synthesize that with some of what they knew of Christianity.

Kant, like the rest, looked at the history of discussions about the world and God and sought to reconcile much of what had been set forth previously. Schleiermacher, Ritschl, Cupitt, and others sought to capitalize and build on Kant's views in order to attempt to fit some understanding of God into such a construct.

Given the abundance of such discussions, what's a Christian to do? How do we begin to understand where to begin to understand?

A Dual View

This section offers a Christian approach to knowing, especially knowing God and (something of) God's own knowing. In saying that this is *a* Christian approach, we are saying at the same time that there are, and have been throughout history, other options proffered by Christians with respect to our subject. There can be little doubt that brilliant thinkers, such as Anselm and Aquinas, Turretin and Jonathan Edwards have developed their own views (whether full-blown or not) within the context of the truth of the Christian position. There seems still to be room for one more, and we will attempt to work through what a self-consciously Christian view of ultimate reality, and therefore of knowledge, could be. More specifically, we will attempt, within the context of historic Reformed theology, to work out the implications of that theology for a Christian-theistic epistemology.[1]

It seems that the doctrine of creation is the most helpful place to begin when attempting to say something Christian about the nature of things. Whatever else Christianity teaches, there is little disagreement that God's creating everything is a kind of rock bot-

1. We will not be spelling out the details of Reformed theology as it applies to our subject. For more on that, see K. Scott Oliphint and Lane G. Tipton, eds., *Revelation and Reason: New Essays in Reformed Apologetics* (Phillipsburg, NJ: P&R, forthcoming).

tom truth, essential to the Christian position.[2] There is something, therefore, that we can know about everything; we can know that everything is created, except, of course, God.

But that brings up another important point. If everything is created except God, then God must be of an entirely different order than everything else. This may seem all too obvious on the surface, but because of its importance it needs to be said clearly here. It is not the case that everything is created, but rather it is the case that everything is created except God, who himself is the Creator. And we would be quick to add that there was nothing that in any way made or created God. It seems, then, that we have a duality of "existences" in our Christian approach: we have things that exist as created, and One who does not.

Now if the duty of metaphysics is to tell us something about the nature of ultimate reality, then it would seem that it should tell us something about the nature of God, given that he alone is uncreated (and, whatever else one might want to import into the concept "ultimate," the fact of being uncreated ought to be included). But now we're forced to ask, in the first place, just how it is that we can know something of this God who is ultimate.

Debates about how one can know God are rich and full in the history of the Western church, of philosophy, and of philosophy of religion. Often the debate is cast in terms of faith and reason. Without engaging those debates here, we can say with some confidence that, no matter how the relationship of faith and reason is discussed, there is little disagreement that at least *one* way to know about God is from revelation. With the exceptions of the deists and modernist thinkers that we might call the Cupitt contingent, virtually all have wanted to affirm that God's revelation is a necessary avenue toward the knowledge of God.

---

2. This is not to say, as we will see later, that there won't be disagreement even on the notion of creation; there is disagreement on virtually everything if one looks hard enough. I am merely acknowledging what has been a central element of Christianity in the East and in the West. The doctrine of creation has implications for Cupitt's discussion above. For a challenge to the doctrine of creation *ex nihilo*, we will look later at Richard E. Creel, *Divine Impassibility: An Essay in Philosophical Theology* (Cambridge: Cambridge University Press, 1986).

So without going into great detail we may simply affirm that (at least part of) the Christian understanding of the character of God has come from his revelation, both in the world and (primarily and centrally) in the Bible. This means that there are two avenues by which we can learn something of God: nature and Scripture. But it also means that in order properly to understand who this God is, it was necessary for him to speak to his creatures, which he has done through his prophets and apostles, and finally through his Son. And that speaking is what we now have in the Bible.

Given that God has revealed himself in the Bible, which is his word to us, it should not be surprising that there have been those in the history of theology and of (certain branches of) philosophy who have attempted, more or less accurately no doubt, to provide a coherent exposition of what Scripture teaches us about the world and about ultimate reality (God). A Christian exposition of the nature of the world, and of God, can follow the lead of much that has already been set forth in one context or another. We can sprinkle our discussion, therefore, with the wisdom of the ages. This may add a certain historical or traditional credibility that might otherwise be lacking in such a discussion.[3]

Hagar and Sarah

Before moving directly to a discussion about the character of God, we should attempt to state clearly just *how* we are approaching our subject matter, and indeed this entire study.

As we saw in chapter 1, the subject of faith and reason usually devolves into the question of faith *or* reason with respect to our understanding of God. The two aspects—faith and reason—are typically meant to point us to the *source* or *authority* of our respective subject matter, faith pointing to its source in revelation and reason pointing to its source in, well, reason.

---

3. The argument set forth here for a Christian notion of the nature of ultimate reality does not *depend* on the sources and authors cited, but it at least shows, in Rortian fashion, that there are (historical) peers that will let us get away with what we are attempting to propose.

If we say that we will approach a particular subject by way of faith, we are admitting our reliance on God's revelation for our content and conclusion(s). If we say that we want to approach our subject by way of reason, we are saying that our source for information and conclusions will be our own understanding, using the tools of reason that have been developed and tested over time.

There must be, however, a way to approach the relationship of faith and reason, and of their respective disciplines—theology and philosophy—so that the two work, not against each other, but in harmony. And there is. With respect to discussions of theology, reason is meant to have a *ministerial* and organic relationship to revelation. Turretin explains:

> A ministerial and organic relation is quite different from a principal and despotic. Reason holds the former relation to theology, not the latter. It is the Hagar (the bondmaid which should be in subjection to Scripture); not the Sarah (the mistress which presides over Scripture). It ought to compare the things proposed to be believed with the sacred Scriptures, the inflexible rule of truth. As when we refer the things we wish to measure to the public standard with the hand and eye. *But reason itself neither can nor ought to be constituted the rule of belief.*[4]

Given the ministerial use of reason, we should be quick to incorporate the best tools of reason in order to help clarify and articulate our theology and its implications. As a matter of fact, when attempting to systematize biblical truth the use of philosophical language, tools, and methods are both (properly) replete in the history of orthodox theology and nearly indispensable. In using the tools of philosophy and reason for doing theology, the Reformed orthodox made a distinction between theological doctrines or questions that are "purely theological" and those that make use of the tools of reason and philosophical terminology. The former were dubbed *articuli puri*, since they used only theological terminology in their assessments; the latter were called *articuli mixti*, since they

4. Francis Turretin, *Institutes of Elenctic Theology*, ed. James T. Dennison Jr., trans. George Musgrave Giger, 3 vols. (Phillipsburg, NJ: P&R, 1992–97), 1:25, my emphasis.

merged both theological and philosophical terminology in their discussions. Muller observes:

> Since theology is a rational discourse and since the truths of theology and of philosophy do not oppose one another, it becomes possible to make statements that include the language and concepts of both disciplines: when theology inquires into the meaning of trinitarian relationships, for example, it asks, in the language of philosophy, whether the persons are really or only rationally distinct from the essence of God. This mixture of language and concepts, in turn, raises the issue of rules for the use of philosophy in theological argument.[5]

Because reason and philosophy are thought to be of ministerial use in theological argumentation, theology is the "higher" truth in relation to philosophy. As a higher truth, theology is not to fall lock-step behind philosophy's pronouncements, especially its pronouncements with regard to the things of the Christian faith. According to Turretin:

> If reason is the principle of faith, then first it would follow that all religion is natural and demonstrable by natural reason and natural light. . . . Second, it would follow that reason is nowhere to be made captive and to be denied, against the express passages of Scripture; and that those possessed of a more ready mind and a more cultivated genius can better perceive and judge the mysteries of faith against universal experience.[6]

At least part of the problem in many discussions in the philosophy of religion is that reason is thought not to be instrumental and ministerial but rather to be *magisterial*. But, given the deep mysteries of God and his ways with the world (Rom. 11:33–36), any application of reason and its tools that seeks to rule over theology or Christianity is doomed to deny the basic principles of Christianity itself. Any philosophy of religion that seeks to understand and to

---

5. Richard A. Muller, *Post-Reformation Reformed Dogmatics: Prolegomena to Theology* (Grand Rapids, MI: Baker, 1987), 247–48.

6. Turretin, *Institutes*, 1:25.

delineate aspects of the *Christian* religion is duty-bound thereby to come under the authority of God's revelation. In doing so, it will discover deep mysteries, mysteries that are beyond reason's ability completely to comprehend. But those mysteries will not be denied; they will form the context in which other truths of Christianity can be better articulated and more clearly set forth. Muller states:

> The consent of reason to the articles of faith in no way implies the dependence of faith on reason, since the relation does not correspond with the relation of cause to effect or of logical foundation to conclusion: faith is prior to reason as a higher to a lower truth, in the context of the essential oneness and self-consistency of truth. What is more, the denial of double truth leads irrevocably to the conclusion that the higher, not unreasonable, truth of faith and revelation illuminates the fallen mind and draws the wreckage of fallen reason toward perfection.[7]

This last statement is itself illuminating. It means, in part, that it is the clarification and articulation of theology, using as it deems necessary the ministerial tools of philosophy and reason, that serves to move the unregenerate toward this "higher truth," that is, toward the truth of who God is and what he requires of us. In other words, the doing of theology, even philosophical theology, when its task is the setting forth of biblical truth, is itself an apologetic. Given that truth is one, setting forth God's truth can serve to impress on "fallen reason" the fact of the existence of the triune God, and the concomitant fact of our obligations to him. Reason and philosophy, then, in the service of faith and theology, provide the content and context for a defense of Christian truth. This is, perhaps, *especially* the case when the topic under review is the topic of God and his revelation.

Knowing God

In our Christian approach to the nature of ultimate reality, it should come as no surprise that we will need to begin to look at

7. Muller, *Prolegomena to Theology*, 247–48.

(1) the character of God, and (2) the possibility of knowing him. We will seek to move in reverse order at this point,[8] looking at the possibility of knowing him beginning in this chapter, and then looking at certain crucial aspects of his character and his relationship to his creation in parts 3 and 4.

Any discussion that purports to be Christian would be remiss, at best, if it did not deal adequately with God as *the* ultimate reality. Though a theology proper is not our immediate concern here, it will be necessary to flesh out some of the main contours of a Christian-theistic structure with respect to reality and knowledge.

There are certain aspects of the character of God that most would simply take for granted: for example, that he is good, wise, holy, and loving. This, it would seem, is about as irresistible a truth as one could imagine. Though there may be some who assert that God, if he exists, must be the devil,[9] most would hold that it is of the essence of any being who is thought to be in any way great, or greatest or Supreme, that he be good, wise, and so on.

There are also, however, certain aspects to the character of God that are less intuitive, harder to hold, abstruse and mysterious, difficult to reconcile with other things we take to be known. There is the notion that God is one, yet as one he exists as three persons. These three persons may not, however, be denominated as three Gods, though each one *is* fully and completely a distinct person and God. There is no room in the Christian tradition for tri-theism; there are not three Gods. This is a difficult notion to explain, much less to comprehend, though the mainstream of Christendom has explicitly held it to be true since at least the third (if not the first) century AD.

There is also the idea, anticipated in the Old Testament and realized in the New, that the second person of this Three-in-One, while remaining God, took on a human nature, came to this earth, and gave up his life for sinful people in order to satisfy the demands

8. That is, we should first understand how it is that we know before beginning to look at what, specifically, we know. Note the order of subjects, for example, in the Westminster Confession of Faith. It deals first with Scripture, then with God and his character.

9. As in the French poet Charles Baudelaire's suggestion that if there is a god, he is the devil.

of his Father's holiness and justice. This is indeed mysterious. It can be discussed—terms can be used to help clarify and commend these truths—but just *how* such things could be remains a mystery for us (though, of course, not for God).

This kind of mystery persists not only in the character of God, per se, but also in God's relationship to other things. In many discussions in the philosophy of religion there has been significant consideration of the relationship of God to time, to our choices, to suffering, and to other things as well. These are fascinating discussions, which provoke intense debate. As interesting as they are, these notions will not occupy our attention in this chapter. They will later on, however, because they are substantial issues in their own right and certainly deserve close attention. Here we will attempt to focus on aspects of the character of God that will help us clarify the parameters of a Christian approach to knowledge. To begin that discussion we turn, first of all, to one particular aspect of the character of God.

Simple Complexity

It is to the traditional teaching on the simplicity of God that we should look to begin our formulation of a Christian approach to (some of) the most acute epistemological (and metaphysical) problems in the philosophy of religion. This discussion will become important as we proceed to part 3, and so the material here should be kept in mind all along. It is necessary to introduce it here because it plays such a crucial part in our understanding of epistemology, as we will see below.

The doctrine of God's simplicity, sometimes denoted as the *unitas simplicitatis*,[10] or the *simplicitas Dei*, says that the characteristics of God are not "parts" of God that come together to make him what he is, but are rather identical with his essence, and thus with him. The simplicity of God affirms not only that whatever God essentially is,[11] he is necessarily. It says even more. The simplicity of

10. In distinction from the *unitas singularitatis*, which holds that God is one.
11. We'll attempt to give more clarity to the notion of essence in chapters 10 and following. For now, we will take its meaning as fairly intuitive.

God holds that God's attributes are not characteristics or properties that exist (in the same way that he exists) in any way "outside" of God, such that his having such a characteristic or property entails his participation in something other than himself. God just *is* his characteristics and his characteristics are identical to him.[12]

The fact that God is truth, therefore, according to the Christian tradition, does not mean that God participates in a property of truth that lies in eternity or exists eternally with or alongside him. Rather, as God, he simply *is* truth, and the truth that he is just *is* himself. As good, God does not partake of a universal goodness in a maximal way such that he has the most of it or its eternal manifestation or anything of the sort. Rather, God's goodness just *is* God himself; to separate him from that goodness would, *per impossibile*, destroy him entirely.[13]

Not only so, but when we think of the simplicity of God, we are also committed to the notion that God's attribute of truth and his attribute of goodness themselves are, since they are God's, attributed to him essentially and thus are his essence. God's truth is a good truth, and his goodness is true goodness, just because the one is included in, and identical with (in God), the other.

Perhaps the best way to think about the simplicity of God lies in the fact that it demands a denial of any composition of parts in God. In this denial is an equally important affirmation. The affirmative aspect of simplicity says that whatever attributes, qualities, or properties inhere essentially in God, they are all identical with his essence. Notice in this denial and affirmation that there is no denial of *distinctions* in God. The doctrine of simplicity, in its best formulations, has never wanted to affirm that God was some sort of being in which no distinctions did, or could, reside. That kind of

12. Whether simplicity is, strictly speaking, an attribute of God need not be decided here. It could be argued that simplicity is not an attribute that God has, so much as it is a description of the way in which his attributes are related. If, however, simplicity is something that is attributed to God, it seems to be an *attribute* of his as well. It should be remembered also that the doctrine of simplicity is, at least in part, a piece of *negative* theology, attempting to articulate what God is *not*, rather than what he is.

13. See part 3 for a discussion and distinction of God's goodness as covenantally qualified.

"simplicity" is more akin to philosophical speculation than to biblical truth. Rather, the distinctions that do reside in God, because they accrue to his essence, are identical with that essence and thus are not parts of God, serving to make up the "whole" of who he is. Simplicity, therefore, applies to the essence of God.[14]

We can think of simplicity, then, in at least the following way: the simplicity of God means that God is simple, [which means] removing from him all kinds of composition, which are five:

(1) of quantitative parts, as a body.
(2) of essential parts, matter and form, as a man consists of soul and body.
(3) of a genus and difference, as every species.
(4) of subject and accidents, as a learned man, a white wall.
(5) of act and power, as the Spirits.[15]

An important aspect of this doctrine of God's simplicity is that these distinctions in God are not thought to exist *realiter*. That is, they are not distinctions that should be thought of as "things," so that the Godhead is a composition of "thing upon thing." Rather, the distinctions of attributes in the Godhead, because identical with his essence, are *formal* or *modal* distinctions, describing for us the ways in which the essence of God exists. Thus, for example, the three persons in the Godhead are not essential distinctions in God, but rather the ways in which the essence of God exists personally.[16]

14. This will become important in future chapters. Because we will argue that God voluntarily takes on covenantal properties, we can say for example that the essentially simple God, in whom there is no composition, is nevertheless jealous, wrathful, vengeful, and so on. These latter properties are not of the essence of God; he takes them on freely and willingly by virtue of his free decision to create. We should note as well that none of these properties negate or in any way change who and what God essentially is.

15. Richard A. Muller, *Post-Reformation Reformed Dogmatics: The Rise and Development of Reformed Orthodoxy, Ca. 1520 to Ca. 1725: The Divine Essence and Attributes*, 2nd ed. (Grand Rapids, MI: Baker, 2002), 277–78.

16. As Muller notes, the Protestant scholastic doctrine of simplicity implies that God is triune, and it was formulated in the face of different opponents who sought to deny the orthodox understanding of the Trinity. See ibid., 271ff.

One can begin to see why objections have been raised against this notion of simplicity. We have no creaturely example of such a thing. It does not seem to fit with anything else with which we are familiar, neither can we lay out *exactly what kind* of attributes these are, which describe, entail, and are identical to God's existence.[17] But limitations of this sort need not arouse an immediate charge of irrationality or demand a call for a radical revision of God's attributes as we understand them. There are, as might be expected, some who have called for just that.

Because the simplicity of God is foundational to so much more that we believe about God, we will attempt, first, to flesh out a possible epistemological context here in order later to develop a metaphysical structure in light of such a context.

Perhaps one of the clearest and most articulate objections, at least in recent time, to the simplicity of God comes from Alvin Plantinga. In his, *Does God Have a Nature?* Plantinga sets out an argument, the conclusion of which calls for a rejection of (his notion of) the traditional notion of simplicity. Plantinga's problem with simplicity is motivated by Thomas Aquinas's discussion of it. So perhaps it would help us to set forth a defense of God's simplicity if we pause to interact with Plantinga and Aquinas on the matter.

According to Plantinga, the notion of God's simplicity is "a dark saying indeed." It goes back, he thinks, to Parmenides, according to whom reality was "an undifferentiated plenum in which no distinctions can be made."[18] Plantinga has good reason to see the doctrine as "dark." He is convinced that if God were identical with his properties, then, *ipso facto*, God would be a property. If Plantinga is right, then simplicity is indeed a dark

17. This latter notion of God's attributes entailing his existence may not itself be intuitively obvious to some. It does, however, seem to be the truth of the matter.

18. Alvin Plantinga, "Does God Have a Nature?" in *The Analytic Theist: An Alvin Plantinga Reader*, ed. James F. Sennett (Grand Rapids, MI: Eerdmans, 1998), 228. This statement seems to miss the mark as far as an attempt to ascertain the basic reason for the assertion of the Christian doctrine of simplicity. It also is wide of the mark in that it fails to recognize the Christian source and discussions of the doctrine. But since Plantinga's criticisms do not depend one way or the other on Parmenides, we can treat the remark as an unfortunate aside.

saying in that its implications wind up denying the Christian God. If God is identical with his properties, so his argument goes, then God himself is a property; and if God is a property, he cannot be Personal.[19]

This seems to be a reasonable objection to the doctrine of simplicity. It is admirable that Plantinga is opposed to any implication that would require a rejection of the personal character of God. Such a rejection would amount to a rejection of the true Christian God. Not only so, but in characteristic fashion, Plantinga's argument is well argued, well reasoned, and logically valid.

What is not so valuable, from a Christian perspective, is that Plantinga, in order to begin to deny (his construal of) the traditional doctrine of simplicity, is forced to deny what he calls the "sovereignty-aseity intuition." That is, Plantinga not only rejects the simplicity of God, but he rejects what he sees as a couple of the main culprits that have caused such a "dark saying" to be put forth in theology in the first place. Thus, for Plantinga, God is neither sovereign nor *a se*.

This conclusion, together with the rejection of God's simplicity, is most troubling. As we will see in the next few chapters, it seems nearly impossible to affirm any Christian notion of God while at the same time rejecting his essential character. Any God whose existence is dependent cannot be the God revealed to us in Scripture. Why reject such a thing as aseity or simplicity?

It could be that there are underlying notions lurking in the background of Plantinga's discussion, notions that could undermine the way in which distinctions are made, and thus resolutions proposed, in the first place.

Doubting Thomas

It took the genius of Thomas Aquinas to set forth and defend the notion of the simplicity of God as an essential aspect of God's character. Thomas attempted to work out his philosophy in a way that would both do justice to the truth of God's simplicity and allow

19. Ibid., 238ff.

for a true knowledge of God.[20] Unlike Aquinas, however, we will attempt to tackle the knowledge question first, which will be front and center for us here, and turn to the metaphysical implications of God's simplicity in part 3. For now, we will merely state that the simplicity of God, as discussed above, is an essential and necessary aspect of his character.

The problem with simplicity for Thomas, however, revolves around the question of predicating something of God. For Thomas, the question of predicating something of God goes hand-in-glove with the notion of simplicity. Thomas recognized that if God's nature is identical with God himself, then to say something like "God is good" is to say something that, at least on the surface of it, denies the unique character of God altogether. It is to predicate something of God, something in which the predicate is distinct from the subject. Worse, it is to predicate of God something that is found in his creatures, and thus to ascribe to God creaturely attributes. Ascribing creaturely attributes to God was not an option for Aquinas.

Just what were the options available to Aquinas? A denial of simplicity was no option. To deny the simplicity of God would mean to attribute something to God that was neither of the creature nor of the Creator; it would mean to attribute, for example, some kind of independent and abstract property, say, eternity, to God. And since eternity was thought to be independent of God, not identical with God, it would necessarily be something "added" to his character. But what would that "something" be? What would the status of "eternity" be if it was independent of God? It could not be Creator, for it was added to him; it could not be created, because it was a part of *God's* character. It would have to be some kind of *tertium quid*, perhaps coming from the nebulous sphere of Platonic properties.

For Aquinas, with his strong notion of creation, this too was not an option. After all, if in the beginning there was God, who then created everything else, what else could there be (or have been) between, beside, or alongside God prior to creation? What would be the status of some "thing" that was neither created by God nor an

---

20. Note here again the necessary and reciprocal relation between the nature of ultimate reality, God, and the nature of knowledge.

essential aspect of his character? Whatever it was, it would have to partake of a number of God's own attributes; for example, it would have to be eternal, existing alongside God in the way that he exists, perhaps participating in him, and so forth. This, too, could not be entertained as a Christian option.[21] The only Christian option available to Thomas, as he thought, was to affirm God's simplicity. In affirming simplicity, the (biblical) character of God is maintained, though other problems may in fact creep in.

And they did. One of the primary problems with respect to affirming the simplicity of God was the problem of speaking of God, of saying something that was true of him. It was the problem, we might say, of theistic predication. What could it mean, really, to say, "God is good" if the goodness that God is is identical with him (thus transcending the notion of a "property" of goodness)? Doesn't the metaphysical doctrine of simplicity leave us with an epistemological (having to do with predication) doctrine of simplicity? If God is *really* simple, aren't we left with saying—if we want to speak truthfully about God—simply, "God"?

Thomas set forth, in response to this dilemma, a notion of analogy[22] that was calculated to respond to the problem of theological predication[23] in the context of the dilemmas posed by affirming the simplicity of God. He developed a notion of predication and

21. We will see later, in Creel, that such an idea will be entertained as a metaphysical option.

22. There is significant debate on the *nature* of Thomas's analogical structure. Ralph McInerny, in *The Logic of Analogy* and elsewhere, argues for Thomistic analogy as a *logical* rather than *metaphysical* construct. If he is right, then proper proportionality relates primarily to terms rather than to things. We cannot enter the debate, but would only interject that, even if McInerny is correct, meaningful predication for Aquinas still *depends* on his metaphysics, and thus his doctrine of analogy would have significant metaphysical implications. Suffice it to say at this point that Thomas's metaphysics requires his notion of analogy in a symmetrical way such that if one is altered, so, to a greater or lesser extent, must the other be. For this latter point, see Scott MacDonald, "Theory of Knowledge," in *The Cambridge Companion to Aquinas*, ed. Norman Kretzmann and Eleanor Stump (Cambridge: Cambridge University Press, 1993), 160–95.

23. We shall think of predication here as an ascription or affirmation of that which is in the mind as concept to an object. Our use of "goodness," for example, will therefore include the concept in the mind and the ascription of it to an object.

designated this as "analogy" in order to distinguish it clearly from both univocal and equivocal predication.

In univocal predication, what is attributed to one thing is identical when attributed to another. So, if we were to speak univocally, when we say that "God is good" and that "people are good," "goodness" would be an identical property, relating as it does both to God and to people. But since we do not want to attribute creaturely attributes to the Creator, nor are we allowed to biblically, univocal predication is ruled out.[24]

In equivocal predication, what is attributed to one thing is in no way similar or identical to the same attribution given to another thing. So, if we were to speak equivocally and say "God is good" and "people are good," "goodness" would mean something completely and totally different when applied to God, on the one hand, and then to people, on the other. Since we do not want to say, nor can we biblically, that our attribution of goodness to God could just as well mean that God is maleficent, we cannot affirm equivocal predication either.

There must, therefore, be a way of predicating that will allow for a true attribution of goodness, or any other proper perfection, to God without ascribing to him any form of creatureliness and without making nonsense of every proposition predicated of God. Analogical predication is Aquinas's way. And by analogy, he means at least the following.

To the question of whether we can ascribe any name to God properly,[25] that is, not *merely* metaphorically, Aquinas first responds by arguing that any perfection found in creation is there because it was caused by One who has that perfection "in a transcendent way" (*modum altiorem*). Thus, analogy, at least in this instance, requires a qualitative distinction between two (or more) predicates. That is, there is one term used in two different senses, yet the two senses

24. It might be worth mentioning here that Duns Scotus rejected the notion of analogy and argued for univocal predication with respect to God and his creation.

25. Thomas Aquinas, *Summa Theologiae: Latin Text, English Translation, Introduction, Notes, Appendices and Glossary*, ed. Thomas Gilby (London and New York: Eyre & Spottiswoode and McGraw-Hill, 1964), 1.13.3: "Utrum aliquod nomen dicatur de Deo proprie."

are somehow related. At issue, therefore, is meaningful predication such that the term used for both the cause and the effect ascribes something meaningful to the cause while relating somehow to its use for the effect as well. It is this "somehow" that needs to be spelled out more clearly.

Thomas attempts to spell out the "somehow," to resolve the impasse in the problem of theistic predication, by his distinction between the *modus significandi* (mode of signification) and the *res significata* (thing signified). According to him, two things must be considered when one attempts to speak meaningfully about the perfections (or attributes) of God. With regard to things themselves ascribed to God—for example, goodness, truth, being—these things are properly (we could say "literally") said of God. These ascriptions are not metaphorical; they reside intrinsically and essentially in God. The thing signified (*res significata*), therefore, refers primarily to God and only secondarily to creatures. As for the *modus significandi*, the way or ways things are signified, however, Thomas says, "these are not properly used of God."[26]

Now how can Aquinas make sense of the *res significata/modus significandi* distinction? First, Aquinas maintains that "everything is named by us according to our knowledge of it"[27] With this assertion comes, not a metaphysical skepticism, but rather an epistemological dependence on metaphysics for knowledge to be coherent. It is because reality is the way it is that we can name something and do so such that the proposition can be judged to be true or false.[28] Thomas affirms that when we name the perfections, we are saying some *thing* literally true of God, though our *saying* itself is an improper mode of signification. The question then revolves around the truth of a given proposition with respect to the *res significata* aspect of that proposition.

Thomas maintains that the *modus significandi* is improper (perhaps "nonliteral" would be a better way to designate it) when speak-

26. Ibid.: "non proprie dicuntur de Deo."
27. Ibid., 1.13.1: "Unumquodque enim nominatur a nobis, secundum quod ipsum cogniscimus."
28. This is, it seems to me, correct as far as it goes. We will attempt to defend this principle in chapter 8.

ing of the names or perfections of God. Such is the case because we must use a subject and predicate when we speak of God, whereas *in God* no such relationship *really* obtains (and remember that, for Thomas, there must be a metaphysical reality behind whatever is predicated truthfully). God *is* what he *is*, or *who* he is, is *what* he is; there can be no real separation between the what and the who in God. The attributes and perfections of God are coextensive with his being.

However, when it comes to the *res significata*, as we have seen, perfections ascribed to God are used *proprie*, that is, used properly, or literally. When we predicate that "God is good," therefore, goodness is signified of God in an improper, or nonliteral way, but goodness properly belongs to God in that it is identical with his essence (given simplicity).

But there are questions that arise based on this construction. How, for example, can Thomas make his theory of analogy and predication coherent with his own understanding of knowledge? As we saw above, we name something according to our knowledge of it. With respect to God, our *modus significandi*, therefore, is the product of our *modus cognoscendi* (mode of knowing). Because Thomas is a metaphysical (moderate) realist, that which we cognize is a product of that which is, the *modus essendi* (essential mode).[29] In lining things up in just this way, it seems, Thomas would have a difficult time affirming anything about God after all.

The problem of the proper predication of God's perfections is what motivates Thomas's discussion of the distinction between the *modus significandi* and the *res significata*. Because he wants to maintain that we cannot properly signify *how* God is identical with *x*, he distinguishes between *x* and its signification. But the question has to be asked as to how we *know* the *res significata*. Just how does the *res significata* become something known to us?

Let us use goodness again as an example. Goodness is, according to Thomas, identical to God and is predicated, secondarily, of crea-

29. For elaborations of this in Aquinas see, for example, Thomas Aquinas, *Commentary on the Posterior Analytics of Aristotle*, trans. F. R. Larcher (Albany, New York: Magi Books, 1970), 1.2, 4; 2.8. This structure, of the *modus essendi* and the *modus cognoscendi*, is one that is crucial to a proper understanding of theology, as we will see.

tures and created things. Such is the case because goodness is essentially who God is. But predication is more than mere ascription.

I may say, "Bill is milliton," and even though I have predicated *something* of Bill, the statement is yet to be meaningful; we just don't know what "milliton" *is*. Now the scenario that Thomas has outlined is not quite as bad as that. He does at least use predicates that are a part of our common language. He uses predicates that are meaningful to us, but are also distinguished from us. But, aside from that, his distinction here seems to be plagued with the same problem of reference. Here the situation can become most complex. It is, however, worth a look, and perhaps focusing on the *res significata* will be as good a place as any to begin looking.

Just what *is* a particular *res significata*? It is one thing to say that a *res significata* is applied literally; it is quite another to say just *what* it is that is known in the first place. According to Aquinas, in this context, what is known is that which God essentially is, a perfection predicated properly of God. But how can we know what God is like? Again, in this context, Aquinas has already attempted to show that we know what God is like by our observation of the world around us. We know goodness, not because of our experience of God, but because of our experience of the world. The analogical relationship that obtains in this context is between goodness as it relates to God *proprie*, and goodness as it relates to creatures secondarily. And, as attributed to God properly, it also exists in him in a higher way.

Now because an analogical term is a species of equivocity rather than univocity, to say that goodness exists in God in a higher way is just to say that it exists in him in a higher, *but different*, way. By Thomas's own construct, there is no road we may take that will lead us in any way toward this difference. Nor is there anything to indicate in any way the delimitations of this difference. Goodness in God can only be predicated *modum altiorem*.[30] The situation looks bleak at this point.

---

30. One might ask to what extent Thomas's argument, or perhaps our analysis of it, falls prey to an ambiguity owing to the use/mention distinction. It doesn't seem that the distinction is in any significant way employed by Thomas or in the analysis of Thomas here. See the next chapter for an affirmation of Thomas's understanding of the relation-

If we cannot determine in any way *what* goodness *is* when predicated of God compared to its predication of creatures, how can we posit any kind of analogy at all? On what basis can analogy rest? That is, how can we determine that there is any similarity at all in a term ascribed to two different things if one of those ascriptions must remain, because of its subject, indeterminate? A determination cannot rest on our knowledge of God because that knowledge always comes by way of abstraction from sensible things, never by way of abstraction from an experience of God, at least not in this life (according to Aquinas). Thus we could just as easily ascribe greenness to God since the best we can do is to take the sensible and project it—inappropriately no less, as a *modus significandi*—to God.

It cannot rest on the predication of *x* in creatures because such predication as referencing the *res significata* is secondary and as *modus significandi* is inappropriate for God. Neither can it rest in what has already been shown to be true about God, because central to that theological construction is God's simplicity such that to predicate goodness would have to be to predicate God, thus reducing God to a property (since goodness is an abstraction). To say, then, that "God is good" and goodness is predicated properly (literally?) of God, says little that is meaningful, since we cannot say what goodness *is* when applied to God, except that it is different from secondary, creaturely goodness, from which the concept came in the first place.[31]

Or to approach it from another angle, that which we know, including the perfections of God, is known by virtue of our way of knowing, our *modus cognoscendi*. The method of the *modus cognoscendi* is, for the most part, according to Thomas, one of abstraction. For example, we know what *bonum* is by abstracting the universal form from the particular thing. *Bonum*, then, as known, cannot apply directly to Socrates, but in its application to Socrates is individuated in a way that excludes its being known as

ship of the nature of reality to knowledge, and thus to predication as well. Thanks to William Davis for bringing this to my attention.

31. It will not help us here to say that the concept is "different, but analogous," since it is the very idea of analogy that is currently being discussed. The fact of indeterminacy seems to result in the fact that the term *analogy*, since without content, when added to the notion of difference, is really no different than difference by itself.

a universal form. It is not the case, therefore, that "goodness" *as known* ever applies to a single *thing*.

> Nevertheless, it cannot be said that the character universal belongs to nature so understood, because commonality and unity belong to the character universal. . . . For if commonality were included in the notion of man, commonality would be found whenever humanity was found. But this is false, because in Socrates no commonality is found. On the contrary, whatever is in him is individuated.[32]

Now since Aquinas is no Platonic realist, the form as abstracted from the matter does not exist except in the matter itself and in the intellect as form. That is, there is no finite realm in which the perfect form *really* exists per se. Goodness, therefore, exists in two different, and seemingly disparate, ways. It exists in Socrates, but not as goodness; and it exists in the mind, but not as it exists in Socrates. How then can a concept abstracted from creatures, a concept existing in the mind only as universal form, be ascribed *proprie* to God of whom we have no experience, in whom is no form, and for whom there can be no *real* predicate?

There is a further handicap in Thomas's construction that can only be mentioned here: that is, that one can never form a concept of God by any experience of God's attributes or perfections. This, therefore, necessitates that whatever is predicated of God must be predicated of him by way of forms that are abstracted *as creaturely* and then transferred to some kind of relationship between what is experienced and what cannot be experienced *as such*.[33]

In the next chapter we will seek to offer some suggestions as to how we might improve on the scenario just developed.

32. Thomas Aquinas, "On Being and Essence," in *Selected Writings of St. Thomas Aquinas*, trans. Robert P. Goodwin (New York: Bobbs, 1965), 48.

33. Without detailing Thomas's account of abstraction and its relationship to knowledge, we must note here that he himself distinguished between abstraction as a mode of cognition, and *separation*. In separation, that which is known is simply conceived separately from something else, given that it cannot be experienced, since, in the case of God, it never exists in sensible matter and is not itself subject to the necessary (for abstraction) distinction of form and matter.

6

God Speaking of God

Therefore, that exclusive definition, encountered everywhere, annihilates all the divinity that men fashion for themselves out of their own opinion: for God himself is the sole and proper witness of himself. —JOHN CALVIN

We saw in chapter 5 that there are problems with Thomas Aquinas's notion of predication with respect to God and his character. How would Thomas respond to this kind of critique? Aquinas would have at least two responses in an attempt to extricate himself from the critique above. First, he would call on his moderate realism as that which grounds his epistemology. That is, he would remind us that it is only because of the *modus essendi* in the first place that one can even *have* a *modus cognoscendi* or a *modus significandi*. As grounded in the real, therefore, goodness can be referenced in predication without being subject to the way in which it is signified. Second, and this follows from the first, Aquinas would remind us that the *causal* factor embedded in creation guarantees us some kind of link between that which we know and signify and that which God is.[1]

The Aquinas Analogy

But there seems still to be a problem with such a response. It seems not to accomplish what it intends. While it is true that Thomas wants to ground our knowledge of things in the way things actually *are*, we have seen that, at the same time, he affirms that one never has cognitive access to the actual thing, but only to its form as universalized in the mind. This does not necessarily lead to skepticism, but it does mean that, whatever we do wind up knowing, what we can never know is a particular thing *as particular*, or *in a particular way*. But God himself is *the* particular thing *par excellence*. We are forced to ask whether we can really know him in any way whatsoever since he is exactly the preeminent and primary *Thing* that could never be experienced.[2]

Thomas's second (assumed) response to the above critique, which response involves his notion of causality, gets us closer to his doctrine of analogy and thus deserves a little more attention. We can ask of Thomas's assumed response how one might ascertain the truth or falsity of a given statement about God.

There seem to be two different aspects to Aquinas's teaching on analogy.[3] At times in his writings he affirms what has come to be called the analogy of proper proportionality. This aspect of analogy highlights Thomas's metaphysical construct in that each "thing" exists to the degree that its respective essence permits. Given that

---

1. This point can be granted and is helpful as long as one begins, not with causality per se, but with the revelation of God as that which determines the limits of causality itself. More on this in the next chapter.

2. Thomas is famous for his insistence that we can know God. To be clearer here in this context, however, we are asking as to whether we can know anything *about* God, ascribe anything to God, that will be more than merely metaphorical.

3. This is a controversial point that need not detain us here since the argument does not depend on the precision of one or the other delineations. Cajetan's notion of analogy as proper proportionality seems to have had predominance until the relatively recent past. Since then differences in emphases have been set forth by Etienne Gilson, Ralph McInerny, James Ross, G. B. Phelan, Charles Hart, and others.

essences particularize, something can be predicated of two different things analogically because each would participate in that thing to the degree that its essence allowed.

But there is another kind of analogy; there is also what is sometimes called intrinsic attribution. The analogy of intrinsic attribution states (among other things) that meaningful theological predication obtains because of the causal relationship between God and his creation. We can thus posit something that is *really* true of God because the effects that he has made are in some way like what he himself is. Analogy of intrinsic attribution, therefore, focuses on a middle term, a term ascribed to the two (or more) analogates that itself is in need of some kind of parameter, a definition or something like one, if such a term is going to be used in a meaningful (and truthful) way.

Goodness, as a middle term, is related to creatures in one way and to God in another, "transcendent" way (*modum altiorem*). Theological predication of goodness as such, in its mode as *res significata*, is properly ascribed to God, according to Aquinas. But the above question returns as to just what this goodness is? In order for us meaningfully to use such a term in a proposition such that it can be ascertained as either true or false, need we not have some idea of the relationship that is posited in the proposition?[4]

So, for example, we say, "Socrates is good." One of the important ways that we ascertain meaning from that statement, particularly given Aquinas's moderate realism, is that there *must be* a relationship between Socrates and the goodness that is ascribed to him. If there is no such relationship, then the statement cannot be determined to be either true or false because the mere structure of the proposition posits *some kind* of *real* relationship. That is, a

4. For a critique similar to the one here, see William P. Alston, "Aquinas on Theological Predication," in *Reasoned Faith*, ed. Eleanore Stump (Ithaca, NY: Cornell University Press, 1993), 145–78. The basic idea here is that, unless we can say *something* determinate about the relationship of the subject to the predicate, when we have committed ourselves to its different sense, we are handicapped with respect to the truth of the proposition. If the truth-value has something to do with the relationship designated in the proposition, and if the term used in the proposition is used in an unspecified but different way, it seems impossible to determine the status of the proposition itself and thus, in this case, to say anything meaningful about God.

condition of truth in a proposition is that there *be* a *modus essendi*, a way of being of the thing signified *and* of the subject. If there is no such way of being, there can be no truthful, meaningful expression. But isn't the problem here that, although Aquinas wants to affirm that the middle term applies to both subjects analogically, he must also affirm that in God there *really is* no relationship of the middle term to its subject (since the two are identical, as the doctrine of simplicity states)?

If so, then it would seem that Thomas's metaphysical system will not allow for a truthful assertion with respect to the character of God at all. Or, to put it another way, the middle term itself, whatever it is, in theological predication, can never apply to God, because in order for it to do so the middle term would necessitate some kind of real relationship in God between himself as subject and the predicate (as middle term). But there can really *be* no such relationship when the simplicity of God is maintained. Thus the analogy would break down since there would no longer be a proportional relation of the middle term to *both* analogates.

Now Aquinas might say here that we are confusing the way in which God is in himself with the way in which we know him. We cannot identify the middle term of the analogy with God because creatures never know him except through the ascription to him of a subject and predicate; such is the creaturely way to know him and we can know him in no other way. This is, it seems, fundamentally correct.

It should be remembered, however, that Thomas wants to affirm our proper understanding of God as far as the *res significata* goes. Goodness, as *res significata*, properly and primarily, as we know it and how we know it, applies to God. The question of *what kind* (creaturely or otherwise) of knowledge of God need not here enter the discussion. Thomas *does* want to say that goodness applies to God *in some way.* He even wants to say that ascriptions of this kind are *proprie*, proper (literal?). For our argument to hold, therefore, we should not at this point discuss the creaturely character of knowledge, but only try to show that goodness cannot meaningfully apply to God in any way, given the Thomistic epistemological system of analogy and theological predication.[5] What's a theological predicator to do?

There seem to be at least two possible solutions to this Thomistic dilemma. One solution would be to deny the simplicity of God. This is Plantinga's (and others') solution. It carries certain strong appeals with it, among which would be the possibility of maintaining a proportional relationship between God and his essential attributes. If such a relationship were maintained, even as it is in the realm of creation, then the analogy of proper proportionality would suffice and the proposition, "God is good" could be evaluated in terms of the *modus essendi* (since goodness would not be identical with God) and not simply as a *modus significandi*, which must be significantly distinguished from the *res significata*. There would be a proportional relationship between God and goodness, on the one hand, and people and goodness, on the other. There would be, therefore, the possibility of an analogical relationship.

This option, however, presents what seem to be insurmountable problems with Thomas's (and the general Christian tradition's) notion of God. For Thomas, God must be identical with his nature. To anticipate Thomas's response to such a suggestion, if there is one aspect or characteristic of God that is not identical with his nature, then God would be in potency with respect to that aspect or characteristic and would not, therefore, be pure act. To put it in more familiar terms, God would not be a maximally perfect being. Furthermore, as Aquinas himself states,[6] to deny the simplicity of God would make God composite and thus he would be dependent on someone or something else to be who he is. To give up the simplicity of God, it would seem, would mean for Aquinas to give up his entire theological-metaphysical system, not just one emphasis within it, since simplicity, for Aquinas, has as its correlates the notion of God as first cause and as first being.

5. We should say here that the creaturely form of knowledge is all-important to the discussion. Given Thomas's epistemology, however, it cannot be interjected here.

6. Thomas Aquinas, *Summa Theologiae: Latin Text, English Translation, Introduction, Notes, Appendices and Glossary*, ed. Thomas Gilby (London and New York: Eyre & Spottiswoode and McGraw-Hill, 1964), 1.3.7.

In other words, if God were not simple, he could not be shown to be what reason, according to Thomas, discovers him to be: the uncaused cause (since without simplicity there must be something that in some way caused God to be what he is) or the first being (since without simplicity God could not be *ipsum esse subsistens* because something that existed, but was not God, would have been needed in order for God to be what he is). There would have to be, if simplicity were given up, both another way or ways developed to get to God, as well as another notion of God and of whatever else was 'consubstantial' (by, with or around) to God.

Whether or not one accepts the categories that Thomas himself applies to his discussion of simplicity, to give up such a notion would seem to be contrary to traditional notions of God as "that than which no greater" is.[7] Not only so (and this will only be stated here, but argued later), but to give up on at least some notion of God's simplicity seems to compromise the truth that God has revealed about himself.

It seems, therefore, that to deny the simplicity of God is too high a price to pay for too little return. That is, though giving up on God's simplicity may resolve the epistemological dilemma, what one must also give up in the process is perhaps the most crucial and essential theistic truth that must be affirmed for a Christian—the truth of the existence of the triune God as *a se*, in the first place, and then the dependent existence of everything else.

But suppose we take Aquinas's own premise.[8] Suppose we take seriously the fact that God as an infinite, eternal, and necessary being is also the Creator of all that is. And suppose, rather than positing "being" as a *transcendental* notion, we posit a twofold or duality theory of being in which being becomes, not a unifying principle, but rather a basic principle of differentiation. That is, if

---

7. Though there have been numerous disagreements with Anselm's argument, none, including Thomas's, have denied that God is the greatest of all possible beings. They have not been for the most part directed at Anselm's concept of God, but rather at the way in which one can prove such a God exists. We must simply state it here, without looking at historical or biblical data, that God has traditionally been conceived to be the one who is the greatest of all that is, including all concepts.

8. For example in Aquinas, *Summa Theologiae*, 1.44.1; 1.45.5.

we start with Thomas's premise, we can start also, not with a transcendental notion of being such that it is set forth to bring unity to all that exists, but with a twofold notion of existence (being) such that the existence (or being) of God is primary and of a different nature than the existence (or being) of everything else, which is secondary. In this way, we cannot simply posit existence without at the same time saying whether it is God's existence that we are positing or something that exists because created by God.

Now Thomas would no doubt quickly agree with such an idea of God. It was for this reason that he was constrained to develop not only an analogy that would have as its controlling motif "proportion" (so that in this kind of analogy we could learn something about those things in which there is a *bona fide* relationship between *esse* and essence), but also an analogy of intrinsic attribution (in which the causal factor is primary). In other words, in speaking of both kinds of analogies, Thomas is aware that there must be a fundamental difference between the being of God, including also the way in which we know him, and the existence or being of his creation, including also the ways in which we know that. Or to say it another way, the reason that there must be *both* an analogy of proper proportionality *and* an analogy of intrinsic attribution is simply because of the different relationships that obtain between things that are created, on the one hand, and between the Creator and creation, on the other. What is more, Thomas is insistent on the differences that must be recognized between God and creation.[9]

Dividing the Difference

So which understanding of being, it may now be asked, has the priority in one's system of philosophical theology? Does "being" have priority over everything else, such that it unifies, governs and undergirds all else? If so, as in Aquinas, it is the responsibility of *reason* to discern who God is and to delineate the differences

9. There are numerous places where Aquinas makes this clear. See, for example, ibid., 1.12.11.

between him and us.[10] Or is there a prior relationship that must be stated, that of the Creator and his creation, which itself must serve to delimit even the concept of being? It seems that Aquinas would want to give an affirmative answer to the first question and a negative answer to the second. We would propose the reverse. The difference, however, in what is proposed above and what Thomas wants to maintain, would be shown in answer to the question of conceptual priority or primacy.

Could it be that one's knowledge of the difference between God and his creation should serve as the presupposition behind everything else, such that the Creator/creature relationship is the fundamental and primary interpretive grid through which everything else must come? If so, then one cannot simply posit "being" without at the same time asking the question, which being? Neither can one speak of goodness without framing it within the context of its exemplification.

There is, in this suggestion, some support from the biblical material that Thomas himself seems not to address.[11] In a passage recognized and utilized by Aquinas, Romans 1:18ff., the apostle Paul seems to be making a fairly strong statement with regard to the creature's understanding of God.[12] The context of the discussion begins with revelation, but moves as well to some of the implications of this revelation to creatures and creation.[13] We can only highlight some of the keynotes here.

10. The relationship between being and reason in Aquinas can be noted, for example, in ibid., 1.5.2.

11. Whatever is said about Aquinas's view of Scripture, he certainly did *not* look askance at biblical authority. Eleanore Stump notes, "Everything in the biblical text is true, he [Aquinas] says, and nothing is contrary to anything else." Eleanore Stump, "Revelation and Biblical Exegesis," in *Reason and the Christian Religion: Essays in Honour of Richard Swinburne*, ed. Alan G. Padgett and Richard Swinburne (Oxford: Clarendon Press; Oxford University Press, 1994), 172. It can be assumed, then, that Aquinas would want his own understanding of God in his philosophical theology to cohere with that which is found in Scripture.

12. We will elaborate on the epistemological implications of this passage in the next chapter.

13. It is interesting that, in Thomas's *Super Epistolas S. Pauli: Lectura*, cura P. Raphaelis Cai, O.P., editio 8, revisa vol. 1 (Taurini: Marietti, 1953), 22, Thomas notes three ways in which one may know God: *per causalitatem, per viam excellentiae,* and *per viam*

Paul begins this epistle with a discussion of the implications of sin in the world. More specifically, his point is not simply to discuss the implications of sin for a select group of people; nor is it to provide the Christians in Rome with some interesting tidbits of knowledge. Rather, Paul sets out to answer the question of the relationship of those without the Bible to God.[14]

Most significant in the first two chapters in Romans is the concept of knowledge presented there, as well as its result. Paul says quite clearly that those against whom the wrath of God is revealed are the same ones who know God (γνόντες τὸν θεὸν—v. 21). The point he is laboring to set forth is that all people are without excuse before God because God has made himself known and has been clearly seen and understood through the things that are made.[15]

What Paul wants the Roman Christians (and us) to understand is that there is a knowledge of God that comes by virtue of God's revelation to people, a knowledge that is a part of our being the image of God, a knowledge, therefore, that is innate or intuitive within us. Thus, the knowledge of God is, *contra* Aquinas, self-evident. It is a knowledge that comes to people *through* creation. And, given Paul's (and Thomas's) schema, *everything but God* is created. There is, therefore, an inescapable knowledge of God that people have by virtue of creation *as* revelation.

Two aspects of this knowledge must here be noted. First, while this kind of knowledge cannot be, at least initially, equivalent to the kind of knowledge Thomas wants to affirm—that which comes by demonstration—it is nevertheless true knowledge. Perhaps Bertrand Russell can help us here. Two quotes from Russell should

---

negationis. Paul's discussion, however, seems to indicate a more *universal* application than Thomas wants to admit.

14. We can view this first part of the book as written to "those without the Bible." Without going into great exegetical detail here, we see hints of Paul's purpose when his explanation in Rom. 1–2 takes an abrupt turn as he begins to discuss how the Jew, who has the very words of God (3:2), relates to God. For more on this passage, see K. Scott Oliphint, "The Irrationality of Unbelief," in *Revelation and Reason: New Essays in Reformed Apologetics*, ed. K. Scott Oliphint and Lane G. Tipton (Phillipsburg, NJ: P&R, forthcoming).

15. More on this in the next chapter.

suffice. In his essay, "Knowledge by Acquaintance and Knowledge by Description," Russell explains the former in this way:

> I say that I am *acquainted* with an object when I have a direct cognitive relation to that object, i.e., when I am *directly aware* of the object itself. When I speak of a cognitive relation here, I do not mean the sort of relation which constitutes judgment, but the sort which constitutes presentation.[16]

Elsewhere Russell notes concerning knowledge by acquaintance:

> The main consideration is undoubtedly to be derived from remembering what "presence" actually is. When an object is in my present experience, then I am acquainted with it; it is not necessary for me to reflect upon my experience, or to observe that the object has the property of belonging to my experience, in order to be acquainted with it, but, on the contrary, the object itself is known to me without the need of any reflection on my part as to its properties or relations.[17]

Second, Paul also wants to make the point that the knowledge that all people have of God, sufficient to render inexcusability before God, is a knowledge that is *true* but also *suppressed*. That is, this is not a knowledge that people will readily acknowledge. Rather, it is a knowledge that sparks a reaction of rebellion and suppression in the ones to whom it is given. Thus, this knowledge will not be readily or automatically acknowledged by those who receive it.[18] Thus, we can at least posit here that there *is*, given Paul's argument,

16. Bertrand Russell, *Mysticism and Logic and Other Essays* (London: George Allen & Unwin, 1917), 209–10.

17. Bertrand Russell, *Logic and Knowledge: Essays, 1901–1950* (New York: Macmillan, 1956), 167. We will note in the next chapter that Thomas, too, seems to affirm this kind of knowledge. He seems also, however, not to apply it to this aspect of epistemology.

18. Though this suppression is an interesting twist on Paul's discussion, it should not distract us from the point he is seeking to make of the character of the knowledge that is given. Though suppressed, it is nevertheless, as it comes from God, still clearly seen and understood. It is the truth (τὴν ἀλήθειαν) that is suppressed, not some vague or obscure notion of something somewhere.

113

a self-evident (though suppressed) knowledge of God and that this knowledge is both clearly seen and understood.[19]

From the Top Down

If what the apostle says is true, it would appear that some revision may help us out of the above impasse. At least the following points seem relevant with respect to this natural or "general" revelation of which Paul speaks: (1) God continually reveals himself to all people; (2) God's continual revelation to all people is specific, not generic; it is not simply a revelation of theism; (3) God's continual revelation to all people is clearly seen and understood; (4) God's continual revelation is both known and suppressed;[20] (5) God's continual revelation is sufficient to render all people inexcusable.[21] These five points should be grouped with the following Thomistic affirmations: (6) God's essence is impenetrable by the human mind; (7) God necessarily exists.

If we combine the above biblical and theological points, the stage is set for a different metaphysical and epistemological construct that may go some distance in resolving the confusion with regard to theological predication. As was said above, it seems that God is known, not first of all by reasonable demonstration, but first of all by revelation. This would entail that the *fundamental* interpretive context with respect to knowledge of God is (the content of God's) revelation rather than abstract being or the combination of being and essence. To ascribe being to God, then, would not entail a reduction of his character (contra Marion et al.), as long as we remember that such an ascription (1) is on the level of creatures and (2) is true by

19. There is some precedent for this in Protestant circles. John Calvin opens the first book of his *Institutes* affirming the coincidence of the knowledge of God with knowledge of self.

20. The suppression of this revelation is as important conceptually as the knowledge of it. We will deal with that in the next chapter.

21. It is worth noting also that, in the Old Testament, Ps. 19 describes a similar situation with respect to the natural revelation of God. Day after day pours forth speech and night after night knowledge is displayed.

virtue of revelation, not metaphysics per se. We can know God to "be," or to "exist" because he has revealed himself.

With a duality of being (that of Creator and creation) rather than a scale of being, as in Aquinas,[22] theological predication could be developed in a different direction, though analogical predication could be maintained. Since the guiding concept is now revelation (not being per se), it might be possible to import some of Thomas's own distinctions in delineating a *phanerotic* structure of reality.[23] In such a structure, we could perhaps propose a "third way" that would provide for meaningful theological predication while also safeguarding essential attributes, such as simplicity, in our notion of God. In this construction, being is no longer the overriding and primary object of the rational intellect, revelation is.

Thus, rather than attempting to maintain knowledge of God through reasonable demonstration, we can now see knowledge of God as something more foundational and fundamental than that. Knowledge of God comes, first of all and immediately, by way of creation. That is, as Paul says (Rom. 1:19), that which is known about God is evident to us because God made it evident *in* us and *to* us, *through* creation. Those things which we see and observe, therefore, including ourselves, are all God's *modi significandi*. They are God's way of *signifying* what he knows (and it cannot be forgotten, since we have not given up the simplicity of God, that what he knows is also who he is). Creation, therefore, has as its basis God's *modus cognoscendi*, and it *is* essentially God's *modus significandi*.[24]

---

22. There will be distinctions between things that exist in creation, but such distinctions will be developed in the context of the original duality rather than in the context of being as a transcendental notion.

23. Such a view was proposed by the contemporary Christian philosopher, H. G. Stoker, in *Oorsprong en Rigting* (Kaapstad: Tafelberg-Uitgewers, 1970).

24. This understanding depends for its cogency on a similarity (if not identity) of meaning between what Paul calls *manifestation* and what we are calling *signification*. Is it legitimate to see God's creation as his signification? It would seem so, especially given the psalmist's language in Ps. 19, wherein he affirms natural revelation as declaration and speech of who God is. Clearly, this is metaphorical language, but it is language that allows for a clear relationship between what God shows, and what he says in and through creation.

We saw that it was the *res significata/modus significandi* distinction that provided confusion in the attempt to affirm the perfections of God. Suppose now, for example, we want to speak meaningfully of the goodness of God.[25] Based on the discussion above, goodness is a concept gleaned first by way of revelation.[26] That is, we know of God's goodness because he has revealed himself as such. And that knowledge comes by way of the revelation of God in creation.[27] Thus, our knowledge of God comes *via* the senses ("clearly seen," says the apostle) *through* creation.[28] We know God, then, not because what is in the effect is also in the cause, though in *modum altiorem*, but rather because the Cause of all things causes, through revelation, a knowledge, also, of himself to be present in his creatures. Our *modus cognoscendi*, then, is revelation. Or, we could say, our *modus cognoscendi* is through God's *modus significandi*, creation.

But what must we say about goodness as a *res significata*? As *modus significandi*? We would have to say, with Thomas, that our *modus significandi* is still on a creaturely level, thus improper for any univocal predication, because inapplicable, as it is, to the Creator. Can we say that goodness as *res significata* is used *proprie* of God? Yes, but with other qualifications.

We will remember that Thomas maintained an analogical relationship between a term predicated of creatures, on the one hand, and of God, on the other. The problem, as we saw, was that there was no way to "connect" the term used in one sense with the same term used in the other. That is, the terms were used in different

25. I see no compelling reason to accept, as in Jean-Luc Marion for example, the perfection of love over any other perfection in God. It seems that it is the ontological character of God that grounds the relational. See Jean-Luc Marion, *God without Being: Hors-Texte*, trans. Thomas A. Carlson (Chicago: University of Chicago Press, 1991).

26. Is our concept of goodness still a universal form? The discussion here does not depend on the form/matter distinction, nor does it explicitly deny it.

27. As we will note below, God's written revelation provides the primary avenue through which we can know God. Our concern here, however, is more with the universal knowledge of God and the implications of such for knowledge generally.

28. "Senses" here need not be restricted simply to that which is seen. The apostle also makes clear that knowledge of God is in us as well. This is one reason why Calvin, for example, argued for a *sense* of deity (*sensus divinitatis*) within all people. More on that in the next chapter.

ways, with no way to determine the content of the analogical term when used to refer to a characteristic of God.

Perhaps now there is a way. When we predicate goodness of God, the concept itself, we could say, is God's *modus significandi*. What is given to us, therefore, in creation, even in its aspect as *res significata*, is God's *modus significandi*. Analogy can now perhaps be reinterpreted and applied. Goodness, when ascribed to God, is ascribed to him *proprie*; he is literally and properly spoken of as good. But *goodness* itself as a term is analogically related to the goodness that he is because, as a term given to us by way of revelation, it is God's *modus significandi* of his *modus cognoscendi*, which essentially *is* also his *modus essendi*.

How can goodness, for example now be delimited? Since the Creator/creature distinction, rather than "being," is basic, and since all that we know of God is by way of revelation, we can say now, *contra* Aquinas, that it is not the case that the goodness as a *modus significandi* belongs to creatures since we know creatures first,[29] but rather that goodness as a *modus significandi* belongs and applies first to God whom we know first (because revealed).[30]

In other words, since all that we know of God is his *modus significandi*, goodness as applied to him is true; it comes from his *modus essendi*. But it is also, as known by us, limited, and analogical, since it is predicated of and by the One who is simple. His *modus essendi* is not and cannot be known *as such* (that is, we cannot fully comprehend the concept of simplicity), but can be known as revealed. There is no reason then to distinguish in theological predication between the *modus significandi* and the *res significata*. The term itself when predicated of God and of creatures is analogous because it is revealed by him, thus based on his essential nature. It is revealed by him but on a creaturely level.

29. Aquinas, *Summa Theologiae*, 1a.13.7.

30. As we will see in chapters to come, because God's *modus essendi* partakes of both essential and covenantal (accidental) properties, the predication of God as good can refer to God's covenantal properties and, thereby, relate also to his essential character. In other words, *as revelation*, the goodness of God is itself a condescension of God to us in order to speak to us in a way that we might meaningfully know him.

It is *revelation* that assures continuity between the term as applied to creatures and the same term as applied to God (though it is still not possible exhaustively to delineate just *what* the term means when applied to God). We can, however, say that, because the term comes from the revealing activity of God, it is true and tells us something meaningful about him (though always on our level) about his character. The foundational point of Thomas's concern, therefore, has shifted from being as a primary guide, to God's revelation as that guide.

The way forward, then, to provide for meaningful predication is not the way of Thomas, in which reason must ascertain its own limits. Nor is it to give up on God's simplicity, thus making him, at best, co-equal with his attributes. Rather it is to ground our predication, not in the *modus essendi* of God, such that goodness requires either indeterminate affirmation, on the one hand, or independent existence, on the other. Our predication is grounded in God's *modus significandi*, which is the entirety of creation (and of Word-revelation). He has *revealed* himself (and himself as good etc.) to us.

Though we cannot exactly determine the limits, or lack thereof, in the goodness that *is* God, the goodness that we ascribe to God is *his* goodness, *revealed* to his creatures on a creaturely level, and thus used *proprie* of God; it comes through his *modus significandi* (creation) and is based on his *modus cognoscendi*, which, of course, is also his *modus essendi* (because God is simple).[31]

This does not exhaust the problem of theological predication. At this point, all we have attempted to do is to provide something of a skeletal framework for a possible *analogia revelationis* that could allow for much of what Thomas desired, while at the same time taking seriously some of the concerns that have shown his own system in this area to be as yet deficient.[32]

---

31. As we will argue later, there seems to be no reason to attempt to map all of the attributes of God directly onto his essential character. Rather, given that he has, by way of condescension, taken on contingent (covenantal) properties that are compatible with and, in some cases, entail his essential properties, predication of God relates itself directly to his condescension and is compatible with who he essentially is.

32. It is difficult to articulate exactly what this *analogia revelationis* is. We'll take a stab at aspects of it in the next chapter. As we will see below, it includes at least the fact

What might an *analogia revelationis* look like? We cannot lay out here an entire philosophy of language. However, there are a couple of fundamental aspects that should be maintained of any philosophy of language that takes God's revelation as its foundation.

First and foremost, the vehicles or *modes* through which and by which God reveals himself tell us something crucial about our own language and speech. And how does God reveal himself? He reveals himself both by way of creation and by way of language. As a matter of fact, the two modes have since the beginning been inextricably linked. It was God's "speech," his language, that first created—He *spoke* and it was—and then it was that very creation which, from the beginning, revealed just who this God is (Ps. 19:1–6; Rom. 1:20).

We should be clear about the fact that language itself is a creation of God. It is something that God himself *uses*, even as he accommodates himself to his creation. And he uses language in order to express how we are to relate to him and to his creation. In that sense, language is the created medium—both used and given by God—that serves to express our connection to God and his world.

Note that it is not that language *is* our connection to the world; we are connected to the world by virtue of creation (cf. Gen. 2:7, 19). Language is employed, by God initially (Gen. 1:28–30; 2:16–17) and then by humans, as a way of expressing the connection with God and with the world that is given to human beings in creation. In other words, the *purpose* of language is *covenantal*. It is to be employed to give expression to God's relationship to us, first of all, and then our relationship to God and to the world.

Second, because God reveals himself by and through (created) words and creation, we should be quick to affirm that words (and creation) do tell us something of who God is. It is not the case, therefore, that words cannot express the essence of God. Certainly words cannot exhaustively express God's essence and cannot express

---

that what we have in creation, and in Scripture, is what exists originally and infinitely in the mind of God. The analogy, then, is between that which is in God's own thinking, on the one hand, and that which (covenantally) he give to us, on the other. Thus, what we have in revelation is God's "translation" of what he eternally (covenantally) knows.

God's essence *as he exists* (since he exists in light unapproachable, and he is altogether beyond the finite). But the words that God has given to tell us something of who he is and what he requires of us are adequate truly to express his own character.

Words (and creation) are, therefore, one of the primary expressive means of God's condescension to us and to his creation. The question of whether or not they point to, or signify, or connect to the world is a question only for those who choose to deny a biblical understanding of creation (and thus of revelation). For Christians, the existence of language is evidence of the *fact* that we are connected, first to God, and then to the world. This does not imply that there is no interpretive *aspect* to language, but it does mean that reality is not essentially linguistic; reality is essentially created (including language), and we express its createdness, and its meaning, by way of language.[33]

Conclusion

It seems that we need to take seriously the revelation of God if we want to know him and to know *how* we might know him. This is old news to those who travel in Christian and theological circles.

33. In this regard, a monumental misunderstanding of one of Cornelius Van Til's now-famous phrases needs clarification. Van Til affirmed that there is no "brute fact." Some have taken this to mean that every fact is in need of interpretation. Thus, the opposite of a brute fact is sometimes thought to be an interpreted fact. This misunderstanding of Van Til's phrase can be explained, at least in part, by the tremendous influence of Hans-Georg Gadamer and others on the discipline of hermeneutics. A Gadamerian would want to emphasize the cultural "horizons" both of language and of experience such that interpretation is directed toward bridging the gap between them. This, however, has the unfortunate result of a relativistic turn with respect to language and truth and knowledge, culminating in extremist views that argue that things such as language, truth, and knowledge are *only* culturally bound and conditioned.

What Van Til had in mind, in opposition to any relativistic view of facts and language, is that the opposite of a brute fact is *not* an interpreted fact, but a fact that is *already given its meaning and interpretation by God*. In other words, meaning is already embedded in reality (including language) by virtue of God's creative and controlling activity in bringing all things about. In this way, language retains cultural and interpretive elements, but such elements do not *define* or *control* creation or language in such a way as to deny a universal connection between man and God, a connection that, at root, is *defined* and *controlled* by God's revelation in language and in creation.

But it seems it is, sadly, new news to those whose orbit is primarily in philosophy of religion and related fields.

We might be tempted to think here, again, that this is as it should be. Those who spend their waking hours thinking theologically *should* be buried in God's revelation, and those who devote themselves to philosophy should work with the tools of reason to ascertain truth, even truth about God. But we should remember again van Inwagen's confession: not only are we free to start wherever we wish in our metaphysical pursuits, but after a few thousand years of beginning with the tools of reason, metaphysics has yet to establish any viable body of knowledge. There is much more to say with respect to this Creator/creature relationship, more to flesh out and more application needed. Before we venture into that discussion, there is a serious problem looming—a problem that relates to our knowledge of God, specifically, and which will have implications for our knowledge more generally. We need to address that problem before we attempt to set out a Christian metaphysical structure.

7

Truth and Consequences

The apostle affirms that,—"that which may be known of God"
(his essence, being, subsistence, his natural, necessary, essential
properties) "is manifest in them"; that is, it hath a self-evidencing
power, acting itself in the minds of all men endued with natural
light and reason. —JOHN OWEN

Truth be told, the problems that plague metaphysics plague epistemology as well. If van Inwagen is correct, then there is no established body of accepted metaphysical results to which one interested in the subject must appeal in order to enter the debate. As it was in the beginning, is now, and perhaps ever shall be, metaphysics remains in a near-total state of flux and chaos.

But so does epistemology. Discussions epistemological abound in the history of philosophy, and it could easily be argued that, as in metaphysics, there is no established body of accepted epistemological results to which one interested in the subject must appeal in order to enter the debate.

Perhaps in epistemology, however, with a few notable exceptions, the situation is even worse. Whereas in metaphysical discussions the topic of God and his relation to the world is (naturally) broached, there is relatively little discussion of God and his relationship to the knowledge situation in epistemology. This, of course, can be explained in terms of the subject matter of the disciplines themselves. Because metaphysics deals with the nature of *ultimate* reality, the topic of God is bound to arise. But because epistemology deals with the subject of human knowledge, it is easier to think that the relationship of epistemology to God is, if not irrelevant, significantly minimal.

This is, however, historically speaking, a rather recent phenomenon. As we noticed in our previous discussion of Cupitt, Immanuel Kant's influence has been vast in its reach, convincing many that the best that we are able to do in this world is to confine ourselves to that which has its ground in experience. Prior to the enlightenment, however, it was more common to think of the things of this world in relationship to God. More specifically, it was quite common prior to the enlightenment to think of everything that we think, do, and are as having its explanation and rationale in the existence and providence of the triune God. Happily, those kinds of discussions are gaining ascendancy in the philosophical literature again (thanks in large part to Alvin Plantinga and others). We can use Plantinga as our springboard into an epistemology that will seek to take seriously the relationship of God and his revelation to the way in which we think about knowledge.

Primal and Simple Knowledge

Any *analogia revelationis* worth its salt will have to take seriously the fact of God's revelation to and in his creation. That revelation includes God's word in Scripture, but it also includes God's "speech" (Ps. 19:2) in and through creation. One of the most encouraging developments in discussions epistemological of late is that an analysis of Calvin's *sensus divinitatis* (hereafter, *SD*), thanks to the work of Alvin Plantinga, has become a central aspect of many of those discussions.[1] Not only is it encouraging that Calvin's thought has become a matter of discussion, but it is significant that such discussion has been prompted by Plantinga, whose stature in the philosophical community is formidable. Just as he has led the way in current debates on epistemological structure and methodology, so also has he introduced into those debates topics and ideas that were heretofore ignored or forbidden.

It would be difficult to overstate the significance of this for a Reformed approach to philosophy and apologetics. As we will see, one of the central aspects of such an approach depends for its cogency on Paul's analysis of unbelief in Romans 1:18ff. In that passage, Paul delimits the parameters of (certain aspects of) an epistemology that has its basis in God's revealing activity, his revelation. Given that revelation, we are able to understand something of how we come to know what we do, and how such knowledge would be impossible without that revelation. We would argue, therefore, that as in a Reformed apologetic so also in a Reformed, Christian

1. See, for example, Gregory Bateson and Mary Catherine Bateson, *Angels Fear: Towards an Epistemology of the Sacred* (New York: Macmillan, 1987); Shlomo Biderman, *Scripture and Knowledge: An Essay on Religious Epistemology*, Studies in the History of Religions, 69 (New York: E. J. Brill, 1995); Andrew Dole, "Cognitive Faculties, Cognitive Processes, and the Holy Spirit in Plantinga's Warrant Series," *Faith and Philosophy* 19, no. 1 (2002): 32–46; Charles Gutenson, "Can Belief in the Christian God Be Properly Basic? A Pannenbergian Perspective on Plantinga and Basic Beliefs," *Christian Scholar's Review* 29, no. 1 (1999): 49–72; Cornelis van der Kooi, "The Assurance of Faith: A Theme in Reformed Dogmatics in Light of Alvin Plantinga's Epistemology," *Neue Zeitschrift Für Systematische Theologie und Religionsphilosophie* 40, no. 1 (1998): 91–106; Jonathan L. Kvanvig, *Warrant and Contemporary Epistemology: Essays in Honor of Plantinga's Theory of Knowledge* (Lanham, MD: Rowman & Littlefield, 1996); Pierre Le Morvan and Dana Radcliffe, "Plantinga on Warranted Christian Belief," *Heythrop* 44, no. 3 (2003): 345–51; Mark S. McLeod, "The Analogy Argument for the Proper Basicality of Belief in God," *International Journal for Philosophy of Religion* 21 (1987): 3–20; Alvin Plantinga, *Warrant and Proper Function* (Oxford: Oxford University Press, 1993); Plantinga, *Warranted Christian Belief* (Oxford: Oxford University Press, 2000); Joseph Runzo, and Graig K. Ihara, eds., *Religious Experience and Religious Belief: Essays in the Epistemology of Religion* (Lanham, MD: University Press of America, 1986); Michael C. Sudduth, "Can Religious Unbelief Be Proper Function Rational?" *Faith and Philosophy* 16, no. 3 (July 1999): 297–314; Julian Willard, "Plantinga's Epistemology of Religious Belief and the Problem of Religious Diversity," *Heythrop* 44, no. 3 (2003): 275–93; Michael Williams, *Groundless Belief: An Essay on the Possibility of Epistemology*, 2nd ed. (Princeton, NJ: Princeton University Press, 1999).

philosophy, the roots must be in a biblical epistemology.[2] What, then, are the primary tenets of that kind of epistemology?

Perhaps the best way to begin to think about this is to set forth, in sum, the crux of Plantinga's epistemological endeavor.[3] The substance of Plantinga's epistemological argument is found in his latest work on epistemology, *Warranted Christian Belief*. A brief perusal of the relevant sections of that work should suffice in laying the groundwork for a discussion of the necessity of the *SD* for epistemology.

In that volume Plantinga argues for (what Andrew Dole has rightly called) an "unresolved conditional."[4] What Dole means by this is that Plantinga's epistemological argument revolves around the *de jure* question, that is, Is Christian belief intellectually acceptable? In attempting to answer that question, he provides a crucial distinction with regard to objections to Christian belief, a distinction between *de facto* and *de jure* objections. *De facto* objections are objections to the *truth* of Christian belief. With these objections, Plantinga is not primarily concerned.

Even more prevalent, however, have been *de jure* objections.

> These are arguments or claims to the effect that Christian belief, whether or not true, is at any rate unjustifiable, or rationally unjustified, or irrational, or not intellectually respectable, or contrary to sound morality, or without sufficient evidence, or in some other

2. This is not to say that the Bible is an epistemology handbook, or that *every* principle or aspect of epistemology is found in Scripture. It is only to say that, given a Reformed view of Scripture, the basis for a biblically founded epistemology must be in God's own revelation. This is, in part, what is meant in the previous chapter by an *analogia revelationis*. As we will seek to argue, only a covenantal approach to knowledge, in which the affirmation of God's revelation, dynamically given to his human creatures, can serve to explain the subject-object relationship. For a clear and excellent account of certain aspects of this, see Esther L. Meek, *Longing to Know* (Grand Rapids, MI: Brazos, 2003).

3. For those completely new to these kinds of epistemological debates, the context for them focuses on the question, "Is knowledge justified true belief?" While positive answers have been given to this question as far back even as Plato, more recent discussions have had to qualify responses, owing primarily to a refutation of those positive answers by Edmund Gettier. See Edmund Gettier, "Is Justified True Belief Knowledge," *Analysis* 23 (1963): 121–23.

4. Dole, "Cognitive Faculties," 39.

way rationally unacceptable, not up to snuff from an intellectual point of view.[5]

While *de facto* objections deal with the truth or falsity of Christian belief and thus can be fairly straightforward, *de jure* objections are less clear; they are diffuse and often opaque, claiming that there is something other than falsity that is wrong with Christian belief. Christian belief is in some way deficient such that one's holding such belief entails that one inherits its deficiency. So, the purpose of Plantinga's book, by and large, is to respond to the *de jure* objection.

Plantinga proposes that no *de jure* objections to Christian belief are independent of *de facto* objections. More specifically, he argues that "the attitude expressed in 'Well, I don't know whether Christian belief is *true* (after all, who could know a thing like that?), but I do know that it is irrational (or intellectually unjustified or unreasonable or intellectually questionable)'—that attitude, if I am right, is indefensible."[6] He wants to clear the way for a discussion of the *de facto* objections by removing obstacles presented to Christian belief by the *de jure* objections. He proceeds by locating the subject matter of theism and of Christian belief within the discourse of his epistemological project on warrant. If warrant is acquired in the way that Plantinga argues, and if theistic belief generally and Christian belief more specifically are consistent with (at least the essential core of) that project, then theism and Christianity too may be warranted.[7]

5. Plantinga, *Warranted Christian Belief*, ix.
6. Ibid., ii.
7. For those unfamiliar with Plantinga's warrant project in epistemology, it is summarized as a "proper function" view of warrant. Warrant is that property or quantity enough of which transforms true belief into knowledge, and warrant is obtained by way of properly functioning cognitive faculties (along with other qualifiers). More specifically: "According to the central and paradigmatic core of our notion of warrant (so I say) a belief **B** has warrant for you if and only if (1) the cognitive faculties involved in the production of **B** are functioning properly . . . ; (2) your cognitive environment is sufficiently similar to the one for which your cognitive faculties are designed; (3) the triple of the design plan governing the production of the belief in question involves, as purpose or function, the production of true beliefs (and the same goes for elements of the design plan governing the production of input beliefs to the system in question); and (4) the design plan is a

Plantinga employs his "proper function" notion of warrant here to argue for the warrant of Christian belief. In *Warranted Christian Belief* the central part of his argument is contained in what Plantinga calls "the A/C Model" (the Aquinas/Calvin model), providing as it does an explanation for the warrant of Christian belief. The A/C model is developed with respect to theism generally and then is extended for the sake of arguing for the warrant, more specifically, of *Christian* belief.

At the center of the A/C model for Plantinga is what Calvin called the *sensus divinitatis*. Plantinga contends that the SD is something on which both Aquinas and Calvin agreed, "(and anything on which Calvin and Aquinas are in accord is something to which we had better pay careful attention)."[8] After quoting Romans 1:18–20 and select passages from Calvin, Plantinga tells us exactly how he understands the SD: "The *sensus divinitatis* is a disposition or set of dispositions to form theistic beliefs in various circumstances, in response to the sorts of conditions or stimuli that trigger the working of this sense of divinity."[9]

The SD works in such a way,[10] according to Plantinga, that, under certain agreeable circumstances, we find ourselves believing in God; that is, we find ourselves with theistic beliefs. In this, notes Plantinga, the SD is similar to memory or perceptual beliefs. I don't simply decide to believe, when I see a tree outside my window, that I see a tree outside my window; I find myself believing such a thing without inference or argument. I don't construct an argument that would seek to conclude for the fact of my seeing that tree. Rather, I know I see the tree by virtue of the fact that I

---

good one: that is, there is a high statistical or objective probability that a belief produced in accordance with the relevant segment of the design plan in that sort of environment is true. Under these conditions, furthermore, the degree of warrant is given by some monotonically increasing function of the strength of S's belief that **B**. This account of warrant, therefore, depends essentially upon the notion of proper function" (Plantinga, *Warrant and Proper Function*, 194).

8. Plantinga, *Warranted Christian Belief*, 170.

9. Ibid., 173.

10. And remember, given a proper function notion of epistemology, just how our relevant faculties "work" is all-important.

see it. According to Plantinga the *SD* is designed to work the same way, or in similar ways.

Not only does the *SD* function similarly to other faculties of mine, but the *SD* is also, in some important respects, *innate*.[11] According to Plantinga, it is likely *not* innate in that knowledge of God is present from birth, but its "innate-ness" revolves around the fact that the *capacity* for such knowledge is present from birth.

> Here the *sensus divinitatis* resembles other belief-producing faculties or mechanisms. If we wish to think in terms of the overworked functional analogy, we can think of the *sensus divinitatis*, too, as an input-output device: it takes . . . circumstances . . . as input and issues as output theistic belief, beliefs about God.[12]

Although there are other factors and qualifiers that help to clarify the A/C model, it seems clear that the *SD*, as a faculty designed to produce theistic belief, *just is* the A/C model. The two are virtually identical.

One important aspect[13] of the *SD* mentioned by Plantinga is spelled out in a section subtitled "Natural Knowledge of God."[14] Here Plantinga deals, not with a natural knowledge of God, as might be expected, but rather with a brief comparison and contrast (to be expanded later in the book) between the *SD* and the internal testimony (called by Plantinga, the internal instigation) of the Holy Spirit. In this section, Plantinga claims that part of our original epistemic equipment includes that we were meant to be endowed with the capacity for knowledge of God.[15]

11. Plantinga, *Warranted Christian Belief*, 173.

12. Ibid., 174–75.

13. There are six features of the *SD* (as the A/C model) developed by Plantinga, some of which are familiar to those who have followed Plantinga's epistemological expedition, and some of which are not. We can pass over the more familiar features, features not directly relevant to our concerns here, which features include basicality, proper basicality with respect to justification, and proper basicality with respect to warrant. The last three, however, are directly relevant to our development here.

14. Plantinga, *Warranted Christian Belief*, 180.

15. This seems to me to be altogether right and true, but may not do justice, at least at this point, to Calvin, following Paul, in their affirmations about the *SD*.

Plantinga then asks whether the *SD* requires that our knowledge of God comes by way of perception; that is, "would it follow that the warrant enjoyed by theistic belief is perceptual warrant? Not necessarily."[16] Rather than maintaining that there must be perceptual experience in order for there to be knowledge of God in us, Plantinga argues that there is another kind of experience necessarily entailed in the *SD, a doxastic experience*, which is "the sort of experience one has when entertaining any proposition one believes."[17]

Important also for our discussion of the *SD* is a key feature of the A/C model: the reality of sin.[18] According to the A/C model, "this natural knowledge of God has been compromised, weakened, reduced, smothered, overlaid, or impeded by sin and its consequences," so that "failure to believe in God is a result of some kind of dysfunction of the *SD*."[19] Here Plantinga is referring to the noetic effects of sin as a hindrance to knowledge. He argues that "the noetic effects of sin are concentrated with respect to our knowledge of other people, of ourselves, and of God; they are less relevant (or relevant in a different way . . .) to our knowledge of nature and the world."[20] Plantinga does admit, however, in this connection that, "were it not for sin and its effects, God's presence and glory would be as obvious and uncontroversial to us all as the presence of other minds, physical objects, and the past."[21] The problem is that the *SD* is corrupted by us.[22] The "deliverances of the *sensus divinitatis*

16. Plantinga, *Warranted Christian Belief*, 180.

17. Ibid., 183.

18. One of the more lucid critiques of (what was initially called) the "Reformed epistemology" proposal of Plantinga dealt specifically with the topic of sin. See Merold Westphal, "Taking St. Paul Seriously: Sin as an Epistemological Category," in *Christian Philosophy*, ed. Thomas P. Flint (Notre Dame, IN: Notre Dame Press, 1990), 200–26.

19. Plantinga, *Warranted Christian Belief*, 184.

20. Ibid., 213.

21. Ibid., 214.

22. This is in keeping with Calvin's discussion of the *sensus divinitatis*. "But, however that may be, yet the fact that men soon corrupt the seed of the knowledge of God, sown in their minds out of the wonderful workmanship of nature . . . must be imputed to their own failing." John Calvin, *Institutes of the Christian Religion*, ed. John T. McNeill, trans. Ford Lewis Battles, Library of Christian Classics (London: SCM, 1960), 1.5.15.

can be compromised, skewed, or even suppressed altogether."[23] For Plantinga, then, the most important cognitive consequence of sin is failure to know God.

> But if we don't know that there is such a person as God, we don't know the first thing (the most important thing) about ourselves, each other, and our world. That is because (from the point of view of the model) the most important truths about us and them is [*sic*] that we have been created by the Lord and utterly depend upon him for our continued existence. We don't know what our happiness consists in, and we don't know how to achieve it. We don't know that we have been created in the image of God, and we don't grasp the significance of such characteristically human phenomena as love, humor, adventure, science, art, music, philosophy, history, and so on.[24]

Thus, the A/C model, as the *SD*, includes such a faculty in order to affirm that theistic belief, when present, is a result of the proper functioning of that faculty. Though sin does hinder and perhaps bury that faculty altogether, the faculty itself, as a capacity for the knowledge of God, remains in us.

In this discussion of the *SD* and the effects of sin on it, Plantinga is basically correct. But certain corrections are needed, corrections that should take into account Paul's discussion of the *SD*. In order to show this, we will attempt a modification of Plantinga's construal of the *sensus divinitatis*. We will attempt to show that the *SD*, at least as it is presented to us by Paul (and we assume that Calvin was following Paul), provides the epistemological foundation that is needed in order to begin to think, not only about the knowledge of God, but about the nature of knowledge itself and its acquisition by us.

Because the *SD* is central to Plantinga's argument—indeed we have argued that it is *the* central focus of his A/C model—it is all the more important that we try to be as clear as possible with regard to its character. It is crucial, it seems to me, that a construal of the *SD*

23. Plantinga, *Warranted Christian Belief*, 216.
24. Ibid., 217.

130

be as accurate, as precise, as exact as possible in order for the model itself to have maximal credibility. Plantinga takes his cue concerning the *SD* primarily from Calvin. That, of course, is a legitimate and natural place from which to take one's cue, given that Calvin was in many ways *the* champion and theological architect of such a notion. Calvin, however, simply saw himself as following the apostle Paul, particularly, as Paul works out this notion in Romans 1:18–2:17. If Calvin's formulation, then, is directly dependent on Paul's (and more generally, on the *biblical* notion), its own warrant is only as strong as its adherence to the biblical teaching on the matter. It would be important for us, then, to see just what Paul says with respect to the *SD* (to put the matter somewhat anachronistically).

Truth Detectors

The *locus classicus* for the *SD* is Romans 1:18–2:17. Although we noted this passage earlier, it is necessary for us to review it again in light of the problems mentioned. In that passage, according to Calvin: "Paul shows that the whole world is deserving of eternal death. It hence follows, that life is to be recovered in some other way, since we are all lost in ourselves."[25] Paul's point, in other words, is initially to show that we are *all* under the grip of sin, and that the way out of that condition requires something outside of us (*extra nos*). It is crucial to note here that Paul's purview in this passage is universal; he is not attempting, in this passage, to describe the way things are or have been in particular circumstances or with particular people only. He is not saying that only *some* people have a *sensus divinitatis* and are therefore rendered without excuse, while others lack such knowledge and are thereby excused from judgment. Paul's point in Romans 1 and 2 is to argue that *we all* are in the same depraved boat. Since we all are under the same curse of sin, the gospel is for *all* of us as well—"to the Jew first and also to the Greek" (1:16).

25. John Calvin, *Commentaries on the Epistle of Paul, the Apostle, to the Romans* (Edinburgh: Calvin Translation Society, 1849).

Beginning in Romans 1, and into Romans 2, Paul's particular purpose is to describe just what our condition of sin looks like, how it works, and what processes it engages in while we remain in our sinful state. It is important that we look, briefly, at Paul's analysis.[26] We will focus our attention on 1:18–25:

> For the wrath of God is revealed from heaven against all ungodliness and unrighteousness of men, who by their unrighteousness suppress the truth. For what can be known about God is plain to them, because God has shown it to them. For his invisible attributes, namely, his eternal power and divine nature, have been clearly perceived, ever since the creation of the world, in the things that have been made. So they are without excuse. For although they knew God, they did not honor him as God or give thanks to him, but they became futile in their thinking, and their foolish hearts were darkened. Claiming to be wise, they became fools, and exchanged the glory of the immortal God for images resembling mortal man and birds and animals and reptiles.
>
> Therefore God gave them up in the lusts of their hearts to impurity, to the dishonoring of their bodies among themselves, because they exchanged the truth about God for a lie and worshiped and served the creature rather than the Creator, who is blessed forever! Amen.

Much could be said about Paul's discussion here. For our purposes, however, we will confine our discussion to elements germane to the *SD*.

Perhaps we can best situate our understanding of the *SD* by seeing its primary aspects as analogous to the primary aspects delineated by Plantinga of (what he calls) the *extended* A/C model. In his elaboration of the *extended* model, Plantinga sets forth three central aspects of it—Scripture, faith, and the internal instigation

26. We should note here Plantinga's affirmation of the teachings of Scripture. We come to believe the great things of the gospel, he says, quoting the Belgic Confession, "because the Holy Spirit testifies in our hearts that they are from God, and also because they prove themselves to be from God." Thus, in looking at what Paul teaches, we are not simply comparing what Paul says to what Calvin says about the *sensus divinitatis*, rather we are attempting to see what *God* says, through Paul, about the *sensus divinitatis*, according to which Calvin sought to be faithful.

of the Holy Spirit. Just as Plantinga develops a tripartite account of the *extended* A/C model (which, we should note, moves from a general theistic belief to more specific *Christian* belief), we would suggest a tripartite account of the *sensus divinitatis*, given Paul's discussion of it here.

So, for example, just as Plantinga's extended A/C model includes God's revelation in Scripture as one of its three central elements, so also the *sensus divinitatis* is itself, as Paul notes in Romans 1, taken from God's revelation in creation; it takes its contents from the revelation of and by God, and thus it is a kind of "speech" itself. Not only so, but just as the extended A/C model includes the internal instigation of the Holy Spirit as its second element (IIHS), so also the *sensus divinitatis* requires an activity of God *from the outside in* to be present. To use Calvin's phrase, the SD obtains due to its being internally "implanted by God." Finally, just as the extended A/C model includes faith as its third element, so also the SD includes (and essentially *is*) knowledge. Our revision of Plantinga's notion of the SD will include these three elements as essential aspects of it. We need, therefore, to flesh out what we mean by each one. We shall take the last element, knowledge, first.

What is Paul telling us in this passage? Notice, first of all, that we *all*, born as we are into our sinful state and continuing in that state by virtue of our wickedness, nevertheless *know God*. The way in which Paul introduces this notion is not, in verse 18, to tell us first of all about our knowledge of God. His initial concern is the revelation of God's wrath and the *reason* for it. And the reason for such an expression by God lies in the fact that, according to Paul, we all in our sins suppress the truth. But Paul immediately realizes, as he writes, that he should explain what he means by "suppression" and by "truth." He takes up the latter first.

He affirms, beginning in verse 19, that there is a universal knowledge of God, in every human creature. He does that in the context of elaborating first our suppression of the truth (v. 18) and then what that truth *is*, which we suppress. In sum, the truth we suppress is not, first of all, truth about nature or about aspects of this world. The truth that we suppress in unrighteousness is simply this: the "clearly perceived" (καθορᾶται) and "understood" (νοούμενα)

133

knowledge of God (v. 20). This is no obscure knowledge; neither is it knowledge that is beyond our capacity to understand. This knowledge we have is both perceived—"clearly perceived"—something that we, somehow, comprehend.

And it is knowledge with significant and substantial content. We know much by virtue of this clearly perceived and understood revelation of God to us. We know his invisible nature (ἀόρατα), namely, his eternal power (τε ἀίδιος αὐτοῦ δύναμις) and deity (or, "God-ness"—θειότης) (v. 20). We know these things to such an extent that Paul can pronounce that, since the creation of the world to the present, human beings are and have always been creatures who "knew God" (διότι γνόντες τὸν θεὸν) (v. 21).

This is strong (and clear) language. It explicitly states that all of us "since the creation of the world" (v. 20) are characterized as those who knew (and know) God—we know his deity and his power, in short, all of those things which are a part of his invisible nature. And what are those things? Charles Hodge in his commentary on Romans says that Paul means to delineate here "all the divine perfections"[27] in his affirmation of those things which we know about God. Presumably, then, human beings are created such that they know God to be a Spirit, infinite, eternal, and unchangeable, in his being, wisdom, power, holiness, justice, goodness, and truth.[28] Important truths such as these (and we could say these truths are really the *most* important ones) God has seen fit not to leave to our own reasoning process to discover; they are not left to the schools or seminaries; they are not in any way dependent on the capacities of human creatures themselves for the process of knowing. They are given to us, revealed to and in us, implanted in us, by the creative power and providence of almighty God the Creator.

This seems altogether consistent with God's character. There would be something amiss if God chose to create creatures such as us, but also chose to hide himself from us, either leaving us without

27. Charles Hodge, *Commentary on the Epistle to the Romans* (Grand Rapids, MI: Eerdmans, 1994), 37. Hodge likely got this from Calvin; see Calvin, *Institutes*, 1.5.11.
28. Westminster Shorter Catechism, question 4.

a witness to himself or, perhaps worse, leaving us to ourselves to try to figure out what he was like.[29] Just what kind of knowledge this is and how it might function is another question, but the import of Paul's pronouncement here should not be lost. He is affirming that human beings, *all* human beings "since the creation of the world," know and have always known the character and attributes of the true God. This would indicate in fairly strong terms that, whatever else we might want to say about the *SD*, it is more than merely a capacity that we have. The *SD* is more than a function of our human constitution. It is, in fact, "*notitia.*"

Plantinga's references to the *SD* shy away from a description of it as knowledge. In keeping with his concern for a "proper function" epistemology, he refers to the *SD*, as a "faculty," a "cognitive mechanism," a "disposition" or "set of dispositions" to form theistic beliefs in different circumstances; it is a kind of "input-output device"; it has its own deliverances, and it resembles perception, memory, and *a priori* beliefs. These descriptions are primarily functional; they look more like functional operators with a view to knowledge rather than knowledge itself. It seems, however, that in Paul's mind the *SD* is more a *deliverance* itself than a device, more content than capacity, more *sensus* than set (of dispositions).

We say that the *sensus* is *more* "this" than "that" because, even if knowledge, it still must presumably have a "capacity" for such. Likely, Plantinga wants to emphasize the functional aspect of the *SD* in order to further support his notion of warrant as proper function. But the fact that it constitutes *knowledge* might change the way in which the *SD* is able to find its place in a "proper function" epistemology. For example, if the *SD is* knowledge and not simply a capacity or functional process toward such, then whatever else we want to say about the *SD*, its content necessarily entails warrant. That is, it is not within the realm of Paul's purview at this

29. It is worth noting here that the Westminster Confession rightly attributes our inability to know and serve God, not, in the first place, to our sinfulness, but to our constitution *as creatures*. As we will see in coming chapters, we are, as created, inherently limited in our ability to understand and to worship God. Thus, the revelation of himself to us, as Paul notes, was necessary, not simply because of or after the fall of man into sin, but at creation's inception (see WCF 7.1).

point that the *SD* would, or even *could*, malfunction. Because of its *source* (God himself) and its *content* (God's "God-ness"), its "function," in this case, is dependent on God's activity, which activity does not and will not fail.[30] Thus, we should insist that the *SD* is knowledge itself.

The second aspect of the *SD* is the internal implanting by God of this knowledge (IIG). Notice, again, how Calvin describes it:

> To prevent anyone from taking refuge in the pretense of ignorance, *God himself has implanted in all men* a certain understanding of his divine majesty. Ever renewing its memory, he repeatedly sheds fresh drops. Since, therefore, men one and all perceive that there is a God and that he is their Maker, they are condemned by their own testimony because they have failed to honor him and to consecrate their lives to his will.[31]

And further:

> Men of sound judgment will always be sure that a sense of divinity which can never be effaced *is engraven upon men's minds*. Indeed, the perversity of the impious, who though they struggle furiously are unable to extricate themselves from the fear of God, is abundant testimony that this conviction, namely that there is some God, is naturally inborn in all, and is fixed deep within, as it were in the very marrow. . . . For the world . . . tries as far as it is able to cast away all knowledge of God, and by every means to corrupt the worship of him. I only say that though the stupid hardness in their minds, which the impious eagerly conjure up to reject God, wastes away, yet the sense of divinity, which they greatly wished to have extinguished, thrives and presently burgeons. From this we conclude that it is not a doctrine that must first be learned in school, but one of which each of us is master from his mother's womb and which nature itself permits none to forget, although many strive with every nerve to this end.[32]

30. Which is why Paul notes, at the end of v. 20, that this knowledge renders all of us "without excuse."

31. Calvin, *Institutes*, 1.3.1, my emphasis.

32. Ibid., 1.3.3, my emphasis.

We know God, not because we have reasoned our way to him, or have worked through the necessary scientific procedures, or have inferred his existence from other things that we know; we know him by way of his revelation. We know what God is like "because God has shown it" to us (ὁ θεὸς γὰρ αὐτοῖς ἐφανέρωσεν—Rom. 1:19).

The knowledge we have *of* God is knowledge that has been given to us *by* God. It is "implanted" in us, "engraven" in our minds, "naturally inborn" in all of us, "fixed deep within" us, a knowledge "which nature permits none to forget." As Creator, God has guaranteed that he will never be without a witness to the creatures who have been made in his image. He has insured that all of his human creatures will (always) know him. The *SD*, then, is not "a doctrine" or teaching that is learned, but rather it is that which is present within us "from our mother's womb." Such is the case because this knowledge is not dependent on us to be acquired; it is given by God. So, we have the *SD*, because we *are* God's image and because, *as* image, God implants the knowledge of himself within each of us. And this knowledge is, *ipso facto*, warranted.

But how could that be? How could something within *us*—flawed and imperfect human beings—be such that its content was always and everywhere warranted? This brings us to the third element of the *SD*: revelation.

Traditionally, this section of the book of Romans has been understood to discuss the topic of natural or general *revelation*. The knowledge of God that human beings possess is *not* a knowledge that depends for its acquisition and content on something that is within us.[33] It is a knowledge that is given, and it is given by God himself. It is the revelation of the character of God, given to God's human creatures, in and through the things that are made. Thus, Paul regards the *SD* as *knowledge itself* that comes directly and repeatedly from God himself through the things that God made and sustains. This, of course, is consistent with the Old Testa-

---

33. To some extent it "depends" on us in that it would be impossible for us to have it if we did not exist, exist as human beings with cognitive capacities, and so forth. The distinction here is akin to that between an externalist and internalist notion of warrant. This knowledge does not depend on us in that it is acquired externally, as God himself implants it in us.

ment understanding of natural revelation as well. The psalmist, therefore, can say,

> The heavens are telling the glory of God;
>   and the firmament proclaims his handiwork.
> Day to day pours forth speech,
>   and night to night declares knowledge. (Ps. 19:1–2 RSV)

Of course, it is not, strictly speaking, *the heavens* that are declaring God's glory, but it is *God* declaring his glory "through the things that are made" (Rom. 1:20). The SD itself, then, is revelation from God, implanted in us by God, and is knowledge of God, the true God, which is clearly perceived and understood by us.

There is another factor that we need to see from Paul's discussion in this passage. We should remember that Paul began his discussion of the SD, not directly, but indirectly, as an elaboration of the notion of "truth," which truth we all, in our sins, suppress. Specifically, it is the *truth* suppressed that is the subject of Paul's description of the SD. It is *not*, we should note, the *suppression* that is a part of the SD, but the *truth* suppressed that is. The suppression itself is, rather, an elaboration of what it means to be ungodly and wicked (cf. Rom 1:18).

This said, I think Plantinga and Calvin are correct to attribute any malfunction or dysfunction with respect to theistic belief, not to the SD per se, but rather to "the *seed* of the knowledge of God," as Calvin puts it, or the *deliverances* of the SD, as Plantinga has it.[34] Thus, while the SD itself is always functioning properly, *im*proper

---

34. There are places in *Warranted Christian Belief* where Plantinga does attribute malfunction and dysfunction to the *sensus divinitatis*. There are other places where the dysfunction relates to *what we do* with the *sensus divinitatis* itself. I suspect the latter is closer to what Paul means. I can't see, at this point, that highlighting this truth would significantly alter Plantinga's model, except to say that dysfunction itself lies somewhere beyond the *sensus divinitatis*. There are two reasons, at least, that the *sensus divinitatis* should be construed as, by definition, warranted. The first reason is that, as was noted above, it just *is* knowledge. The second reason, however, as we have seen, is as important. The *sensus divinitatis*, as knowledge, is in its nascent form *given* by God. The process by which human creatures acquire that knowledge is the process of God's "implantation." Thus, both the process of acquisition and the status of the *sensus divinitatis* guarantee its warrant. So how should we think of that knowledge once it is suppressed, exchanged, subverted, and perverted? We should, it seems, see these processes as presupposing the

function lies elsewhere; *that* malfunction lies somewhere "beyond" the knowledge of God, clearly perceived and understood, given to us *by* God *in* natural revelation. The implications of this for epistemology, and for Christian apologetics and philosophy generally, are multifold and abundant, exciting and stimulating. We can only touch on certain elements here.

First, as was said above, it seems to be altogether true and right, that human beings, by virtue of their being created in the image of God, always and everywhere carry the knowledge of God with them. This knowledge does not come by the proper and diligent exercise of their cognitive, emotive, or volitional capacities; it rather comes by God's own revelatory activity within them.[35] Here, it seems to me, David Reiter is right. In his article, "Calvin's 'Sense of Divinity' and Externalist Knowledge of God,"[36] Reiter argues (among other things) the following concerning "Calvin's Sense of Divinity" (CSD):

> (CSD) For any sane human being S, if S has any propositional knowledge at t, then S knows at t that God exists.[37]

This formulation has numerous implications for a "proper function" epistemology. One implication is that it allows for an explanation of the attainment of knowledge for those who, perhaps for reasons of age, lack of effort, or malfunction in some other faculty, would otherwise be deemed cognitively incompetent to know such things. It allows, in other words, for the knowledge of God to reside in *all* human beings to the extent that they can attain knowledge at all.[38]

---

true knowledge of God, as Paul does, and thus as secondary to and dependent on the *sensus divinitatis* itself.

35. Notice Paul's point that what is known about God is made manifest within us (διότι τὸ γνωστὸν τοῦ θεοῦ φανερόν ἐστιν ἐν αὐτοῖς—Rom. 1:19), and Calvin's point that "God himself has implanted" this knowledge (*Institutes*, 1.3.1). The actor, clearly, according to both Paul and Calvin, with respect to the acquisition of any knowledge of God, which is the *SD*, is God, not us; we are the (unwilling?) patients.

36. David Reiter, "Calvin's 'Sense of Divinity' and Externalist Knowledge of God," *Faith and Philosophy* 15, no. 3 (1998): 253–70.

37. Ibid., 256.

38. Ibid. Reiter does take note of the difficulty of attributing knowledge to infants and to those who are judged to be insane. I think Paul allows for knowledge in such cases, but to argue the point here would take us too far afield.

One important qualifier needs to be added here and should be developed, but cannot be elaborated. Since this knowledge of God that all people have is both *knowledge* and *implanted* by God through the dynamic of his revelatory activity, it is a knowledge that is in many ways quite different from most (if not all) other kinds of knowledge that we acquire. It is a knowledge, we could say, that is presupposed by any (perhaps all) other knowledge. For this reason, it may be best to think of it as more *psychological* than *epistemological*.[39] It is a knowledge that *God* infuses into his human creatures, and continues to infuse into them, even as they continue to live out their days denying or ignoring him. It is a knowledge that he implants "through the things that are made." Thus, it comes, always and anon, whether or not the human creature claims to know God or to have reason for not knowing.

Another implication of our now modified formulation of the *SD* is that theistic belief of this kind always and everywhere has warrant. That is, there can be no situation in which God implants the knowledge of himself and in which the person to whom this knowledge is given fails to know God.

We may now ask, what does this mean for epistemology? There are significant implications to what we have said thus far, implications that could go a long way in helping us understand what a Christian epistemology might require.

A "Basic" Problem

In discussions of epistemology of late it has become customary to think, not so much about the *source* of our knowledge as about its *structure*. So, for example, where epistemological debates were once preoccupied with questions of empiricism or rationalism (i.e., the source of knowledge being either our senses or our ideas, respectively), current discussions center on questions of foundationalism or coherentism, reliabilism or causalism, and so forth (all of which seek to highlight the structure of knowledge). The structure of

39. That is, knowledge that is initially and centrally focused in the soul, rather than centrally focused in the mind.

knowledge for which Plantinga argues in the context of his "proper function" epistemology is, generally speaking, foundationalism, and, more specifically, what he calls "Reidian foundationalism."[40]

Reidian foundationalism has two basic elements: (1) It maintains the basic structure of foundational epistemology. In any foundational epistemology there are two categories of belief. There are beliefs that are basic, and there are beliefs that are inferred. Basic beliefs are beliefs that are not inferred but rather acquired by another means or mode of belief acquisition. They are acquired, for example, by way of memory, perception, testimony, and the like. Furthermore, these basic beliefs, acquired as they are more "immediately," without recourse to argument or inference, are nevertheless not thought to be irrational. They are instead held to be (as Plantinga says) "properly basic." Proper basicality obtains for someone, S, with respect to a belief, B, just in case B is basic for S and S is not in any way irrational in holding B.[41] (2) Reidian foundationalism, unlike other

40. Thomas Reid (1710–96) is credited with developing and articulating, in opposition primarily to David Hume, a school of philosophy known as "Common Sense Realism" or "Scottish Common Sense Realism." In opposition to Humean skepticism, Reid argued that philosophy's inability to justify and prove certain things that we all take for granted (e.g., cause and effect) is not due to a defect in (or absence of) those things, but rather a product of defects in much of what passes for philosophy. We should rather, according to Reid, rely on our common sense as adequate to justify much of what we believe instead of counting on philosophy to justify those beliefs for us. For example, says Reid: "I take it for granted that all the thoughts I am conscious of, or remember, are the thoughts of one and the same thinking principle, which I call *myself* or my *mind*. Every man has an immediate and irresistible conviction, not only of his present existence, but of his continued existence and identity as far back as he can remember. If any man should think fit to demand a proof that the thoughts he is successively conscious of, belong to one and the same thinking principle—if he should demand a proof that he is the same person today as he was yesterday or a year ago—I know no proof that can be given him: he must be left to himself, either as a man that is lunatic or as one who denies first principles, and is not to be reasoned with." Thomas Reid, Ronald E. Beanblossom, and Keith Lehrer, *Thomas Reid's Inquiry and Essays* (Indianapolis: Hackett, 1983) and quoted in Plantinga, *Warrant and Proper Function*, 51. For a summary description of Reidian foundationalism, see Plantinga, *Warrant and Proper Function*, 183f.

41. One of the motivations behind Plantinga's epistemological project was to argue that the (so-called) "evidential objection"—that it is wrong always and everywhere to hold anything except on the basis of evidence—is itself incoherent. So, a properly basic belief, while not obtained on the basis of evidence or argument, can nevertheless be rational.

versions of foundationalism, allows for a wider and broader inclusion of categories of basic beliefs, beyond those allowed by the "classic" version of foundationalism.[42] So, Plantinga widens the "base" of foundationalism in that categories other than the ones previously accepted are added to the foundation.[43]

The primary motivation, however, for Plantinga's attachment to a Reidian foundationalism is that he wants to argue for one's belief in God to be included among the set of properly basic beliefs. Unlike the classic version of foundationalism, a Reidian version would extend the categories of proper basicality such that one's belief in God, if present, itself can be properly basic. Standard versions of foundationalism will not allow for such a belief. Since belief in God fits none of the three categories of properly basic belief—that is, since belief in God is not a self-evident belief, is not a belief evident to the senses, and is not an incorrigible belief—it is irrational to hold such a belief until and unless it can be inferred from other (basic) beliefs one holds. What is needed for belief in God to be rational, therefore, given classical foundationalism, is evidence and inference. Plantinga's epistemology is, in part, an argument *against* the illegitimate constraints imposed by classical foundationalism, and *for* the rationality of one's believing in God's existence without producing reasons, which is another way of saying that he argues for properly basic theistic belief.

In his critique of a classical foundationalist structure, Plantinga sees proper basicality as its "fundamental principle." That is,

(1) A proposition p is properly basic for a person S if and only if p is either self-evident to S or incorrigible for S or evident to the senses for S.[44]

42. In classical foundationalism, generally speaking, the three typical categories of basic belief allowable were (1) self-evident beliefs, (2) beliefs evident to the senses and (3) incorrigible beliefs.

43. We say "widens the base" because foundationalism is often pictured as a pyramid, the bottom of which depicts properly basic beliefs, and the two sides of which show beliefs inferred from those basic beliefs.

44. Alvin Plantinga, "Reason and Belief in God," in *Faith and Rationality*, ed. Alvin Plantinga and Nicholas Wolterstorff (Notre Dame, IN: University of Notre Dame Press, 1983), 59. It is important to understand that from the writing of this article to

Plantinga sees at least two serious problems with the above "fundamental principle" of classical foundationalism. First of all, he is willing to concede that a belief is properly basic if it is self-evident, incorrigible, or evident to the senses. So far, so good. What he will not concede is that such is the case *if and only if* the above conditions are met. The reason being that, in this case, classical foundationalism's problem consists in its inability to account for much of what we take to be true.

> We should note first that if this thesis, and the correlative foundationalist thesis that a proposition is rationally acceptable only if it follows from or is probable with respect to what is properly basic—if these claims are true, then enormous quantities of what we all in fact believe are irrational. . . . Relative to propositions that are self-evident and incorrigible, most of the beliefs that form the stock in trade of ordinary everyday life are not probable. . . . Consider all those propositions that entail, say, that there are enduring physical objects, or that there are persons distinct from myself, or that the world has existed for more than five minutes: none of these propositions, I think, is more probable than not with respect to what is self-evident or incorrigible for me.[45]

We see here, in Plantinga's argument against classical foundationalism's conditions for proper basicality, an appeal to those things which are generally accepted to be true, and true perhaps without evidence, yet which (generally accepted) truths have no place in a classical foundationalist structure. Thus, classical foundationalism is suspect as an epistemological structure because it says too little. It has nothing to say to my belief that I was in Boston last year or that I did not just appear at my desk five minutes ago or that you,

---

the production of the warrant trilogy, Plantinga's *response* to the epistemological problem of evidentialism and classical foundationalism underwent some significant modification. Specifically, Plantinga moved from a more internalist approach to an externalist epistemology, emphasizing the *function* of our epistemic faculties rather than our own (subjective) rationale for our beliefs. The general analysis of the problem, as we have it here, did not substantially change during this time.

45. Ibid., 59–60.

like me, are a person. Classical foundationalism's proper basicality, in this sense, is far too restrictive.

But it is also far too ambitious, and destructively so. Not only does it say too little but it also says too much. We have just noticed Plantinga's problem with the "only if" aspect of (1) above, but now notice that (1) itself is not consistent with its own criterion. Consider that (1) either must itself be a properly basic belief or must be believed on the basis of some other, more basic, belief(s). The classical foundationalist, believing (1) above, must be able to support that belief by way of some beliefs that are self-evident or incorrigible or evident to the senses. But no argument has been forthcoming from the classical foundationalist. Therefore, since (1) is not inferential, it must be itself properly basic in order to be rationally believed. But (1) cannot meet conditions of being evident to the senses, self-evident, or incorrigible. Therefore, the fundamental principle of classical foundationalism, with its insistence on and conditions of proper basicality, is itself, as Plantinga likes to say, "self-referentially incoherent."[46] Foundationalism's own basic principle is insufficient to support the very position for which it seeks to argue.

It is Plantinga's contention, therefore, that an epistemological structure should make room for the proper basicality of more and more "kinds" of beliefs than the standard versions of foundationalism are prepared to do, including theistic belief.[47] Such is the case, it seems, because an epistemological structure must make room for the things we all take to be obvious, for example, the existence of other persons. And if belief in other persons is obvious to everyone without itself satisfying classical foundationalism's conditions for

---

46. Ibid., 61f. George Mavrodes seeks, among other things, to show Plantinga's notion of self-referential incoherence as erroneous. George Mavrodes, "Self-Referential Incoherence," *American Philosophical Quarterly* 22, no. 1 (January 1985): 65–72.

47. It is *not* Plantinga's contention that an epistemological structure *must* include theistic belief or that theistic belief *should* be contained somewhere within the structure. Rather, argues Plantinga, any epistemological structure worth its salt must include memory beliefs, beliefs about other persons, and theistic belief as beliefs that are warranted without the constraints of propositional evidence. It must, therefore, make room for theistic belief, and theistic belief, when included, can be properly basic.

proper basicality or for inferential belief, then the existence of God (himself another person) must be given at least the same status.

In a Reidian foundationalism, however, there are categories or kinds of knowledge included in the foundation of one's noetic structure that allow for a much broader and wider range of beliefs to be included as basic, and properly so.[48]

But is this approach sufficient for a *Christian* epistemology?

---

48. For a more detailed account of Plantinga's warrant project, see K. Scott Oliphint, "Plantinga on Warrant," *Westminster Theological Journal* 57, no. 1 (Spring 1995): 81–102; K. Scott Oliphint, "Epistemology and Christian Belief," *Westminster Theological Journal* 63, no. 1 (Spring 2001): 151–82.

8

Common Sense and Common Ground

The weightiest Testimony only that can be brought to prove that there is a God, is to produce the Testimony of God speaking in his own word. None other in the world can have equal authority.
—EDWARD LEIGH

Perhaps the best critique of a Reidian approach to epistemology can be found, not in a critique of epistemology per se, but rather in a critique of an apologetic approach that, it is argued, has its roots deeply embedded into Thomas Reid's common sense philosophy.

Common (Non)sense?

In his excellent article, "The Collapse of American Evangelical Academia,"[1] George Marsden attempts to show the (partial) historical progression in which scholarship has divorced itself from

1. Ironically, this article, which provides a substantial refutation to Plantinga's Reidianism, is found in George Marsden, "The Collapse of American Evangelical Academia,"

Christianity, beginning in the eighteenth[2] and continuing into the nineteenth centuries. One of the key elements in this progression was the adoption of, in evangelical apologetics (as well as the consequent failure of), Reid's common sense philosophy. The primary reason for this failure, according to Marsden, was that it was never able to provide a ground, or foundation, for its most basic principles; it was never able to account for its understanding of "common sense" itself.

As Marsden follows the historical progression up to the middle of the nineteenth century, he notes the inability of evangelical apologetics to deal with the destructive elements of Darwinism. Marsden's central question, given such an inability, is this: "What . . . about this mid nineteenth-century American evangelical apologetic made it particularly vulnerable to onslaughts of the scientific revolution associated with Darwinism?"[3] Now the "mid nineteenth-century American evangelical apologetic" of which Marsden speaks is that promoted by, among others, Mark Hopkins, Archibald Alexander, Charles Hodge, and B. B. Warfield. With regard to the approaches of these men, says Marsden, "Common-Sense philosophy was the starting point."[4]

An apologetic with its roots in Reid's common sense philosophy means that one would begin (and notice the affinity with Plantinga's views on the matter) with the "immediate, noninferential beliefs . . . as Reid proposed, such as the existence of the self, the existence of other personal and rational beings, the existence of the material world, the relationship of cause and effect, the continuity of past and present." These were called, by Reid, "principles of common-sense."[5] In defending Christianity, those who adopted this philosophy began by attempting to show how the basic truths

---

in *Faith and Rationality*, ed. Alvin Plantinga and Nicholas Wolterstorff (Notre Dame, IN: University of Notre Dame Press, 1983), 219–64.

2. It is interesting to note that Marsden sees Jonathan Edwards as the only one among the specified group who saw the necessity of grounding common sense beliefs in biblical revelation. See ibid., 247.

3. Ibid., 241.

4. Ibid., 235.

5. Ibid.

and principles of Christianity could fit within the *already estab-lished truths* of common sense. In other words, they would argue, belief in God can fit with other, common sense beliefs that we all already have (which, we should note, is just another way to phrase Plantinga's argument for theistic belief as properly basic).

Without reproducing Marsden's penetrating article, we should note carefully his analysis of the failure of the Reidian (via Hopkins et al.) approach. As Hodge (following Reid) remarked in stating his assumptions, common sense truths were "given in the constitution of our nature." Having been so purposely designed, they could be relied on with perfect security. This is because Reid himself argued that it is possible to establish once for all a universal code of agreed-upon common-sense principles.[6] So, asserted Hodge, the design of nature was assumed to involve the creation of a single universal human nature. Hence the presumption made by Hodge and others was that common sense principles were universal and unalterable.

But there are serious problems with Reid's assumption. For example, when Darwinism came on the scene, one of its most seri-ous challenges was that it could retain its evolutionary principle *without* recourse to theism. The problem was not so much that Darwinism needed atheism, which would have been easier (because more explicit) to deal with, but rather that Darwinism needed only agnosticism. In other words, it was not that Darwinism had to con-tend, "There is no God, but there is design," but only, "We see design in everything, though we are not sure whether or not God exists," which is far less radical (and thus *more* challenging) than blatant atheism. So Darwinism challenged Christian theism's contention of the certainty of God's existence by postulating agnosticism *along with a thesis for design.*[7] Tragically, those married to Reid's philosophy

6. Ibid., 243. Plantinga has not gone so far as Reid in assuming that there is a *univer-sal* code of principles. Some, however, have seen that such is exactly what Plantinga must affirm with regard to theistic belief if he wants to include them in the so-called "paradigm cases" of properly basic beliefs. See McLeod, "The Analogy Argument for the Proper Basicality of Belief in God," *International Journal for Philosophy of Religion* 21 (1987); James F. Sennett, *Modality, Probability, and Rationality: A Critical Examination of Alvin Plantinga's Philosophy* (New York: Peter Lang, 1992).

7. See ibid., 241–44.

could only respond by positing that Darwin's position excluded an intelligent Designer, which was all too obvious even to need asserting.[8] As Marsden points out, all that Hodge (for example) could do in the face of Darwinism was assert that large parts of the population still believed in an intelligent Designer. What, then, would happen to this "defense" when the next generation would show belief in an intelligent Designer to be far from universal?

Most damaging to the philosophy of common sense, therefore—and, according to Marsden, the fatal blow to Reidianism—was demonstrated in the nineteenth century in the apologetic responses to the introduction of Darwinism; and the fatal blow is summarized by Marsden in this way: "Common sense could not settle a dispute over what was a matter of common sense."[9]

Common sense philosophy, therefore, when tried in the fire of apologetic methodology, and thus also of epistemology, failed in its attempt to defend the truth of Christianity in the face of a hostile science. In other words, the problem with a strict Reidian approach to epistemology is that there is no way, no method or mode, by which one might be able to determine just what beliefs *are* common and what beliefs are not. One man's properly basic belief, therefore, could easily be another man's irrationality. How might we address this problem?

8. Marsden, "Collapse of American Evangelical Academia," 243–44.

9. Plantinga is not unaware of this problem. In assessing how we might find criteria sufficient to determine which beliefs are properly basic and which are not, Plantinga says: "And hence the proper way to arrive at such a criterion is, broadly speaking, *inductive*. We must assemble examples of beliefs and conditions such that the former are obviously properly basic on the latter, and examples of beliefs and conditions such that the former are obviously *not* properly basic in the latter. We must then frame hypotheses as to the necessary and sufficient conditions of proper basicality and test these hypotheses by reference to those examples." Alvin Plantinga, "Rationality and Religious Belief," in *Contemporary Philosophy of Religion*, ed. Stephen M. Cahn and David Shatz (New York: Oxford University Press, 1982), 276.

At least one of the reasons for this is that common sense beliefs were thought to function as *principia*, basic and fundamental principles of knowledge itself. But it was "common" knowledge that common sense beliefs were only *generally* common and not absolutely so. Therefore, there was no criterion by which to determine which views were and which were not "common sense." Or, to say it another way, since these beliefs were thought to be on the level of *principia*, there was no way to give a *rationale* for such common sense beliefs.

Thomas to Thomas

Common sense is not able to stand on its own; it needs to be grounded or situated such that its principles are or can be universally accessible and applicable. So, one of the implications of our understanding of the knowledge situation is that there must be something behind and beyond the most basic principles of epistemology that can provide a reference point and ground for the theory itself. As Marsden notes, common sense philosophy, in seeking to ground knowledge in itself alone, was hoist with its own petard.

In order to resolve the problems entailed in epistemology generally, and demonstrated in the common sense philosophy specifically, we need to move back in time from Thomas Reid to Thomas Aquinas. While incorporating our (now revised) understanding of the *SD* into the discussion, we will also look into Thomas's epistemology in order to think through the relationship of our knowledge to the fact of God's existence, a relationship, we will argue, that requires an explicit and inextricable link between epistemology and metaphysics.

Before we do that, however, we should make clear the general structure into which we will incorporate Thomas's epistemology. As we noted in chapter 1, crucial to any understanding of epistemology, or of knowledge in general, is the existence of *principia*.

Principia were set forth, in the history of thought, generally, and of theology, more specifically, as those beginning points,[10] indemonstrable in themselves, out of and by which one could think about and know reality. In that sense, they were fundamental to everything else that we could know.

As we saw previously, in the Protestant tradition, the notion of *principium* was adapted from philosophical discussions in order to underline the importance of foundational starting points with respect to our knowledge. Thus, necessary for any theological knowledge was, first, a *principium essendi* and, second, a *principium cognoscendi*. The *principium essendi* was that which provided for

10. Remember that, *principium*, historically, is the Latin translation of the Greek word, ἀρχή.

the reality itself. It was that without which the thing to be known would not exist. Of course, in theology this is the triune God himself. Given this *principium essendi*, the *principium cognoscendi* is that principle, or "starting place," for knowledge, which itself depends on the *principium essendi*. And the starting place for knowledge, it has been rightly argued, is God's revelation.

> In theology, the foundation (*principium*) is twofold: of being and of knowing (*Essendi et Cognoscendi*), namely, that by which it is and that by which it is known; the former establishes or presents the knowable object (lit., the knowable thing and the object: *scibile et obiectum*); the latter brings forth knowledge and gives form to the subject: the former is God, and the latter is the word of God himself, as is manifestly expressed and indicated in holy Scripture.[11]

What this means, with respect to theology at least, is that knowledge must be grounded in something else. It cannot have or find its ground within itself. With respect to the *principia*, knowledge must be grounded in the nature of (ultimate) reality itself.

As it turns out, this emphasis is found in Aquinas's epistemology as well.[12] First, we will outline some general principles of Thomas's approach, then we will seek to incorporate our understanding of the *SD* into the main contours of that approach.

According to Thomas, "demonstration," by which he means syllogistic reasoning, must "proceed from principles that are immediate either straightway or through middles."[13] It is necessary, therefore, for the reasoning process that the knowledge gained thereby rest on knowledge that is not inferred. So far, we might think that Thomas

11. Muller is quoting Hoornbeeck here in Richard A. Muller, *Post-Reformation Reformed Dogmatics: Prolegomena to Theology* (Grand Rapids, MI: Baker, 1987), 298.

12. In the previous chapter, we were concerned more specifically with the relationship of Thomas's metaphysics to his theory of theological predication. Here we are concerned with the structure of Thomas's epistemology more generally. We will borrow freely from Scott MacDonald's fine article, "Theory of Knowledge," in *The Cambridge Companion to Aquinas*, ed. Norman Kretzmann and Eleanor Stump (Cambridge: Cambridge University Press, 1993), 160–95.

13. Thomas Aquinas, *Commentary on the Posterior Analytics of Aristotle*, trans. F. R. Larcher (Albany, NY: Magi Books, 1970), 17.

is simply affirming here the basic structure of foundationalism. It sounds as though he is classifying our knowledge as either inferred or immediate. And so he is.

But there is a difference in what Thomas is saying from what many modern foundationalists want to affirm. It is certainly the case that Thomas affirms knowledge of propositions that are indemonstrable. Such is his meaning of immediate propositions. If immediate propositions were in need of demonstration, they would not, therefore, be immediate. They would be mediated by way of demonstration.

Immediate propositions, however, are those in which "the predicate is included within the notion of its subject."[14] These propositions are known by virtue of themselves and not by virtue of any inference from predicate to subject. Thus, immediate propositions are stronger than mediate and are known with more certainty. Immediate propositions, therefore, are not simply epistemic grounds for other, mediate, propositions, but (even more importantly) they are propositions that themselves are grounded metaphysically. So, says Scott MacDonald, "Immediate propositions, then, are capable of being known by virtue of themselves and are, therefore, proper objects of non-derivative knowledge."[15] This much could be said by virtually any foundationalist. What is more significant, however, is the following sentence: "But their actually being known by virtue of themselves *requires that one be acquainted with the facts expressed by those propositions* which requires that one conceive the terms of those propositions."[16]

In other words, one of the key elements necessary for a proposition to be immediate is that there be a particular structure of reality. What propositions are immediate depends on the nature of the world. Or as MacDonald explains, "Which propositions are immediate, then, depends solely on what real natures there are and what relations hold among them, that is, on the basic structure of the world, and too on the psychology or belief-structure of any given epistemic subject."[17]

14. Ibid., 21.
15. MacDonald, "Theory of Knowledge," 172.
16. Ibid.
17. Ibid., 170.

We can highlight the difference in Thomas's view here perhaps by recalling one of the typical ways that foundationalism has been pictured in comparison to coherentism.[18] Foundationalism has been pictured as a pyramid, the base of which represents basic, non-inferential beliefs, and the two sides of which represent beliefs inferred from those basic beliefs. Coherentism, on the other hand, has been pictured as a raft, that is, a set of beliefs, each of which is consistent with the rest. The problem with this picture, however, if we take our cue from Thomas's formulation, is that the pyramid itself is a raft. While it may have some kind of base, it nevertheless is "floating" around on its own without anything to tie it down. For Thomas, the structure of knowledge is not a pyramid. Rather, it is a pyramid that needs its own ground, a pyramid that is grounded in the way the world is made. Thus, says MacDonald, "Propositions are immediate by virtue of expressing what might be called metaphysically immediate relationships or facts, the relationships that hold between natures and their essential constituents."[19]

Thomas, therefore, sees a necessary and direct link between what we know and the nature of the world. This takes knowledge out of the realm of epistemology per se, and requires, for a justification of knowledge, a metaphysical structure such that facts, natures, and their constituents, and the relationships between them, themselves *be* and be known, and known immediately. This is contrary to virtually any current understanding of foundationalism. Foundationalism, as presently discussed, with its allegiance to Immanuel Kant, will allow for no intrusion of metaphysics.

> This metaphysical picture allows us to see the kind of objectivist requirement Aquinas incorporates into the theory of demonstration. When he claims that the first principles of demonstration must be immediate and indemonstrable, he is claiming that they must express metaphysically immediate propositions and not just propositions that are epistemically basic and unprovable for some

18. Ernest Sosa, "The Raft and the Pyramid: Coherence versus Foundations in the Theory of Knowledge," in *Knowledge in Perspective: Selected Essays in Epistemology*, ed. Ernest Sosa (Cambridge: Cambridge University Press, 1991), 165–91.

19. MacDonald, "Theory of Knowledge," 170.

particular epistemic subject. That a given proposition *P* happens to be indemonstrable *for some person S* because there are no other propositions in *S*'s belief-structure on the basis of which *S* would be justified in holding *P* is no guarantee that *P* is, on Aquinas' view, an immediate, indemonstrable proposition. The structure of demonstration, then, is isomorphic with the metaphysical structure of reality: immediate, indemonstrable propositions express metaphysically immediate facts, whereas mediate, demonstrable propositions express metaphysically mediate facts.[20]

It is the nature of the world, therefore, that gives us a foundation for foundationalism. The pyramid itself needs a place on which to stand. That place is creation.

The *Sensus* Consensus

Thomas's epistemology fits within the context of the *principia* noted above. We can have knowledge because of the way things are, the way the world is made. Thus, our *principium cognoscendi* is dependent on the *principium essendi*. The principle of knowledge depends on the essential principle, the latter of which provides the context and the foundations for the possibility of knowledge itself.

We can also begin to see just how Thomas's approach to epistemology fits most comfortably with our previous discussion of the *SD*.[21] If the *SD* constitutes knowledge, knowledge given by God himself, then, while there can easily be similarities between the *SD* and other basic ways of acquiring knowledge—ways like perception and memory—we need to affirm that there are important and crucial differences between the *SD* and other ways of acquiring knowledge or warranted belief. Thomas's way of spelling out those differences is helpful.

20. Ibid.
21. As far as I can tell, Thomas would not have countenanced a view of the *SD* that we have set forth. That remained for Calvin to do. There is no question, however, that Thomas was thinking of theology (as well as natural science) as paradigmatic illustrations of the structure of knowledge he advocates. See MacDonald, "Theory of Knowledge," 174.

Specifically, given that immediate propositions are those in which the predicate is included in the notion of the subject, any knowledge of God that people have by virtue of God's general revelation is, necessarily, knowledge in which the predicate is included in the notion of the subject. To know that God is, for example, is to know that existence is included in the very idea of God. So also to know that God is good is to know that goodness has its ground in the character of God himself.

Fundamental to the *SD*, however, is the fact that this knowledge of God—given that all people have it, and given that it is had by virtue of our being made in the image of God—is a knowledge that is both *universal* and *immediate*. The fact that it is universal has already been explained above. The "immediacy" of the knowledge of God that we all have does not mean that this knowledge is not mediated through anything. For surely it is mediated, as Paul says, "through the things that are made." Rather, it is immediate knowledge because it is not gained by way of inference. There is nothing that we do—no demonstration, no syllogism—that is the ground for the acquisition of this knowledge. It is, as our Christian forefathers would say, *cognitio insita*. It is *implanted* (or inserted) knowledge of God, given to us, through the things that are made, by God himself.

It is knowledge, therefore, that depends on the nature of the world. It requires that the nature of the world be such that God is always and everywhere revealing himself through it, and that this revelation is not something that is resisted, or even resistable, by us, but is rather something that we do indeed take.

It may very well be that this knowledge is not propositional. Our analysis of the *SD* might indicate such. But if it is not, that is no problem for a theory of knowledge that seeks to be grounded in the real nature of things. To insist that such knowledge be propositional is to revert back to a narrowing of epistemology, and thus perhaps to a pyramid with no place to stand.[22]

---

22. Some, like Aquinas, would hold that truth accrues only to propositions and the statements that represent them. If the knowledge of God given in the *SD* is not propositional, then, under this construal, it cannot be true. This does not, however, seem to be the way Paul understands the truth that we have by way of God's revelation in creation.

If it is the case, therefore, that all of us know God, and we know him by virtue of being created in his image (itself a metaphysical notion), then there is a universal, metaphysical ground for anything, and everything, else that we can and do know. Given that all of us begin our cognitive awareness with sure and certain knowledge (of God), all else that we know will have that knowledge as its anchor. If we know anything, it will be consistent with that knowledge. It would be impossible for us to know something, therefore, that in any way contradicted or contravened that essential, fundamental, metaphysical knowledge of God. Since God is *the* immediate, metaphysical fact *par excellence*, anything else that comes to us as knowledge will have that knowledge as its Archimedean point.

What might this mean for non-inferential knowledge or belief? Given Thomas's delineation of knowledge, we know immediately, when we do, because of the nature of the world and its constituent parts. That is, knowledge is inextricably linked with the way things really are. As we have seen, we first and foremost know God. And, as Paul says, we know him through "the things that have been made." Entailed, therefore, in our knowledge of God is a knowledge of the things made, through which we know God. Paul is not arguing that our knowledge of God comes through the things that are made without at the same time our knowing the thing itself. Thus, it seems, the way in which we begin with respect to knowledge is by being confronted with the reality of God's creation in all its splendor and, because of sin's effects, in all its ugliness as well.

How might we explain this kind of knowledge? Remember Mac-Donald's analysis above. He notes that, on Thomas's view, knowing things by virtue of themselves "requires that one be *acquainted* with the facts expressed by those propositions which requires that one conceive the terms of those propositions." The notion of "acquaintance" with respect to knowledge, we may remember, is similar to the "Knowledge by Acquaintance" that we looked at in chapter 6. Remember that Russell noted that I may say that I am *acquainted*

Taking Paul's context, we might simply want to say that truth obtains whenever our cognitive content, propositional or not, corresponds to the way things really are.

with an object when I have a direct cognitive relation to that object, that is, when I am *directly aware* of the object itself.

Now that which is indubitably, relentlessly, clearly, and comprehensibly "present" to and in all of us is the revelation of God. We know him by virtue of his presence.[23] But we also know the things made, the things of this world—including at least other people, the world around us, the testimony of others, our own memories—because as present to us these things are the conduits through which God himself is revealed and known.

It is not the case, therefore, that "common sense" beliefs or non-inferential beliefs (or knowledge) must be universal in order to be justified. Rather, what *is* universal is the knowledge of God. And it is universally the case that this knowledge comes through all that God has made, including ourselves. It will be expected, therefore, that, included in being the image of God is the fact that we are covenantally bound to the rest of creation such that our knowledge of it and interaction with it is an essential aspect of who we are as image. The "connection," therefore, between our own knowledge and the world as known is made by God himself, who always and everywhere is revealing himself to his covenant creatures (creatures made in his image) such that, in knowing what he has made, we know him. What is "common sense" to us all, therefore, is not necessarily a specific set of non-inferred beliefs, but rather the knowledge of God that all of us have, and the concomitant knowledge of the created world that brings that knowledge of God to us.

At least one of the implications of this for epistemology is this: just as in theology there must be a *principium essendi* that grounds our *principium cognoscendi*—that is, just as the existence and character of God ground our knowledge of him, since that knowledge presupposes his existence and character (as given to us in Scripture)—so also in epistemology generally. With respect to knowledge in general, it must be that the existence and character of God ground our knowledge of him *as given to all through all that is made*. All knowledge, therefore, if it *is* knowledge, presupposes,

23. One will readily note the covenantal implications that are central to this kind of knowledge.

first, the knowledge of God (the universal *principium cognoscendi*) and, second, his existence (the universal *principium essendi*).

Foundationalism, therefore, cannot bear the weight of its own claims. Rejecting, as it is wont to do, any appeal to "the way things are" with respect to reality itself, it cannot find a universal consent with respect to beliefs that are thought to be basic. That universal consent is found in the knowledge of God, knowledge that is immediate and is grounded in the metaphysical nature of God (as revealer) and of the world he has made (as revelation).

The Cretan Condition

But things are not quite that simple. There is now a significant problem with the "way things are" relative to the "way we come to know" them. The problem, as Paul makes clear in Romans 1, is that we suppress the truth, we seek to hold down the very knowledge that we all have, that knowledge which is ours and universally so by virtue of God's revealing activity in and through us. The problem, and we must admit this is the quintessentially maximal problem, is sin. Thus, we seek to suppress the very thing that would give us all that we need for a proper and full account of knowledge.[24]

Here again is where there will need to be some substantial modification with respect to any theory of knowledge that has as one of its crucial elements the notion of proper function. More specifically, if an essential aspect of the proper functioning of our cognitive faculties is that they operate according to a design plan, and if sin's effects have substantially altered that plan, then it would seem that the cognitive faculties are not, when enslaved by sin, operating at any one time according to that plan. Thus, whatever "proper" means in the notion of proper function must take account of such *dys*function.[25]

24. Of course, it's much worse than that. We suppress the very thing that would give us all that we need for a proper and full *life* in this world, and the next.

25. Plantinga does mention, in *Warrant and Proper Function*, that we all know, at least to some extent, what it means that, say, a kidney is functioning properly, and presumably we all should know what it means for our cognitive faculties to function properly as well. While this comparison is undoubtedly legitimate in some respects, there are also

Assume that, except for the entrance of sin in the world and its influence on our cognitive faculties, we would all know and believe in (in the biblical sense) and acknowledge the existence and character of the true God. Given what Paul has said in Romans 1, we would all acknowledge that fact, in part, because we would acknowledge our constant perception of God through the things that are made; we would see God everywhere and acknowledge that we do. Not only so, but this God who is revealed in creation, reveals himself also by speaking to us. We take that speech for what it is, the very word of God (now given to us in Scripture).[26] *That*, it seems, describes in part the *proper* functioning of our noetic faculties.

But our faculties no longer function that way. They have been damaged, fractured, broken, impeded, hindered, hampered, thwarted from doing what they were designed to do, since the effects of sin have enslaved and influenced them. Whereas we were designed to do all things to the glory of God—whether eating, drinking, thinking, knowing, and so forth—sin has constrained us so that, enslaved to it, we do all things to our own glory, or to the glory of something or someone other than God. If every fact is such that it reveals God, we may take that fact and believe it to be what it is, but in our sin we believe such without acknowledging the God who is revealed in that fact. In every aspect of knowledge or belief, therefore, in which the effects of sin's enslavement are operating, our cognitive faculties fail to function as they were designed to function. There is, we could say, in every functioning of our cognitive faculties in which sin dominates, an element, perhaps a strong element, of self-deception.

---

properties of our cognitive faculties that are exclusive to them alone. Unlike other organs of the body, for example, our cognitive faculties can ponder, think, analyze, synthesize, carry on internal conversation, and so forth. It is our cognitive faculties as well that play a crucial role in assuring that we properly make our way in the world in which we live. They do that by believing, knowing, understanding, perceiving, etc. those things given to us in the world.

26. For the best articulation of the relationship of general revelation to special revelation, see Cornelius Van Til, "Nature and Scripture," in *The Infallible Word: A Symposium by the Members of the Faculty of Westminster Theological Seminary*, 2nd ed., ed. N. B. Stonehouse and Paul Woolley (Philadelphia: Presbyterian and Reformed, 1967), 263–301.

There are fascinating and stimulating aspects of self-deception that cannot be explored here. In order to flesh this out a bit, however, it may be helpful to highlight some of the properties of self-deception that are relevant to this discussion.[27]

According to Paul, there are things about God that we all know yet suppress. One way that we suppress those things is by believing things that are false, "exchanging the truth of God for a lie." In other words, because of sin, we are all Cretans (who, as Scripture notes, were reputed to be perpetual liars). There is, therefore, a process of self-deception that takes place wherein we choose to believe things that are false in order to avoid acknowledging things that we know to be true.

Could it be, then, that we hold contradictory beliefs, believing at one and the same time that (1) God exists and (2) that God does not exist, or that we are not sure whether or not he exists? It certainly seems so. It would seem that we are capable of holding beliefs that are in direct conflict with each other. Indeed it would seem that because of our sinfulness we are determined to hold such beliefs with respect to God and his character. But how could that be?

It might be, as Robert Audi has suggested, that in holding contradictory or conflicting beliefs, one of the beliefs is, as a matter of fact, an unconscious belief.[28] According to Audi, a person, S, is in a state of self-deception with respect to a proposition, *p*, if and only if:

(1) S unconsciously knows that not-*p* (or has reason to believe, and unconsciously and truly believes, not-*p*);

27. Most of these properties can be found in Brian P. McLaughlin, "Exploring the Possibility of Self-Deception in Belief," in *Perspectives on Self-Deception*, ed. Brian P. McLaughlin and Amelie Oksenberg Rorty (Berkeley: University of California Press, 1988), 29–62.

28. See Robert Audi, "Self-Deception, Rationalization, and Reasons for Acting," in *Perspectives on Self-Deception*, ed. Brian P. McLaughlin and Amelie Oksenberg Rorty (Berkeley: University of California Press, 1988), 92–122. "Unconscious," for Audi, simply means that the belief cannot be known "without special self-scrutiny or outside help." This would be the case for one who is self-deceived by way of unconscious beliefs, given that such self-deception cannot be known until and unless one begins to see it as a product of one's sinful state (special self-scrutiny), which, according to Plantinga's extended A/C model, would not take place without Scripture and the Holy Spirit (outside help).

(2) S sincerely avows, or is disposed to avow sincerely, that
   p; and

(3) S has at least one want that explains in part why S's
   belief that not-p is unconscious and why S is disposed
   to avow that p even when presented with what he sees
   as evidence against it.[29]

In this case, a person would know that God exists, but would
deny such knowledge, or at least deny that he had such knowledge,
and would deny all that such knowledge entailed.[30] He would look
at the world, not as created, but as somehow getting by on its own.
In terms of the classical understanding of sin, the driving force
behind his interpretation of the world would be to assert its, and
his, autonomy from anything like a Creator. No matter how difficult
it might be to give a coherent account of his life, his beliefs, his
thoughts about the world, his family, and so forth, he would maintain a staunch belief in his own independence. We could even say
that he maintains a staunch belief in his own autonomy—he looks
around and sees so much evil in the world that he simply cannot
sustain anything like a belief in God. This would lend itself to a
view of self-deception that would see the knowledge of God given
by God as an unconscious knowledge. This person would thus be
self-deceived with respect to his knowledge (entailing belief) of
God.

But maybe the situation is worse than that. It may be that the
self-deception is of such a nature that, given (at least two) conflicting beliefs, we simply have no access to one (or more) of the
beliefs. Using Brian McLaughlin's characterization of inaccessible
beliefs,[31] it might be that, due to the ravages of sin, one desires his
own autonomy to such an extent that he denies his known dependence on God.

29. Ibid., 96.

30. It wouldn't be possible to deny *all* that the knowledge of God, as the SD, entails,
however, since that knowledge entails any other knowledge we might have. What *would*
be possible, and is actually the case, is that all knowledge of God that is entailed by the
SD would be denied.

31. McLaughlin, "Possibility of Self-Deception," 48f.

Consider "Jim," who knows that God exists by virtue of Jim's being created in the image of God. Jim thus has a true knowledge of God; as a person made in God's image, he has within him a *sensus divinitatis*. But, because of the sin into which Jim was born, and because he delights to do things that are in opposition to the God he knows, Jim wants desperately to assert his independence; he will admit dependence on no one and nothing. He does not want to believe in God. Owing to these desires, Jim acts in ways that assert his presumed independence—he makes up his own moral code, which consists chiefly of the principle that he always be happy.

Thus, he drinks too much alcohol, abuses people who get in his way, and even abuses his own family. These things serve to support Jim's strong desire for independence and provide him evidence for it. His actions support his belief in his own independence to such an extent that the knowledge of God that Jim has, and continues to have, is such that Jim cannot access it. Even if someone were to come to Jim and give him a good argument or evidence of this God whom he knows, Jim would not be able, in and of himself, to access his knowledge of God.

That scenario, too, is consistent with the effects of sin, in that our enslavement to sin entails that we simply cannot do the things that are necessary to free ourselves from it, without intervention from the outside.

Whether the self-deceived person holds some beliefs unconsciously, or whether they are inaccessible or perhaps suppressed in some other way, the truth remains, it seems, that we all are, in our sins, self-deceived. And it seems we are self-deceived about *everything*.

Being self-deceived about everything, however, does not mean that everything that one believes is necessarily false or irrational or unwarranted. My wife calls the office and says that she is baking a cake for me for dessert tonight. I come home from the office and find a cake in the kitchen with the inscription, "From Your Wife" written on it. For some unknown reason, I may deceive myself into thinking that this cake was formed in my kitchen through an elaborate, albeit virtually instantaneous, confluence of events. I may believe that materials present in my kitchen, combined with a fortuitous consecution of random events served to produce this cake.

Does my being self-deceived in this situation mean that I hold no rational beliefs whatsoever about this situation? It doesn't seem so. I still believe that what was concocted was a cake and not a telescope; I still believe that it sits in my kitchen and not on Jupiter; I still believe that I am in my house and not in heaven; and so on. Thus, there are beliefs that I still hold that are true and thus rational to hold, beliefs about the very situation in which I am self-deceived. I am deceived about this cake, but there are still beliefs that I hold that comport with the nature of things surrounding this cake.[32]

So suppose I am self-deceived about *everything*. It still could be the case, and I would suggest actually *is* the case, that many of the beliefs that I hold are true; true, that is, as far as they go. If my brother were to come into the kitchen and begin quizzing me about the cake, we might have a pleasant conversation in the beginning. He might ask me what is on the kitchen counter, what the inscription says, and so forth. The questioning would not have to go on too long, however, until the irrational beliefs would begin to manifest themselves.

So it is with the *sensus*/suppression dynamic. There is an aggressive acedia present such that we seek diligently to deny what is obviously the case. This would suggest that, however we understand proper function, we should be quick to qualify such a designation as limited in scope and content. If Calvin, following Paul, is right, we all suffer, when enslaved to sin, from a kind of spiritual dysesthesia, a condition in which we simply do not function properly with regard to the way the world actually is, the way in which it operates and according to which it is maintained.

---

32. The situation is actually more complex than this. I may believe that I am in the kitchen, but because of other beliefs I hold I may not be able to give an adequate account even of *that* belief. Not only so, but the kitchen in which I rightly believe I am, is not, according to me, "the kitchen in which my wife baked a cake," or, "the kitchen in the house in which my wife baked a cake." The kitchen in which I rightly believe, then, has different properties than the real kitchen, properties with respect to my wife, the cake, the house, and so forth. So, deception at the point of the baker of the cake extends to the surrounding context as well. This has sweeping ramifications for Christian apologetics that cannot be discussed here.

Or perhaps we should say that the proper functioning of the cognitive faculties can only obtain when the extended A/C model is applied to us. Perhaps, that is, we should say that, apart from the breaking of the bonds of sin and the re-creation of our natures such that we are renewed unto knowledge, righteousness, and holiness, whatever knowledge we do obtain is present without a significant degree of warrant, due to the fact that our cognitive faculties are mired in self-deception and thus are not functioning according to the design plan.[33]

One final point should be made here. There *are* epistemological aspects of Christian theism that are wholly unique according to the Christian construal of things. That uniqueness relates to the *sensus divinitatis* and to the acquisition process of Christian belief. It comes to focus in Plantinga's development of the internal instigation of the Holy Spirit, but also in the second part of the tripartite account of the *SD* given above. Here we can only touch briefly on something that has already been broached.

It seems more needs to be done to conjoin the notion of cognitive *processes* with cognitive *function*. If our knowledge (in the case of the *SD*) and our faith (in the case of the internal instigation of the Holy Spirit) are *given* to us by God, then it seems also that, whatever role our cognitive faculties play, they play a less-than-direct, subsidiary role with respect to that knowledge and that faith.[34] Not only so, but given that the process itself is instigated and motivated by God, and that the content of knowledge or faith is put there, implanted, given, by him, it seems impossible that such a process could be in

33. Could it be, given this understanding of the design plan, that even after regeneration and renewal our cognitive faculties are *still* not functioning according to the design plan, since that plan did not include the fall into sin? Perhaps, but it seems plausible to maintain that the regeneration and renewal of our cognitive faculties bring us back to the situation of the original design plan to such an extent that the two conditions, *in that sense*, are virtually identical.

34. What is meant here by "less-than-direct" is hard to define precisely. At least what is meant is that the external instigation in each case, rather than the functioning of our faculties, is the initial *sine qua non* of the faith and knowledge produced. It is also true that, unlike other, perhaps most other, cognitive situations, in these cases we are relatively passive in the gaining and acquiring of the knowledge or faith. It is *given, implanted, instigated* within us.

any way liable to error or falsehood. That, of course, is not the case with typical cognitive function. As Andrew Dole put it,

> I find it difficult to imagine better credentials for an item of human knowledge besides its being produced directly by God. If beliefs produced by our cognitive faculties deserve to be called knowledge when they display satisfactory epistemic credentials, then beliefs produced directly by God, it seems to me, have even more right to the title whether or not they satisfy the criterion for warrant as this applies to the productions of our cognitive faculties.[35]

Given God's activity in this process, it seems what we have here is an argument for the truth, not simply the warrant, of Christianity. Given that it is God who implants these truths in us, who reveals himself to us, who causes us to believe in him, we can claim that certain things are indeed free from error and altogether true, not because we have produced them and can trust our cognitive faculties never to err, but precisely because we *have not* produced them and can trust the One who has given us such knowledge and has himself never erred.

Conclusion

We have only begun to flesh out the implications of what it means for all of God's human creatures to have, essentially, the knowledge of him. We have not been able to broach such important topics with respect to, for example, defeaters to our knowledge or the problem of irrationality.[36]

Enough has been said, however, so that we can begin to get an inkling of what a Christian epistemology will need, initially, to affirm. Without this universal knowledge of God, for example, there is no way to begin properly to assess the "connection" that we all have,

35. Andrew Dole, "Cognitive Faculties, Cognitive Processes, and the Holy Spirit in Plantinga's Warrant Series," *Faith and Philosophy* 19, no. 1 (2002): 43.

36. I attempt an initial foray into these in K. Scott Oliphint, "Epistemology and Christian Belief," *Westminster Theological Journal* 63, no. 1 (Spring 2001): 151–82; and "The Irrationality of Unbelief," in *Revelation and Reason: New Essays in Reformed Apologetics*, ed. K. Scott Oliphint and Lane G. Tipton (Phillipsburg, NJ: P&R, forthcoming).

and know we have, to the world that God has made. Not only so, but, given the suppression of the truth—the denial of the knowledge of God that we all have—because of sin, we can also begin to see just how complex the knowledge situation is. Since the fall, man has done with his intellect what he has also done with the rest of his life. He has taken the good things that are given by God, used those things to his own temporary benefit, all the while refusing to acknowledge the very One who has given such good gifts, the very One in whom "we live, and move, and have our being."

This not only makes life at times unbearably perverse, but also makes the knowledge situation unbearably perverse, in that we have sought for millennia to justify ourselves and our knowledge without even a hint of our total and complete dependence on God for all that we think, do, and are.

In the next part, we will begin to think about the implications of the nature of reality for philosophy generally, and philosophy of religion more specifically. We will attempt to apply our *analogia revelationis* to metaphysics and one of its primary problems: the relationship of ultimate reality (God) to everything else.

Metaphysics

9

Being and Essence—
Take Two

*We are given to know the divine attributes or essential proper-
ties by revelation and rational reflection on revelation in such a
way that God's nature is truly known by means of the revealed
attributes.* —TURRETIN

Existence/essence, form/matter, being/nonbeing—these and
other categories are attempts to come to grips with the nature
of reality and thus also with the nature of human knowledge. Some
of these categories have been applied to the character of God as
well, in an attempt to explain his relationship to everything else.
None of these dualities, it seems, has been satisfactory as a Christian response to the way things really are. For that reason, I would
propose another option, one that has its foundation in Reformed
theology. That theology, taking seriously as it does the aseity of God,
is alone able to provide for philosophy a Christian metaphysical

structure such that God's own essential character will not be denied, nor will his interaction with his creation be minimized.

Basic to everything that we think and do is the fact that God is, and he alone always is and always is who he is. Everything else is created, controlled, and sustained by his omniscient, omnipotent, sovereign hand. Given this basic distinction, there are two, and only two, kinds of "reality." There is the reality that is the triune God himself, and there is the reality that is everything else.

Since this is the case, we should not simply discuss notions of "being" or of "knowledge" in general without first recognizing that such notions take their place in two different contexts, two different "realities." Therefore, the categories of existence and thought should be set out as two (related but) distinct realities. That, we should note, is perhaps easier said than done, at least if the history of philosophical theology is any indication.

In postulating God and his character as being of a distinct order and kind from everything else that exists, we are really saying a mouthful (and "brainful") in just a few words. We are saying that everything within the experience of the creature (centrally, people created in God's image), just *is, fundamentally and essentially, immutably and invariably, creaturely*. That is, creatures think as creatures, know as creatures, exist as creatures, and so forth. God, on the other hand, has nothing essentially creaturely about him. He exists as a non-creature, thinks as a non-creature, knows as a non-creature, and so on. All that he essentially is and does, he is and does as one who is not in any way, nor could in any way be, essentially creaturely.

The Mind of God

The implications of this are many, and we'll need to spell out some of the significant ones below, but let's just note one initially that is significant. God knows things. As a matter of fact, God knows everything, and knows everything exhaustively.[1] But just *how* is it that

---

1. The knotty problem of God's omniscience, anything but accepted in philosophy of religion, will not be discussed here. Like the church for over two thousand years, we simply affirm it.

this one who is perfect and complete, who has always existed, and who has no external constraints on his essential being, knows?

Different answers have been given to that question. Alvin Plantinga, for example, asks just how it can be that God can know such difficult propositions as future contingents and counterfactuals of freedom. After delineating four such propositions,[2] from least to most complex, and after a discussion of his notions of warrant, design plan, and so forth, Plantinga concludes: "By way of conclusion, it is indeed true that we don't see how God knows or could know such propositions. . . . For we don't see how God knows *any* of the things he knows; all we know is that necessarily, for any proposition p, p is true if and only if God believes it."[3]

Compare this discussion with that of George Mavrodes. Mavrodes too is concerned to ascertain how God knows what he knows.

2. You can see the four difficult propositions that Plantinga uses as examples in Alvin Plantinga, "Divine Knowledge," in *Christian Perspectives on Religious Knowledge*, ed. C. Stephen Evans, Merold Westphal (Grand Rapids, MI: Eerdmans, 1993), 40–65. It should be mentioned here that the primary reason that some (including Plantinga) struggle with God's knowledge of such propositions is their presupposition of libertarian freedom, a presupposition with which we heartily and happily disagree.

3. Ibid., 65. The question of whether or not God has beliefs cannot be entertained here. Suffice it to say that there seems to be no reason to assume that he does, especially since the holding of beliefs would entail some kind of noetic lack or privation. The view that God has beliefs seems to be an erroneous corollary of the view that God knows by way of propositions. This way of thinking has historically been denied in Christianity, since to know by way of propositions is to know by way of a process of reasoning. Pictet explains: "Concerning the manner (*modus*) in which God knows all things, we must speak cautiously and not attribute anything unbecoming or unworthy to the ultimate majesty. . . . Now we must not at all imagine that God knows things in the same manner as men, who understand one thing in one way, and another thing in another way, and the same thing sometimes obscurely and at other times more clearly, and who, from things known proceed to things unknown. The divine knowledge is of such a mode, as not to admit of any discursive imperfection, or investigative labor, or recollective obscurity, or difficulty of application. God comprehends all things by one single act, observes them as by a single consideration, and sees them distinctly, certainly, and therefore perfectly." Quoted in Richard A. Muller, *Post-Reformation Reformed Dogmatics: The Rise and Development of Reformed Orthodoxy, Ca. 1520 to Ca. 1725: The Divine Essence and Attributes*, 2nd ed. (Grand Rapids, MI: Baker, 2002), 413. See also Thomas Aquinas, *Summa Theologiae: Latin Text, English Translation, Introduction, Notes, Appendices and Glossary*, ed. Thomas Gilby (London and New York: Eyre & Spottiswoode and McGraw-Hill, 1964), 1.14.14.

His argument, contra Plantinga (and Aquinas), is that God knows by way of inference. Says Mavrodes:

> The proposal to be explored is that God knows everything that He knows *by inference*. More explicitly the thesis at hand is
>
>> (T) For every proposition that God knows, He knows that proposition by inferring it from one or more other propositions that He knows.
>
> This thesis really is intended here to apply to *everything* that God knows—including, for example, his knowledge of his own essence, his will, and so on.[4]

So, which is it? Does God know everything by inference, or do we say that we do not know how he knows, but that truth follows necessarily from God's own beliefs?

Both discussions seem significantly wide of the mark (though Mavrodes's discussion is "wider" than Plantinga's) given what we can infer from a knowledge of God's own character. That is, instead of starting from the "bottom up" by attempting to flesh out how God can fit into what is created, more (and more biblically accurate) analysis could take place if our inferences began with what we know about God and his character from his revelation.

To use one example, Turretin understands God's knowledge to be consistent with the character of One who is perfect and complete in himself:

> Concerning the intellect of God and the disquisition of his knowledge, two things above all others must be attended to: the mode and object. The mode consists in his knowing all things perfectly, undividedly, distinctly and immutably. It is thus distinguished from human and angelic knowledge: perfectly because he knows all things by himself or by his essence. . . . (2) Undividedly, because he knows all things intuitively and noetically, not discur-

---

4. George I. Mavrodes, "How Does God Know the Things He Knows?" in *Divine and Human Action: Essays in the Metaphysics of Theism*, ed. Thomas V. Morris (Ithaca, NY: Cornell University Press, 1988), 345–46. Mavrodes says explicitly what Plantinga's position may imply—that God's knowledge is propositional.

sively and dianoetically (by ratiocination and by inferring one thing from another). . . . (3) Distinctly, not that by a diverse conception he collects diverse predicates of things, but because he most distinctively sees through all things at one glance so that nothing, even the most minute, can escape him. (4) Immutably, because with him there is no shadow of change, and as he himself remaining immovable gives motion to all, so he sees the various turns and changes of things by an immutable cognition.[5]

More needs to be said, and more will be. The point to be made here is simply that our understanding of God must come, first, from who he is as revealed, not first from what creation is like. In that way, we are able to maintain the central metaphysical structure of the Creator/creation. But just what is a knowledge that is non-inferential, immutable, undivided? We have no experience of such a knowledge at all. We can describe it, but we cannot imagine what it would be like actually to have something like this.

Perhaps a less controversial example would help. God is present everywhere; he is omnipresent. There is no place where God is not. This is the case because, as infinite, God is not constrained by space in any way. But this presence of God, in the way we are thinking about it here, is a nonspatial presence. That is, it is a presence that does not depend on space for its actuality. Since it is *God's* presence, it does not depend on anything at all beyond himself. What *kind* of presence could this be? We have never experienced this kind of presence, nor could we since, when we are present, we are present as creatures with all of the limitations that entails.

We need, then, to begin to come to grips with God's wholly other-ness, and to do that in such a way that is true to the theology of the Reformation. Any other theological foundation will necessarily undermine the sovereignty and aseity of the triune God. So, how shall we think about this other-ness?

---

5. Francis Turretin, *Institutes of Elenctic Theology*, ed. James T. Dennison Jr., trans. George Musgrave Giger, 3 vols. (Phillipsburg, NJ: P&R, 1992–97), 1:207.

"I Am" Revealed

Although Aquinas's notion of God[6]—taken as it is in part from
Exodus 3:14—is incomplete, he does, it seems to me, approach
the central truth of the matter. A brief look at Exodus 3 will help
us see that.

It is instructive to note in Exodus 3 that God announces himself
to Moses in two different ways. In the first place, God announces to
Moses that he is the God of Abraham, Isaac, and Jacob (v. 6). This
ascription of God's character by God himself is no doubt intended
to highlight that God had entered into a covenant with Abraham, a
covenant in which he promised to redeem his people. That notion
of redemption is the Lord's primary concern in this chapter. He
comes to call Moses to the task of mediating the exodus of Israel
from Egypt. So, God initially tells Moses that he is the covenant
"LORD," the One who has initiated and entered into a relationship
with his people, including Moses himself, and therefore has determined to bring them out of their slavery in Egypt.

But, in the course of the dialogue between God and Moses,
Moses asks for God to identify himself, so that Moses might be
better able to defend his actions in mediating the exodus. God does
identify himself. Only this time, he does not repeat the ascription he
earlier gave himself as covenant "LORD," which he certainly could
have accurately done. Rather, he speaks to Moses in a phrase that
is as peculiar as it is illuminating. He tells Moses, first, who he is:
"I am that I am." He then tells Moses, that if the children of Israel
want to know by whom Moses has been sent, he should tell them,
"I AM has sent me to you" (v. 14).

There is no reason to read more, philosophically, into this
ascription *of* God, *by* God, than is warranted in Scripture. But
there is no reason to read less into it either. What is abundantly
clear from the text is that this ascription is meant to highlight
that God, while entering into a special covenant relationship with
his people, is and remains, nevertheless, *a se*. He and he alone is

---

6. That is, his notion of God as *ipsum esse subsistens*.

independent. He *is*, in a way that no one or nothing else *is*.[7] God alone is the "I AM."

This means that God is of a character and nature such that we creatures can never and will never be. We cannot know what it is like to be completely and exhaustively independent, self-contained, self-fulfilled, perfect, and complete. No matter what measure of independence we think we might have, we nonetheless depend on our parents for our birth, on food and air and space and gravity, and so on, in order to be who and what we are. God has no such dependence. *He is who he is*, and thus his existence is of a totally and radically different order than ours.

There is, then, a "distance" between God and his creation, including creatures made in his image. There is such a distance that, as his creatures, we cannot experience anything that is "on his level." The Westminster Confession of Faith (7.1) puts it succinctly:

> The distance between God and the creature is so great, that although reasonable creatures do owe obedience unto Him as their Creator, yet they could never have any fruition of Him as their blessedness and reward, but by some voluntary condescension on God's part.

There is in this scheme a vast—we could say, infinite—distance between God and his creatures. And we should notice that this distance is not owing to sin. The confession's concern here is not a *moral* distance, but rather, we could say, a *metaphysical* (or ontological) one.

This may sound initially like bad news for limited creatures like us. With this kind of distinction, we could despair of knowing anything at all about God, except what we could project with our own limited resources, albeit with little confidence. But God has spoken, and it is his speaking that provides the foundation and the

---

7. One of the clearest indications of this interpretation of God's ascription is the burning bush that Moses first encountered (Ex. 3:2–4). This was an important point for Moses, and later Israel, to grasp. They needed to know that their salvation, their exodus, was not dependent in any way on what they would do, or on what Pharaoh would do, but was sovereignly carried out by God himself. See below.

"fruition" (to use the language of the Westminster Confession) of our knowledge of him and of the world. God has told us what he is like; he has communicated to us through his works[8] and, pre-eminently and primarily, through his Word, working with the Holy Spirit.[9] So, basic also to the Christian tradition is that God has spoken definitively and infallibly.[10]

Because God has spoken, we can know who he is, something of what he does, even why he does what he does; and we can know that who he is, what he does, and why he does what he does is revealed to us to know *as* creatures, not as creators. In other words, it is not the case that since we have the truth of Scripture, what we know is identical[11] with what he knows. While it may be that when we believe the truth, "what we believe is one of [God's] thoughts,"[12] I should hasten to add that we believe God's thoughts, but *after him*. We believe them, if we do, as creatures, not as God. God's thoughts are his alone, and ours are ours, each partaking of the nature of the one whose thoughts they are.

8. See, for example, Ps. 19:1f. and Rom. 1:18ff.

9. See 1 Tim. 3:16–17; Rom. 8:16.

10. The question of infallibility is debated, but should not be debated within the context of the Bible as God's word. Given that it is *God's* word, it could be nothing but infallible.

11. We can define "identical" here as sharing at least one property, not necessarily all properties. So, if *a* and *b* share only one property, they are identical *at that property*, whatever other properties they might share. The point to be made here is that there is no sharing of any property between the knowledge God essentially has and that which we have as creatures. There is no sharing of *any* property of God's with anyone or anything else. Since God's properties are not universals in which he shares, but are uniquely identical to and with him, it is impossible that such properties would be shared in any way. It would seem that this point is the central one made historically and is behind distinctions with respect to God and our knowledge of him, distinctions such as God as *in se* and God as *quoad nos*. The distinction is identical to that made between archetypal and ectypal knowledge. It seems to me, however, that such language can obscure rather than clarify the eikonic nature of all language, including language of God's revelation. In that regard, given the reality of God's covenantal condescension, rather than asserting, for example, that we can know *that* God is eternal, and so forth, but not *what* God is, it is clearer and more helpful to affirm that we can know the *that* and the *what* of God only to the extent that he reveals such things, and all only eikonically (or ectypically). For an example of this kind of distinction (*in se* and *quoad nos*) in Calvin, see Paul Helm, *John Calvin's Ideas* (Oxford: Oxford University Press, 2004), esp. 11–34.

12. Plantinga, "Divine Knowledge," 62.

Let us say, for example, that I see a rose bush. I now know that rose. But I know it as a creature knows it—I myself being one of God's creations. I know its color, say, yellow; its approximate height, say, three feet; and so forth. In that sense, I now have that rose bush "in mind."[13]

Does God have the same rose in mind? Of course he does. God's knowledge of that rose, however, is in no way dependent on its existence as created; it is a knowledge that is eternal, infinite, independent, perfect, and so on. God knows the exact height of the rose, its exact color, and how the height, color, and so forth relate to every other rose, to the rest of the world, to the whole universe, and to him.[14]

Our knowledge of the rose is completely dependent on its created existence, its location (and ours), its time (and ours), and similar factors. There can be no identity between the rose as it exists in the mind of God and the rose as it exists in my mind (though the rose itself is the same rose, and yet it always existed in God's mind).[15] So there is the Creator's knowledge and there is ours. Is there a way to understand this duality?[16]

13. Granted there are knotty problems here with respect to the subject-object relationship. We pass over those in the interest of the current discussion.

14. There is, we should mention here, a difference between the rose as it is eternally and infinitely in the mind of God, and the rose as it exists by virtue of God's creating activity. In that way, the "thing" known is radically different, depending on its context. But since the rose in the mind of God is the foundation upon which the rose in creation exists, God's knowledge of the rose takes on an eternal and infinite dimension that our knowledge never could.

15. That is, though that rose has always existed in the mind of God, it was also created, and thus, since God is omniscient, he knows that same created rose that we know. The objective thing thus provides for the consonance in knowledge between God and us. The objective thing itself is, fundamentally, a revelation of and from God.

16. This may be the best place to mention a classic distinction in Reformed orthodoxy that, itself, was designed to help us understand the relationship of God's knowledge to ours. Junius, according to van Asselt, in his archetypal/ectypal distinction, also made a distinction between ectypal theology that exists *in the mind of God* and archetypal theology. Ectypal theology *in the mind of God*, call it EG, is that theology that is internal to God's own mind, but is the *source* of the external ectypal theology given to us. EG is delineated *theologia simpliciter dicta* in its internal instantiation, and it becomes *theologia secundum quid*, that is, relational theology, in its external (to God's mind) instantiation. We can expand the notion of theology here to include, not only archetypal theology, but all of God's knowledge of things external, including the eternal decree, such that God's ectypal theology becomes the foundation for ours, all the while remaining fully

It seems to me that this is a good place to introduce new terminology into our discussion. There is no reason to introduce new terminology just to be new; that would smack of postmodern vacuity. The reason for introducing new vocabulary at this point is that much of the standard terminology used in these discussions is already filled with so much theoretical baggage that it can sometimes be obtuse, fuliginous, and murky, lending more darkness than light. Of course, new vocabulary can be risky as well, in that its newness guarantees an unfamiliarity that necessitates more explanation. The latter risks, however, outweigh the former problems.

One way to think about our metaphysical and epistemological situation is in terms (supplied by biblical data) of what *is*, in distinction from an image of what is.[17] God's existence, knowledge, character, and so forth simply *are*. That is—to go no further than the etymological sense of the word—all that God is, he is as the only genuine, essential, fundamental One. In the classical construction, God is the archetype.[18] He alone is original. He is the "I AM." God, and God alone, is *Eimi*.[19]

We, however, are completely and exhaustively God's image; we (and we could add here, though with qualifications, *everything else except God*) are "eikonic."[20] That is, all that we are, think, do, and become is derivative, coming from or out of something else; we depend on, as well as mirror, the real, the Original, the *Eimi*. In

and completely *God's*, and thus partaking of the fullness of his deity. See Willem J. van Asselt, "The Fundamental Meaning of Theology: Archetypal and Ectypal Theology in Seventeenth-Century Reformed Thought," *Westminster Theological Journal* 64, no. 2 (Fall 2002): 329.

17. Here we use the word *is* in the sense in which God himself used it with Moses. What *is* in this sense is (just to use some of the dictionary synonyms) genuine, fundamental, essential, complete. As the only one who *is*, God exists whether or not anyone believes he exists. Furthermore, in the way that we're using the term, what *is* is original and completely independent; God exists in and for himself. In that sense, the personal God is the only thing that *is*; everything else is an image of the real.

18. Note again, for an excellent discussion of the archetypal/ectypal distinction in theology, van Asselt, "The Fundamental Meaning of Theology." The Greek word ἀρχή carries connotations of all these.

19. This is the transliteration of the Septuagint version (ἐγώ εἰμι) of the Hebrew אֶהְיֶה.

20. Taken from the Greek word for image, transliterated as *eikon*.

classical terminology, we are "ectypal."[21] The *kind* or *type* of people we are, knowledge we have, thoughts we think, things we do, is always and everywhere a copy, pattern, impression, image, taking its metaphysical and epistemological cue from the only One who truly *is*, that is, from God himself.

A person is, in the deepest sense of the word, an image, an *eikon*, made according to the "pattern" of the Original, the triune God. This means that whatever we are, think, and do, we are, think, and do *as image*. We will never become, at any time and in any way, original.

It may be helpful to illustrate this by way of a photograph. Just what is that image in the photograph? It is a picture, looking much like the original, but without the context, the dimensions, the "substance" of the original. No matter how accurately a photograph reflects the original, it will never be, nor should it ever be confused with, that original itself. It has, embedded within it *as image*, necessary and essential limitations. The photograph would be nothing, literally, except for the original that it copies. It is entirely dependent for its meaning and interpretation on that from which it came.

So it is with people. No matter how closely we might resemble God, the Original, we will always lack his context, his "dimensions," his "substance." As a matter of fact, as image, a photograph will lack all that the substance has. It is no different for us. All thinking, being, doing, and so forth by us is always and everywhere on a creaturely level and is therefore eikonic. We would be literally nothing without God, the Original, and all that we are depends on him each and every second. The meaning of what we are can only be understood in the light of who he is—in the light of the Original.

Not only so, but the world, though not created in God's image in the way that people are, is itself an *eikon*. It declares God's glory; it displays his attributes. In that way the universe, too, shows forth the characteristics of God. It "images" God in that it is created after

21. The language of archetype/ectype may be best and is certainly the one with good historical precedent, but it too can seem like a kind of *analogia typi* in a way that could mis-communicate. For that reason, we'll steer clear of such terminology here though, properly understood, it is quite sufficient as well.

the original pattern that always exists in the mind of God, and in that it reveals, as creation, something of its Creator.

This puts a different light on the way in which we think about the world and about ourselves and our activities. Instead of thinking about the subject of the nature of ultimate reality as the "study of being *qua* being," as Aristotle and Aquinas would have it, we think of metaphysics and epistemology (not to mention all of life itself) in the context of the relationship of things created to the Creator.

We must begin, then, with this basic and fundamental distinction—the *Eimi/eikon* distinction—the distinction of the "I AM" and his image.[22] If we begin in that way, then all of our discussion about "reality," "individuality," "externality," "objectivity," "knowledge," "truth," and the like has that distinction as its context and as its defining character.[23]

So, to review, while it is true that the Christian's responsibility is to think God's thoughts after him, the actual thoughts of God cannot be thought by us. God's thoughts are always thoughts of the One who is *Eimi*. As such they are eternal, infinite, exhaustive thoughts, archetypal, original with him, always and only true, exhaustively and eternally independent, not gleaned over time, and so on.

The thoughts that we think, even when in conformity with God's, are still at root eikonic. They are patterned after his thoughts; they are formulated in the context of his image; they depend on and necessarily relate to him as the Original, but they are never

22. This language best suits our discussion of essences. I am avoiding the language of Creator and creature here simply because, as we will see, being Creator is not of the essence of who God is and thus could serve to confuse our discussion of God's essence. Though it is certainly true that we are essentially creatures, every other created thing is too. Only human beings, however, are essentially *image*. So, the language is designed to highlight the *essential* distinction between God and us.

23. What is meant by "begin" with this distinction is, in part, described by Alvin Plantinga: "My point is that the Christian philosopher has a right (I should say a duty) to work at his own projects—projects set by the beliefs of the Christian community of which he is a part. The Christian philosophical community must work out the answers to its questions; and both the questions and the appropriate ways of working out their answers may presuppose beliefs rejected at most of the leading centers of philosophy. But the Christian is proceeding quite properly in starting from these beliefs, even if they are so rejected. He is under no obligation to confine his research projects to those pursued at those centers, or to pursue his own projects on the basis of the assumptions that prevail there." Alvin Plantinga, "Advice to Christian Philosophers," *Faith and Philosophy* 1, no. 3 (1984): 263.

identical to his thoughts, nor could they be. That would necessitate "eimic" thoughts, of which creatures, by definition, as "eikons," are incapable. So, we think God's thought, but *after him.*

This, then, is the *Eimi/eikon* relationship. It is the relationship of the "I AM" to the "image." That relationship will have a surfeit of implications, which we will discuss. Before doing so, however, we should note something that this *Eimi/eikon* relationship entails.

God's Translation

Whenever we work with a foreign language, we quickly become aware that the relationship of that language to our own can be confusing. Not only must one be able to translate the actual words of the other language, but those words must make sense within their context, and the translation must provide fluency to that context. In order to translate the statement,

καὶ ὁ λόγος ἦν πρὸς τὸν θεόν
(*kai ho logos ēn pros ton theon*—John 1:1),

it would be most helpful to know what comes before the καὶ, and what comes after θεόν. Of course, the verse itself could be translated without knowing the before and after, but the coherence of the translation would suffer to the degree that knowledge of the context were avoided or unknown. These matters need not detain us here. There are certain things that are true of all translations that can help us understand something of this *Eimi/eikon* distinction.

First of all, though different language is used (typically) in the process of translation, and though the person reading a translation may not know the original, the state of affairs expressed by a good translation will be the same as that expressed by the original language. For example, taking our quotation of John 1:1 above, it can be translated as,

and the word was with God.

This translation, to be accurate, would need to express the same reality the original does. The words in Greek need to mean the same things as do the words translated into English. Thus, while the words are different, the reality to which they refer is not. This is an important part of translation theory and relates directly to any translation's accuracy.

So whenever translation takes place, the translator engages in the process of taking something that is original in its form and context, and "carrying it across" to another form and context *without losing the original meaning and context*. To the extent that a translation is able to do this, it is a successful translation, providing accuracy, equivalence, and fluency.

Much more could be said with regard to translation, but the point to appreciate here is that we may view God's creative activity as a kind of divine translation.[24] Granted, God's translation is *sui generis*; it nevertheless has some of the typical characteristics of a translation. We can note a few.

We should recognize that, when God created, what was created resided first in the triune God's mind (Heb. 11:3; Rev. 4:11). What God made, therefore, came from the original, that is, his thoughts. He did not create those very thoughts, but what he thought he then spoke into existence, and from that speaking what he thought was created. That creation, however, was a kind of translation of God's thoughts. It could not be identical with his thoughts (in part, because, as the doctrine of simplicity requires, his thoughts just are his being). Rather, creation was his taking the original as it resided in his mind and "carrying it across" *as* and *into* the created realm. Creation, then, is God's translation of that which was in his mind from eternity.[25]

---

24. Cornelius Van Til, because of his insistence on the ontological distinction between the Creator and the creature, pressed this kind of ingenious and illustrative language. He often referred to creation as God's *interpretation*. By that he meant, I take it, that what God spoke into existence was that which was always in his mind, and what was produced by that speaking was his interpretation of the same.

25. Turretin notes that all things created were first ideas pre-existent in God's mind and, therefore, were "nothing else than the very divine essence itself." He goes on to argue that, "in man, the things themselves are the exemplar and our knowledge is the image; but in God the divine knowledge is the exemplar and the things themselves the image or its expressed likeness." Turretin, *Institutes*, 1:312. For a contrary view, see James F. Ross, "God, Creator of Kinds and Possibilities: Requiescant Universalia Ante Res," in *Rationality, Religious Belief, and Moral Commitment*, ed. Robert Audi, William J. Wainwright (Ithaca, NY: Cornell University Press, 1986).

It is a translation (from God's thought to creation), not simply of things and essences, but of *being* as well. This is an important point, in part, because it separates our understanding from (at least some of) the discussion of metaphysics in the medieval period.

According to W. Norris Clarke, the medievals objected to the notion that, in creating, God would have created more being. If such were the case, then God's infinity would not reach to his being, since "more being" would *be* at the point of creation. "As the medievals put it, God + creatures = *plura entia, sed non plus entis.*"[26]

The problem with this medieval metaphysical notion, however, is that the starting point of the discussions, which (as for Aristotle) was "being *qua* being," requires a univocal conception and use of the word *being.* Such a conception does not allow for a fundamental (ontological) difference between God and his creation. Norris thinks that the medieval principle of participation answers the problem in that it provides for more "*sharers* in being" without affirming any kind of "*qualitative intensity* of the perfection of being itself."[27]

But this confuses the issue. We should be able to affirm *both* that God's being is infinite *and* that, by virtue of creation, there is "more being." We can affirm that, however, only if we begin our discussion, not with a univocal notion of being, but with the *Eimi/ eikon* distinction. Beginning with that distinction, we can affirm that God's existence is infinite, independent, immutable, and so on. His being is *Eimi.*

At the same time, we can affirm that God's creative activity results in being that is fundamentally and essentially eikonic; it is dependent, finite, mutable, and so forth. Does this mean that there is "more" being? In one sense it does, just as it means that there are more people, more things, more relationships. The "more," however, is the "more" of a different kind; it is "more" within a class that is in no way identical to—and certainly not equal to—God's existence, person, inter-Trinitarian relationships, and so forth. Nothing, there-

---

26. That is, more beings, but not more being. W. Norris Clarke, "Charles Hartshorne's Philosophy of God: A Thomistic Critique," in *Charles Hartshorne's Concept of God: Philosophical and Theological Responses*, ed. Santiago Sia (Boston: Kluwer Academic, 1990), 108.

27. Ibid.

fore, not even being, is "added to" God in any essential way (though, as we will see, something *is* added to God in a covenantal way).[28]

This provides for both continuity and discontinuity with respect to the relationship of our knowledge to God's knowledge, as well as the overall relationship of *Eimi/eikon*. There is continuity in that God's translation can be counted on to be wholly accurate, true to the original, referring to the same thing, and meaningful. That which God thought from eternity "comes across" at a point in time—"in the beginning"—such that it becomes something that it was not prior to "the beginning." What it becomes is not identical with the original; that would be impossible. The thoughts of God could not be, by definition, created. But it becomes a proper and true translation, or interpretation, of that which has always been, that which God has eternally thought.

But there is discontinuity as well. No matter how accurate the translation, the original does not and could not become the translated. Just to use our example above, no matter how similar the Greek word λόγος (*logos*) is to the English word *logic*, the two can never be identified such that one could in every case be substituted for the other.[29] They cannot be interchangeable because, among other reasons, the two words necessarily function and reside in different contexts, relating to different words, which themselves have different contexts and syntax.

So it is with God's translation, his creation. No matter how accurately it represents God's thoughts (and it does represent them accu-

---

28. Thomas at points falls prey to a univocal notion of being and thus denies that anything contingent or accidental can pertain to God: "For being cannot participate in anything that is not of its essence, although that which is can participate in something. The reason is that nothing is more formal or more simple than being, which thus participates in nothing. *But the divine substance is being itself*, and therefore has nothing that is not of its substance. Hence, no accident can reside in it." Thomas Aquinas, *Summa Contra Gentiles*, trans. Anton C. Pegis (Notre Dame, IN: Notre Dame University Press, 1957), 1:121–22. We would agree with Thomas that no accident can reside *in* God, but would also argue that, given creation as another *kind* of being, God can "have" properties that obtain in creation, without in any way changing who he essentially is. As we will see, our supreme example of such is in the person of Christ.

29. To use another example, the English translation of Heb. 3:1 uses the same word, "apostle," in the accusative that it would use were it in the nominative case, whereas in the Greek text the word ἀπόστολον must be used since it is in the accusative.

rately), the fact is that it *re-presents* those thoughts; it re-presents them *as created*, which in their original form they were not. There is nothing in creation that can ever be identified with those thoughts, since God's thoughts necessarily function in a different context (an infinite, eternal, holy, incomprehensible context), a context that has different constituent "parts," a different "syntax."

There is an impermeable (for us), ontological boundary, therefore, between God and creation. It is a boundary that is impossible to transgress. It would be just as impossible for God essentially to become a created being as it would for creation to become in any way identical to God. The boundary is creation.[30]

How, then, are we to know God and to think any thoughts at all *after him*? If the boundary is as radical as all that, what does that mean for our knowledge of God and of his character (not to mention creation itself)?

Creation and Revelation

As God creates, he establishes the boundary between creation and himself, *and* (this is the point so often missed) he crosses that boundary (just what this means for our understanding of God we'll look at later). He establishes that boundary by creating something that essentially is not, and could not be, what he essentially is. He crosses that boundary by communicating *into* creation. He communicates into creation in his word, in his works, and supremely in himself.[31] This communication is God's revelation both *to* and *in* his creation.

Creation, then, is inextricably linked with God's revelation. It *is* revelation in that God "speaks" through what he has made. As we saw above, God's attributes have been revealed and seen through the things that were made "since the creation of the world" (Rom 1:20). Not only so, but since the creation of the world, God has spoken. In speaking, he has revealed something of who he is, as well as his will for his creation.

---

30. This is, in part, what is behind the philosophy of the South African philosopher, Hendrik Stoker, in his *Die Wysbegeerte van die Skeppingsidee*.

31. In himself, that is, as the Word of God becomes flesh (John 1:14). More on that below.

Given the dual metaphysical construct of *Eimi/eikon*, the "I AM"/ image, therefore, we should begin to see that, just as the very being of creation was given by and is dependent upon God the Creator, so is our knowledge of God and of creation dependent upon him. This dependence requires not just an acknowledgment so that we can tip our philosophical hat to God and then go our merry way in pursuit of the truth (which is what much of theistic philosophy appears to do). It invites us, instead, to see the entire knowledge situation as dependent, first of all, on what God has said and done.

The implications of this for philosophy and other disciplines are legion. One of the primary implications is that philosophy's boundaries and parameters should be set by the truth of God's revelation *first of all*, and thus should be dependent on the theological conclusions gleaned from that revelation. In this way, philosophy should be dependent on theology.

This may sound strange, particularly to philosophic ears. It may sound as though theologians are trying to usurp the domain of philosophy. Consider, however, that philosophy has, almost without argument, trespassed on the grounds of theological territory, and often without so much as a hint of impropriety. Just to use one example, in a recent book *Time and Eternity*, the author states:

> The present book is written for Christians who want to grapple seriously with the concept of God's eternity. Unlike some other writers on the attributes of God, I am convinced that the best tool we have for really understanding what is meant by the affirmation that God is eternal is not poetry or piety, but analytic philosophy.
>
> Some readers of my study of divine omniscience . . . . expressed surprise at my remark that someone desiring to learn more about God's attribute of omniscience would be better advised to read the works of Christian philosophers than of Christian theologians. Not only was that remark true, but the same holds for divine eternity. In the Middle Ages students were not allowed to study theology until they had mastered all the other disciplines at the university, but unfortunately today's theologians generally have next to no training in philosophy and science and so are ill-equipped to

186

address in a substantive way the complex issues raised by God's eternity.[32]

This is an interesting statement indeed. Not only does it read like a certain philosophical hegemony, but it assumes a host of tenets that are questionable at best. Let's look at a few.

Why should we agree with the author that the "best tool we have" for understanding God's eternity is analytic philosophy? Does that mean, as it surely seems to, that the best tool we have for understanding *God* is analytic philosophy? If so, that would be quite a shock to the thousands upon thousands of theologians who, because untimely born, never had access to the pearls of wisdom offered by this twentieth-century philosophical oyster. Not only so, but, if true, this means that God's own revelation of himself is, at best, secondary and, at worst, relatively useless in our pursuit to discover what God is like; analytic philosophy can accomplish that without any need of what God himself has told us about his character.

Protestant scholasticism had a phrase for this approach—*usus rationis magisterialis*. In their use of this phrase they did not deny that philosophy could help theology in its task, nor did they imply that philosophy had nothing to say to theology that was useful. They only wanted to deny philosophy the right to set theology's limits and to define theology's truth. When those things happen, there is an illegitimate, magisterial use of reason that in effect denies the importance and necessity of God's revelation for understanding who he is.

As to the point concerning medieval students: while it may be true (generally) that students in the Middle Ages were not allowed to study theology until they had a university education, the history of theology in that era does not necessarily display a more truthful or accurate way of doing theology, which is one of the reasons some in the late Middle Ages were convinced of the need for a reformation of theology. A study of philosophy prior to theology, at least in the Middle Ages, provided inadequate protection against heterodoxy.

32. William Lane Craig, *Time and Eternity: Exploring God's Relationship to Time* (Wheaton, IL: Crossway, 2001), 11. My review of this book is found in K. Scott Oliphint, "Review of God and Time," *Westminster Theological Journal* 63, no. 2 (Fall 2001): 439–45.

This one example can be multiplied. The number of philosophers at present who want to pronounce on and argue for theological truths is vast and increasing. That, on the one hand, is quite encouraging. The fact that now more than in the recent past philosophers *can* work with and promote theological tenets within their own discipline is a new and hopeful development. The fact that theology is not given its due, on the other hand, is most disappointing and ought to be rectified if real progress is to be made in—to use one example—a philosophy of religion that moves beyond bare theism to the truth of who the triune God is and what his world is like.

The proposal I am describing is that we see theology, perhaps not as the queen of the sciences, but, better, as the *scientia prima inter pares*.[33] We should see theology in this way for at least two reasons.

First, it is the task of theology to deal with the most fundamental problems and issues of the universe. Theology's task is to help us understand who God is, how he relates to us and to the world, what pleases him, who we are, and so on. *Those* questions, contra many modern-day philosophers, need to be answered within the context *first of all* of what God has said. They are not questions that can be answered simply by an appeal to our own thoughts and ideas. God's revelation must control the discussion of those issues.

Second, and perhaps more importantly, it is from, through, and to God *alone* that all things are (Rom 11:36). Since that is the case, just how a particular "thing" is from, through, and to God is an important set of facts about that thing, facts to be understood, *first of all*, theologically. That is, a thing is to be understood within the context of God and his relationship to it. That, again, turns us *first of all* to God's own revelation to see what, if anything, he has said about himself and his relationship to his creation. These two areas—who God is and how he relates to his creation—are two areas in which philosophy of religion, perhaps unwittingly, persistently errs.

---

33. For a discussion of theology's relationship to philosophy in this regard, see Hendrik G. Stoker, "Reconnoitering the Theory of Knowledge of Professor Dr. Cornelius Van Til," in *Jerusalem and Athens: Critical Discussions on the Theology and Apologetics of Cornelius Van Til*, ed. E. R. Geehan (Nutley, NJ: Presbyterian and Reformed, 1971), esp. 92ff. I am aware that calling theology a science is in itself controversial. I am arguing here for its *place* with respect to philosophy, rather than its definition as a discipline.

One thing is for sure. God has said *something* about *everything*. He has told us that all things are created and that all things are sustained by him. He has told us that all things are to be done to his glory and that all things work according to the counsel of his own will. These notions have sweeping ramifications for any *thing* that we pursue, and so the revelation of God about that thing and his relationship to it is crucial for our understanding. Theology's task is, at least, to help us understand the revelation of God. Given that objective, philosophy's task is set.

It simply is not the case, therefore, that analytic philosophy holds the key to unlocking the attributes of God or his relationship to us or to his world. Theology has been given that key. Thus, the *Eimi/eikon* relationship must be understood, *first of all*, theologically so that it can be applied and implemented philosophically (and in other areas) when the need arises.

This would lead us to something like a *usus revelationis magisterialis*—a magisterial use of revelation. That is, it would affirm that God's revelation to his creatures is both central and necessary in our understanding of some of the problems that have plagued philosophy, and humanity.

There is no doubt that in our use of revelation we must also use our reasoning faculty. It is likely true as well that philosophy can be most helpful in helping us clarify and explain the truths that are gleaned from God's revelation. It is *revelation*, however, as *God's* revelation, that must be used, consulted, pursued, mastered, and heard if we are to begin to address the problems (both intellectual and otherwise) that confront us.[34]

If revelation becomes our guide in these matters, we should understand at the outset that there will be many things, perhaps *most* of the "big" things, in which we will have to be content, in the end, with mystery. This, too, might grate on the nerves of many theologians and philosophers of religion. Once there is an assumption (either implicit or explicit) of a certain kind of rationality, it

---

34. Theology has historically contended for an organic use of philosophy, in which philosophy helps theology in analysis and the like. That help, however, was seen as *ministerial*, not magisterial, as we have seen, and thus gave due weight to theology's place in the process.

becomes difficult to admit that some things simply cannot be comprehended by virtue of what (or Who) they are. Contrast this aversion to mystery with the great Dutch theologian Herman Bavinck, in his monumental study about God. The first sentence of that work begins, "Mystery is the lifeblood of dogmatics."[35] Perhaps instead of restricting mystery just to dogmatics, we should also say that mystery is the vital element of all of life. If all things are from, through, and to God, then all things are from, through, and to the One who is ultimately mysterious, utterly incomprehensible (to us, not to himself). Because of that, all things, too, will contain a vital element of mystery. Theology (that is true to God's revelation) helps us to acknowledge that. Some theologies and philosophies of religion may have a more difficult time with it.

Given that everything about which we speak is first of all *God's*—for from him and through him and to him are all things—it behooves us to recognize that the relationship of those things to him is of utmost importance. Also, to the extent that we have knowledge of those things which are his, to that extent has he given us that knowledge, either immediately or mediately, so he is the One who controls, maintains, and preserves it. He should, therefore, be the One who is central to all of it. This, I think, is at least in part what Calvin meant in opening his *Institutes* with the necessity of knowledge of God for self-knowledge. We begin with knowledge of God, and that comes *first of all* by God's own revelation.

---

35. Herman Bavinck, *Reformed Dogmatics: God and Creation*, ed. John Bolt, trans. John Vriend (Grand Rapids, MI: Baker, 2004), 29. See also, Herman Bavinck, *Gereformeerde Dogmatiek* (Kampen: J. H. Kok, 1967), 1: "Het mysterie is het levenselement der dogmatiek."

10

It Is What It Is

The essence of God is Deity itself or the divine nature, one in number but three in the community of persons: known to us both by names or by distinct properties. —JOHANN H. HOTTINGER

Now that we have the basic metaphysical structure in place—the *Eimi/eikon* relationship—and now that we have seen something (in the previous chapters) of the epistemological methodology that should be our guide in these matters, the need of the hour is to see just how this structure and this methodology can serve to transform some of the methodological procedures in the philosophy of religion, procedures that seek to ascertain who God is and how we are to think about him.

Philosophy of religion, in the main, because of its anti-revelational bias with respect to matters philosophical, seems to be significantly wide of the mark when it comes to its understanding of who God is and of how he relates to his creation. Virtually any article or book on the topic will conclude with some god who is (at best) far inferior to the triune God of Christian theism. The best one can hope for in current discussions concerning the character of God in philosophy of religion is a conclusion that will steer us toward a kind of super-man rather than the triune God.[1] How should we begin to address this predicament?

The "Essential" Problem

Perhaps the best way to begin is to highlight the problems that seem to persist in these discussions. The basic problem can be summarized (though certainly oversimplified) in three methodological steps: (1) take any of the essential attributes of God; (2) argue that God, because of the nature of creation, cannot have this attribute; and (3) conclude that we must give up believing that God has this attribute.[2]

Given this methodology, where should our analysis begin? It might be best to begin by asking whether, in fact, there *are* any essential attributes in God. An answer to that question can go in any number of directions. We might begin by working through biblical passages exegetically to see if revelation tells us of any characteristics of God's that are intrinsic to who he is; we might look at the history of theology to see if there are convincing arguments that point us in a certain direction; or we might look at the discussions

1. This is true, as well, of much current-day discussion of the character of God in some theological circles. See, for example, Gregory A. Boyd, *God of the Possible: A Biblical Introduction to the Open View of God* (Grand Rapids, MI: Baker, 2000); Clark H. Pinnock, et al., *The Openness of God: A Biblical Challenge to the Traditional Understanding of God* (Downers Grove, IL: InterVarsity, 1994), and *Most Moved Mover: A Theology of God's Openness* (Grand Rapids, MI: Baker, 2001).

2. Any book on the philosophy of religion will prove the point. See, for example, Michael L. Peterson, ed., *Philosophy of Religion: Selected Readings* (New York; Oxford: Oxford University Press, 1996); Louis P. Pojman, ed., *Philosophy of Religion: An Anthology* (Belmont, CA: Wadsworth, 1987); or Robert Audi and William J. Wainwright, eds., *Rationality, Religious Belief, and Moral Commitment: New Essays in the Philosophy of Religion* (Ithaca, NY: Cornell University Press, 1986). There are, of course, a (relatively) few arguments that do not fall prey to this methodology, arguments calculated to show how any of God's essential attributes *can* be philosophically defended, but since our focus here is on some of the methodological weaknesses of philosophical theology, we will confine our discussion to certain delineations of those problems.

in philosophy to see if any of them provide a way for us to answer the question. Without prejudice to any of the approaches mentioned (or any not mentioned), it might help us to think initially about the notion of "essence" itself. Just what is an essence, and how do we know if there is such a thing?

An essence can be construed as a property, or set of properties, that something[3] has necessarily. That is, without a given essence, a given thing would not be, or would not be what it is. As simple as this may sound, it gives rise to a complex set of philosophical (and perhaps, by extension, theological) issues that are perhaps not readily apparent.

For example, in his highly complex and erudite work, *Logic and Theism*, J. Howard Sobel questions whether there can be such things as essences. While not dismissing philosophical discussions that make use of essences, Sobel suspects that essentialism (the doctrine that some things have properties essentially and others contingently) founders for lack of grounding. In a discussion of God's omnipotence, Sobel notes:

> While, as can be observed, some people are really blind, if any are essentially blind, that they are would need to be told by means [of] special powers of observation. I want to say that no one is essentially blind. I want to say that no one *could* be essentially blind. Similarly, I find, for my intuitions concerning the essentially sighted, honest, and, to move to our subject, omnipotent. "I understand in theoretical terms these characters, but . . ." The problem is with what would be "the grounds" for such essential attributes, their "real grounds" in the natures of their possessors.[4]

Sobel's suggestion is sobering for some. He cannot affirm essentialism, because he cannot see a reason why some things are deemed essential and others not. There seem to him to be no "grounds" on which to posit necessity or contingency. By "grounds" Sobel

---

3. I am using the notion of "something" here in the broadest sense so that it includes anything that exists.

4. Jordan Howard Sobel, *Logic and Theism: Arguments for and against Beliefs in God* (Cambridge: Cambridge University Press, 2004), 351.

seems to mean something like criteria or constraints or conditions under which a thing must be a certain way or necessarily possesses certain properties. If there are such criteria, constraints, or conditions, then what are our modal intuitions about *them*? And would those criteria, constraints, or conditions be even more *essential* than the essential properties themselves?[5] And how would we go about discerning what *they* are? On what basis, to use his example, could we say that someone is essentially omnipotent?

These are perplexing questions, questions that need to be addressed within a Christian-theistic context. In order to address them, let's begin with the *real* problem that Sobel, by his own admission, is addressing: the problem of whether or not God has essential properties.

In order to clear the field for our discussion of God's essential attributes, we should first look at the philosophical context in which questions of this kind are often discussed. One of the more current approaches to the question of essence—called by some, "essentialism"[6]—is by way of a discussion of possible worlds.[7] One of the reasons for this approach is that it provides a context in which to discuss basic ideas of possibility and necessity.[8]

---

5. Or perhaps they are simply essences of essences. See Alvin Plantinga, *The Nature of Necessity*, Clarendon Library of Logic and Philosophy (Oxford: Clarendon Press, 1974), 77.

6. Essentialism is discussed by Saul Kripke, *Naming and Necessity* (Cambridge, MA: Harvard University Press, 1982), and by Plantinga, *The Nature of Necessity*. See also Christopher Hughes, *Kripke: Names, Necessity and Identity* (Oxford: Clarendon Press, 2004), and James E. Tomberlin and Peter van Inwagen, eds., *Alvin Plantinga* (Dordrecht: D. Reidel, 1985), esp. 73–76. While essentialism fell into disrepute in philosophy a number of decades ago, only to be revived again by Kripke, Plantinga, and others, some version of it has always been stock and trade for orthodox theology, since the distinction between God and the world entails a distinction between that which is essential and necessary and that which is not. We will use the word *essentialism* as shorthand for *Christian-theistic essentialism*, given that such a notion presupposes the ontological Trinity.

7. While there are debates as to the nature of possible worlds themselves—some wanting to define them in terms of propositions, others in terms of "ways things might have been," still others in terms of "maximal states of affairs"—we will follow the description of possible worlds as maximal states of affairs.

8. Problems persist for a Christian in discussions of possible worlds, but we should note that the basic idea is not hostile to Christianity. Because we believe that creation was an act of God's free decision, we understand (1) that it was possible that God not create

For example, what is of the essence of a thing is just what that thing has by necessity. But what does it mean for something to inhere in something else "necessarily"? And if something, *x*, has some property, *np*, necessarily and another *cp*, contingently, then *x* could remain *x* without *cp*, though *cp* could nevertheless be a part of what *x* is? The notion of possible worlds is designed to help philosophers work through possibility (and impossibility) and necessity (and contingency), and therefore, in part, to help us see just what properties a thing *must* have and what properties it merely *might* have. It would seem, then, that the discussion of possible worlds is one way to engage in a discussion of essences.

How, then, does one use possible-worlds semantics to discuss the notion of essence? Given our definition of essence—a property, or set of properties, that something has necessarily—we can readily see that entailed in the concept is a notion, or a *mode*, of necessity. Part of the design of possible-worlds semantics is to help us see just what we mean when we ascribe modalities, like necessity (and contingency), to things.

In "possible-worlds speak," something has a property necessarily if it has that property in every world in which it exists. That is, if *W* equals "a possible world," then we could define essence as

E_{df} = For any thing *x* and any possible world, *W*, in which *x* exists and any property *P*, *x* has *P* in *W*.[9]

Since, therefore, *x* has *P* in any possible world in which it exists, *P* is essential to it; it does not exist in any world at all unless its existence includes the property *P* (this entails, of course, that it is impossible that *x* exist without *P*). Contrast this with properties that are not essential to a thing—contingent properties. In such cases, we could define these properties as

---

and (2) that it was possible that God create a different world than the one he did create. Thus, there *are* possible states of affairs that differ from the actual ones. Qualifiers will be given to this discussion below.

9. Assumed in this discussion, without argument, is a notion of the actual such that only those things that exist have properties. See, for example, Alvin Plantinga, "Actualism and Possible Worlds," *Theoria* 42 (1976): 139–60.

C_{df} = For any thing x and any possible world, W, in which x exists and any property P, x has P in W and x does not have P in W_1.

There are some worlds, W, in which x has P and some worlds, W_1, in which x does not have P.[10] This means that P is a contingent property of x.

The trick in all of this discussion, as Sobel notes above, is in attempting to postulate the "grounds" on which one might suppose P to be essential or not. On one level, this is not difficult. If we were to ask the question of whether or not "being a professor of apologetics" (BPA) is essential to me—whether BPA is of the essence of me or is accidental to me—we could simply postulate a maximal state of affairs, that is, a possible world, and ask if BPA must obtain for me in that world.[11]

It seems obvious enough, given the configuration of events that conspired to my being a professor of apologetics, that it need not obtain; it is not a necessary or essential property of mine. I could have existed in another possible world and "not BPA" obtain in that world. Other events than the ones that actually happened might just as well have happened in another world. To think that BPA *must* obtain for me would be to think that there is no possible world in which I exist and in which I am not BPA; I would then have BPA

10. This account of contingent or accidental properties depends for its cogency on the S5 system of modal logic. The details of the various systems are beyond the bounds of our discussion here. Suffice it to say at this point that, to the extent that modal logic and possible-worlds semantics are useful, S5, including (and advancing) as it does its lesser cousins, S4 and T, seems to make the most sense. For a helpful summary of the differences in these systems, see Jay Wesley Richards, *The Untamed God: A Philosophical Exploration of Divine Perfection, Simplicity and Immutability* (Downers Grove, IL: Intervarsity, 2003), 53–54, n. 14.

11. Plantinga defines a maximal state of affairs in the following way: "A state of affairs S is *complete* or *maximal* if for every state of affairs S', S includes S' or S precludes S'." Plantinga, *The Nature of Necessity*, 45. That is, a maximal state of affairs is not one in which everything that *could* obtain *does* obtain, but rather it is one in which, for example, if you are the first child in your family in the actual world, it is impossible that you not exist in the actual world, or that someone else be the first child in your family in the actual world. A maximal state of affairs, in other words, is a consistent and complete set of circumstances at a given possible world.

essentially.[12] But that would mean that, in any possible world in which I exist, essential to me would be BPA. In order to affirm *that*, we would have to argue that the choices I have made, and make, were, and are, together with their consequences, all essential to me and thus necessary as well; we would have to say that in any world in which I exist BPA must obtain.

But that seems to be false, intuitively and otherwise.[13] There are numerous choices that I have made that I could have refrained from making, and others I could have made but didn't. So, there is nothing about me that is incompatible with there being a possible world in which I am a rancher in Texas, and another possible world in which I am an auto mechanic, and so on. Even more radically, there are plenty of possible worlds in which I never existed at all, in which case it would be difficult to be a professor of apologetics. So, neither my existence nor my present occupation is a necessary property; neither obtains in every possible world.

If we think of possible worlds as "a way things might have been," then we can begin to see how we might postulate some properties as essential to a thing, and some as not essential. Those which are essential obtain in every possible world in which the thing exists, and those not essential obtain in at least one, but not all, possible worlds in which the thing exists.

From here, however, things become fuzzy. Given that I do not have to exist, what properties are essential to me if I do exist? To put it another way, if my existence is contingent, how can we begin to determine what is essential or necessary for something that is fundamentally contingent?

---

12. BPA *is* essential to me in the actual world, but then BPA is an essential *world-indexed* property, which is not to say an essential property of mine, given E above. However, the reason for Sobel's hesitation to affirm essentialism looms in the background here. Just what is it that makes our modal intuitions true or false? One possible candidate is that it is the actual world. See James F. Ross, "God, Creator of Kinds and Possibilities: Requiescant Universalia Ante Res," in *Rationality, Religious Belief, and Moral Commitment*, ed. Robert Audi, William J. Wainwright (Ithaca, NY: Cornell University Press, 1986).

13. We will deal with what kind of contingency this is later. Here the burden of proof might be shifted to the objector. Just what argument could be given that would conclude for the necessity of every consequent? How could one go about proving that the proposition "If I exist, necessarily BPA will obtain for me" is true?

Fortunately, we need not deal with that here. Given our interest in the character of God, we can move directly to a discussion of that without settling the question of contingent existence, individual essences, and so forth.[14]

The Essence of God

It should be said at the outset that, contrary to much confused language in some of the literature about whether or not one can know God's essence, orthodox theology has consistently held that God's essence can indeed be known as it is revealed to us, but cannot be known per se, that is, as it is in God himself. Hence, Muller:

> As Turretin indicates, the way in which God is what he is in the simplicity of the divine essence cannot be known by the human mind, granting that the human mind knows things only by composition and composite attribution—nonetheless, we are given to know the divine attributes or essential properties by revelation and rational reflection on revelation in such a way that God's nature is truly known by means of the revealed attributes.[15]

Two historical points bolster our discussions here. First, the history of Christian thought is replete with discussions of the essential attributes, or the essence, of the triune God. Second, as Muller notes, though some might want to see Calvin's approach as decidedly anti-essentialist, Calvin "belongs as much to the theological tradition, with its interest in the divine essence and in its understanding

---

14. Aristotelian essentialism, the forerunner in all of this discussion, held that there were no such things as individual essences. Leibniz, and others after him, held that each thing actually has an individual essence, or *haecceity*, that consists of all the properties associated with that thing. See Michael J. Loux, "Essentialism," in *The Cambridge Dictionary of Philosophy*, ed. Robert Audi (Cambridge: Cambridge University Press, 1995), 241–43.

15. Richard A. Muller, *Post-Reformation Reformed Dogmatics: The Rise and Development of Reformed Orthodoxy, Ca. 1520 to Ca. 1725: The Divine Essence and Attributes*, 2nd ed. (Grand Rapids, MI: Baker, 2002), 195–96. For a discussion and defense of "essence language" among the Protestant orthodox, see ibid., 227–28. Note especially, "Thus, in answer to the question of 'What' or 'Who' God is, the orthodox set themselves first to describe the 'nature' or 'essence' of God" (ibid., 232).

of Scripture as containing references to the divine being, as any of the later Reformed writers."[16] What Calvin rightly opposed was not essentialist language, but abstract speculation with respect to the character of God.

When considering the essence of God, it would be difficult to overstate the significance of God's self-identifying name in Exodus 3:14: "I AM." As we noted earlier, it would be possible to pour philosophical content into the implications of the name that may stretch its real meaning. That should certainly be avoided. The simple point to see, however, is that such a name, given the context of its declaration and the interpretation given it by God himself, requires us to attribute to God absolute independence, sovereignty, and power. We should note two points in this regard.[17]

First, the interpretation of the name itself is given by God. The miracle of the *un*burning bush was meant, not simply to show Moses something extraordinary, but rather to give Moses a visible illustration of just what it was that God was saying to Moses about his own character. The fire, often (as here) illustrating the presence of God in Scripture,[18] is a fire that is both *with* the bush, without in any way *needing* the bush in order to burn. So, the Lord comes to Moses and announces that he is the God of Abraham, Isaac, and Jacob; he is a God who is *with* his people. But he also announces his name to Moses. He is with them *as the* "*I AM,*" as the One who is in no need of them or of anything else he has made.[19] The interpretation of that announcement, of the "I AM," is visibly represented to Moses (and now to us in God's revelation) by God in the miracle of the fire.[20]

16. Ibid., 250.
17. We will expand on this section of Ex. 3 in the next chapter when we look at the notion of God's condescension.
18. See, for example, Gen. 15:17; Ex. 13:21; Num. 14:14; Deut. 4:24; 2 Chron. 7:1; Neh. 9:12, 19; Ps. 105:39; Isa. 4:5; Matt. 3:11; Heb. 12:29; Rev. 1:14; 2:18; 19:12.
19. It is significant that Paul makes this point to the philosophers at Athens in Acts 17:25. Paul is drawing, in this address, not on his audience's knowledge of the Old Testament, but rather on their God-given understanding (Rom. 1:18ff.) of what kind of God the triune God must be.
20. This is, in redemptive history, a common way for God to communicate to his people. Many of Christ's miracles were meant to point people to the greater reality of his

The second point to be made is that this revelation of God's name to Moses takes on such significance that it is used over five thousand times in Scripture. The announcement in Exodus 3 was clearly meant to resonate throughout the whole of Scripture.[21]

It is the *Eimi* (I am) aspect of God's name that is our focus when we begin to discuss the essence of God. As we have noted, possible-worlds semantics might (at least minimally) help us discuss that essence.[22]

Whether or not Anselm's ontological argument is sound, *the* crucial premise to that argument is that God is that than which no greater can be conceived. Whenever discussions of the existence or nature of God take place, entailed in those discussions is the concept of God as one who is as great as one could be.

But just what does it mean to be "great"? With respect to God it typically means, at least, that there is no lack, no privation, no want of anything at all. It means he is a perfect being. The notion of "perfect" in "perfect being" is not altogether perspicuous. In the way that I use it here, it refers to the lack of lack; God as perfect means, in the first place, that he is in need of nothing and is there-

---

person and work. For a fuller biblical exposition of this principle, see K. Scott Oliphint, "Most Moved Mediator," *Themelios* 30, no. 1 (Autumn 2004): 39–51.

21. As Calvin notes, "Contrary to grammatical usage, [God] used the same verb in the first person as a substantive, annexing it to a verb in the third person; *that our minds may be filled with admiration as often as his incomprehensible essence is mentioned.*" Commentary on Exodus 3:14, quoted in Muller, *The Divine Essence and Attributes*, 250, my emphasis. As we will see, this means that we are to think of God both as the "I AM" (*Eimi*) and as the one who has condescended to save a people for himself.

22. I should say here that I am not convinced that the language of possible worlds is the most helpful as a context in which to discuss God's existence and character. Given that any possible world is simply a maximal state of affairs, it could perhaps be (carefully) affirmed that God's existence is such a state of affairs. That is, without getting into a discussion of the differences in *de dicto* and *de re* modalities, the state of affairs "God necessarily exists" obtains, so the proposition "God exists" is true. It seems rather odd, grammatically at least, to refer to the necessary existence of the triune God as a possible world. While the concept behind such locutions might be agreeable to the biblical view of God, it seems better, and clearer, to affirm that he is the presupposition behind any and every notion of possibility and necessity. His existence, then, is not so much a possible world as it is that which allows for the existence, and any true predication, of any world whatsoever. We should note, therefore, that our use of this philosophical tool is for precision more than clarity. More qualifiers are still needed and will be mentioned below.

fore complete. To lack something would mean that there would be something missing, something needed, in order for one to be more, or more complete. God is one who does not lack anything.

Some have questioned the perspicuity of "perfect" as an ascription for God. William Hasker, for example, notes:

> The difficulties with perfect being theology do not, in my view, stem from the assumption that God is an absolutely perfect being—that he is "whatever it is better to be than not to be." Rather, difficulties have arisen because people have been too ready to assume that they can determine, easily and with little effort, what perfection is in the case of God—that is, what attributes a perfect being must possess. Yet it clearly is no simple matter to say what is the best kind of life for a human being or what are the ideal attributes (or virtues) for a human being to possess. So why should we assume that this is simple in the case of God? I do not think it should be taken as obvious, without long and thoughtful consideration, that it is "better" for God to be temporal *or* timeless, mutable *or* immutable, passible *or* impassible.[23]

Hasker is correct here, perhaps, that it is not a simple matter to determine exactly what "perfect" means with respect to God. But, given that God has spoken and has told us who he is, given that his name, "I AM," is replete through Scripture as a designation of his "incomprehensible essence" (as Calvin says), then we can say with some certainty that anything that is entailed by God's aseity is included in the notion of perfection, when we think of God as the perfect being.

It is certain, therefore, that God cannot lack with respect to existence. He exists necessarily. There can be no potentiality to his essential existence, since, if there were, he would lack some measure of existence, or would be in need of more existence, more "to be," in order to be perfect.

Within the domain of possible worlds, the argument for the necessity of God's existence entails the fact that God exists in every possible world. If there were a possible world, *per impossibile*, in

23. Pinnock, et al., *The Openness of God*, 132.

which there were no God, then God's existence would be merely possible, and he could not be One without lack or privation, since his existence would be reduced to a contingency. That is, there would be a possible world in which God did not exist. If that were true, then his existence would be dependent on a certain possible world obtaining, in which case he would be dependent on something independent of his own existence, that is, possible worlds.

In this vein, it is instructive to note that perfect-being theology, though going back as far as Augustine, was developed in more detail later by Anselm. Anselm's ontological argument has embedded within it a notion of God as the maximally perfect being. In fact, the appeal of (at least Plantinga's version of) the ontological argument is that, *given* the possibility of God's existence (and *that* is, of course, the controversial point), assuming God to be the most perfect being, his existence is, thereby, necessary.

In other words,

(1) God's existence is possibly exemplified,

means that there is a possible world in which God exists. But since God's existence includes no lack, it cannot be the case that he could exist in one world and not in another. To exist in that way would be to lack existence in at least one possible world, which would mean that his existence is *dependent* on a given possible world, or on the notion of possibility itself (an absurd notion, given that no possible world is either possible or actualized without him). So, the possible exemplification of God's existence entails its necessary exemplification, such that there is no possible world, nor can there be, in which God does not exist.[24]

24. Plantinga's (simplified version of the) ontological argument includes the following four propositions (my numbering):

[1] There is a possible world in which unsurpassable greatness is exemplified.

[2] The proposition *a thing has unsurpassable greatness if and only if it has maximal excellence in every possible world* is necessarily true.

[3] The proposition *whatever has maximal excellence is omnipotent, omniscient, and morally perfect* is necessarily true.

[4] *Possesses unsurpassable greatness* is instantiated in every world. (Plantinga, *The Nature of Necessity*, 216).

Entailed in the notion of God's necessary existence is God's essence. Assuming for the moment that existence is a property, p, the proposition,

(1) God has p in every world,

extends not only to his existence but (remembering E_{df} above) to anything else that God has (or *is*) essentially.[25]

How then do we construe God's essential attributes, given (1) and E_{df}? One way, though admittedly not the only (or even, perhaps, best) way, would be to take those attributes which are necessarily exemplified in every possible world—attributes, we could say, that are related strictly to God (quite apart from anything else), attributes that are entailed by his character as *Eimi*—and affirm them to be of the essence of who he is. In other words, given that God is essentially *a se*, we could begin to posit attributes or properties that are entailed by his essential independence, which would themselves, therefore, also be exemplified at every possible world.

For example, is God essentially infinite? If we affirm that God is a perfect being who lacks nothing, if we affirm his character as *a se*, then it cannot be the case that he is in any way limited by anything outside of himself, since to be limited would, by definition, be a lack; it would be a constraint placed on God by something else, be it space or time or human choices or some other factor. We can affirm, then, that God is essentially infinite. Entailed in his independence and his perfection is infinity itself.

As we have said, the crucial and controversial premise is (1). It is that premise that serves to diminish the argument *as an argument for God's existence*. In our context, however, given that (1) is true, the argument is both valid and sound. For an analysis and critique of Plantinga's ontological argument, see James F. Sennett, *Modality, Probability, and Rationality: A Critical Examination of Alvin Plantinga's Philosophy* (New York: Peter Lang, 1992), 17–48.

25. We should note here that to say that God *has* a property is not to undermine the biblical doctrine of simplicity. It is merely to say *what kind of* God we are talking about, without pronouncing, at this point, on the relationship of his properties or of him to his properties. The doctrine of simplicity, together with an essentialist understanding of God's properties, would affirm that whatever properties or attributes are essential to God are, themselves, identical to him. They are not parts or properties in some way added to or divisible from him.

On the other hand, is the property "Creator" of the essence of God? One way to answer that question is to ask if there is a possible world in which God is not the Creator.[26] Or, to put it another way, is it possible that God not create anything? The orthodox answer to this question is, of course, yes. To answer no would mean that God *had to* create the world, in which case there is no possible world in which God is not the Creator, and, therefore, the creation of the world would itself be a necessary property of God's.[27] But then God would have a necessary property that (1) was not entailed by his independence (since the necessity of God's creative activity would entail a dependence on something besides God) and (2) implied some kind of lack in God (since the necessity of something *ad extra* would mean that God was in need of it in order to be who he essentially is). So "being Creator" is not an essential property that God has.

It would seem, then, that God has essential properties and others that are not essential to him. How should we delineate between these two? What is it that helps us to see God's essential properties as essential, and what is it that helps us to see God's other properties as nonessential? According to E_{df}, essential properties are essential in that they are exemplified at every possible world. Not only so, but that which is exemplified at every possible world (and thus necessary) is anything that is entailed by the fact that he is the "I AM." That is, God's properties are properties that God has that in no way depend on anything but himself in order to obtain at every world. Since God has these properties in every possible world, they are essential properties; they are necessary attributes of his. It is not possible, then, that God not have these properties (i.e., there is no possible world in which God does not have these properties).

But so far we have simply delineated the *mode* of God's properties—they are essential, necessary properties that always obtain.

26. We may be tempted to say that there is no possible world in which God is not Creator, since for any possible world to exist at all, God has to create it. However, this is to think of a world as something actualized, rather than as a maximal state of affairs.

27. The Reformed scholastic notion of hypothetical necessity, as pertaining to creation, is not denied here, because contained in that notion is the possibility of no creation at all.

Just what properties *are* they that are essential and necessary? This is the burden of Hasker's question above with respect to perfect-being theology.

From what we have seen thus far, given that we can affirm that God is *Eimi*, the "I AM," perfect and perfectly independent (for how could God be God if he were dependent on something else?), God's essential attributes will certainly include any properties that are entailed by his aseity. It is the divine name of God, then, that gives us a way into his essential attributes,[28] and any attribute that would be entailed by God's absolute essential independence would necessarily be included in God's essential attributes.

Among the most basic of essential attributes historically attributed to God is, as we saw in chapter 5, the simplicity of God. It is easier to see why this is essential to God than it is to explain just how it can be. It is essential to God because if God were essentially composed of something other than himself, then he would be essentially dependent on that thing, or things, in order to be who he essentially is. So, he would not be "I AM" in that case, but would rather be one whose existence consisted of (at least in part) something or some things outside of himself. The burden of the notion of simplicity as an essential attribute of God is to affirm what "I AM" is meant to affirm; it is to reiterate the independent character of God.

The central concern in delineating and developing just what properties of God are essential to him is to attribute properties to him that will make clear his perfect and complete autonomy, that is, a total lack of need of anything outside himself. If we use Plantinga's description of God as one in whom unsurpassable greatness is exemplified, then he cannot be dependent on something else in order to be who he is. If he were, then there would be a possible world in which there were one who both exists at every world and

---

28. This, we should note, is nothing new: "The divine names present a biblical point of entry into the rather abstruse and necessarily metaphysical discussion of the essence and attributes—indeed, as far as the Protestant orthodox were concerned, the names of God, the biblical identifiers of who and what God is, provided the natural point of contact between the biblical language of God and a more strictly philosophical discussion." Muller, *The Divine Essence and Attributes*, 248.

is not dependent on anything in order to be who he is. In that case, there would be a possible world in which one is greater than the one in whom unsurpassable greatness is exemplified, which is impossible.

So how do we think about all of those properties of God that are essential to him, are indeed distinct, but that also reside in (as?) him? Just how do these properties or attributes relate to the personal God himself? As we have seen chapter 5, one way to think about such a relationship is to opt for the rejection of the simplicity of God, and to affirm that God is made up of things that are external to him, things perhaps even eternal that reside alongside him. In this case, as we saw with Plantinga, a rejection of simplicity brings with it a rejection of God's aseity and sovereignty. It is a rejection of his aseity because he is *dependent* on properties *ad extra* in order to be God, and it is a rejection of sovereignty because necessity is defined in such a way that no one, not even God, may have *control* over those things in which necessity obtains. To have control over those things would mean that they could be essentially different than they are, thus not necessary at all. While this rejection of simplicity is wildly popular in current philosophical literature, this option has not been seriously entertained in orthodox Reformed thought.[29]

So, in keeping with Reformed thought, how *do* we think of God's properties relative to his being? Perhaps the best we can do is to affirm that all of these essential properties, while being identical to each other, are, nevertheless, in some way *modally* distinct. That is, their distinctions lie in their mode of existence within the Godhead. Somewhat analogous to our understanding of the Trinity, we can affirm *both* that there are distinctions within the Godhead *and* that there is only one essence, who is God. As in our understanding of the Trinity, therefore, we do not posit that what we have in God's properties are essentially different "things"; what we do posit is that what we have is a distinction with no essential difference. God is,

29. Note that "all of the Reformed orthodox assume the simplicity of the divine essence, and all understand the attributes as in some sense distinct." Ibid., 296. Contra Plantinga, the notion of divine simplicity had nothing to do with Parmenides and everything to do with God's own revelation of himself.

as triune, both one (essence) and three (persons). So also we affirm that he is essentially *both* one (essence) *and* many (properties), without in any way allowing for essential composition in God or for a real essential difference in him.

Exactly what the essential properties of God are depends on how they are characterized. We are suggesting (because it seems Scripture suggests this) that if we characterize them by way of entailment with aseity, then we would include, at least, simplicity, immutability, immensity (which includes infinity and eternity), and perfection as essential to God, all of which pertain to his personal faculties of knowledge and will and affection. But they would pertain to him as he is in himself, essentially. And they would pertain to each of the three persons, all of whom are both essential with respect to God and are themselves the one God.[30]

It is these (and other) essential attributes of God which have become a stumbling block to some philosophers of religion, and to some in certain theological contexts. The stone of stumbling, however, is not a result of God's inability to lift it from the path, but rather the result of a structure and methodology that, if not removed, is bound to trip up even the ablest of minds.

In coming chapters, we will seek to analyze and ferret out that structure and some of the implications it entails. We will also seek to provide a biblical corrective to it.

Conclusion

The triune God of Scripture is "I AM." He is the one who alone is essentially independent; he does not need anything. He is not composed of any parts that are external to his essential being, and he is not essentially constrained by anything outside of himself.

To the extent that we can begin to grasp the implications of what this means, the problems that seem to plague philosophers of religion will begin to dissipate. Once we see God as having essential

---

30. As Muller notes, distinctions were often made among the Reformed with respect to the essential properties, on the one hand, and the personal properties that accrue to each of the three persons of the Godhead. The personal distinctions were just that, *personal*, and not essential. See ibid., 215ff.

properties, however, we see as well that there are properties that God has taken on, properties that are not essential to his character, but that nevertheless remain as a true description of who he is. How might we begin to think about this distinction of properties in such a way that we can be true to God's own revelation of himself and thereby develop a biblical philosophy and, more specifically, a biblical philosophy of religion?

11

Reality as Covenantal

God cannot be known otherwise than in Christ. . . . Hence all that think that they know anything of God apart from Christ, contrive to themselves an idol in the place of God; as also, on the other hand, that man is ignorant of Christ, who is not led by him to the Father, and who does not in him embrace God wholly. —JOHN CALVIN

T he problem is creation. No matter how many or what kind of arguments are given to show the incommensurability, if not the outright contradiction, between God's essential existence and other aspects of that existence, or other aspects of creation, the tension inherent in every one of these arguments is located in the attempt to come to grips with the relationship of God to creation.[1]

---

1. It should be noted here that, contrary to much discussion about God these days, to locate the problem in creation is to presuppose that it is the existence of creation, not of God, for which an account must be given. Contrast this, for example, with the analysis set forth in Philip Clayton, *The Problem of God in Modern Thought* (Grand Rapids, MI: Eerdmans, 2000).

The Creation Relation

We saw the tension developing as far back as Plato. Just how Plato's forms actually related to the particulars "down here" in the sensible world was never clearly articulated. Aristotle's "thought thinking itself" had to remain completely aloof from everything else in order to be in some way absolute. Thomas's being seems to be either divorced from the world or in some ways identical to it.[2]

There is a problem, a tension, that inevitably develops between what is thought to be ultimate and supreme, and everything else. This is especially true as philosophers of religion (and some theologians) seek to work out a relationship between God and the world; tension always ensues.[3] Whenever there is an intellectual tension of which God is one part, however, the problem is not with God; the problem is with creation.

Theodore Drange marks out two primary categories of atheological arguments (arguments for the nonexistence of God). The first category consists of "incompatible-properties arguments." These arguments seek to show that there are properties that God is assumed to have that cannot reside in the same person. The second category consists of "God-vs.-world arguments," in which it is argued that there is a serious incompatibility between the supposition of God's existence and the nature of the world

2. Though this has not been argued, the argument would look something like this: Thomas holds being to be a transcendental notion. It pertains to all that is. Metaphysics is thus the study of being *qua* being. How, then, does the being of God relate to the being of everything else? Since being is the category that encompasses them both, either God is the highest being on a scale of being, or he is divorced from the being of everything else. There is, therefore, either a univocal predication of being, with diversity explained by way of essence, or an equivocal predication, in which the being of God is in no way like the being of everything else. Thomas's notion of analogy, as we saw in chapter 2, does not succeed in overcoming this problem.

3. Besides Drange's article (see below), there are numerous articles that attempt to work out this relationship. See, for example, Anthony John Patrick Kenny, "Omniscience, Eternity, and Time," in *The Impossibility of God*, ed. Michael Martin (Amherst, NY: Prometheus, 2003), 210–19; Norman Kretzmann, "Omniscience and Immutability," in *The Impossibility of God*, ed. Michael Martin (Amherst, NY: Prometheus, 2003), 198–209. For a refutation of these kinds of arguments, see K. Scott Oliphint, "Something Much Too Plain to Say," *Westminster Theological Journal* 68, no. 2 (Fall 2006): forthcoming.

such that we are compelled to conclude for the nonexistence of God.[4]

While Drange's categories might point to different nuances in certain atheological arguments, category one—incompatible-properties arguments—is really just a subset of category-two arguments—God-vs.-world arguments.

For example, the first incompatible-properties argument that Drange gives is "The Perfection-vs.-Creation Argument," which proceeds as follows:

1. If God exists, then he is perfect.
2. If God exists, then he is the creator of the universe.
3. A perfect being can have no needs or wants.
4. If any being created the universe, then he must have had some need or want.
5. Therefore, it is impossible for a perfect being to be the creator of the universe (from 3 and 4).
6. Hence, it is impossible for God to exist (from 1, 2, and 5).[5]

Whatever the merits of this argument (and there seem to be none), it is strange for Drange to set this out as an "incompatible-properties" argument, when clearly the problem here is God's creating activity. It is because God's creating comes into the equation that Drange sees conflict in God. No less strange for Drange is that he seems unaware of some of the most basic elements of Christian theology with respect to the attributes of God. So, for example, he notes, "If the creation were accidental, then that in itself would imply that God is imperfect (since perfect beings do not have accidents), and that would be another basis for the Perfection-vs.-Creation Argument."[6]

We will respond to these arguments below. For now, the point to be kept in mind is that, as we have said, the problem is creation.

4. Theodore M. Drange, "Incompatible-Properties Arguments: A Survey," in *The Impossibility of God*, ed. Michael Martin (Amherst, NY: Prometheus, 2003), 185.
5. Ibid., 186.
6. Ibid., 187.

More specifically, once God determines to bring into existence something that is contingent, finite, and of a different metaphysical order than himself, the relationship of that existence to his own becomes a problem. It is in response to that problem that we have sought to understand the essence of God (as has been done historically) in the context of an essentialism that implies a distinction between essential and nonessential properties. Given such a distinction, the question as to just how these two might relate becomes all the more pressing. We will seek to work out elements of that relationship, first, by way of contrast; that is, we will look first at arguments that attempt in some way to confuse, merge, or otherwise conflate the two, and then we will attempt to set forth some positive principles that help define that relationship.

The Eternity of God

Historically, God's eternity has been seen as an aspect, or corollary, of his infinity. Since God's essence is not limited by anything external to himself, it follows that his essence is not limited by time. This is a basic truth in theology; God is essentially eternal.

Recent discussions about God's eternity, however, seem to confuse and equivocate with respect to just what eternity *is*. In some discussions, eternity seems to be equated with a *context* or *environment* in which God operates as God. Eternity is seen primarily in terms of God's relationship to time.

Though this sheds light on a biblical understanding of eternity, it is not the way a discussion of eternity should begin. The way to think about eternity is to articulate what it is first in relation to God and then in relation to time. First, eternity is an essential property of God, quite apart from time. Eternity is God's unlimited essential duration.[7] It is the affirmation that God, unlike time, has always

7. That is, because eternity is a corollary of infinity, it is an affirmation of God's aseity, denying the possibility in God of any essential change or succession. Thus, "resident in the scholastic concept of eternity . . . there is a distinction parallel to that between immensity and omnipresence—namely, between eternity utterly apart from time because prior to the creation of time, eternity strictly so-called; and eternity in relation to the temporal sequence, eternity understood as everlasting duration." Richard A. Muller, *Post-*

been; he never began to exist, nor was his existence (eternally) caused, nor will it end, but it simply *is*, without past, present, or future (just as infinity simply *is* without spatial categories). Eternity, therefore, references something of the *duration* of God's "is-ness." It points us to the fact that God's necessary existence has always been, and has always been without temporal categories.[8]

Given this truth concerning God's essence, eternity also tells us something of the relationship of God to his creation.[9] Unlike many current discussions of theism in philosophy, an understanding of God's eternity, with its roots in exegetical theology,[10] has historically been discussed in the context of his immediate and direct relationship to temporal succession. Most current-day philosophical discussions, however, seem to ignore the vast majority of historical discussions, and thus present God's relationship to time as a new problematic. One example should suffice.

Reformation Reformed Dogmatics: The Rise and Development of Reformed Orthodoxy, Ca. 1520 to Ca. 1725: The Divine Essence and Attributes, 2nd ed. (Grand Rapids, MI: Baker, 2002), 356–57. Note also, for example, "Following a different approach than either Turretin or Brakel, Pictet derives eternity from the divine necessity or self-existence, inasmuch as 'what necessarily exists, is incapable of not existing, and therefore can have neither beginning or ending.'" Ibid., 346–47.

8. Though words suggesting time must be used to describe God's eternity, such does not imply that eternity (thus also God) is time conditioned any more than use of propositions to describe what God knows implies that God's knowledge is propositional. The burden of Reformed theology has been to emphasize that there is no essential change in God, yet there is duration. For example, ". . . the Leiden Synopsis: 'eternity is the attribute of the duration of the essence of infinite God,' and Turretin, 'eternity is the essence of God as lacking *terminus* in duration.' Ridgely similarly notes that 'we firmly believe that God exists *throughout* all the changes of time, and yet that his duration is not measured thereby.'" Muller, *The Divine Essence and Attributes*, 357. A distinction has been made historically between successive and non-successive duration, with God's eternity including the latter.

9. So much so that eternity has been thought to be a relative, rather than an absolute, characteristic of God's.

10. William Craig, in the same text in which he avers that theologians should yield to the expertise of philosophers with respect to understanding God's essential character, notes that "the doctrines of divine simplicity and immutability . . . find no support in Scripture." William Lane Craig, *Time and Eternity: Exploring God's Relationship to Time* (Wheaton, IL: Crossway, 2001), 31. Muller, on the other hand, notes extensive exegetical support in the history of orthodox theology for the doctrines of simplicity, immutability, eternity, and so forth. See Muller, *The Divine Essence and Attributes*, 254–364.

If God is eternal, according to Stephen Davis, then the following sentences are either meaningless or necessarily false:

God existed before Moses.
God's power will soon triumph over evil.
Last week God wrought a miracle.
God will always be wiser than human beings.[11]

These statements are thought to be meaningless or necessarily false because, obviously, they postulate something time-conditioned of one presumed to be eternal.

But Davis's concerns run deeper than this. He is convinced that the traditional understanding of eternity, in which God is not subject to time, serves in the end to deny the existence of the Christian God. The following argument illustrates his point:

(1) God creates x.
(2) x first exists at T.
(3) Therefore, God creates x at T.[12]

Now (3) is ambiguous, notes Davis, between (3a) and (3b):

(3a) God, at T, creates x.
(3b) God creates x, and x first exists at T.

The defender of divine eternity will opt for (3b) as the proper understanding of (3).[13]

Given this argument, says Davis, a timeless God cannot create anything at all. He cannot create because, he argues, we do not have a usable concept of atemporal causation that would allow for (1) and (2) to be meaningful. "Therefore, we are within our rights in concluding that [(1)] and [(2)] entail that God is temporal, i.e. that a timeless being cannot be the creator of the universe."[14]

---

11. Stephen T. Davis, "Temporal Eternity," in *Philosophy of Religion: An Anthology*, 4th ed., ed. Louis P. Pojman (Belmont, CA: Wadsworth, 2003), 211.
12. Ibid., 211, my numbering throughout.
13. Ibid., 213.
14. Ibid.

Furthermore, says Davis, the Christian God's existence must also be denied by the defender of divine eternity because of the ways in which Scripture speaks of God.

> He makes plans. He responds to what human beings do, e.g. their evil deeds or their acts of repentance. He seems to have temporal location and extension. The Bible does not hesitate to speak of God's years and days. . . . And God seems to act in temporal sequences—first he rescues the children of Israel from Egypt and later he gives them the Law.[15]

Davis is to be commended for his motive here. He seeks to do justice to the Christian view of God as he is presented to us in Scripture. He is not, like those who set forth atheological arguments, attempting to prove God's nonexistence.

The price he pays for this worthy motive, however, is too high. In order to try to safeguard the Christian God, Davis ends up denying him his rightful status as God.[16] In order to argue for God's essentially limited existence, he argues for a god that is contrary to the triune God of Christianity. The god of which Davis writes is a god who is constrained by the (limited and dependent) duration of the temporal world. He is able to act only within such constraints. Clearly, the notion of One who exemplifies maximal greatness is absent here. Clearly God as orthodox Christianity has historically conceived him is dead. We'll say more on that later.

There are any number of "incompatible-properties arguments" and "God-vs.-world arguments" that we could peruse in order to note the ways in which philosophers of religion attempt to work out the presumed tensions.[17] One more, however, should suffice in this regard.

15. Ibid.

16. As do many philosophers of religion who have found it necessary to give up on God's eternity. See also Nicholas Wolterstorff, "God Everlasting," in *God and the Good: Essays in Honor of Henry Stob*, ed. Henry Stob, Clifton Henry, and Lewis B. Smedes (Grand Rapids, MI: Eerdmans, 1975); Richard Swinburne, *The Coherence of Theism*, rev. ed. (Oxford: Clarendon Press; Oxford University Press, 1993).

17. See, just to take a few examples, the typically erudite discussion of omnipotence in Alfred J. Freddoso and Thomas P. Flint, "Maximal Power," in *The Existence and Nature*

God as Impassible

The Westminster Confession of Faith, 2.1, says:

There is but one only living and true God, who is infinite in being and perfection, a most pure spirit, invisible, without body, parts, or passions; immutable, immense, eternal, incomprehensible, almighty, most wise, most holy, most free, most absolute. . . .

Included in this standard, orthodox description of God is the fact that he is "without . . . passions." But how are we to understand this of One who is revealed to us in Scripture as essentially personal?[18]

Richard Creel provides as good an analysis as any of impassibility from a philosophical perspective. We will use his study as a typical example. After a brief survey of some representative discussions of impassibility, Creel lists the varying definitions surveyed:

1. "Lacking all emotions"
2. "In a state of mind that is imperturbable"
3. "Insusceptible to distraction from resolve"
4. "Having a will determined entirely by oneself"

---

of God, ed. Alfred J. Freddoso (Notre Dame, IN: Notre Dame University Press, 1983); and discussions of omnipotence and omniscience in Jordan Howard Sobel, *Logic and Theism: Arguments for and against Beliefs in God* (Cambridge: Cambridge University Press, 2004), 346–97; Louis P. Pojman, ed., *Philosophy of Religion: An Anthology* (Belmont, CA: Wadsworth, 1987), 231–56; William L. Rowe and William J. Wainwright, eds., *Philosophy of Religion: Selected Readings*, 3rd ed. (Fort Worth: Harcourt Brace College Publishers, 1973), 24–77. Two considerations argue against using these attributes as our examples here. First, with respect to omnipotence, the discussions seem either to discuss a view of omnipotence that is no part of the Christian tradition, or to be ambivalent as to whether such discussions apply to God. Second, with respect to omniscience, we will touch on the relationship of God's knowledge to libertarian freedom in the next chapter.

18. Impassibility should be seen as a subset of immutability. If God cannot change, then it follows that he cannot be altered in any essential way, thus he is impassible. In this sense, it is difficult to see if impassibility is an "incompatible-properties argument" or a "God-versus-world argument." Nothing in our discussion necessitates that we clear up this confusion, so we need not do that here. For an argument that impassibility does not entail immutability, see Brian Leftow, "Immutability," *The Stanford Encyclopedia of Philosophy*, ed. Edward N. Zalta (Fall 2002 edition), http://plato.stanford.edu.

5. "Cannot be affected by an outside force"
6. "Cannot be prevented from achieving one's purpose"
7. "Has no susceptibility to negative emotions"
8. "Cannot be affected by an outside force or changed by oneself"[19]

In his analysis of these eight definitions, Creel sees number five as summarizing the concern and the content of defenders of God's impassibility.

This seems to be right. Theological discussions of causality generally hold that the action and the patient[20] are mutually dependent. The common adage—*actio est in passo*—notes that a transeunt action (an action that has effects outside the agent, rather than merely internal to it) exists in the patient. The relation of causal dependence is signified by the term *action* or *acting*, on the one hand, and by the term *passion* or *being acted upon*, on the other.

A passion, in this context, is that which is causally dependent on an acting agent, and it affects the patient intrinsically. So, as the confession denotes God to be "without passions," what it affirms, again, is that however and whatever God essentially is and whatever he experiences, he is and experiences according to his own sovereign plan and not because he is caused to *re*-act to something external to himself that has moved his action.[21] We must conclude, in this context, therefore, that God is essentially without passions.

19. Richard E. Creel, *Divine Impassibility: An Essay in Philosophical Theology* (Cambridge: Cambridge University Press, 1986), 9, my numbering.

20. A "patient" here is one upon whom an action is given; to be a patient is to change internally as a result of an external action upon one.

21. Note Thomas Aquinas, for example: "There are two kinds of power, namely passive and active. The first is not at all in God, but the second is his supremely. Precisely as being actual and complete, each thing shows itself an active principle of something, and as being wanting and incomplete a passive principle. We have shown that God is sheer actuality (*quod Deus est purus actus*), simply and wholly complete, and not wanting for anything. Hence his it is above all to be a principle of activity and in no way to be a passive principle. To be an active principle directly spells active power. Active power is a principle of acting on another, *while passive power is a principle of being acted on by another*, as Aristotle explains." Thomas Aquinas, *Summa Theologiae: Latin Text, English Translation, Introduction, Notes, Appendices and Glossary*, ed. Thomas Gilby (London and New York: Eyre & Spottiswoode and McGraw-Hill, 1964), 1.25.1, my emphasis.

But does this conclusion do an injustice to the teaching of Scripture? What do we do, for example, with passages that clearly indicate God's own empathy toward his people? To use just one example:

> For he said, "Surely they are my people,
> > children who will not deal falsely."
> And he became their Savior.
> In all their affliction he was afflicted,
> > and the angel of his presence saved them;
> in his love and in his pity he redeemed them;
> > he lifted them up and carried them all the days of old.
> > (Isa. 63:8–9)

What does it mean that God was afflicted in Israel's suffering? How can a God without passions be afflicted? Adding fuel to the fire of this discussion is the fact that this kind of question does not simply sit casually on the surface of intellectual curiosity; it can, and rightly *should*, be an intensely personal question.

Nicholas Wolterstorff, for example, who argues against the notion of impassibility, does so at least in part in order to think through God's own relationship to him in the loss of Wolterstorff's son. How does an impassible God "relate to" such a death? Is there any comfort in God, when such tragedies strike, if God remains aloof and removed from the intensity of our pain? If God cannot empathize with our most excruciating experiences, how can he comfort us, or can we be comforted? The debate over impassibility is meant to address some of these questions.

In order to work out a solution to these questions, Creel is (at least initially) on the right track when he discusses the notion of God's impassibility in the context of (four aspects of) God's character.

> Specifically, an incorporeal personal being could conceivably be impassible with regard to his *nature*, his *will*, his *knowledge*, or his *feelings*. To say that God is impassible with respect to his nature would be to say that his nature cannot be affected by an outside force. To say that God is impassible with respect to his will would

218

be to say that his will cannot be affected by an outside force. To say that God is impassible with respect to his feelings would be to say that God's feelings, or the quality of his inner life, cannot be affected by an outside force. To say that God is impassible with respect to his knowledge would be to say that what he knows cannot be affected by an outside force.[22]

When divided in just that way, it becomes fairly uncontroversial to affirm that God's *nature* is impassible. As Creel notes, whatever is of the essence of a thing is, by definition, not able to be changed; such change accrues only to accidental characteristics.[23]

From here, however, things move in a less fortunate direction. Having affirmed God's impassibility with respect to his nature, Creel maintains that God is impassible in his will as well. His will is based on what he can know, and he can know only all possibilities. That is, God's will is impassible because, like his knowledge, it is indexed only to contingencies (and not to actual events). Because Creel accepts a libertarian view of freedom (as do the vast majority of philosophers who declare on such matters), God does not have the capacity *independently* to know concrete occurrences with respect to his human creatures. He can only know these occurrences once an action has been freely decided.[24] God cannot know, for example, according to Creel, whether or not Katie will wash her car at time "T":

> God, then, has given free creatures the capacity and responsibility to participate with him in creating this world, and not even God knows in advance which possible world we will bring into actuality. Consequently, God must be passible in relation to change in the world in which Katie washes her car at T or not. To be sure, God does know eternally the parameters within which our choices will take place, and the consequences that will flow from

22. Creel, *Divine Impassibility*, 11.
23. Ibid., 13–14.
24. There are differences among libertarians as to when or how God might know a particular occurrence. The point to be made here is that libertarianism entails ignorance in God until and unless a choice is made by a free creature, whether that choice be known prior to creation, as in Molinism, or at a created moment.

our various possible actions, but the full actuality of the world is a joint product of the decisions and actions of God and free creatures. Which possible world the actual world is is still being decided—but the only decisions left to be made are those by us. Because they are free they cannot be foreknown by God knowing his will or possible worlds.[25]

It is up to us, quite literally, therefore, given a libertarian view of freedom, as to what God can know of actual events and actions in the world with respect to us. "It follows that free creatures have some degree of control over what God will know in the present. I, for example, can cause God to know me as finishing this paragraph before or after I eat lunch today."[26]

It is in this sense that Creel can argue for the impassibility of God's will. His nature is impassible, given that Creel wants to continue to affirm that God does, indeed, have essential characteristics. But now also his will is impassible as well, not because God's decisions are rooted in his sovereign majesty, but rather because his decisions are grounded in mere possibility; his will is determined only by possibilities, possibilities that depend on us, for the most part, to become actualities.

Though God's impassibility has historically been seen as a logical extension of his aseity, Creel strikingly presents an apologetic for the impassibility of God's will by arguing for his dependence. In order to be impassible, then, God must be ontologically dependent.

For example, in order to argue against the Christian doctrine of creation *ex nihilo* (CEN) and to affirm his own permutation of the traditional notion of impassibility, Creel attempts to convince us that God is metaphysically dependent on what he calls the "plenum." The plenum is an entity that contains all possibilities that are not inherent in God. In arguing for the necessity of the plenum, Creel wants to hold CEN to be incoherent.

His reasoning here is not altogether transparent, but he seems to move in this general direction: in order for God to create, he had

25. Creel, *Divine Impassibility*, 91–92.
26. Ibid., 99.

to make actual what was, prior to that, passively possible.[27] And, according to Creel, "theism rejects the idea that such possibilities are resident in God because that would imply pantheism, i.e., that God becomes what is created and that, therefore, the world is God."[28] In other words, Creel seems to think that if there are passive potentialities in God, which then become actualities by virtue of God's creative activity, those actualities, since they originally inhere in God, would themselves in some essential sense *be* God, and thus pantheism would be the inevitable outcome.

It is surely true that Christian theism would reject pantheism; there is no inkling in historic Christianity of an identity between God and his creation. Creel's argument, however, begins in the wrong place. So, as is the case with all such arguments, it will inevitably reach the wrong conclusions. The "wrong place" in which Creel begins is with a univocal understanding of potentiality and actuality with respect to reality. Or, perhaps better (and simpler), a univocal understanding of reality. According to Creel, "actualities and possibilities are exhaustive of reality."[29] The reason he argues for the incoherence of CEN is that (given that actuality and possibility are the same for God and for us) God either creates on the basis of actualized possibilities inherent in him, or from nothing. Because the latter is absurd, the only option available for the doctrine of CEN is that God create from actualized possibilities inherent in him. But if that is the case, then those actualized possibilities become actualities inherent in him, and thus, creation is of the character of God himself.

The "work-around" to this problem is what motivates the idea of Creel's plenum. As a repository of passive potentialities independent from God (thus, not inherent in him), the plenum gives God the option of picking out possibilities that are not inherent in him, and thus of creating, or actualizing, possibilities that do not participate in his character at all.

27. Questions of time-conditioned language should be held in abeyance for the sake of argument here.
28. Creel, *Divine Impassibility*, 65.
29. Ibid., 66.

But why think that actualities and possibilities are exhaustive of reality in the same way for God as they are for creation? Consider that prior to creation there was nothing but the triune God of Scripture. What would a possibility or potentiality *be* in this context? Creel is right to think that, according to traditional Christianity, whatever it would be, it would have to be identical with God, since in God there can be no composition of parts that are or could in any way be external to him. What would "creation" be at this point? It would have to be something that inheres in the mind of God, one of God's thoughts, say, or something on which God thinks. Since God thinks what he is, creation prior to its actualization by God would have to be either identical to him (given simplicity) or a contingent noetic property of his (more on this below).

But if God's thoughts of creation were identical to him prior to creating, why think that God could not then actualize that which was identical to him in such a way that it becomes something else, something not identical to him, something that, while remaining true to his idea of it, was nevertheless not in any way identical with that idea, or with his thinking? It seems the only reason to disallow such a possibility is because Creel has begun his own thinking with the presupposition that actuality and possibility must be the same for all of us—for God and for his creation. But this kind of univocal thinking on the part of Creel begins with the denial of the most basic metaphysical truth of historic Christianity. It begins with a denial of the distinction made between the *Eimi* and the *eikon*, from the outset, in order then to conclude that such a distinction cannot account for the reality of either of its parts.

Thus, Creel wants us to entertain the notion of a *tertium quid*, a plenum, which is neither *Eimi* nor *eikon*, "a different kind of actuality from the things that are actualized from it."[30] But, if one is going to allow for a different kind of actuality in the plenum, why not dispense with such a strange and peculiar notion and allow for a "different kind" of actuality, and of potentiality, which comes from the triune God?

30. Ibid., 71.

To put the matter in the starkest terms, why argue that there is something that, as Creel says, is "not this or that," that "does not exist as an individual or as a thing," that is entailed by the existence of God such that "either the plenum is eternal and uncreated, along with God, or there is no God," that requires one to say, *not*, "In the beginning was God," *but*, "In the beginning was God and the plenum"?[31] Surely such an argument, to put it mildly, borders on the absurd to those who have even a passing familiarity with the theology of the Christian tradition.

The Triune Essence

In attempting to do justice to (some kind of) impassibility of God, Creel considers it necessary to invent another metaphysical entity, the plenum, in order to guard against pantheism (thus allowing God to actualize possibilities that were not inherent in him). He has to, in the process of working this out, restrict God's own sovereignty, power, and knowledge (just to name a few attributes) in order to allow for the impassibility of God's will. Because possibility and actuality are, in this sense, more ultimate than God (in that God is dependent on them, and they are not an essential part of his character), creation becomes something that determines what God knows and when God knows it. This, in the name of impassibility.[32]

As we said, the problem is creation. This does not mean that creation per se is a problem. God saw all that he had made and it was very good. It means rather that the fact of creation and its status *as created* seem almost invariably to get in the way of clear, Christian thinking on these matters. From an essentially time-bound God to a metaphysical *tertium quid*, from a god who is (to a greater or lesser degree) essentially and hopelessly time-conditioned, to a metaphysical repository of passive potentialities,

31. Ibid., 71, 68, 69.

32. Given our explanation of impassibility above, that it refers primarily to the impossibility of an agent being caused to "move" by something external to himself, it is strange indeed that Creel can maintain impassibility only by affirming that God is, routinely and necessarily, "moved" by what we decide to do, and when.

too many discussions about God and his relationship to creation conclude with a god who is in some way, like his creation, essentially needy. The triune God of Scripture takes a back seat to a host of wants, needs, and aspirations as philosophers and theologians, supposedly safeguarding intellectual respectability, debate his nature and character. Is there any way to maintain the integrity of the revelation of the triune God in the midst of such a bleak and anemic context?

Given what we saw earlier of van Inwagen's invitation, we are suggesting that a Christian theory of ultimate reality begin with the fundamental distinction between the triune God as he is in himself and creation as that which God produced and controls. Admittedly, such a beginning can take place only in a context in which God's revelation in Scripture provides the content of that starting point. And, admittedly again, that revelation is marginalized at best when many philosophers and theologians set their tasks with respect to theism.

But that need not be the case. As a matter of fact, given van Inwagen's admission, and given that philosophy has had a few thousand years of beginning its work with virtually every starting point *but* the basic truth provided in Scripture, a good argument could be made that a change of thinking is long overdue. It seems high time to introduce into the discussions something altogether different, perhaps aberrant, that can provide both for a discussion of the triune God of Scripture (who alone is the true God) and of our relationship to him. Perhaps a philosophical deracination is the order of the day.

We have thought about essentialism in the context of possible worlds. Though the language itself can at times obscure rather than clarify, the notion of possible worlds should not be seen as altogether inappropriate.[33] For example, we should remember, the Christian tradition has always held that God did not have to create. If that is true, then we could say there is a possible world in which God does

---

33. Inappropriate, that is, in certain contexts. We will note in the next chapter some serious concerns with possibility and similar notions that are utilized in these discussions.

not create. Such a world would include only God, but it would be, in the way that we're now using the terms, a possible world.[34]

How, though, would an essentialist understanding of God be able to reckon with the fact that God is triune? Given that God is essentially triune—that is, that there is no possible world in which the Godhead consists of two persons in one, or four in one, or anything but three in one—how does one go about thinking of the three persons in relation to the one essential God?

This is a problem inherent in any discussion of God's characteristics, and so it is not unique to those who affirm that God has essential attributes (and we should remember that those attributes are not distinct from him). The best that one can do, it seems, is to affirm that there are essential properties of God, all of which apply to each of the persons, and that there are essential properties of each of the persons that are unique to each one. That is, in line with historic Christianity (in this case, the Athanasian Creed), orthodox theology has historically affirmed that

> the Godhead of the Father, of the Son, and of the Holy Spirit is all one, the glory equal, the majesty coeternal. Such as the Father is, such is the Son, and such is the Holy Spirit. The Father Uncreate[d], the Son Uncreate[d], and the Holy Ghost Uncreate[d]. The Father Incomprehensible, the Son Incomprehensible, and the Holy Ghost Incomprehensible. The Father Eternal, the Son Eternal, and the Holy Ghost Eternal and yet they are not Three Eternals but One Eternal. As also there are not Three Uncreated, nor Three Incomprehensibles, but One Uncreated, and One Incomprehensible. So likewise the Father is Almighty, the Son Almighty, and the Holy Ghost Almighty. And yet they are not Three Almighties but One Almighty. So the Father is God, the Son is God, and the Holy Ghost is God. And yet they are not Three Gods, but One God.

While affirming this truth, we must also affirm, with the same creed, that

34. That is, it is not the case that God's existence per se is a possible world. Rather, given God's existence, there is a consistent and coherent state of affairs in which he determines *not* to create anything.

the Father is made of none, neither created, nor begotten. The Son is of the Father alone; not made, nor created, but begotten. The Holy Ghost is of the Father, and of the Son neither made, nor created, nor begotten, but proceeding.

Thus, while everything that God is, the Father, Son, and Holy Spirit are, there are properties of each of the three that do not apply to the one essential God *as one*. The one triune God, for example, is not from the Father; only the Son is from the Father.

Muller, in explicating the differences between the persons and the essence (and, in part, quoting Rijssen) explains:

> [The persons] differ from the divine Essence not *realiter*—that is to say, not *essentialiter, ut res & res*—but *modaliter, ut modus à re*: "the personal properties by which the persons are distinguished from the Essence, are modes of a sort, by which they are charac-terized, not formally and properly as in creatures who are affected in certain ways by their properties, but eminently and analogically, rising beyond all imperfections."[35]

So, there are essential properties of each of the persons that do not apply to the one God, though the reverse is decidedly *not* the case.

One of the best ways, perhaps the only orthodox way, to distin-guish these properties is with respect to the *proprietates essentiales* and *proprietates personales*.[36] That is, the distinctions made between the persons and essence of God are *personal*, rather than *essential* distinctions. Here, the use of the word "essential" is different from the way in which we have used it with regard to essentialism, in that it refers to the essence of God in distinction from the persons

---

35. Richard A. Muller, *Post-Reformation Reformed Dogmatics: The Rise and Develop-ment of Reformed Orthodoxy, Ca. 1520 to Ca. 1725: The Triunity of God* (Grand Rapids, MI: Baker, 2003), 190.

36. For an elaboration of this distinction, see Muller, *The Divine Essence and At-tributes*, 213ff. Muller notes, "As Alexander of Hales had argued, there cannot be any *distinctio realis* between the attributes—nor can there be such a 'real distinction' between the divine persons and the divine essence—but the persons as identified by the *propri-etates personales*, must be distinct from one another, indeed, really (*realiter*) distinct" (ibid., 215). See also Muller, *The Triunity of God*, 167–95.

who comprise the Godhead. Thus, there are essential properties of the persons—what we might call personal properties—and there are essential properties of the essence, applying as they do to each of the three persons equally and without dividing those properties in any way.

While there is no way for finite human beings completely to circumscribe the relationship of the one God to the three persons, we may rest content, with the history of the orthodox Christian tradition, with the fact of God's triunity and its evidence of God's utter incomprehensibility (Rom. 11:33–34).

The Covenant God

Given God's essential, triune character, the crux of our concern is the way in which we are to think of God and his relationship to his creation in the context of theological and philosophical discussions, primarily in the philosophy of religion. Or, to put the matter in the form of a question, why are philosophical arguments routinely formulated to end up either (1) denying the (exegetically and historically) overwhelming evidence for the essential character of the triune God or (2) denying the existence of God altogether? What kinds of principles are lurking in the background that compel virtually all philosophers who deal with theism to conclude with a less-than-Christian god?

With regard to Davis's argument above, we will remember that he argues against God's essential eternity because "we do not have a usable concept of atemporal causation" that would allow for an eternal God to do x at t. But why think there is no such concept? Presumably because the "we" who do not have such a concept are those who begin their understanding of causation "from below," rather than from above. That is, since causation always presupposes the constraints of time, God must be essentially time-bound in order to cause anything. But is this the way God reveals himself to us in Scripture?

To use another example alluded to earlier, William Craig wrestles with God's eternity relative to time. He is asking, fundamentally, whether a personal God can stand in some kind of relationship to the world and yet not be constrained by time. His answer:

> It is very difficult to see how He can. Imagine once more God existing changelessly alone without creation, but with a change-less determination of His will to create a temporal world with a beginning. Since God is omnipotent, His will is done, and a temporal world comes into existence. Now this presents us with a dilemma. Either God existed prior to creation or He did not. Suppose He did. In that case, God is temporal, not timeless, since to exist *prior* to some event is to be in time. Suppose, then, that God did not exist prior to creation. In that case, without creation, He exists timelessly, since He obviously did not come into being along with the world at the moment of creation.
>
> This second alternative presents us with a new dilemma. Once time begins at the moment of creation, either God becomes temporal in virtue of His real relation to the temporal world or else He exists just as timelessly with creation as He does without it. If we choose the first alternative, then, once again, God is temporal. But what about the second alternative? Can God remain untouched by the world's temporality? It seems not. For at the first moment of time, God stands in a new relation in which He did not stand before (since there was no "before"). Even if in creation of the world God undergoes no *intrinsic* change, He at least undergoes an *extrinsic* change. For at the moment of creation, God comes into the relation of *sustaining* the universe or, at the very least, of *co-existing with* the universe, relations in which He did not stand before. Since He is free to refrain from creation, God could have never stood in those relations, had He so willed. But in virtue of His creating a temporal world, God comes into a relation with that world the moment it springs into being. Thus, even if it is not the case that God is temporal prior to His creation of the world, He nonetheless undergoes an extrinsic change at the moment of creation which draws Him into time in virtue of His real relation to the world. So even if God is timeless without creation, His free decision to create a temporal world also constitutes a free decision on His part to exist temporally.[37]

37. Craig, *Time and Eternity*, 86–87.

Although there are elements in this quotation that seem to be headed in the right direction (specifically, that there may be no *intrinsic* change in God at the point of creation), the conclusion of the matter disappoints. According to Craig, God's "timeless, free decision to create a temporal world with a beginning is a decision on God's part to abandon timelessness and to take on a temporal mode of existence."[38]

Though this is the direction that most philosophers who deal with theism want to go—that is, arguing for a limited, constrained, and relatively ignorant God (because, again, of the presence of creation or of free creatures in creation)—the other direction, absorbing (at least some of) the temporal into God, is sometimes argued as well. Calvinistic philosopher Paul Helm, in order to account for God's timelessness, supports a notion of eternal creation. In other words, since God's eternity is not qualified by anything temporal, his dealings with creation must themselves be eternal dealings. The priority of God's eternity over creation, according to Helm, is not a temporal one, but is rather like the priority of the queen over the prime minister: there is a logical relationship there, but no temporal one. Helm goes further in his support of this idea; he sets out the notion that the incarnation itself is eternal.

> The point is . . . there is no preexistent Christ with a life history independent of and prior to the incarnation. There was no time when the eternal God was not Jesus of Nazareth. There is no other life story . . . of God than the incarnation. There was no time when the Son of God was not willing himself to be incarnate in our history.[39]

One could perhaps interpret this in such a way as to allow for some latitude with respect to God's relationship to time. It is, of course, true that "there was no time when the Son of God was not willing himself to be incarnate in our history." But is it true that "there was no time when the eternal God was not Jesus of

38. Ibid., 241.
39. Gregory E. Ganssle and David M. Woodruff, *God and Time: Essays on the Divine Nature* (Oxford: Oxford University Press, 2002), 54.

Nazareth"? Scripture certainly doesn't seem to see the incarnation in that way (especially since both "Jesus" and "Nazareth" require the presence of creation, and thus of time).[40] Neither does it seem to allow—explicitly, implicitly, or by good and necessary consequence—for a notion of eternal creation.

And what are we to make of Creel's discussion of impassibility? He does want to affirm it as a characteristic of God, but in order to do so, not only does he "rob Peter to pay Paul" (in that he takes away from God's essential character at one point in order to affirm impassibility at another), but he also has to create his own metaphysical repository (the plenum) in order to justify his position.

What would motivate such strange behavior? Why, for example, insert such a thing as the plenum into a discussion of God's relationship to the world? Creel seems to need something like that in order to guarantee that creation is not God. The tension that gives rise to such a view is that God as pure act cannot have anything but active potentialities in himself, and thus a domain suited to passive potentialities is needed.

What's a Christian to do with all of this? How do we negotiate our way through this murky metaphysical morass in order to affirm the triune God of Scripture, on the one hand, and his real relationship to us and to his creation, on the other?

To approach an answer to these questions, two things are needed. First, a little biblical theology is in order.[41] Second, given

---

40. More recently, in attempting to explain (what he thinks to be) Calvin's view of the incarnation, particularly with respect to the tension of eternity and time, Helm notes: "Perhaps Calvin's view amounts to this: in the Incarnation there is uniquely powerful and loving and gracious focusing of the divine nature upon human nature, rather than a transfer of the Son of God to a spatio-temporal location. This focusing makes it possible for us to say that God the Son is so present with human nature that there is a union of natures in Jesus Christ. God in the person of the Son, through whom all things are created, focuses upon one unique aspect of his creation in uniting to human nature in the person of Jesus Christ. God the Son was not simply present by being active, he was present by being in union. The character of this divine presence sanctions the language of person with respect to the result." Paul Helm, *John Calvin's Ideas* (Oxford: Oxford University Press, 2004), 64. This, too, seems to break significantly with orthodox notions of the incarnation.

41. Because there are various forms (and contents) of biblical theology, we should be clear here as to how we are using the phrase. To put it simply and in the words of

biblical theology, we need an application of such to the discussions concerning God's properties and how those properties are to be understood relative to his creation.

Princeton's biblical theologian, Geerhardus Vos, "Biblical Theology is that branch of Exegetical Theology which deals with the process of the self-revelation of God deposited in the Bible." In the way that we're thinking of it here, it is the work of biblical theology to relate exegetical conclusions to each other, all within the context and process of God's revealed history. It organizes exegesis, arranging it so that the text itself is properly understood within the context of God's work in history. To some extent, and in a mutually dependent way, biblical theology provides a check both for exegesis and for systematic theology. It checks exegesis in that it provides a historical background and situation in which a particular text must be understood. It checks systematic theology in that it roots its organizing principle firmly in the historical outworking of God's redemptive purpose, rather than in, say, an abstract principle of truth or unity. Biblical theology, then, provides the unity within diversity of biblical studies—properly contextualizing both exegesis and systematics.

12

Christian Covenantal Condescension

This certainly is an inestimable pledge of special love, that God should so greatly condescend for our sake. —JOHN CALVIN

The Westminster Confession notes, as we have seen, that, if it weren't for God's voluntary condescension, we, as creatures made in his image, could have no "fruition" of him. The scope and depth of this may not be immediately obvious.

From the beginning, we see God bringing into existence what did not exist previously. Even if we affirm, as we must, that creation was known by God "prior to" his creating it, it is still the case that, when he brings creation into existence, it did not exist *as creation* until that point.

Cosmic Condescension

But just what does this voluntary divine condescension entail? We should note that, as far as God's relationship to that which he creates, it entails everything that he does, says, and, as we will see, *is* with respect to that relationship.[1] For example, the very fact that God brings something into existence to which he himself is in some way related entails, automatically, an act of condescension.

It entails condescension because of who God is essentially. Given that God is supremely perfect and without need or constraint, to begin to relate himself to that which is limited, constrained, and not perfect is, in sum, to condescend.[2] For example, the very fact that Scripture tells us that "the Spirit of God was hovering over the face of the waters" (Gen. 1:2) is evidence of God's own condescension; he had to "come down" to hover over the waters. God, as infinite Spirit, has no need to constrain himself by hovering over the face of the waters. He is altogether infinite, without constraint. But he does hover, and he condescends to do so.

Or, to use another example, the very fact that Scripture tells us that "God said, 'Let there be light,' and there was light" (Gen. 1:3) is evidence of condescension. God did not have to speak at all. He is not in need of language in order to communicate (especially since, in this case, there was no one with whom to communicate except himself) or to create. Neither does he *need* to speak in order to create. He could create without saying a word. But he spoke, and it was. He condescended to speak, and it was. His word is evidence of his condescension to us.[3]

Not only so, but just after Adam and Eve sinned, "they heard the sound of the LORD God walking in the garden in the cool of the day" (Gen. 3:8).[4] God condescended to his creation in order to begin and

1. As we will see, when we say that God's condescension involves everything that he *is*, we are not saying that all that he is is exhausted in this act of condescension; that would be to deny what we have already affirmed with respect to God's essential character.

2. To say that creation is not perfect is not to say that it was not good, as God himself declared it to be good. It is simply to say that it was inherently dependent and thus not in any way necessary, as a perfect being would be.

3. It is not central to the argument here that God literally, with words, *spoke* creation into existence (though it seems this is exactly what he did). Even if God did not literally speak creation into existence, the fact of creation itself entails God's condescension. In creating, he also "stooped down" to relate himself to that creation. As we will see, his Word-become-flesh is the supreme evidence of God's condescension.

4. For an analysis of this "theophany," see James A. Borland, *Christ in the Old Testament* (Chicago: Moody Press, 1978), 83–86.

maintain a relationship with that creation, more specifically, with those whom he had made in his image. Evidence of (something of) the extent of that condescension is found in the next verse as well: "But the LORD God called to the man and said to him, 'Where are you'" (v. 9)? In condescending to relate to Adam and Eve, he is, like them, (not essentially, but covenantally) restricted in his knowledge of where they might be hiding in that garden.

It is for this reason that the confession wants to summarize God's condescension in the word *covenant*. That is, the condescension itself includes a contract that God makes with his human creatures, a contract that requires, first, God's relating himself to us and, second, an understanding of our relationship to him.[5] In the garden, since there was no sin yet introduced into the cosmos, the contract consisted of Adam's obedience to God's specific commands, especially with respect to the tree. Those commands presuppose God's condescending communication to Adam, and Adam's responsibilities as he relates to his Creator.

When, however, sin did enter the cosmos such that the whole creation fell (cf. Rom. 8:18–23), while the *goal* of God's condescension changed, the *fact* and *mode* of it remained the same. He continued in his relationship to us (though admittedly that relationship was characterized by wrath and by grace in a way that it was not before the fall into sin). The goal of that relationship, after the fall, was (in part) the redemption of some who had fallen into sin.

As we noted in chapter 9, the quintessential example of that goal in the Old Testament is found in Exodus 3.[6] Another look here will bring out at least three truths evident in this passage that will help us to see more clearly the nature of the condescension of God. First, notice how God initially identifies himself to Moses: "And he said, 'I am the God of your father, the God of Abraham, the God of Isaac, and the God of Jacob'" (Ex. 3:6). The first way in which the

5. Once God relates himself to us, there is no reciprocal decision on our part. We necessarily relate to God. The onus is then placed on us to understand that relationship obediently. Even if we fail so to understand it, however, it is always and everywhere present, into eternity.

6. For a more extended discussion of what follows, see K. Scott Oliphint, "Most Moved Mediator," *Themelios* 30, no. 1 (Autumn 2004): 39–51.

Lord describes himself, is as *Moses'* God, the God of Moses' father, Abraham. This is typical throughout the Old Testament when God wants his people to know that he is *their* God (note Ex. 6:7, for example, as well as Jer. 7:23; 11:4; etc.). He identifies himself as the covenant God. Notice, just prior to this passage in Exodus 3, we read, "And God heard their groaning, and *God remembered his covenant with Abraham, with Isaac, and with Jacob.* God saw the people of Israel—and God knew" (Ex. 2:24–25).

The mention of Abraham, Isaac, and Jacob is meant to remind us of God's relationship to his people, a people of his own choosing (John 15:16), a people for God's own possession (1 Peter 2:9). Exodus 3 opens with the reminder that God is a covenant God and that he knew the sufferings of his people in Egypt.

When God appears to Moses in the burning bush, he announces himself as the God of the covenant, more specifically, as the God of Israel, and thus as Moses' God. The passage is, therefore, under-girded with covenant language. What God is actually saying to Moses, however, is an elaboration of his initial announcement to him. He is telling Moses what it means that he is a covenant God. It means, in part, that God has identified himself with his people. There is an intensity about the language in this chapter that communicates clearly that God is moved by the sufferings of his people. That intensity is communicated, in the first place, when God says that he has "surely seen" the suffering of his people.[7] In the second place, we are told twice (once in Ex. 2:25 and again in 3:7) that God knows the suffering of his people.

In the context of God's covenant faithfulness to his people, it would be impossible to understand God's "knowing" in these passages as something intellectual or strictly mental, as if God learned something at a given point in the history of his people. The "knowing" here is covenantal knowing. It is the kind of knowing, for example, that we see in Genesis 4:1, where Adam "knew" Eve and she conceived. It is a knowing of identity, a knowing of intimacy, a knowing that highlights the union of the ones known to the Knower (see Isa. 63:9ff.). Just how it can be that this triune

---

7. The intensity of the language is clearer in the original Hebrew.

God, who is essentially impassible, can be moved by this suffering will be discussed below.

The second thing to note in Exodus 3 is that Moses realizes that, if he is to be God's instrument, he needs to know as much as possible about the authority of the one who is sending him. So, he asks for God's name. He wants to know what God is like; he wants to know exactly who it is that is sending him into Egypt. And God says to Moses, "I AM WHO I AM" (v. 14).

This revelation of God's name has prompted significant discussion among commentators. Without reproducing the controversies surrounding this text, we should highlight a few points that are crucial for understanding what God is revealing here.

The traditional view of this text is that God is revealing himself as the self-existent One.[8] Though he initially announces himself as the God who is *with* his people, and thus *in* history, when he is asked to give his name, he announces himself as the God who is also above history; he alone is the "I AM."

One reason that some commentators are confused about what God is saying here is their fascination with the etymology of the Hebrew phrase itself, to the neglect of its revelational context. The significance of the divine name is to be seen, not simply from etymological considerations, but particularly from revelational considerations. Rather than isolating the pronouncing of the divine name from the context in which it is revealed, we can only properly understand it within that very context.

Yahweh does indeed reveal his divine independence. In the context of the Exodus narrative he proves himself to be unlimited, not constrained by temporal categories. More generally, he announces himself as one who is independent of the created order and therefore sovereign over it. "I AM WHO I AM" indicates that, by contrast, for

8. This is criticized by many contemporary Old Testament scholars on the grounds that issues like the aseity of God would not cross the mind of an ancient Israelite. But that certainly cannot be the case, given the history of God's dealings with his people. That interpretation speaks more about the influence of Immanuel Kant on current hermeneutics, than about the text itself. See Richard A. Muller, *Post-Reformation Reformed Dogmatics: The Rise and Development of Reformed Orthodoxy, Ca. 1520 to Ca. 1725: The Divine Essence and Attributes*, 2nd ed. (Grand Rapids, MI: Baker, 2002), 49–52, 227ff.

example, with Moses—who is what he was and will become what he is, who had a beginning and an end in human history—God possesses his existence without beginning, without end, without explanation beyond himself. The ultimate fact of divine revelation is that God is who he is, without cause and without need. God gives Moses a name that only he could give (and have)—"He is who he is."

Remember, as we noted previously in chapter 9, that the reason we can be confident of what God was saying in this name is that its meaning is precisely what was modeled for Moses in the *event* of divine revelation given with the word-revelation.[9] It is not an insignificant detail that what draws Moses into God's presence on that mountain is a picture of who God is. There is no analogy in the creation for the independent and the uncreated. So God creates a picture of his character in the burning bush. He gives Moses a sign: an "independent" fire. The fire does not derive its burning from the context in which it burns. It is self-generated, contradicting all rules of creation. The bush is on fire, but the fire is not dependent on the bush; it possesses its own energy. There is, it seems, a deliberate and *revelational* sign given by God to unveil the significance, both of God's covenantal revelation to Moses (because the fire is *with* the bush), and of his revelation of the divine name—"I AM WHO I AM."

We should see, then, that the *un*burning bush shows, on the one hand, the absolute independence of God—that he possesses being in and of himself in a manner that is without precedent in all of creation. God's sign revelation points to an ontological truth. The ultimate fact about God that makes the human mind stagger and reel, because we have no categories to describe or understand this element of the existence of God, is that he simply *is*.

But it also shows, on the other hand, that, while remaining the "I AM," while remaining *a se*, while remaining *God*, he is nevertheless

9. This "show and tell" method of God's revelation seems to have been all too often underemphasized. God often tells us who he is by giving us an earthly picture, or analogy, of who he is. This is understood more clearly in the New Testament. For example, we understand something of what it means that Christ is the true Bread as we see him miraculously feed five thousand. This "show and tell" method of revelation should be seen more explicitly throughout Scripture.

with his people, just as the fire was *with* the bush. The significance of the bush that did not burn, was that, in any other circumstance, the fire would need the bush in order to be fire. Not only so, but once used as fuel, the bush itself would be consumed by the fire. In what Moses saw, however, neither did the fire need the bush, nor was the bush consumed. The "I AM" has covenanted with his people. Therefore, as he abides with them, they are not destroyed either. Here, then, is the beauty of God's character. It is the wonderful mystery of the God who is *a se*, eternally and immutably dependent on nothing but himself, covenanting with us, relating to us, in such a way that we can know and love him.

Within the context of our previous discussion of the *Eimi/eikon*, we should note here that what we see in Exodus 3 (and elsewhere in Scripture) is the "I AM," the *"Eimi," taking on* an *eikon*, an image, in order to show his limited creatures just who he is and what he is like.[10]

Third, once we understand this, once we see the supreme significance of God's announcement of his name in the context of his covenant, the most important phrase to understand in this passage is in these four words in verse 8: "I have come down."[11] These four words could easily serve to frame the core of our understanding of God from Genesis to Revelation. There is no way to understand both who God is and his dealings with his creation without seeing this principle running throughout Scripture: God has come down climactically in the person of Jesus Christ; Christ is the *Eimi/eikon*, in one supreme person. He *is* the principle of the covenant.

In order for us to have anything to do with God whatsoever, God had first to "come down," to stoop to our level. So, says Calvin:

> For who even of slight intelligence does not understand that, as nurses commonly do with infants, God is wont in a measure to "lisp" in speaking to us? Thus such forms of speaking do not so much express clearly what God is like as accommodate the knowl-

10. The *eikon* (image) that God takes on here is not, strictly speaking, the sign of the burning bush, but is rather the nature of the angel of the Lord himself who, as it turns out, *is* the Lord.

11. The four words in English are actually just one Hebrew word וָאֵרֵד.

edge of him to our slight capacity. To do this he must descend far beneath his loftiness.[12]

What does God's divine "stoop" look like? From a biblical-theological perspective, it looks like the Lord God walking in the garden in the cool of the day (Gen. 3:8); it looks like the angel of the Lord (which is the Lord himself) calling to Abraham (Gen. 22), or to Moses (Ex. 3), or to Israel (Judges 2). Because of his voluntary condescension, the Lord protects and delivers his people (e.g., Ps. 34:7), and he fights for them (e.g., Isa. 37:36). Supremely, it looks like Jesus Christ, the Son of God taking to himself the created properties of a human nature in order to accomplish what only he can accomplish, our redemption. All of this "relationality" on the part of Yahweh, the "I AM," can happen only because he willingly decides to condescend to our level, to the level of the created.[13]

This condescension can take place only in the context of the union of the *Eimi/eikon* principle. It is shown to us in the symbol of the burning bush and its manifestation of God's inner being. It is shown to us in the fact of the angel of the Lord himself. The transcendent One is not a prisoner of his own transcendence, but in his transcendence is able to condescend to dwell among his people. As the transcendent One, he nevertheless is immanent; he

12. John Calvin, *Institutes of the Christian Religion*, ed. John T. McNeill, trans. Ford Lewis Battles, Library of Christian Classics (London: SCM, 1960), 1.13.1.

13. This condescension helps us to understand, for example, how it can be that God, who eternally loves us, can in history also hate us. A less-than-satisfactory solution to this dilemma highlights the problems one encounters, even among theologically orthodox philosophers, if one assumes that God's dealings with us are always and only with respect to his *Eimi* character. In order to avoid the appearance of change in God, Paul Helm describes wrath and grace in this way: "So the truth about atonement, about reconciliation to God, has to be represented to us as if it implied a change in God, and so an inconsistency, an apparent contradiction, in his actions towards us. But in fact there is no change in God; he loves us from eternity. There is however, a change in us, a change that occurs as by faith Christ's work is appropriated. The change is not from wrath to grace, but from our belief that we are under wrath to our belief that we are under grace." Paul Helm, *John Calvin's Ideas* (Oxford: Oxford University Press, 2004), 395. Thus, change from wrath to grace is attributed only to us and our beliefs. This seems far from the biblical understanding of God's disposition toward us.

is "above" all that is created, while determining in his love to be "with" it as well.

This union *by* God, *in* God and *for* us, of the *Eimi/eikon* principle is, in one sense, the most basic truth for us to understand if we want to know who God is; it is basic to a proper understanding of God, creation, and all of Scripture. It is the principle that we must use to understand how God can remain who he is while at the same time interacting with his creation.[14]

And here is the central truth of it all: *The unified* Eimi/eikon *principle of the exodus becomes the Emmanuel principle of the new exodus, the deliverance of the Lord's people from bondage to sin.*

It seems all too likely that philosophers who deal with theism have not seen this *Eimi/eikon* principle. As basic as this principle is, because God's revelation of himself is no part of most philosophizing, it is no part of most philosophical-theistic discourse. But, things ought not to be this way. If we are interested in a truly *Christian* theistic philosophy, we must commit to taking seriously the fact that the *Eimi/eikon* principle, summed up as it is in the person of Jesus Christ, provides the foundational metaphysical structure for all discussions of God and his relationship to his creation. How, specifically, does the person of Christ help us to understand who God is and how he relates to us?

We must first recognize that Christ is *the* climactic, quintessential revelation of God *par excellence*. He is the one who is, as Paul reminds us, "the image [*eikon*] of the invisible God" (Col. 1:15) and "in him all the fullness of God was pleased to dwell" (Col. 1:19). He is, as the angel announced, Emmanu-*el*, that is, *God with us* (Matt. 1:21). "He is the radiance of the glory of God and the exact imprint of his nature" (Heb. 1:3). As Christ himself said to the Pharisees, in the clearest possible identification of himself with the Lord of the Exodus—"I am" (John 8:58).

This is Paul's point in Philippians 2:5–8.[15] He wants us to see that Christ emptied *himself* by becoming something that he was

14. What we're saying here, in other words, is that understanding who Christ is is the way for us to understand who God is and how he relates himself to his creation.

15. For an exegetical discussion of this text, see Oliphint, "Most Moved Mediator." We see this principle displayed for us, albeit in nascent form, in the Old Testament as

not previously, something that by definition required humility and, ultimately, humiliation (Phil. 2:8). For Christ to make himself nothing is for him to humble himself, and he humbles himself by being born in the likeness of men and then by becoming obedient to the point of death.

But this "emptying" is no undoing, undermining, constraining, or limiting of who he essentially is as God; such a feat would be impossible, given what we have understood about essentialism as it applies to God. Rather than a change of essence (which is impossible), the self-emptying that Paul articulates is in fact a self-*adding*. Hence Turretin:

> Here also belongs the verb *ekenōse*, which is not to be taken simply and absolutely (as if he ceased to be God or was reduced to a nonentity, which is impious even to think concerning the eternal and unchangeable God), but in respect of state and comparatively because he concealed the divine glory under the veil of flesh and as it were laid it aside; not by putting off what he was, but by assuming what he was not.[16]

---

well. We remember Moses' bold request that the Lord display the fullness of his glory to Moses (Ex. 33:18). This, Moses was told, would bring certain death. Instead the Lord in his mercy showed Moses his glory, but only as veiled; Moses could only glimpse the back side of the Lord as he passed by the cleft of the rock in which Moses was hidden. Was the Lord less than fully God as he passed by Moses? Certainly not. His proclamation as he passed by—what Luther called the "Sermon on the Name"—was meant to remind Moses that the "I AM" was present. Rather, he was accommodating himself to Moses in a way that demonstrated both his glory and the veiling of the fullness of that glory. "THE LORD" came down and showed himself to Moses even as he hid himself from Moses.

16. Francis Turretin, *Institutes of Elenctic Theology*, ed. James T. Dennison Jr., trans. George Musgrave Giger, 3 vols. (Phillipsburg, NJ: P&R, 1992–97), 2:314. Though it cannot be pursued here, it is instructive to note that Turretin links an understanding of the Trinity to an understanding of the hypostatic union: "For as in the Trinity, the unity of essence does not hinder the persons from being distinct from each other and their properties and operations from being incommunicable, so the union of natures in the person of Christ does not prevent both the natures and their properties from remaining unconfounded and distinct" (2:311). The serious point to be made here is that a confusion or ignorance or, worse, denial of the orthodox notion of Christology could imply the same with respect to the Trinity, such that Christianity would then be replaced for another religion altogether.

The *Eimi/eikon* principle, summed up as it is (in history) in the person of Christ, should therefore be our guide in understanding who God is and how he relates to us and to his creation.

The triune God made a decision—a decision of humiliation. That decision has its focus on the second person of the Trinity, who would uniquely condescend. This decision carried with it no necessity; it was not necessary for the second person of the Trinity to decide to humble himself. He had every right to refrain from such a decision and not add to himself the humiliating status of humanity. But he determined not to. This second person—one who is equal to God, who is in the form of God, who is himself God (John 1:1)—did not stop being God (such a thing would be impossible), but rather he took on something that was not a part of his essential character previously. He took on human nature (John 1:14).

To be clear, Christ does not become the opposite of himself by taking on human nature. Moreover, it is not as though he gives up deity in order to become man. This pattern is nowhere given in Scripture; it is, as we have said, an impossibility (given what we understand of God's essence). Rather, just as the "I AM" remains Lord while coming down to be the God of Abraham, Isaac, and Jacob, so the second person of the Trinity remains God, while coming down to assume human nature and therefore becomes the God-man. This, as we have said, *is* the covenant; as the Westminster Confession reminds us, Christ is the *substance* of the covenant (WCF 7.6, WLC 35; cf. Col. 2:8ff.). It is covenant condescension, inconceivable to comprehend fully, but nevertheless central to a basic understanding of God and his relationship to creation.

Perhaps here we need to qualify and clarify our theology of the incarnation with respect to the condescension of the Son of God. As we might expect, the question of just what kind of union took place between Christ's human and divine natures has been delineated with care and precision in the history of theology. There is no reason to repeat all of that discussion here. What seems most pertinent to our argument concerning the essential and contingent properties of God, given that Christology provides the primary and quintessential warrant for such an argument, is whether the union of the human nature with the divine nature in Christ was an *accidental* union. If the argument we are making is opposed to some central christological concepts in the history of the church, then we may need to go back to the drawing board. We shall note two objections to the notion of an accidental union in Christ, and then seek to provide a response to those objections. Whether the response will vindicate our argument, the reader will have to judge.

In his elaboration of the hypostatic union of the two natures in the person of Christ, John Owen is concerned to note that this union was a "substantial" union, "because it was of two substances or essences in the same person, *in opposition unto all accidental union*, as 'the fullness of the Godhead dwelt in him bodily.' "[17] The notion of an "accidental union," which Owen rejects, may seem to be exactly what we are affirming when we speak of the Son of God taking on contingent properties. Surely, if those properties are contingent, then they are not essential to who he is (viz., the Son of God), and thus could be construed to be accidental.

Thomas Aquinas is even more specific. He objects to the idea of an accidental union of a human nature with the Son of God. Since we need not detail the entire argument here, we will pick out aspects of the argument that are specifically germane to our discussion.

The relevant question in Thomas is this: "Was human nature united to the Word in the manner of an accident?"[18] Thomas's answer is this:

> Whenever a predication is accidental, substance is not the predicate (*non praedicat aliquid*), but quantity, quality or some other modifier of the subject. If, then, human nature came to Christ in the manner of an accident, when we say that he is a man, we would not be predicating substance of him (*non praedicaretur aliquid*), but quantity, quality or some other accident.

17. John Owen, *The Works of John Owen*, ed. W. H. Gould (Edinburgh: Banner of Truth, 1977), 1:293, my emphasis.

18. Thomas Aquinas, *Summa Theologiae: Latin Text, English Translation, Introduction, Notes, Appendices and Glossary*, ed. Thomas Gilby (London and New York: Eyre & Spottiswoode and McGraw-Hill, 1964), 3.2.6: "Utrum humana natura fuerit unita Verbo Dei accidentaliter?"

In light of the objections of Aquinas and Owen (and others),[19] it is crucial for us to make some fine distinctions.

First, we should note that the way in which we are using the notion of "contingent" (and its possible synonym "accident") is with respect to those things which are *de re* necessary and those which are not. In other words, we are confining our use of those two concepts to our notion of essence relative to possible worlds. So, what is contingent or accidental, in this context, is something that is not necessary, that is, something that does not obtain at every possible world.

Second, and important for a proper understanding of Thomas and Owen, it was the metaphysics of Thomas (and of Owen as well in this case) that disallowed any notion of accidental union in Christ.[20] For Thomas there were only three modes of union available to him, given his metaphysical structure, and none of them was sufficient to describe the mode of union of the incarnation. The first mode of union would be a union in nature, wherein different component parts were united in one nature.[21] The second mode of union would be a combination of substantial form and the matter it configures to form one supposit.

The third mode of union, which is the one most relevant to our discussion, is the union of an accident with a supposit. Thomas rejects this option because, for him, a nature could not be an accident. A nature is, rather, in the case of a human being, a substantial form of a particular material thing. Because it was a human *nature* that Christ assumed, and not simply a combination of properties

19. Turretin, for example, argues against "accidents properly so called" in God such that God is essentially composed of parts. See Turretin, *Institutes*, 1:311–12. We are in full agreement with this statement, which is one reason why it is helpful to make the distinction of essential properties and covenantal properties.

20. The following material is taken from the discussions of Thomas's metaphysics of the incarnation in Eleonore Stump, "Aquinas' Metaphysics of the Incarnation," in *The Incarnation*, ed. Stephen T. Davis, Daniel Kendall, and Gerald O'Collins (Oxford: Oxford University Press, 2002), 197–218; and Eleonore Stump, *Aquinas* (New York: Routledge, 2003).

21. As Stump notes, "the collection of the species-conferring properties a thing has in virtue of having a substantial form of a certain sort is a 'nature.' A thing's nature is given by its substantial form." Stump, "Aquinas' Metaphysics of the Incarnation," 201.

(properties such as, "having brown hair," "being x inches tall," etc.), there can be no union of accidents with a person (supposit). The properties conferred on Christ by virtue of this union were all those properties that are essential to a human nature.

The objection to any kind of "accidental" union, therefore, takes its place, not in the context of what is ultimately necessary and what is merely possible, but rather in the context of a substance metaphysic, in which concepts such as "human nature" were thought to entail a substantial form.[22]

The Christology we have been delineating here is nothing new. Any cursory glance at the church's position on the hypostatic union will bring out these same basic points. Moreover, the position of the Chalcedonian Creed is ample evidence that much of theistic philosophy (not to mention so-called "open theism") needs a heavy dose of orthodox Christology. That creed reminds us that the incarnation has never been seen as God's abandoning any of his attributes. As a matter of fact, it is in the incarnation that we see supremely how God can relate to his creation without in any way changing his essential character or becoming less than God.

The creed affirms that the Son of God, as God, is to be "acknowledged in two natures inconfusedly [ἀσυγχύτως], unchangeably [ἀρέπτως], indivisibly [ἀδιαιρέτως], and inseparably [ἀχωρίστως]." It goes on to affirm, concerning this hypostatic union, that with regard to these two natures,

> the distinction of natures [is] by no means taken away by the union, but rather the property of each nature [is] preserved, and concurring in one Person and one Subsistence, not parted or divided into two persons, but one and the same Son, and only begotten, God the Word, the Lord Jesus Christ.

Generally speaking, it seems philosophers are wont to see the profound implications of this for their discussions of theism. If not

22. The conclusion to the matter of the *mode* of union in Christ, for Aquinas, is agnosticism. Stump notes: "So what does configure the components of the whole into one thing? Aquinas himself concedes that he has no answer to this question." Stump, *Aquinas*, 424.

arguing for atheism outright, many who want to maintain some kind of theism seem to fall prey to a kind of philosophical Eutychianism, in which there is no way that God can take on another nature until and unless he abandons (at least part of) his own essential nature.[23]

While there are careful distinctions here that must be maintained with respect to God (e.g., that God's essence is identical with

23. This might be a good place to note what has come to be called the *extra Calvinisticum*. Eventually in response to the Lutheran notion of ubiquity, the Reformed have maintained the historic (Chalcedonian) position with respect to Christology (thus, the "extra" in Christology seems to come, not from Calvin, but from Lutheran theology), that though the Son of God took on human nature, he is not thereby confined to that nature, nor does his human nature take on divine properties. He did not give up or otherwise "humanize," for example, his omnipresence when he assumed human nature. One quotation from Calvin summarizes the position well: "But some are carried away with such contentiousness as to say that because of the natures joined in Christ, wherever Christ's divinity is, there also is his flesh, which cannot be separated from it. As if that union had compounded from two natures some sort of intermediate being which was neither God nor man! So, indeed, did Eutyches teach, and Servetus after him. But from Scripture we plainly infer that the one person of Christ so consists of two natures that each nevertheless retains unimpaired its own distinctive character. And they will be ashamed to deny that Eutyches was rightly condemned. It is a wonder they do not heed the cause of his condemnation; removing the distinction between the natures and urging the unity of the person, he made man out of God and God out of man. What sort of madness, then, is it to mingle heaven with earth rather than give up trying to drag Christ's body from the heavenly sanctuary?

"They bring forward these passages for their side: 'No one has ascended into heaven but he who descended from heaven, the Son of man, who is in heaven'; and again: 'The Son, who is in the bosom of the Father, he has made him known.' It is equally senseless to despise the 'communication of properties,' a term long ago invented to some purpose by the holy fathers. Surely, when the Lord of glory is said to be crucified, Paul does not mean that he suffered anything in his divinity, but he says this because the same Christ, who was cast down and despised, and suffered in the flesh, was God and Lord of glory. In this way he was also Son of man in heaven, for the very same Christ, who, according to the flesh, dwelt as Son of man on earth, was God in heaven. In this manner, he is said to have descended to that place according to his divinity, not because divinity left heaven to hide itself in the prison house of the body, but because even though it filled all things, still in Christ's very humanity it dwelt bodily, that is, by nature, and in a certain ineffable way. There is a commonplace distinction of the schools to which I am not ashamed to refer: although the whole Christ is everywhere, still the whole of that which is in him is not everywhere. And would that the Schoolmen themselves had honestly weighed the force of this statement. For thus would the absurd fiction of Christ's carnal presence have been obviated." Calvin, *Institutes*, 4.17.30. For an excellent current discussion of the *extra Calvinisticum*, see Helm, *John Calvin's Ideas*, 58–92.

God himself), there is no question that what orthodox Christology has always taught is that God came down, in the second person of the Trinity, who is, was, and remains fully God, and he took on a human nature without thereby in any way changing his essential nature as God.[24] To think that, because God interacts with creation, he must necessarily change or in some way limit his essential deity, is in effect to fail to see the incarnation for what it is. It is to fail to see Christian theism for what it is. It is, we could say, to fail to see the most basic truth of Christianity as in any way relevant to philosophical discussions of theism.[25]

A truly Christian philosophy (and especially a truly Christian philosophy of religion) will take seriously the principle that God came down; while remaining who he is essentially, he condescended, in order first to create something other than himself and then to relate to that creation by taking on that which is and was in no way essential to him.

A Christian philosophy, based on a Christian theology, will have little connection to philosophies that seek to make problematic what is essential to the Christian religion. To reference just those examples we used above: Recall Drange's comment, "If the creation were accidental, then that in itself would imply that God is imperfect." It can readily be seen that such would only be the case if that which is in some way accidental or contingent is also

24. The fact that God the Son "came down" means that he took on covenantal properties, including properties relative to time. Though not denying this, Paul Helm's summary of Calvin on this point might be mildly uncomfortable with such a notion. Says Helm, "Perhaps Calvin's view amounts to this: in the Incarnation there is uniquely powerful and loving and gracious focusing of the divine nature upon human nature, rather than a transfer of the Son of God to a spatio-temporal location. This focusing makes it possible for us to say that God the Son is so present with human nature that there is a union of natures in Jesus Christ," Helm, *John Calvin's Ideas*, 64. Whatever the merits of Helm's description of Calvin here, it seems that Scripture is in no way hesitant to affirm that, in fact, the Son of God *did* come down to a spatio-temporal location. Not only so, but, though we should affirm that the incarnation is indeed a special presence of God, we should also be quick to affirm that the person of the Son of God united himself with human nature, in time, all the while remaining fully who he is.

25. Though we cannot comprehend just what it means for one person fully to possess two distinct natures, we must affirm it in order for the gospel, in its fullest biblical sense from Genesis to Revelation, to be what it is.

essential to God. We have seen that such is not the case. Nowhere in the history of orthodox theology is it held that creation, or *being* Creator, is essential to God. This, then, is a false problematic, and it exemplifies an ignorance of the rudimentary truths of Christian theology.

What about Stephen Davis's argument against God as eternal? Is it the case that the propositions, "God existed before Moses," "God's power will soon triumph over evil," "Last week God wrought a miracle," and "God will always be wiser than human beings" are all "either meaningless or necessarily false"? Not if the basic truth of Christian theology is granted: that God condescended climactically in Christ. While remaining the "I AM," God, at the point of creation and beyond (culminating in the incarnation), took on (nonessential) properties (including, if we agree with Thomas, a *nature*) that were a part of his covenant contract with creation generally and with his people more specifically.

Given God's condescension, given that, *in* God, the *Eimi* (as essential)/*eikon* (as nonessential) union/duality is present, the scenario that Davis articulates is perfectly natural:

> He makes plans. He responds to what human beings do, e.g. their evil deeds or their acts of repentance. He seems to have temporal location and extension. The Bible does not hesitate to speak of God's years and days. . . . And God seems to act in temporal sequences—first he rescues the children of Israel from Egypt and later he gives them the Law.

All of this God does, because he has first come down, adding to himself such properties as are not and were not essential to who he is, and which do not in any way require a change in his essential nature.

With respect to impassibility as discussed earlier, the situation becomes a bit more complex. Creel is certainly right that God's nature is impassible. Given our definition of impassibility above, God is not essentially moved by something independent of, or external to, himself.

But what about the will of God? We will remember that Creel wants to argue for an impassible will of God, but in order to grant such a thing, he is forced (1) to index God's will to contingencies only and (2) to invent the notion of a plenum in order to account for passive possibilities' (which do not inhere in God) becoming actualities.

It seems, however, that if we understand God to have two sets of properties—those essential to him, and others that are "covenantal"—then there is no need to slight the essential properties in order to account for the covenantal.[26] Just what are these properties that are not essential to God?

Covenant Properties

If we think, for example, of the will of God, we immediately realize that important distinctions must be made.[27] Surely, as a personal being, God wills. Scripture tells us that he does choose and decide; he makes promises and determinations.[28] Such things could not be possible without a will. But how can a necessary being, one whose essential nature is immutably what it is, will something that is contingent? If God's will is a property of his essential nature, must it not also be necessary?

This problem can be addressed if we think again about the distinction made concerning God's own properties. Given the status of the *Eimi/eikon* metaphysical structure, we distinguish God's will according to its object or its referent. Hence, Turretin:

> God wills himself necessarily, not only by a hypothetical necessity but also by an absolute necessity. He is the ultimate end and

26. That is, God *can* contain passive potentialities, but only on the suppositions (1) that such potentialities are not essential to him and (2) that such potentialities are covenantally qualified, that is, qualified in terms of God's taking on covenantal properties by virtue of his divine condescension.

27. This is another one of those subjects taken up by many philosophers, though from the perspective of theology they seem to be woefully ill-prepared for such a discussion. Any cursory glance at the history of theology shows careful and helpful distinctions made with respect to God's will, distinctions that seem for the most part to be ignored in philosophical discussions about God.

28. See, for example, Deut. 12:5; Acts 18:21; Ps. 147:4; Prov. 16:33; Josh. 21:45.

the highest good which he cannot but will and love, not only as to specification (that he can will and love nothing contrary), but also as to exercise (that he never ceases from willing and loving himself), for he cannot nill his own glory or deny himself.[29]

When the object of God's will is himself, it is in fact, like him, absolutely necessary.[30] God cannot deny himself because, as God, he is not "free" to change his essential nature.[31] On the other hand, when the object of God's will is *other* than himself (i.e., creation), then his will is free to do whatever seems best to him, whatever he decides to do.

But how are we to construe this "free will" of God that is at one and the same time a property of his? How can such a property have contingency embedded within it? Here Owen's explanation is helpful. While this free will of God "naturally and eternally resides in God," it is also the case that it is a relative property with respect to its "egress and exercise."

To put it in terms of our distinction, the free will of God should be seen as a covenantal attribute, extending as it does from his essential attributes. Given that, in this case, it is a decision God makes with respect to objects, or things, or existences outside of him, God's free will is directed covenantally; it is a decision entailing condescension. In that sense, we could say, God "takes on" something else, some other properties, when he determines to will something that is not him. His consideration of "something else"

29. Turretin, *Institutes*, 1:219. Turretin is following Aquinas here. See Thomas Aquinas, *On the Truth of the Catholic Faith: Summa Contra Gentiles* (Garden City, N. Y.: Hanover House, 1955), 1.19.3.

30. This is in direct conflict with Karl Barth's notion of God's will, in which freedom is primary, to the extent that God even chooses his own nature. Aside from the fact that there is no scriptural support for such an idea, the history of orthodox theology stands steadfastly against it.

31. Muller notes that, contra Arminianism, a Reformed notion of freedom is "the faculty of doing what one wills." While Arminians, and, we could say, virtually all philosophers who deal with theism, think that God's freedom, to be freedom, must be completely and totally unconstrained, the historic Reformed position is that, like his essential properties, God's freedom is unconstrained by anything but himself. God's freedom is not "the ability to do or not do what is necessary, rooted in a fundamental indeterminacy." See Muller, *The Divine Essence and Attributes*, 447.

(i.e., creation) is *itself* a condescension (as is his knowledge of possibilities that he did not actualize).

How could it be otherwise? Given that there are two and only two kinds of existence—God's and creation's—anything that God *does* with respect to creation is, by definition, a "coming down" from the majestic heights of his own independent and immutable deity, without in any way compromising that deity.[32]

Those things in God, those properties or attributes, which have to do with creation, therefore, partake *both* of the *Eimi and* of the *eikon*; they are, as Owen notes, naturally and eternally *in* God, but, with regard to their egress and exercise, they are relative, not in any way essential; they are potential, possible states of affairs.

Does this mean that there are potentialities in God, the one who is *actus purus*? This, we will remember, was Creel's conundrum. The conundrum can, at least in part, be addressed when we recognize that God, in determining to covenant with creation, made that creation an object of his will. In so doing, he condescended. He came down to the level of that creation, without losing anything of his essence, in order to establish the covenant by way of creation. Thus, it is not the case that God cannot himself "contain" passive potentialities. He can, and does "contain" those potentialities as a covenant God, as a God who makes the object of his will something other than himself.[33]

Once God wills what he wills, as Aquinas and others affirm, there is a necessity inherent in it. Once God determines to create what he creates, inherent in creation is a "hypothetical necessity" in which God, having decided what he will do, will not change his will with respect to what he will do.

32. This is perhaps the primary difference between Arminian and Reformed theology (and, likely, philosophy as well). While Arminian theology wants to affirm the possibility (and actuality) of God's denial of (at least part of) his essence, Reformed theology does not. It would seem, however, that once one acknowledges the reality of the *Eimi/eikon*, climactically brought together in the person of Christ, the biblical and theological warrant for such a denial is gone.

33. The relationship of God's knowledge to his will, and of his knowledge of himself to his knowledge of creation, is complex. The only point to be stressed here is that, once the object of God's *will* is anything other than himself, there is, *because inherent in the act*, a condescension on God's part.

Hence, since God's goodness subsists and is complete independently of other things, and they add no fulfilment to him, there is no absolute need for him to will them. However, there is an hypothetical necessity here, for on the supposition that he does will a thing it cannot be unwilled, since his will is immutable.[34]

This will, which Thomas argues cannot change, is God's free will, a will that, prior to its determination, was under no constraint one way or the other with respect to its object.[35]

One final word with respect to God's covenantal, condescending character. We should remember the *analogia revelationis* (chapter 6) whenever we think about God's relationship to creation. This analogy seeks to affirm that *everything* that we have from God as revelation is, *ipso facto*, accommodated to us.[36] It is sometimes said that, for example, when Scripture speaks of God's changing his mind, we are to read that anthropomorphically, that is, as God's simply speaking according to our way of

34. Aquinas, *Summa Theologiae*, 1.19.3.

35. There are knotty problems here concerning possibility, potentiality, God's will and its relationship to creation. Without attempting to address those problems in detail, a couple of things seem obvious. First, there is no necessary connection between God's essential character and his decision to create; that decision was a free decision. It was a decision that presupposes God's condescension such that contingent properties were assumed by God. It was a decision, therefore, of which we can speak only in temporal terms. God's essential properties, identical with him, are atemporal. His contingent properties are not, but are presupposed by the fact of creation itself. His decision to create was free because it was not constrained by his essential character (nor did it conflict with that character) in that it was not necessary. Once he did decide and did create, other possibilities, while remaining possible perhaps in the abstract, became impossible with respect to God's will and action. Thus, as we will see again in the next chapter, there is something to James Ross's contention that actuality is not something that is added to possibility. Prior to creation, possibility, impossibility, and necessity were simply nonexistent (in a covenantal sense; they may have existed in God, but would have then been identical to him in some way). Thus, says Ross, "God creates the kinds, the natures of things, along with things. And he settles what-might-have-been insofar as it is a consequence of what exists." James F. Ross, "God, Creator of Kinds and Possibilities: Requiescant Universalia Ante Res," in *Rationality, Religious Belief, and Moral Commitment*, ed. Robert Audi, William J. Wainwright (Ithaca, NY: Cornell University Press, 1986), 319.

36. That is, the analogy is between revelation as it exists in God, on the one hand, and as it is revealed to us, on the other. In this way, we see revelation, as we said in chapter 4, as *interpretation*.

understanding. Along with this we are told that when Scripture says that God is not a man that he should change his mind, we are to read that "literally."

It could perhaps be more helpful if we were to begin to see that *all* of God's revelation to us is anthropomorphic. It is, then, essentially accommodated revelation; it is revelation accommodated to our mode of being and our mode of understanding. It is not, therefore, that God's revelation is accommodated to us when it speaks, say, of God's eyes or his arm or his repentance, while it is not accommodated to us when it speaks of his eternity. One quotation from Calvin may help us see the matter more clearly:

> What, therefore, does the word "repentance" mean? Surely its meaning is like that of all other modes of speaking that describe God for us in human terms. For because our weakness does not attain to his exalted state, the description of him that is given to us must be accommodated to our capacity so that we may understand it. Now the mode of accommodation is for him to represent himself to us not as he is in himself, but as he seems to us. Although he is beyond all disturbance of mind, yet he testifies that he is angry toward sinners.[37]

While there can be no question that there are truths given to us in God's revelation that point to his essential character, and others that point to his covenantal character, we should be careful to note that those covenantal attributes of God's are no less "literal" than are his essential attributes. God's repentance, then, is not simply something that "seems to us" like repentance. It is *literal* repentance, he is (covenantally) changing directions because of his faithfulness to his covenant. But it is repentance of a condescended, covenant God who has come down, taking on the form of a creature, in order to glorify himself, and it is repentance that does not in any way sacrifice, undermine, or otherwise alter his

37. Calvin, *Institutes*, 1.17.13. This way of thinking was common among the Reformed. Note, for example, Muller's analysis of Daneau's distinction between God's essential attributes and those others which were spoken of figuratively or anthropopathically, in Muller, *The Divine Essence and Attributes*, 215f.

essential character as *a se*. He repents, all the while remaining the eternal, immutable "I AM."

We can think of it this way. Once the second person of the Trinity took on a human nature (as he did in history), was that nature "literal" or something that represented to us a certain way, a way of "seeming"? Of course, to think that Christ's human nature is something that only seems human to us is to fall prey to the historical heresy of docetism. His human nature is something that he *literally* has (and is central to, though not exhaustive of, who he *is*); it is what he took on in order to accommodate himself to us. Having taken that nature, Christ experienced the limits of the created world. He got hungry and tired; he was moved to act; he was only in a particular place at one time.

So it is true of this one who is *Eimi/eikon* in one person that he was limited, thus was subject to the limitations of (his own) creation. But it is also true that he alone had the power to calm the winds and the seas (Mark 4:35–41). He experienced the limits of this world, but he was sovereign and powerful over it as well. This is the case because the One who is and remains essentially God at the same time condescends, covenantally, to accommodate himself to us, to become one of us, in order to fulfill his perfect plan.

Conclusion

It should go without saying that the centrality and reality of the Christian faith ought to play a central role in Christian thinking, and especially Christian thinking about God and his relationship to his creation. *The* crucial truth of the faith is that God has come, climactically in Christ. God has accommodated himself to his creation—really and truly (not seemingly and metaphorically)—without in any way compromising or denying who he essentially is.

It may be that this truth will require theology, philosophy, and especially philosophy of religion, to give due weight to the mystery of God. Though argumentation for God's character can be, and is, profound and complex at times, we may need to realize that arguments concerning exactly *how*, for example, the Son of God can be one person who is both created and uncreated, sovereign and limited in power, *a se* and hungry, may never be forthcoming.[38] The incarnation teaches us that God can *be* in ways that simply are not readily conducive to intellectually satisfying argumentation. The fact, for example, that God can remain eternal while at the same time interacting with his creation on a day-to-day basis does not always make for good philosophical fodder. It does, however, (if we are correct here) make for the truth of the matter, and we would be hard pressed to want anything less from our theological and philosophical meanderings.[39]

But what does the truth of God's *Eimi/eikon* character (pre-eminently in Christ) teach us about, say, the problem of sin and evil in our world?

---

38. Though how we may articulate such things will be discussed below.

39. Note, in this regard, Owen, *Works*, 1:293: "That the same person should be 'the mighty God' and a 'child born,' is neither conceivable nor possible, nor can be true, but by the union of the divine and human natures in the same person. So he said of himself, 'Before Abraham was, I am,' John 8:58. That he, the same person who then spake unto the Jews, and as a man was little more than thirty years of age, should also be before Abraham, undeniably confirms the union of another nature, in the same person with that wherein he spoke those words, and without which they could not be true. He had not only another nature which did exist before Abraham, but the same individual person who then spoke in the human nature did then exist. This union the ancient church affirmed to be made . . . , without any change in the person of the Son of God, which the divine nature is not subject unto;— . . . with a distinction of natures, but 'without any division' of them by separate subsistences;— . . . 'without mixture' or confusion;—. . . 'without separation' or distance; and . . . 'substantially,' because it was of two substances or essences in the same person, in opposition unto all accidental union, as the 'fullness of the Godhead dwelt in him bodily.' "

Implication and Application

13

Calvinizing Evil

The new goddess contingency could not be erected until the God of heaven was utterly despoiled of his dominion over the sons of men, and in the room thereof a home-bred idol of self-sufficiency set up, and the world persuaded to worship it. But that the building climb no higher, let all men observe how the word of God overthrows this Babylonian tower. —JOHN OWEN

The fact that God himself takes on covenantal properties, properties that are not essential to him, but that nevertheless serve to characterize him, is the central focus of the good news of Scripture. It defines *the* good news for us—the news that God has come in the flesh and has, as God in the flesh, accomplished salvation for sinners. This is the preeminent truth of Scripture. It *is* the covenant, and it defines what we mean by covenant. In creating, God has "come down"; he has taken on that which is foreign to his essential being in order to relate to that which is essentially different from him. It is in the light of this truth, that we should begin to evaluate the problems that are standard fare in philosophical discussions of theism.

Before proceeding to the task at hand, it may be helpful to

remember Paul's argument in this regard in Colossians 2. His concern is that (some of) the Colossian Christians have been duped by "plausible arguments" (v. 4). They are in danger of being captivated by a philosophy that is empty, deceitful, and lost in the darkness of mere human tradition rather than thriving in the light of Christ. In Paul's own words, they are to watch out (or to see to it) that they are not taken in by "philosophy and empty deceit, according to human tradition" (v. 8). They are, rather, to walk in Christ, even as they have received him (v. 6). The reason that Paul gives for this command, even as he issues this warning, is deep and rich enough to occupy us for a lifetime; it is this: "for in him the whole fullness of deity dwells bodily" (v. 9).

One of the initial points to be made here is that our understanding of God is to be guided, directed, formed, and fashioned by who Christ is. The reason, therefore, that we are not to be "delude[d] . . . with plausible arguments" (v. 4) is that "all the treasures of wisdom and knowledge" (v. 3) are found only in Christ.

Paul's overall concern for the Colossians is that they walk in a manner worthy of the gospel. He is not, in this epistle, delineating an abstract Christology. As Calvin notes, "Paul does not speak of an imaginary Christ, but of a Christ preached, who has revealed himself by express doctrine."[1] This Christ is revealed. As revealed, he tells us something—something crucial and necessary for us to understand—about who God is. And though Paul's general concern is the reality of the gospel in the lives of those whose trust is in Christ, he is explicit about the fact that it is in our understanding of the person of Christ that we begin to see the deceitfulness of arguments that proceed, though perhaps plausibly, without such an understanding. Since all the treasures of wisdom and knowledge are in Christ, those treasures are inaccessible apart from him. To attempt to find wisdom and knowledge without Christ is a vain and fruitless exercise.[2]

---

1. Commentary on Col. 2:9 in John Calvin, *The Comprehensive John Calvin Collection*, CD-ROM (The Ages Digital Library System, 2002).

2. The Old Testament equivalent of this principle can be found, for example, in Prov. 1:7, "The fear of the LORD is the beginning of knowledge; fools despise wisdom and instruction."

One will search in vain, however, for a philosophical theology, a philosophy of religion, or a theistic philosophy that takes seriously the reality of Christ as the quintessential revelation of God, and thus as the climactic and central means (as revealed to us now in God's Word) by which we can know God. The reasons for this seem to be primarily two. First, as we have seen, there is a (mostly) unwritten bias against the use of or appeal to Scripture for any kind of philosophical endeavor. Since philosophy's task is assumed to have its focus in our capacity as human beings to think and reason, and in the tools available to us for such reasoning, the use of Scripture, it is thought, illegitimately smuggles in a "religious" authority that automatically excludes certain ideas and concepts (e.g., those of Muslims and of atheists) from the discussion. The second reason is like unto the first. The use of Scripture is automatically *exclusive*; it has the effect of narrowing the philosophical task in such a way that prejudices the discussion at the outset.

By way of (brief) response, we should note, first of all, that the use of Scripture, as a central component of the knowledge had by Christians, can only be excluded as a legitimate source of knowledge (and especially knowledge of God) at the Christian's (including the Christian philosopher's) peril. Every philosophical position must rely on some outside source(s) of authority; a Christian philosophy must rely on God's revelation of himself in his Word. Second, it is just the exclusivity of Christianity that is supposed to be (in part), not a reason for avoiding its use, but the motivation behind the communication of biblical truth. We tell others who are outside of Christ about him so that, by God's Holy Spirit, they might repent and believe. If it were the case, as some (e.g., John Hick) would hold, that Christianity is meant to be *all*-inclusive, then there would be little need for the communication of biblical truth. Because, however, orthodox Christianity has always held that there is no salvation outside of Christ, we speak of him and teach him and preach him, for it is by that very communication that God is pleased to bring some to himself. A Christian philosophy, in this context, is simply another way in which we might attempt to set forth the truth as it is found in Christ.

It should now be clear that one of the best ways for a Christian to think about things metaphysical is to begin with the *Eimi/eikon* distinction. Given this distinction, we would do well to divide our thinking, and the categories of our thinking, into two. So, for example, when we say that, God exists, on the one hand, and we exist, on the other, we should understand two very different modes of existence, each applied to the objects of existence in different ways, according to the nature of those objects. God's existence is *a se*, it is *Eimi*; our existence is eikonic, it is an image, dependent, limited, finite, and (since the fall) marred by sin. There is not one existence exemplified in two different ways; there are, rather, two different existences—God's and creation's.

Given God's revelation to us, therefore, we should see that those things which pertain to God and to us—goodness, for example—presuppose a relationship to God as "I AM," in the first place, and then a relationship to things created after that. In that sense, they should be seen as two *essentially* different properties, yet connected by God's condescending revelation to us.

The Crying Need

Perhaps nowhere in philosophical discussions is the need for a specifically Christian philosophy more evident than in discussions that have to do with the assumed incompatibility between the existence of the triune God and the existence of evil in this world. The challenge that comes to Christianity, in light of this incompatibility, must be taken with all seriousness and addressed. This, it seems to me, is the apologetic task *in excelsus*; it is *the* premier challenge to Christianity. It is a challenge that comes most often from those wanting to show Christianity to be false. It is a challenge that, at least *prima facie*, takes seriously much of what we believe about God and much of what we experience in this world. A response to this challenge, therefore, cannot be set aside; it must be careful and biblical.[3]

---

3. To be clear here, some have wanted to respond to the problem of evil by intimating that, since atheists believe there is no god, they have no standard for good or evil. Therefore, they cannot pose the challenge themselves because they have no standard by which to judge what is evil and what is good. This kind of response, however, confuses the issue and has a ring of disingenuousness to it. The problem of evil is a

But just what *is* the problem, and how should we respond to it?[4]

We need first to look at the problem of evil in the context of its most erudite philosophical response in order afterward to show the implications and application of a Christian philosophical apologetic to one of the most pressing concerns for Christian theism.

Alvinizing Evil[5]

There is little dispute that the most extended, sophisticated, and (in some ways) effective[6] argument for the logical compatibility of God's existence and the existence of evil is that offered by Alvin

---

problem, first and foremost, of theists, and a problem fundamentally of Christianity (since only Christian theism is *true* theism). It is a problem because of what we know of the character of the Christian God, as revealed to us in Scripture, and the real and virtually relentless presence of sin and evil. We should not, therefore, simply dismiss the challenge as illegitimate. It is a legitimate challenge; and it is a decidedly *Christian* problem.

4. There are numerous ways to articulate the problem of evil and numerous ways to begin to respond to it. Because of the specifically philosophical concern of this chapter, we will work within that context. We should realize, however, that it is not the only, and not the most pressing, context within which to work on this problem. The best expositions of this problem, it seems, are found in the area of theology. See, for example, John Calvin, *Institutes of the Christian Religion*, ed. John T. McNeill, trans. Ford Lewis Battles, Library of Christian Classics (London: SCM, 1960), 1.16–18; and Francis Turretin, *Institutes of Elenctic Theology*, ed. James T. Dennison Jr., trans. George Musgrave Giger, 3 vols. (Phillipsburg, NJ: P&R, 1992–97), 1:515, 538.

5. It was Daniel Dennett who coined the verb *alvinize* (taken from *Alvin* Plantinga), defined as, "to stimulate protracted discussion by making a bizarre claim." It should be said at the outset that Plantinga recognizes the all-important truth that the logical problem of evil does not go to the heart of what many recognize to be the *real* problem of evil. Says Plantinga, "The chief difference between Christianity and the other theistic religions lies just here: the God of Christianity is willing to enter into and share the sufferings of his creatures, in order to redeem them and his world. Of course this doesn't answer the question *why does God permit evil?* But it helps the Christian trust God as a loving father, no matter what ills befall him." James E. Tomberlin and Peter van Inwagen, eds., *Alvin Plantinga* (Dordrecht: D. Reidel, 1985), 36. This is admirable and unique in that few theistic philosophers have acknowledged as much. We would like to think that the solution to the problem of evil as it is found in Christ pertains to the logical problem as well.

6. So effective that Robert Adams notes, "I think it is fair to say that Plantinga has solved this problem." Robert Merrihew Adams, "Plantinga on the Problem of Evil," in ibid., 226.

Plantinga.[7] In his "Free Will Defense" (hereafter FWD), Plantinga attempts to show just how it is possible that both God and evil can exist in the same world. Plantinga's most extended treatment of the problem is found in his work, *The Nature of Necessity*.[8] We will work through his argument, in the first place, and then make application of our previous discussions in order, then, to attempt a Reformed Free Will Defense (RFWD).

The reader should be warned: There is no easy way through Plantinga's discussion on this matter. (Readers not interested in the technicalities of philosophical discussion in this context may want to skip to the next section. The fundamental points to be made in the argumentation below is that, because Plantinga holds to libertarian freedom, there are possible worlds that God cannot actualize, among which might be all the worlds in which Adam and Eve refrain from eating the forbidden fruit). Because he seeks to work out the *possibility* of the compatible coexistence of God and evil, he turns to (one of) his favorite tool for such discussions—possible-worlds semantics.

The problem itself is set out by Plantinga in two propositions:

(1) God is omniscient, omnipotent, and wholly good.

and,

(3) There is evil.[9]

---

7. We're thinking here of the so-called logical problem of evil. The other primary context in which the problem of evil is discussed is called the evidential or probabilistic problem of evil. Though Plantinga deals with that as well, we will not deal with it here. It should be noted that Plantinga's latest attempt to formulate a satisfactory view of the problem of evil is more explicitly Christian in that it incorporates the notion of Christ's atonement. See Alvin Plantinga, "Supralapsarianism, or 'O Felix Culpa,' " in *Christian Faith and the Problem of Evil*, ed. Peter van Inwagen (Grand Rapids, MI: Eerdmans, 2004), 1–25. Plantinga's basic point is that a world that includes atonement and reconciliation is better than a world in which people always remain good.

8. Although my discussion below will be heavily dependent on Plantinga's (and Sennett's, see below), some of the material he includes will need to be passed over. For his complete analysis of the matter, see Plantinga, *The Nature of Necessity*, Clarendon Library of Logic and Philosophy (Oxford: Clarendon Press, 1974), 164–95, and Tomberlin and van Inwagen, eds., *Alvin Plantinga*, 25–55, 371–82.

9. My numbering throughout. The number (2) is absent here for reasons that will become clear below.

In order to work through the possible compatibility of these two propositions, four initial points need to be kept in mind. First, Plantinga gives a helpful description of the difference between a defense and a theodicy. A theodicy attempts to answer the question of *why* with respect to evil. In its etymological sense, it attempts to "justify God" given the presence of evil in the world that he has made. A defense, however, is not as ambitious as that. In a defense, the goal is to stave off an objection or objections that are lodged against a particular position. In his FWD, Plantinga is attempting a *defense*, not a theodicy. Thus his goal is simply to hold the objector at bay, diffusing his objection, so that the objection itself loses its punch.

Second, as Plantinga notes, there is no logical contradiction between (1) and (3). The logical problem of evil, then, is not really a logical problem per se, but rather a problem of the consistency or compatibility of the two propositions. So, says Plantinga, the one who objects to the compatibility of the two propositions means, not that there is a contradiction, but "that the conjunction of these two propositions is necessarily false, false in every possible world."[10]

But in order to show *that*, one must produce a proposition that is plausible and necessary, and, in conjunction with (1) and (3), produces a contradiction. No such proposition has been forthcoming. So at this point in the discussion the objector is left with an intuitive sense of dis-ease with respect to the two propositions.

Third, as was said, the objector must hold that the conjunction of (1) and (3) is *necessarily* false. This is because, if the conjunction of (1) and (3) is only *possibly* false, then it could be *possibly* true, as well, such that the charge of incompatibility could not stick. That is, because the objector, in order to maintain incompatibility, is tied to a *necessary* incompatibility, all that needs to be shown (in a defense) is that the perceived incompatibility is not necessary at all; it is, at worst, only possible. And a possible incompatibility is no strong objection to any view.[11]

10. Plantinga, *The Nature of Necessity*, 165.

11. To say that a view is possibly incompatible is to say, in effect (given that the propositions are not necessarily true), that there is a possible world in which the propositions in view cannot both be true. But, if such is the case, there is a possible world in which

Fourth, and this will prove to be the most important point in our response, in order to set forth the FWD, a notion of freedom typically dubbed "libertarian" must be assumed, and assumed to be true. Libertarian freedom is such that no external conditions or laws determine which action one performs.

> More broadly, if I am free with respect to an action *A*, then God does not *bring it about* or *cause it to be the case* either that I take or that I refrain from this action; he neither causes this to be so through the laws he establishes, nor by direct intervention, nor in any other way.[12]

Libertarian freedom is freedom that is autonomous, literally. It is a law unto itself; God has nothing to do with it (other than choosing to make it a part of who we are), and there is nothing external to it that constrains it in any way. Unless this is understood throughout the argument, the argument itself cannot be understood.

Now to the defense. In order to defend the possible compatibility of (1) and (3), all that is needed is a proposition, (2), that is consistent with (1) and that entails (3).[13] If such a proposition can be found, then it is thereby false that (1) and (3) are necessarily incompatible. Plantinga sets out, therefore, to find (2).

There are two key ideas related to the notion of possible worlds that together form the foundation for Plantinga's development of the FWD.[14] The first idea is Leibniz's notion that the world we live in is the best of all possible worlds.[15] The second idea is Mackie's notion that God, since he is omnipotent, could have created a world

---

the propositions in view are both true, and thus the perceived incompatibility is simply a contingent property at a given world.

12. Plantinga, *The Nature of Necessity*, 171.

13. More formally, as Plantinga notes, a generic defense would look like this: $(\Diamond(P\&R) \& ((P\&R)\to Q)\to \Diamond(P\&Q))$.

14. Here I am borrowing from James F. Sennett, *Modality, Probability, and Rationality: A Critical Examination of Alvin Plantinga's Philosophy* (New York: Peter Lang, 1992), 49–79. His chapter is, in my view, the best analysis available of Plantinga's FWD.

15. See Gottfried Wilhelm Leibniz and Austin Marsden Farrer, *Theodicy: Essays on the Goodness of God, the Freedom of Man, and the Origin of Evil* (London: Routledge & K. Paul, 1952).

wherein every human being does only good. In seeking to counter these two positions, Plantinga formulates his FWD.

The first project that faces the FWD is an analysis of the notion that this world is the best of all possible worlds. Leibniz, holding to the omnipotence of God, argued that, because of that omnipotence, God could actualize any world he wanted. In choosing to actualize this world, given omnipotence, God must have chosen the best of all possible worlds. The basic thrust of this argument is also a central contention of any atheological argument from evil.[16] If it is the case, an atheologian would say, as Leibniz wants to maintain, that God is omnipotent and thus could have created any possible world at all, then the fact that there is (so much) evil in the world disproves the notion of an omnipotent God. Plantinga sees flaws in this contention and therefore argues against Leibniz (and, more importantly, against the atheologian) that there are a number (perhaps an infinite number) of worlds that God could not create. How would such an argument proceed?

Plantinga ponders the possibility of a world, *W*, in which, just to use one example, Curley freely takes a bribe, and another world, *W**, in which he does not. Before looking at the argument's details, we should have before us Plantinga's summary of his disagreement with Leibniz, and with any atheological argument that agrees with (at least this point of) Leibniz:

> There are possible worlds such that it is partly up to Curley whether or not God can actualize them. It is of course up to God whether or not to create Curley, and also up to God whether or not to make him free with respect to the action of taking the bribe. . . . But if he creates him, and creates him free with respect to this action, then whether or not he takes it is up to Curley—not God.[17]

16. An atheological argument is one that seeks to conclude for the nonexistence of God. Leibniz is not in agreement with atheologians at this point. As Sennett remind us, "One person's *Modus Ponens* is another's *Modus Tolens.*" Sennett, *Modality, Probability, and Rationality*, 54. Thus, while Leibniz wanted to argue *for* this world's being the best possible, the atheologian wants to conclude *against* the existence of God, since this world is so horribly evil, and God, if he existed, would have, since he could have, done better.

17. Plantinga, *The Nature of Necessity*, 184.

In order to see why the argument must conclude in this way, two other distinctions are needed. First is a distinction calculated to allow for the fact that God, who is the Creator, is nevertheless unable to actualize certain states of affairs. This distinction, then, is between what God might create, and what he might actualize. The proposition, (a) "God creates the world" is true, but it is not equivalent to the proposition, (b) "God actualizes all states of affairs in the world." Second, a distinction is made between *strong* actualization and *weak* actualization.

> In the strong sense, God can actualize only what he can *cause* to be actual; in that sense he cannot actualize any state of affairs including the existence of creatures who freely take some action or other.[18]

Weak actualization, however, requires some other condition if that which is to be actualized obtains. When God, for example, strongly actualizes *x*, *x* obtains by virtue of that action alone. When God weakly actualizes *x*, *x* can only obtain if something else conspires with God to bring about *x*. When discussing possible worlds within a libertarian context, God cannot strongly actualize any possible world in which there are free creatures. To do so would deny that freedom. God can strongly actualize *states of affairs* within possible worlds, but he cannot strongly actualize any state of affairs that would have "S does *x* freely" as its conjunct.

With respect to Plantinga's illustration of Curley, it is possible that God cannot strongly actualize a state of affairs in which Curley freely takes a bribe. To actualize such a state of affairs would mean that Curley would not have taken the bribe *freely*. While we may affirm that God indeed created the world, that is a different thing from affirming that God brings about every state of affairs included in the world. He cannot strongly actualize states of affairs in which free creatures make their decisions freely.

Suppose, therefore, that there is a possible world, W, in which Curley freely takes a bribe. The question that the Free Will Defender will pose is whether or not God could actualize such a world, W. If,

18. Ibid., 173.

by actualize, we mean strongly actualize such that God brings about *W* and the state of affairs of Curley's freely taking a bribe, the answer given in the FWD is no. God could not strongly actualize such a world because to do so would violate Curley's freedom. Conversely, God could not strongly actualize a possible world in which Curley freely rejects the bribe either, and for the same reason.

This, then, would cast serious doubt on Leibniz's contention (Plantinga calls it Leibniz's Lapse), and the contention of atheological arguments from evil. If there are possible worlds that God could not strongly actualize, then it is entirely possible that this is not the best of all possible worlds (contra Leibniz), and it is no refutation of God's existence that this world contains so much evil; perhaps it was just not within God's power (once he decided to create, to create Curley, and to create Curley free) to actualize the best of all possible worlds.

So, Plantinga offers as proposition (2) the following:

(2) God is omnipotent and it was not within his power to create a world containing moral good but no moral evil.[19]

But as we can see from (2) this does not end the matter. All that has been shown thus far is that God cannot strongly actualize just any possible world.

What has not been shown yet is that God cannot actualize a world that is only morally good. This contention is a rejoinder to the FWD so far construed. Even if God cannot actualize *every* possible world, it might be said, surely he could have actualized a world in which there is no moral evil, but only moral goodness. Plantinga's response? "Perhaps, but perhaps not."

In order to answer the question of whether or not God could actualize a world that is only morally good, Plantinga introduces the notion of "transworld depravity." Transworld depravity is not an intuitive idea; it is difficult to understand, for a variety of reasons. The summary

19. Ibid., 184, my numbering. We should remember that (2) must be consistent with (1) and entail (3). In this case, both conditions are satisfied. We must also note here that (2) need not be a plausible proposition. For the argument to succeed, plausibility is irrelevant. All that is needed is that (2) be possible.

of it that we will give here will avoid the bulk of the fine print while seeking to capture the primary principles behind the idea.

In order to get straight what transworld depravity is, we must concede two further points.[20] First, we must assume that there are counterfactuals of freedom and they can have a truth-value. Counterfactuals of freedom are conditions contrary to fact containing in their consequents the predication of a free action performed by an agent. A distinction is to be made between genuine counterfactuals of freedom and subjunctive conditionals. For a counterfactual of freedom to be genuine, the falsity of the antecedent must be assumed. This is not the case in subjunctive conditionals.[21] Furthermore, it must be the case that some counterfactuals of freedom are true. If this is not the case, then the counterfactual

(CFF) If God had actualized a possible world, *W*, then Adam and Eve would have remained morally perfect

would have no truth-value and there would be no need, therefore, for the notion of transworld depravity. In order for CFF to succeed, and thus for the rejoinder to the FWD to hold, it must at least be assumed that at least some counterfactuals of freedom are true.[22] Second, we must assume that all propositions of the form

20. I say "further points" because we have already conceded, as a part of the argument, the notion of libertarian freedom, with its implication of strong and weak actualization. Presupposed in this discussion of transworld depravity, though not essential for understanding it, is the notion of transworld *identity*. According to van Inwagen: "One will see that 'transworld identity' is just good, old-fashioned numerical identity, the relation that Tully bears to Cicero, 2 + 2 bears to 4, and heat (they say) bears to molecular motion. The proponent of 'trans-world identity,' one will come to see, does not say that Socrates must somehow be identical, in some novel and difficult sense of 'identical' that philosophers are going to have to work hard to spell out, with something (else?) having a different set of properties. On the contrary, the proponent of trans-world identity—the philosopher who believes that objects can exist in more than one world—holds that there is only one Socrates, wise and snub-nosed and all the rest, and that he is identical with himself (who else?) and has just the properties he has (what others?)." Peter van Inwagen, *Ontology, Identity, and Modality: Essays in Metaphysics* (Cambridge: Cambridge University Press, 2001), 202.

21. This point is taken from James F. Sennett, "Why Think There Are Any True Counterfactuals of Freedom?" *Philosophy of Religion* 32 (1992): 106.

22. Whether counterfactuals in fact *can be* true is still a matter of debate. Sennett, in ibid., takes his cue from Robert Merrihew Adams, "Middle Knowledge and the Problem

(TD) A person, S, has transworld depravity

is a contingent state of affairs. There is no necessity attached to the idea of transworld depravity such that "S has transworld depravity" obtains in every possible world.

So just what is transworld depravity? It is an implication of the situation entailed by the fact that there are some worlds that God cannot weakly actualize. If there are some worlds that God cannot actualize, it is certainly possible that at least some of those worlds contain propositions of the form

(AENE) Adam and Eve refrained from eating the forbidden fruit,

and thus are worlds in which God cannot actualize and in which there is only good.

The argument is this:[23] Consider that if God weakly actualizes a possible world, he necessarily strongly actualizes a largest state of affairs that he can strongly actualize. Call the largest state of affairs that God can strongly actualize T(W). So, says Plantinga,

> For every world W in which God exists, God could have weakly actualized W only if $G(T(W)) \rightarrow W$.

Which says that if W is a possible world God could have weakly actualized, then the counterfactual

> If God had strongly actualized T(W), then W would have been actual

is true.[24]

of Evil," *American Philosophical Quarterly* 14 (1977): 109–17; and Adams, "Plantinga on the Problem of Evil." See also Plantinga's response to Adams in Tomberlin and van Inwagen, eds., *Alvin Plantinga*, 371–82.

23. Here I am following Plantinga's discussion in Tomberlin and van Inwagen, eds., *Alvin Plantinga*, 51ff.

24. Ibid., 50–51.

Now consider a possible world, *W*. If *W* is weakly actualized by God, then T(*W*) necessarily obtains. But *W* cannot include (AENE). Now consider a world, *W*, in which AENE is true. Though *W* includes T(*W*), it cannot include AENE, since AENE is a contingent proposition presupposing libertarian freedom. In the same way, if God weakly actualizes *W** (which includes his strongly actualizing T(*W*)), and AEE (Adam and Eve ate the forbidden fruit) is true, it cannot include AEE. So, it is certainly possible that God could strongly actualize the same states of affairs and

(AEE) Adam and Eve ate the forbidden fruit

could be true. Thus, we have two worlds, *W* and *W**, both including God's strongly actualizing the same range of maximal state of affairs that he can actualize. But because God, in strongly actualizing the range of maximal state of affairs that he can actualize, cannot thereby actualize a possible world containing free creatures in which, at the one world, *W*, AEE is true and, at the other world, *W**, AENE is true, there are at least two possible worlds that God cannot actualize. He cannot actualize a world, *W*, in which AEE is true, and he cannot actualize a world, *W**, in which AENE is true.

If, therefore, God cannot actualize a world, *W*, in which AENE is true, then, according to Plantinga, Adam and Eve are caught in the serious condition of transworld depravity. There are worlds that God cannot actualize in which Adam and Eve refrain from eating the forbidden fruit. In other words, Adam and Eve have transworld depravity if God actualizes a world, *W*, and if AEE is true. For any world that includes Adam and Eve, therefore, if God were to weakly actualize any of them and AEE is true, then our first parents have transworld depravity. Not only so, but it is possible that God could not actualize a world that includes Adam and Eve and in which AENE is true. To put it in Plantinga's own (complex) words:

An essence *E* *suffers from transworld depravity* if and only if for every world *W* such that *E* entails the properties *is significantly free* in W and always does what is right in W, there is a state of affairs T and an action A such that

> (1) T is the largest state of affairs God strongly actualizes in W,
>
> (2) A is morally significant for E's instantiation in W,

and

> (3) if God had strongly actualized T, E's instantiation would have gone wrong with respect to A.[25]

Thus, transworld depravity responds to the rejoinder that God could have created a world that is only morally good.[26]

Christian Compatibilism

In the FWD, Plantinga sets out to show the (possible) compatibility of the existence of God with the existence of evil. But behind the argument for this compatibility lies the affirmation of a fundamental *in*compatibility between the sovereignty[27] of God

25. Plantinga, *The Nature of Necessity*, 188.

26. Just a note on the "fine print" of this discussion that I promised above to avoid. Michael Bergmann, "Might-Counterfactuals, Transworld Untrustworthiness and Plantinga's Free Will Defense," *Faith and Philosophy* 16, no. 3 (1999): 336–51, argues *against* Plantinga's notion of transworld depravity and *for* transworld *untrustworthiness* as he seeks to show that a denial of transworld depravity is epistemically possible. He further argues that even a denial of transworld untrustworthiness is epistemically possible, and thus that the FWD is weaker than first supposed.

In (brief) response, however, we should note that what is epistemically possible is itself quite shaky philosophically, requiring a host of assumptions and presuppositions that need not detain us here. Important for our discussion is Bergmann's concession toward the end of his article. In characterizing his own notion of transworld untrustworthiness as requiring "might-counterfactuals," in distinction from the notion of transworld depravity's requirement of "would-counterfactuals," Bergmann notes, "It is the atheist objector who needs would-counterfactuals; it is by means of God's knowledge of would-counterfactuals of freedom that God is supposed to be able to actualize a world with free creatures who always freely do what is right. Thus . . . Plantinga is giving the atheist objector all her assumptions and only *then* responding" (p. 348). The advantage of transworld depravity, therefore, over transworld untrustworthiness is that the former responds more directly to the atheist's objection.

27. We'll take as a working definition of God's sovereignty here the notion that God has complete and exhaustive control over all that he has made.

and (libertarian) human freedom.[28] Put simply, the argument goes
something like this:

(1) If humans are to be free, God cannot be sovereign.
(2) Humans are to be free.
(3) Therefore, God cannot be sovereign.

Given this affirmation, the key feature of the FWD is that we have
freedom such that it is not up to God which possible world is actualized and which is not. As a matter of fact, God cannot (strongly)
actualize any world in which there are creatures with libertarian
freedom.[29] There are, of course, some things that are up to God
and God alone. For example, what *is* up to God is which world,
if any, he would create. But, having created a particular (possible) world in which there are free creatures, just what that world
would be and would look like, God simply cannot determine. If he
did determine it, then it would not be a world in which there are
free creatures. And the creation of free creatures, it is thought, is
a good far outweighing any possibility or actuality of evil.

Entailed in the entire discussion of the FWD, therefore, is the
notion of incompatibilism with respect to God's sovereignty and
human freedom. Incompatibilism can be defined as:

Agent A is free at time t with respect to situation s if and only if
A has it in his power at t to bring it about that s and A has it in
his power at t to refrain from bringing it about that s.[30]

---

28. Unless otherwise indicated, *free* and *freedom* will be used in the libertarian sense.

29. That is, if we define a possible world as a *maximal* state of affairs. God needs his
free creatures to co-actualize if any possible world in which there are free creatures is to
become actual.

30. William E. Mann, "God's Freedom, Human Freedom, and God's Responsibility
for Sin," in *Divine and Human Action: Essays in the Metaphysics of Theism*, ed. Thomas
V. Morris (Ithaca, NY: Cornell University Press, 1988), 183. Mann is defining what he
deems the "liberty of indifference" here. While Mann's liberty of indifference is not identical with libertarianism, we can see the two as sufficiently identical in this context without doing an injustice to either.

The point to be made here is that the power of *A* to bring about *s* at *t*, or to refrain from bringing about *s* at *t*, belongs exclusively and only to *A*. If anything or anyone else contributes in any way whatsoever to *A*'s bringing about *s* or to *A*'s refraining from bringing about *s*, then *A* is considered, by the incompatibilist, not to be free.

As William Mann says, "An exhaustive list of all the causal laws governing the world, conjoined with an exhaustive list of all the situations that obtain or have obtained in the past (relative to *t*), entails neither that *A* brings about *s* nor that *A* brings about not-*s*."[31] Therefore, God cannot in any way whatsoever influence, either positively or negatively, the decision of *A* to bring about *s* or to refrain from doing so. God's sovereignty, under this construal, is thought to be incompatible with our activity as free creatures (given our definitions of sovereignty and of freedom). Thus, in order for libertarian freedom to be affirmed, a full-orbed sovereignty must be denied with respect to God.

How might we respond to such an idea? More specifically, what guidance can Reformed theology give to such an idea? An answer to this question must first take into account the theological boundaries beyond which a Reformed theology cannot go, and then attempt to provide a response that is true to those theological boundaries while taking seriously the philosophical tensions that arise in discussions of this kind.

There are (at least) a couple of possible avenues available for a Reformed response at this point. The first avenue would be to attempt to define more precisely, in this context, what is meant by compatibility. Part of Plantinga's complaint against the atheologian's argument is that there has yet to be an argument for the incompatibility of (1) and (3). What they would need to show, remember, is that (1) and (3), to be incompatible, would have to be "false in every possible world," that is, impossible. Compatibility, in this context could therefore be defined as "true in at least one possible world." That is, for two (or more) properties or propositions to be compatible does not mean that they necessarily exist or are necessarily true, but rather that it is possible for them to exist (or be true) in at least

31. Ibid., 183–84.

one possible world. But this does not serve to define in a general way just what compatibility (or incompatibility) is. It is surely the case, with respect to incompatibility, that two propositions could be deemed false in every possible world just because of their respective meanings, not because of any inherent incompatibility between them. The propositions, "God is essentially evil" and "Plantinga was born in Australia in the actual world" are both false in every possible world, and the notion of compatibility or incompatibility is not even relevant to the two propositions.

The further point to be made is that, with respect to two or more propositions or entities, there must be properties in (or of) one or more of them that are thought to be in some way contradictory or inconsistent with properties of the others. To use the example above, there are no properties inherent in "God is essentially evil" that seem to conflict with properties inherent in "Plantinga was born in Australia in the actual world."[32] So, what is implicit in the notion of incompatibility is that the propositions or entities in question contain properties that are, at least *prima facie*, in conflict of some kind.

With respect to our current context, whence, specifically, the perceived incompatibility? As Plantinga notes, incompatibility lies in the perceived conflict between God's omnipotence, omniscience, and goodness, and the existence of evil in the world. Plantinga's solution to the perceived incompatibility is to postulate a possible world in which God's omnipotence is such that it cannot in any way impinge on human freedom. Thus, the compatibility of God's existence and evil is achieved by making God's properties compatible with a libertarian notion of human freedom. God's omnipotence is defined in such a way that it cannot have power over human choice. Not only so, but God's omniscience is defined in such a way as to make God's own knowledge of what free human creatures do dependent on their choices. God can only know such things once he sees what humans decide. There is, therefore, a delineation of God's properties that serves to make him compatible with his creation, specifically his human creation.

32. We are assuming, perhaps groundlessly, that being born in Australia is not an evil, such that it would be evidence of God's maleficence.

But such a move is not an option in a Reformed Free Will Defense. Let's say that God's omnipotence and omniscience are covenantal properties of his—properties he takes on by virtue of his decision to create—that are grounded in God's aseity. That is, the reason God is omnipotent and omniscient is that, even though he does create, he nevertheless remains who he essentially is. He does not in any way give up his aseity. He remains independent of his creation, even while present with and operating within the confines of that creation. Thus, his omnipotence, whatever else it may be, is a power that can in no way be constrained by anything outside of God. His omniscience as well is a knowledge that is in no way dependent on anything outside of him. So such a move as Plantinga's is not open to us because, if we are correct in our understanding of who God is, there is no possible world in which God can change his essential properties. He remains, even in the light of creation, essentially *a se*.

14

Diversity to Unity

The orthodox hold that the providence of God is so occupied about sin as neither idly to permit it nor efficiently to produce it, but efficaciously to order and direct it. —TURRETIN

W e need to think again about compatibility. How shall compatibility (and incompatibility) be defined, given a Reformed doctrine of God?

Two in One

Given that perceived incompatibilities have their focus in different properties, we might begin by defining compatibility initially in terms of properties. Compatibility, therefore, would obtain when differing or opposing properties were in some way unified. We can begin, then, in this way:

PC = two (or more) things, $x_1, x_2, \ldots x_n$, in which differing or opposing properties inhere, are unified by another thing that has

278

its own essential properties, *U*, without altering the essential character of any of the properties concerned.

On this scheme, however, there will be different *kinds* of compatibility. For example, water and oil both have properties that are incompatible. Suppose we put both together in a glass. In that case, given PC, "there is water in the glass," and "there is oil in the (same) glass" could be deemed PC compatible if the essential properties of oil and water are not altered, given that both are predicated of the same, unifying thing, that is, the glass. But this kind of compatibility (if there is such) makes little difference to the glass itself. There is no relevant relationship between the (same) glass that holds the oil and the water, and the oil and water themselves.

So we need another qualification in our notion of compatibility. The kind of compatibility of particular interest in these discussions is the kind wherein there is a supervenient[1] relationship between the properties of the unifying entity and the differing, or opposing, incompatible properties. Perhaps we should define our understanding of compatibility, then, as *supervenient property compatibility*. Thus,

SPC = two (or more) things, $x_1, x_2, \ldots x_n$, in which differing or opposing essential properties inhere, are unified by another thing, which has its own essential properties, *U*, without altering the essential character of any of the properties concerned, and wherein there is a supervenient relationship, *SR*, between the essential properties of *U* and the essential properties of $x_1, x_2, \ldots x_n$.[2]

1. We will take a fairly standard definition of supervenience here: "Properties of type *A* are supervenient on properties of type *B* if and only if two objects cannot differ with respect to their *A*-properties without also differing with respect to their *B*-properties." See Robert Audi, *The Cambridge Dictionary of Philosophy* (Cambridge: Cambridge University Press, 1995), 778.

2. In music, for example, we could think of harmony, in which the musical score (*U*), supervenes on *SR*, the individual, differing notes and parts $(x_1, x_2, \ldots x_n)$, to form a unified whole without any of the essential properties of the respective entities being lost. There is, then, a union in and among diversity.

Given supervenience, the kind of compatibility utilized in these discussions will be such that there is a dependence relation between the essential properties of U and the differing or opposing essential properties $x_1, x_2, \ldots x_n$. This definition may (likely, *will*) need modification in order to be more generally useful, but it should suit our purposes here.

In the FWD, there are initially two propositions: (1) God exists, and (3) There is evil. The compatibility (what we might want to call "modal consistency") of those propositions is maintained by way of (2). But, as we have seen, (2) cannot be a part of a Reformed approach to this problem. It is not possible that God's ability to actualize or not actualize a world is dependent on libertarian human freedom. Not only so, but, *given our definition of compatibility*, we have yet to show that (1) and (3) are really compatible.[3]

Part of the burden of delimiting a notion of *property* compatibility is due to the tension that still resides in Plantinga's solution to the problem of evil. Even if (1) and (3) are modally consistent by way of (2), the problem of evil, as articulated, still remains, given any historic understanding of God.[4] The tension still remains, in part, because the fact of God's creating activity, given that he did not have to create, is still at the root of the problem; the reason for God's taking the "risk" of creation is still left unresolved. While it may be true that a defense *simpliciter* will not concern itself with such tensions (perhaps consistency at a possible world is all that is needed), the fact that, even given the FWD, the decision of God to create is still in tension with the existence of evil puts the point of tension right back onto the character of God.[5] That is, in the

3. To be clear, Plantinga *has* shown them to be compatible, given his notion of compatibility.

4. See John S. Feinberg, " 'And the Atheist Shall Lie Down with the Calvinist': Atheism, Calvinism, and the Free Will Defense," *Trinity Journal* 1, no. 2 (Fall 1980): 142–52, for an argument that the Reformed view of God, at least in terms of his aseity, is presupposed by many atheist objections to the FWD in response to the problem of evil.

5. Possibly attuned to this tension, Plantinga does give a hint as to why God took the risk to create: "A world containing creatures who are significantly free (and freely perform more good than evil actions) is more valuable, all else being equal, than a world containing no free creatures at all." Alvin Plantinga, *God, Freedom, and Evil* (New York: Harper & Row, 1974), 30. Just how one could determine such a world to be more valuable (to

context of the FWD, the question of why God would create any world, knowing his own severe limitations (limitations inherent in the FWD) with respect to that world, still looms large in the discussion. So, in highlighting the essential properties concerned of the entities that are, though differing or opposed, nevertheless brought together by one thing (and thus compatible, at least, with that one thing), SPC seeks to work toward a resolution of that tension.

In order better to fit SPC into the discussion of the problem of evil, we need to make explicit in the beginning of Plantinga's argument what he makes explicit in that argument later—that the two entities under consideration, God's existence and the existence of evil, are thought to be truths inherent in the same (possible) world. That is, they are predicated of the same world. This may be too obvious to make explicit early on in Plantinga's argument, but it is crucial, given SPC, to understand initially in ours. If it were not the case that God's existence and the existence of evil were predicated of the same world (and thus states of affairs obtaining *at* that same world), compatibility would not be at issue. Thus, Plantinga's two propositions can be more explicitly stated as (1) God exists in W, and (3) there is evil in W.

Given SPC, (1) and (3) will be equivalent to x_1 and x_2, and (2) (referenced to W) will be equivalent to U. Because of the relationship of supervenience, there is a dependence between x_1 and x_2, and U, such that U supervenes on x_1 and x_2. In other words, the essential properties of a possible world U supervene on the essential properties of God's existence (x_1) and of the existence of evil (x_2) such that x_1 and x_2 are brought together by U. There is, then, a congruent dependence relation between U and x_1 and x_2. This seems to fit Plantinga's own discussion in that it is the character of the possible world itself that supervenes on God's existence and the existence of evil. It is because a possible world contains humans with libertarian freedom that God's omnipotence is restricted by that freedom,

---

God? to us?) is difficult to imagine. And just how one might configure all things such that they are equal is equally mysterious. The point to be made, however, is that lying behind the FWD is God's deeming it "more valuable" for free creatures to exist, given a created world, than not to exist. This seems to move beyond a defense *simpliciter* and is a (at least partial) theodicy that is behind the FWD.

and that Adam's decision is libertarianly free and thus sinful. In that sense, then, it is the nature of the (possible) world that brings together otherwise incompatible things like God and sin.

But herein lies a problem. Our notion of compatibility is calculated further to highlight the tensions that remain with respect to the FWD. It does so, because the first proposition, (1), in the FWD, is a necessary proposition (i.e., true in every possible world), while the second, (3), is contingent (i.e., true in at least one possible world). Not only so, but (2) is itself a contingency (i.e. "W exists" is only possibly true). Given SPC, then, it is the essential properties of a possible world, U, that bring together the essential properties of God, x_1, and the essential properties of evil, x_2, such that compatibility of x_1 and x_2 is had by the supervenience of U on x_1 and x_2. As we have noted, however, in order to conclude for modal consistency, the FWD must have as a necessary constituent a God who is unable strongly to actualize any world. But then the consistency comes at a cost not available to SPC; God loses some of his essential properties (such as aseity). If SPC requires that no essential properties be lost (since none can be), it cannot be the case that the FWD provides for the compatibility of x_1 and x_2 by way of U. It would appear, therefore, that, given our definition of compatibility (and our understanding of a covenantal metaphysic),[6] we cannot set (Plantinga's) propositions (1) and (3) as the initial "problem set" and then propose a possible state of affairs, (2) or (for us) U, that would make (1) and (3) modally consistent.

To put it another way, the fact of the matter is that any possible world, W, and any existence (other than God's) *necessarily* have as their presupposition the existence of God (Plantinga's (1)). That is, there is no possible world in which W and (3) obtain (or are true) unless (1) obtains, which it necessarily does. Given SPC, therefore, the compatibility question revolves around the existence of W and the existence of evil, both of which have their ultimate source, U, in God.

6. Since a covenantal metaphysic takes the *Eimi/eikon* relationship as basic, and since God is the "I AM," there is no possible world in which God is ever essentially dependent on his creation.

The Crux of Evil

At this point, we might be able better to formulate the crux of the "problem of evil," given our metaphysical structure of the *Eimi/eikon*. We should keep in mind as well what we said earlier: that the reason that Plantinga was able to postulate a possible consistency between God's existence and the existence of evil was that he diminished God's essential character in order to make it consistent with libertarian freedom. God/evil consistency, therefore, depended on God/human consistency.

But this is not how God has revealed himself. He does not tell us in Scripture that he determined to change his essential character. Rather, he tells us that he comes down, that he stoops, that he—while remaining himself essentially—assumes contingent properties in order to relate the things of his creation to himself. He is the initiator and preserver of this covenant relationship.

All of this is to say that it is *God* who has made compatible what would have otherwise remained incompatible (recall the Westminster Confession, 7.1). To put it in terms of SPC, there are two properties (or two sets of properties) that differ essentially. There are essential properties of God and essential properties of creation. These properties differ; they could even be said, perhaps, to be opposites.[7] Thus, there are two entities, x_1 and x_2, creation and Creator, that appear to be incompatible. What then serves as *U*? What unifying entity will supervene on x_1 and x_2 in such a way as to make them compatible without at the same time altering any of their essential properties? In a word, condescension; in two words, *God's* condescension.

It is God condescending, his *act* of condescension that, *ipso facto*, brings together the properties of Creator and creation in such a way as to preserve the essential properties of both, all the while placing them both within the same, unified, context. The unifying element, then, is *covenant*, the bringing together, by God, of the *Eimi* and the *eikon*. To put it in theological terms, the infinite gap that exists between God and creation is bridged by God's covenant condescension with respect to his creation.

---

7. If we were to take infinite to be the opposite of finite, or, independent to be the opposite of dependent.

This is the "bigger" picture with respect to the problem of evil; it is the picture Plantinga painted by assuming that God determined to reduce himself down when he determined to create creatures with libertarian freedom. And this was calculated to make God compatible with his creation so that evil could then be something of which God has had nothing whatsoever to do. But, as we have said, this will not suffice for RFWD.

Given the fact of covenant compatibilism, that is, given the fact that God has condescended to assume contingent properties, while at the same time sacrificing or altering none of his essential properties, how might we now begin to think more specifically about the problem of evil? Plantinga was correct to point out that there were particular properties attributed to God that seem incompatible with the existence of evil. His solution was a philosophical expression of the theology of Molinism. But perhaps we can put the matter in terms familiar to those within the Reformed context. The "compatibility problem" might be better focused on the relationship between the decree of God,[8] on the one hand, and the free and responsible decision of Adam, on the other. In terms of the fundamental problem, then, the following two propositions could now become the problem set:

(x_1) God ordains "whatsoever comes to pass,"

and

(x_2) Adam freely[9] and responsibly decided to eat the forbidden fruit.

The incompatibility between x_1 and x_2 lies in the fact that one of the essential properties of God's decree is that it necessitates what

8. Defined thus by the Westminster Confession of Faith, 3.1, "God from all eternity did by the most wise and holy counsel of his own will, freely and unchangeably ordain whatsoever comes to pass; yet so as thereby neither is God the author of sin; nor is violence offered to the will of the creatures, nor is the liberty or contingency of second causes taken away, but rather established." We should be reminded that God's decree, though eternal, was also a product of his free will; there was nothing in God that necessitated the decree.

9. We define "freely" according to the Westminster Confession of Faith, 9:1: "God hath endued the will of man with that natural liberty, that it is neither forced, nor by any absolute necessity of nature determined, to good or evil."

is decreed.[10] Yet one of the properties of Adam's action in eating the forbidden fruit is that he did so freely and responsibly. To be more specific, the incompatibility lies in the essential property of God as altogether perfect,[11] and the essential property of Adam's will, as free and responsible, which is itself controlled ultimately by God.

Now in order for there to be compatibility, according to SPC, we first need at least two things in which essential properties inhere. In x_1 God has the essential property of his aseity, which, given his decision to create, includes his ordaining whatsoever comes to pass; in x_2 we have Adam as essentially free and responsible for his actions. We have two things in which essential properties inhere, properties that seem to be incompatible, both of which are included in God's decree. What is needed, then, is U—some unifying thing whose essential properties supervene on x_1 and x_2 such that there is a dependence relationship between the essential properties of U, on the one hand, and the (seemingly incompatible) properties of x_1 and x_2, on the other. What might U be?

In order to answer that question, it may help to think about Christology again. The fact that God interacts with his creation, as we have seen, has given rise to a number of substantial problems in much of the literature. If we begin our thinking, however, with

10. We will make distinctions with regard to what *kind* of necessity this is in the next chapter.

11. Given our distinction between essential and covenantal properties of God, how does God's decree relate to this distinction? As we noted above, because theology can be distinguished between archetypal, ectypal (in God), and ectypal (for us), God's decree would fall into the second category and thus would be a covenantal property of his. Turretin's explanation serves us well here. After affirming that the decree has its foundation in God's essential perfection and omniscience, he says, "The divine acts admit of a threefold distinction. (1) There are immanent and intrinsic acts having no respect to anything outside of God [what we call essential properties]. . . . (2) Others are extrinsic and transient acts which are not in God, but from him effectively and in creatures subjectively (as to create, to govern)—these are temporal acts and God is denominated extrinsic only from them [these would be covenantal properties]. (3) There are acts immanent and intrinsic in God, but connoting a respect and relation . . . to something outside of God (such are the decrees, which are nothing else than the counsels of God concerning future things out of himself [these would be covenantal properties of God which flow out of his essential character, given that they are ectypal in God, implying his archetypal knowledge]. Francis Turretin, *Institutes of Elenctic Theology*, ed. James T. Dennison Jr., trans. George Musgrave Giger, 3 vols. (Phillipsburg, NJ: P&R, 1992–97), 1:311.

the quintessential example of God's interaction with the world as given to us in the person of Jesus Christ, we might begin to emerge from the fog and to see more clearly as to what compatibility might entail. Christ is the supreme example of the *Eimi/eikon*; he is the "I AM" who is also image (man). Christ, as the Son of God made flesh, reveals to us how it is that God can remain God and at the same time genuinely participate in the limitations (including the suffering) of a finite world.

We should be clear here. The incarnation is *sui generis*. There is nothing in Scripture or in all of history that compares to that one climactic and historic act of God's condescension. But we must be equally clear that divine condescension has biblical precedent prior to the incarnation. As we have seen, God's condescension is coincident with his act of creation. He condescended in order to create, since creation is the bringing into being of something other than God, and anything other than God would be, by definition, less than God. *If* God desires to interact with that creation, condescension would be necessary. He would need to "stoop down" in order to be in a relationship with that which is essentially (ontologically, metaphysically) beneath him.

And this "divine stoop" is historically and preeminently given to us in Jesus Christ, the Son of God, who took on human flesh. It should help us understand something of what compatibility is, therefore, from a Reformed Christian perspective, if we understand just what the incarnation entails.

> But I speak of the person of Christ as unto the assumption of the substantial adjunct of the human nature, not to be a part whereof his person is composed, but as unto its subsistence therein by virtue of a substantial union. Some of the ancients, I confess, speak freely of the composition of the person of Christ in and by the two natures, the divine and human. That the Son of God after his incarnation had one nature, composed of the Deity and humanity, was the heresy of Apollinarius, Eutyches, the Mono-thelites, or Monophysites, condemned by all. But that his most simple divine nature, and the human, composed properly of soul

and body, did compose his one person, or that it was composed of them, they constantly affirmed.[12]

There is much to be said in explanation of John Owen's description here, but we can only highlight the main points relevant to our discussion. First, it should be noted that in the incarnation the second person of the Trinity assumed a human nature. Because of that assumption, he was such that he was one person with two distinct natures. He was not two persons,[13] neither did the assumption of the human nature absorb that nature into one, other, nature.

Second, as Owen notes, it was not the case that, upon assuming the human nature, Christ was a person who had a mixture of human and divine natures. As we noted in chapter 12, the relationship of the natures of Christ is defined most succinctly in the Chalcedonian Creed. Christ's two natures are neither confused nor changed, divided nor separated.

It was not the case, therefore, that, in taking on a human nature, the Son of God changed his essential divine nature (we have already argued that such a change is impossible). It was not that the essence of God underwent essential change when the second person of the Trinity, himself fully and essentially God, took on human flesh. While the two natures in the one person of Christ are distinct, they are not divided "by separate subsistences." This point is crucial in order to safeguard the reality of the one person's identity. He is not schizophrenic, alternating between two divided personalities.[14]

12. John Owen, *The Works of John Owen*, ed. W. H. Gould (Edinburgh: Banner of Truth, 1977), 1:36.

13. Gordon Clark, in a biting critique of the entirety of historic orthodox Christology, both Catholic and Protestant, and in order to make Christology fit his logic, argued that Christ is indeed two persons. Given his awkward definition of a person, however, (viz., a collection of propositions), any definition including the word *person* cannot in this case be taken seriously. See Gordon Haddon Clark, *The Incarnation* (Jefferson, MD: The Trinity Foundation, 1988).

14. Although one might think this point need not be stated, given what revelation tells us about Christ, ideas that depict Christ as schizophrenic have, unfortunately, begun to surface in discussions of Christology and the incarnation. For example, according to N.T. Wright, "My case, has been, and remains, that Jesus believed himself called to do and be things which, in the traditions to which he fell heir, only Israel's God, YHWH, was to do and be. I think he held this belief both with passionate and firm conviction, and with

Not only so, but the two natures were in no way mixed, as if one could combine them in such a way as to produce a *tertium quid*, something neither fully divine nor fully human but partly both. The composition of two natures in one person allows for no separation of those natures.

But just how should we think of these two natures, the divine and the human? At this point, we should recall our earlier distinctions with respect to essential and contingent properties. Recall

E_{df} = For any thing x and any possible world, W, in which x exists and any property P, x has P in W.

Given E, the divine nature that belongs to the Son of God is equivalent to God's essence. When we think of the two natures that come together in the one person of Jesus Christ, therefore, we should remember that the divine nature is that which is of the essence of God. There is no possible world in which there is no such nature, and the Son of God necessarily is (and has) that nature.[15] It was not the divine nature, in other words, that was "assumed" in the person of Christ. Neither was the divine nature some universal

---

the knowledge that he could be making a terrible, lunatic mistake." N. T. Wright, "Jesus' Self-Understanding," in *The Incarnation*, ed. Stephen T. Davis, Daniel Kendall, and Gerald O'Collins (Oxford: Oxford University Press, 2002), 59. What Wright seems to ignore in this assertion is the biblical and historical-theological point that Christ's humanity, given its contingent character, never overrides his deity, given its essential character. His humanity is displayed *through* his divinity, and not vice versa. Thus, his divine self-consciousness was and is a necessary property of his, without which he would not be the person that he is, whereas his human self-consciousness is not a necessary property, but is rather a contingency of his person. Note, for example, as Thomas Weinandy reminds us, Cyril of Alexandria's *mia physis* emphasis. Jesus is μία φύσις τοῦ λόγου σεσαρκωμένη "the one nature of the Word incarnate." Cyril used *mia physis*, not to deny that Christ was both divine and human, but to emphasize that Christ is one being or reality—one entity. See Thomas G. Weinandy, *Does God Suffer?* (Notre Dame, IN: University of Notre Dame Press, 2000), 192. For a helpful discussion of "the psychological problem" with respect to the incarnation, see Eleonore Stump, *Aquinas* (New York: Routledge, 2003), 418–22; and Thomas Aquinas, *Summa Theologiae: Latin Text, English Translation, Introduction, Notes, Appendices and Glossary*, ed. Thomas Gilby (London and New York: Eyre & Spottiswoode and McGraw-Hill, 1964), 4.19.1.

15. He also has whatever properties are essential to being the Son (and not the Father or the Holy Spirit), but those need not concern us here.

that was particularized by the second person of the Trinity. The divine nature is and was the eternal God in the second person of the Trinity.

Recall also

C_{df} = For any thing x and any possible world, W, in which x exists and any property P, x has P in W and x does not have P in W_1.

Given C, human nature is itself contingent. There are some possible worlds in which it exists and others in which it does not. In any possible world in which it *does* exist, it has properties essential to it, but it only has those essential properties because of a prior contingency, namely, God's free decision to create. Not only is human nature itself contingent, such that it is possible that it not exist, but the assumption of that nature by the second person of the Trinity was a contingency as well. Christ did not have to take on that nature; there was no absolute necessity for the Son of God to become man.[16] The human nature of Christ, which was assumed by the Son of God, is therefore something contingent, as is the fact of that assumption. The divine nature of Christ, however, is something essential and necessary.

This is not to say that Christ could have been who he was with only a divine nature. Once there is an assumption of the human nature by the Son of God such that two natures combine in the one person of Jesus Christ, it is necessarily[17] the case that Jesus Christ have both a human and divine nature. What is *not* the case, however, is that the human nature has the same essential, modal status as the divine nature; nor is it the case that the Son of God, by absolute necessity, take on a human nature.

Furthermore, it is theologically crucial to understand that the hypostatic union did not result in an entirely new person. The union of two natures was not the union of two persons into another person. Nor did the Son's taking a human nature result in a completely "other" person. Rather, the hypostatic union was the assumption of

16. Traditionally, theology has grounded the decision of Christ to become man in the *pactum salutis*, a covenant of salvation decided and determined within the Godhead.

17. It is hypothetical necessity of which we speak here.

that which was formerly abstract and impersonal—a human nature by the second *person* of the Trinity, the Son of God, the result of which was the person Jesus Christ. This union did not effect a change in the essential nature of the Son of God (an essential nature which *is* God), but it added to that essential nature a nature that is contingent, and with the addition of that nature, the person of the Son of God became the (essentially same, but contingently different) person of Jesus Christ. As Thomas notes:

> The divine and human nature are not referred uniformly to the divine person. The divine nature has precedence, in being one with the divine person from eternity. The human nature, however, is related to the divine person secondarily as assumed in time, and not in such a way that the nature should be the person, but that the person subsists in the nature. The Son of God *is* his divinity, but is not his humanity. Therefore, for the human nature to be assumed by a divine person can only mean that the divine nature is united by a personal union to the entire assumed nature, i.e. to all its parts.[18]

So, the human nature is added to the Son of God, who himself has his divine nature essentially. As Turretin notes:

> The human nature in the God-man (*theanthrōpō*) can be called both its adjunct and part in a sound sense. Adjunct, not that it is adjoined or adheres to it as the accident to the subject or a garment to the body, but because to the Logos (*Logō*) (existing without flesh from eternity) it was conjoined in time in the unity of person. It may be called a part also analogically and in a wider sense; not as if the person of Christ compounded or consists of two incomplete natures, as parts properly so called . . . ; but because it subsists not in one, but in two natures and agrees with both.[19]

To clarify, the reason Turretin wants to say that the human nature is not accidental as "a garment to the body," is that, once adjoined to the Son of God, a person heretofore nonexistent in the

18. Aquinas, *Summa Theologiae*, 3.3.7.
19. Turretin, *Institutes*, 2:312.

flesh began to exist in the flesh. This "beginning to be in the flesh" is a new, covenantal relationship, grounded in the personhood of the Son of God; it is a beginning to "be," historically, in the incarnation. Thus, the *mode* of existence of the second person of the Trinity has changed (by way of addition, not subtraction), without in any way changing his essential character.

This might be a good place to address the notion that the incarnation was (is) eternal. We referred to this idea in chapter 11, but perhaps one other quote would help us to see the burden of the position proffered. In her brilliant book, *Aquinas*, Eleonore Stump notes:

> There is no succession in eternity, no *before* and *after*. So it is not the case in eternity that after this moment *t* but not before it God has assumed human nature. On the contrary, each moment in time is simultaneous with the whole of God's atemporal life. The whole of God's life is thus simultaneous with the assumption of human nature at *t*. So the assumption of human nature which takes place at *t* in time is not something new that occurs in the life of atemporal God in eternity. Rather, there never was a part of God's life when the second person of the Trinity had not assumed human nature. The incarnation is thus not a change in God.[20]

This argument seems more plausible than others that seek to reduce God down to something less than *a se*. Given Stump's defense of God's atemporal eternity, the notion of God's giving up such an essential attribute is (rightly) not coherent. Instead, she opts for the notion that the incarnation is itself—like and with God—eternal. She opts for bringing the incarnation "up" (as it were) into the eternal life of God. And she does this in order to conclude that "the incarnation is thus not a change in God."

But there is no reason to think that contingent changes with respect to God are changes that obtain eternally, or are temporal occurrences that are attached to God's essential character. To think in this way is to ascribe essential properties to that which is not essential. If it is the case that "there never was a part of God's life

20. Stump, *Aquinas*, 408.

when the second person of the Trinity had not assumed human nature," then must it not also be the case that the assumption of human nature is an essential property of the second person of the Trinity? Must it not also be the case that there is no possible world in which the Son of God is not also Christ in the flesh? But how could such a thing be when the existence of "the flesh" as well as the rest of creation is itself a contingency?

And if that is the case, then the incarnation is necessary per se, that is, absolutely, and is not simply hypothetically necessary as a remedy to the problem of sin. The incarnation becomes essential and necessary, in this case. If that is true, then are we not forced to deny the historical understanding of the incarnation?[21]

It seems better, theologically and biblically, to see the incarnation as the principal, contingent act of God's covenantal condescension. As such, rather than bringing the incarnation "up," so that it becomes an essential property of God's, we see the source of the incarnation in God's taking on contingent properties; it is God who bridges the gap between his eternal character and his temporal creation. It is God who comes down. In coming down, he takes on properties, attributes, and, in the case of the incarnation, another nature, in order to relate to his creation, which is essentially, ontologically "other" than him.[22]

21. The notion of an eternal incarnation does not necessarily mean that the incarnation is of the essence of God; there is, for example, an eternal decree that itself is contingent. But do Helm and Stump have an option, given their notions of atemporality? It seems it *would* mean that creation is of the essence of God because without creation there can be no incarnation. Anything that is both of the essence of God and created is essentially incompatible.

22. Brian Leftow, "A Timeless God Incarnate," in *The Incarnation*, ed. Stephen T. Davis, Daniel Kendall, and Gerald O'Collins (Oxford: Oxford University Press, 2002), 273–99, seems to come close to this line of reasoning. He does, however, think that *if* God the Son is timeless, he timelessly has properties that have their source in events in time. What Leftow lacks in this discussion is a view of covenantal condescension such that God's (or, more specific to his argument, the Son of God's) knowing what I am writing *now* entails, not a God whose timeless properties are due to this temporal event, but a God whose covenantal condescension includes the property of knowing temporal events *as temporal*. God, whose essential character is atemporal, comes down and covenantally takes to himself our past, present, and future as contingent properties of his (even as Christ did).

With respect to the person of Christ, then, there are two distinct natures, but not two natures that are on a par with each other. The divine nature is essentially what it is necessarily and immutably. The human nature is what it is by virtue of the triune God's creating it as it is; it is thus contingent and limited. Given this truth, we should note that, as the *Eimi/eikon* is combined in the person of Jesus Christ, it is not combined in a way that makes the two equal. Christ, as the Son of God, is always and immutably *Eimi*. The *eikon* that he assumes is contingent and created.[23]

These two natures, by virtue of the incarnation, coexist in the one person of Jesus Christ. They coexist, as we have seen, without confusion, division, mixture, or separation. Again, Turretin:

> The divine essence cannot be communicated to a creature because a created thing cannot be made an uncreated, otherwise it would be God. Therefore none of the essential properties of God which are identified with the divine essence may be communicated. The same nature would be at the same time created and uncreated, immense, and finite, which is contradictory.[24]

With respect to the two natures, therefore, while we recognize a difference in their respective properties, we also recognize that neither nature can "merge" into the other. To do so would deny the essential character of each. Rather it is the one person, the Son of God become Jesus Christ, who has these natures in himself.

We can return now to the question of compatibility. In the context of our discussion above, we may now ask: how may we think about compatibility, given the incarnation of Christ? At least this much is true; given Christ's individual essence (which includes his deity and humanity), we should not think, as was said above, that the reality of his existence since the incarnation consists of a kind

---

23. As Helm notes in explaining the *communication idiomatum* in Calvin: "The Word depends on nothing and on no one; retaining all the properties of Godhood while his human nature utterly depends on him. Thus the Incarnation is an assuming of human nature by the eternal Word. The Word willed to become incarnate, but his human nature did not similarly will to be incarnated by the Son, for apart from that union it had not existence." Paul Helm, *John Calvin's Ideas* (Oxford: Oxford University Press, 2004), 71.

24. Turretin, *Institutes*, 1:323.

of theanthropic schizophrenia. That is, the two natures of Christ are not in constant tension or fundamentally *in*compatible. This, in part at least, is because they exist together in and thus define this one person. There is, then, SPC compatibility between the two natures. There seems to be no tension or conflict in Christ that is a result of these two natures.[25] As Owen notes, while "each nature doth preserve its own natural, essential properties, entirely unto and in itself," and while "each nature operates in him according unto its essential properties," nevertheless:

> The perfect, complete work of Christ, in every act of his mediatory office,—in all that he did as the King, Priest, and Prophet of the church,—in all that he did and suffered,—in all that he continueth to do for us, in or by virtue of whether nature soever it be done or wrought,—is not to be considered as the act of this or that nature in him alone, but it is the act and work of the whole person,—of him that is both God and man in one person.[26]

We can now return to our definition of compatibility:

SPC = two (or more) things, $x_1, x_2, \ldots x_n$, in which differing or opposing essential properties inhere, are unified by another thing, U, without altering the essential character of any of the properties concerned, and wherein there is a supervenient relationship, SR, between the essential properties of U and the essential properties of $x_1, x_2, \ldots x_n$.

Given SPC, the person of Christ provides for us a perfect model. There are two natures, each with differing (some might say, opposing) properties. Thus, we have

25. This is not to say that Christ did not suffer or that he was not tired, and so forth. It is not that kind of tension that we mean here. Rather we are thinking of a tension of incompatibility such that two differing things are not, or cannot be, unified or harmonized. Thus, even as Christ lived with those experiences, there is no indication that his divine nature was warring against them or attempting to root them out, so that he might be more divine than such experiences would allow. Neither did those experiences in any way undermine or diminish the full deity of his person.

26. Owen, *Works*, 1:234. See also Aquinas, *Summa Theologiae*, 3.16.

(x_1) Human nature is finite, etc.

and

(x_2) Divine nature is infinite, etc.

These two properties, finite and infinite, though mutually exclusive with respect to essential properties, are now brought together, unified, by way of the one person, U, the Son of God, who is, in the flesh, Jesus Christ. In this union neither x_1 nor x_2 loses its essential properties, nor does U. Furthermore, U supervenes on x_1 and x_2 in such a way that a change in any of the essential properties of U would effect a change in the essential properties of x_1 and x_2 as well.

This seems to be a way to think of compatibility from a Reformed, Christian perspective. Two essentially different entities, two seemingly incompatible properties, brought together in one person who acts in such a way that the two do not meld into one nature, nor are they in any way incompatible (since they are unified) in the one person. It is the person of Christ who came and who died and who was raised again and who now reigns over all things for the church. It is not that the human nature came and died and was raised, while the divine nature reigns and rules. It is *Christ*, as the God-man, who performs all of these acts. And they are acts, we might add, which could only be performed by one whose essence consisted of the two natures so defined.

Will this help us with respect to our original compatibility problem above? Recall,

(x_1) God ordains "whatsoever comes to pass,"

and

(x_2) Adam freely and responsibly decided to eat the forbidden fruit.

As we said above, what is needed is U—some unifying entity in which essential properties supervene on x_1 and x_2 such that there is a dependence relationship between the essential properties of U, on the one hand, and the (seemingly incompatible) properties of x_1 and x_2, on the other. Given our christological example of SPC compatibility, what might U be?

A couple of theological points need to be remembered here with respect to x_1 and x_2, and we can reiterate them most succinctly by way of the Westminster Confession of Faith. After affirming that God controls whatsoever comes to pass, the confession is quick to provide two other affirmations that might otherwise be deduced from the fact of God's decree.

First, says the confession, ". . . yet so, as thereby neither is God the author of sin . . ." If God decrees whatsoever comes to pass, and sin and evil come to pass, then God decrees sin and evil. And if that is true, it might be thought, then surely it must be that God actually commits sin.[27] But this cannot be a "good and necessary consequence"[28] of the fact of God's sovereign decree. Just why it cannot be is in part due to God's essential character. God is good; there is no possible world in which he acts in an evil way toward his creation. His goodness is a property of his being. So, initially God cannot commit sin because of who he is.

But there is another, contingent, reason why God cannot commit sin, and it is explained in the next clause: ". . . nor is violence offered to the will of the creatures; nor is the liberty or contingency of second causes taken away, but rather established." How shall we understand this?

The first thing we must understand (which we will elaborate below) is that whatever happens in this world happens according to God's decree and is carried out according to God's providence.[29] In that regard, a word of explanation from Turretin:

27. We take the metaphor of "author" here to mean one who actually performs a particular act, even as an author actually writes the words of a book.
28. See the Westminster Confession of Faith, 1.6.
29. Providence is defined in Westminster Confession 5.1: "God, the great Creator of all things, doth uphold, direct, dispose, and govern all creatures, actions, and things, from the greatest even to the least, by his most wise and holy providence, according to his infal-

These two things we derive most clearly from the Scriptures: That the providence of God concurs with all second causes and especially with the human will; yet the contingency and liberty of the will remain unimpaired. But how these two things can consist with each other, no mortal can in this life perfectly understand. Nor should it seem a cause for wonder, since he has a thousand ways (to us incomprehensible) of concurring with our will, insinuating himself into us and turning our hearts, so that by acting freely as we will, we still do nothing besides the will and determination of God.[30]

This, of course, is testified to us in Scripture: "This Jesus, delivered up according to the *definite plan* (ὡρισμένη βουλῇ) and *foreknowledge* (προγνώσει) of God, you crucified and killed by the hands of lawless men" (Acts 2:23). Note, in agreement with Turretin, that there are two reasons, two causes, given for the delivering up of Christ here. He was delivered up according to God's own plan and foreknowledge. Thus, the most grievous sin in all of history was according to God's plan and decree. But he was also crucified and killed by the hands of wicked men. Both things are true of Christ's crucifixion. As Calvin reminds us:

Luke intreateth, indeed, of Christ; but in his person we have a mirror, which doth represent unto us the universal providence of God, which doth stretch itself throughout the whole world; yet doth it specially shine unto us who are the members of Christ. Luke setteth down two things in this place, the foreknowledge and the decree of God. And although the foreknowledge of God is former in order, . . . yet doth he put the same after the counsel and decree of God, to the end we may know that God would nothing, neither appointed anything, save that which he had long before directed to his [its] end.[31]

---

lible foreknowledge, and the free and immutable counsel of his own will, to the praise of the glory of his wisdom, power, justice, goodness, and mercy."

30. Turretin, *Institutes*, 1:511.

31. John Calvin, *The Comprehensive John Calvin Collection*, CD-ROM (The Ages Digital Library System, 2002).

This biblical truth can help us with our compatibility problem. It is the case that Christ's death was planned and designed by God.[32] Its ultimate reason for happening, then, is the plan (including the will) of God. Indeed, if all things happen according to the counsel of his will, if he ordains whatsoever comes to pass, then the plan of God is the reason behind all that happens.

This is the case, we should note, because God took on contingent properties, including the property of "working all things by the counsel of his will." These are covenantal properties, properties not essential to him (since they presuppose the actuality of creation). The cross of Christ, therefore, can be seen in the context of, and as a part of, the purpose of a covenant God for his creation. It is because of his condescension that he "works" all things in creation.

But those who crucified and killed Christ are called "wicked men" (NIV—ἀνόμων). And their wickedness is just *because* of their act of crucifixion and killing. They are wicked because they determined to put Christ to death. How can these two truths be brought together? Can they be compatible?

The answer is that they are harmonized, brought together, by God. God brings them both together, he unifies them, by way of his covenantal providence. That is, the plan and foreknowledge of God are carried out by way of God's own providential working out of that plan. So also, the deeds of wicked men who crucify and kill Jesus are also a part of God's providential work, according to his eternal plan.

What then do we affirm in this regard? With respect to SPC, we have two differing things—the decree of God and the wicked acts of men—that appear initially to be incompatible. They are unified, however, by the covenantal property of God's *providence*. God's providence is that entity (act) which brings together both God's eternal decree and the wicked acts of men. This providence supervenes both on God's decree and on the wicked acts of men; there is a dependent relationship between them. Not only so, but the essential properties of God's decree—its immutability, its design—and the essential properties of the wicked acts—that they be performed,

---

32. Note, for example, Isa. 53:10, "Yet it was the will of the LORD to crush him."

responsibly and freely by man,[33] that they be wicked—are not in any way lost or changed.

Moreover, when the confession says that the "liberty or contingency of second causes" is not "taken away, but rather established," it is affirming that liberty and contingency are only properly thought of within the context of God's providential working in the world. So, says Turretin:

> God so concurs with second causes that although he previously moves and predetermines them by a motion not general only but also special, still he moves them according to their own nature and does not take away from them their own proper mode of operating. The reason is because as the decree of God is occupied not only about the determination of things which ought to be done, but also of the means according to which they are to be done relative to the nature and condition of each, thus actual providence (which is the execution of this decree) secures not only the infallible futurition of the thing decreed, but also its taking place in the very manner decreed (to wit, agreeably to the nature of each; i.e., necessary things take place necessarily, free and contingent things, however, freely and contingently).[34]

Perhaps we can now see how our original compatibility problem can be articulated more fully. Recall, there is a need to make compatible the following two things:

(x_1) God ordains "whatsoever comes to pass,"

and

(x_2) Adam freely and responsibly decided to eat the forbidden fruit.

Both of these, we should now see, are unified, U, by virtue of the providence of God. It is that providence, which looks "backwards," as it were, into eternity and which carries out the decree, and it

---

33. "Free" as defined by the Westminster Confession above.
34. Turretin, *Institutes*, 1:513.

is that providence which guides and governs any and all activities that take place in God's creation. But it is, as well, that providence which neither alters nor eliminates the essential properties of God's decree and of Adam's choice. Providence does not overrule or make absolutely necessary that which is free and contingent.

Nevertheless, we surely cannot see exactly *how* God goes about unifying these two things. But that is not a requirement for compatibility. We cannot see *how*, with respect to Christ, two complete natures, one necessary and one contingent, can coexist in one person, who himself takes on contingent properties. But the exact *way* in which God works these things out is never available to the human mind. This should not tempt us, however, to undermine or otherwise limit God's providential control.

> For providence is so connected with the divinity that it cannot be asserted or denied without either asserting or denying God himself. Hence the Scriptures everywhere separate God from idols by the argument of providence (Is. 41:22, 23; 42:8, 9; Job 12:7–9). By the heathen, God and providence . . . are used promiscuously. Not only they who deny the existence, but also they who deny the providence of God, are condemned as atheists.[35]

Providence is a necessary element of Christian theology, and thus of a Christian philosophy. Not only so, but it does in fact serve to bring together two otherwise incompatible properties, properties relative to God's decree and to the sin of Adam. It thus fulfills the requirements of SPC, that is, that there be something that serves both to supervene on and to unify things that would otherwise be incompatible. The providence of God serves that purpose in this case.

Conclusion

We will have more to say about Christian compatibility, and the way(s) in which we might articulate and defend our understanding of it, in the next two chapters. But perhaps we can conclude this discussion by reworking the FWD. Is it possible to provide modal

35. Ibid., 1:492.

consistency in RFWD? We should remember that, in order for modal consistency to obtain, we need a middle proposition, (2), such that it is consistent with (1) and, together with (1) entails (3).

So, what might we substitute for (2) in light of

(1) God exists,

and

(3) There is evil?

Why not the following?

(2) There is a possible world in which God condescends and thereby providentially works in and through all things so that the eating of the fruit by Adam, as immutably decreed by God, was eaten by Adam freely and responsibly.

On this scenario, (2) has the advantage of maintaining the essential character of God, and that of Adam. Its disadvantage is that it is difficult to see how one thing, like God's condescending providence, could bring together both the decree of God and the free act of Adam as a part of that decree. But surely, in a world in which God, in Christ, takes on a human nature all the while remaining God, it is no conceptual stretch to assert such a thing of God and his providence. That is, just as the person of Christ combines the divine and the human without losing the essential properties of each, so also providence combines the divine (decree) and human (decision) in such a way that no essential properties are lost in each of them.

But how shall we speak of these things which seem initially incompatible, but which become compatible by virtue of God's plan?

15

The Best of All Actualized Worlds

No other cause can be assigned why the Lord has done this or that than this—because he so willed. If you ask further, why he so willed, you seek something greater and more sublime than the will of God. Therefore human temerity ought to restrain itself and not to seek what is not, lest perchance it fail to find that which is. —TURRETIN

We have been looking at a Christian understanding of compatibility. What has motivated us to look more carefully at this is the fact that we need to be able to articulate, as far as is possible with us, what we mean when we say that the existence of God is not incompatible with the existence of evil. It is the problem of evil, therefore, that is the catalyst for a proper understanding of compatibility.

But the problem of evil is just a specific problem to which we are applying our overall metaphysical (and epistemological) structure.

So, given the incarnation, we have been attempting to show (1) that two entities with differing essential properties can be united by way of one unifying entity and (2) that compatibility, particularly with respect to properties essential to God and properties essential to human beings, can be (must be) maintained even when we can't be sure exactly *how* such things can be.

As a matter of fact, according to a Reformed theological context, we simply do not have the option of arguing for essential change in God. Nor do we have the option of arguing that God's control over his creation is such that the decisions and actions that his human creatures take are all related to his decree in such a way as to be absolutely necessary. Nor do we have the option of maintaining that, since God ordains whatsoever comes to pass, our decisions and actions are not free or responsible.

There are (at least) two further, and final, questions that remain for us, and we will attempt a response to those questions in this chapter. First, if two differing entities are unified by way of another entity, how might we begin to speak of such things? This problem is not as urgent when the two entities unified remain physically separate. For example, the biblical concept of marriage is such that it unifies a man and a woman. It is not difficult to see how we can speak of such things, because the union achieved is spiritual. We have little problem, therefore, of predicating with respect to the man and the woman.

When the compatibility is by way of a union (as in the incarnation), or a union of properties (which properties, nevertheless, remain distinct, as in God's providence bringing together both God's decree and human decisions), then predication becomes more difficult. It is with this latter kind of compatibility that we will deal.

Second, just how should we think about the fact that God's decree imposes some kind of necessity on events as they happen in the world? How can we maintain this and also maintain that human choices can be, at the same time, contingent and free events?

You Can Say That Again

First, how might we begin to speak of initially incompatible properties that are, nevertheless, unified by way of a single entity? More specifically, how might we articulate the kind of compatibility that has its focus in the incarnation? Here we might receive some initial help from Thomas Aquinas.

The quandaries that are encountered by virtue of an orthodox doctrine of the incarnation[1] would not have escaped the genius of Aquinas. Thomas was convinced that Chalcedon had properly identified the mode and means of the incarnation.[2] Given, therefore, that Christ was a person with two natures, the questions arose as to how we might predicate truthfully with respect to this one person who was both God and man. To take one example, the question is asked as to whether this statement is true: "Christ, as man, is God." Thomas replies:

> Whatever pertains to Christ as man pertains to all men. If, then, Christ, as man, is God, it follows that every man is God. This is evidently false. . . . The term "man" when placed in reduplication may be taken in two ways. Firstly, as referring to the nature. And in this way it is not true that Christ, as man, is God, since there is a difference of nature between human and divine nature. Secondly, it may be taken as referring to the subsisting subject. And in this way, since the subject subsisting in human nature in Christ is the person of the Son of God to whom it belongs essentially to be God, it is true that, Christ, as man, is God. Taking into consideration, however, that a term placed in reduplication is more naturally taken for the nature than for the subsisting subject, as has already been said, then the following statement should rather be denied than affirmed, "Christ, as man, is God."[3]

1. More specifically, a Reformed orthodox doctrine of the incarnation. It is important to keep in mind in this discussion that we are assuming a Reformed, rather than a Lutheran, view of the *communicatio idiomatum* with respect to Christ's properties.

2. Thomas Aquinas, *Summa Theologiae: Latin Text, English Translation, Introduction, Notes, Appendices and Glossary*, ed. Thomas Gilby (London and New York: Eyre & Spottiswoode and McGraw-Hill, 1964), 3.2.1.

3. Ibid., 3.16.11.

This has been one traditional way of attempting to understand what kind of compatibility is present in the person of Christ. The strategy has been to work out a means of predication that will allow for meaningful discussion about Christ, such that we are not left with bare contradiction. It is a strategy, we could say, of predicative compatibility. Thus, one can say, "Christ is omnipotent" as long as it is understood that what is meant is "Christ, as God, is omnipotent," which would entail as well that "Christ, as man, is not omnipotent."[4]

But this strategy has been challenged. Thomas Morris believes that it does nothing, in the end, to avoid contradiction.

> Consider any conjunctive reduplicative proposition of the form "x as A is N and x as B is not N." If the subjects of both conjuncts are the same and the substituends of N are univocal across the conjunction, then as long as (1) the reduplication predicates being A of x and predicates being B of x, and (2) being N is entailed by being A, and not being N is entailed by being B, then the reduplicative form of predication accomplishes nothing except for muddying the waters, since in the end the contradiction stands of x being characterized as both N and not N.[5]

In other words, argues Morris, suppose one affirms both that "Christ as God is infinite, and Christ as man is not infinite." Given that the subject of both conjuncts is the same, which it is, and that "infinite" is used in the same way in both conjuncts, which it is; and as long as the reduplication predicates "being God" of Christ and "being man" of Christ, which it does, and "being infinite" is entailed by being God, and not being infinite is entailed by being man, which each is; then, says Morris, the contradiction stands since Christ is characterized as being infinite and not being infinite.

4. It should be noted here that, to the extent that Calvin used reduplicative language, he seems to reserve it for the *person* of Christ, rather than the natures. See Paul Helm, *John Calvin's Ideas* (Oxford: Oxford University Press, 2004), 69.

5. Thomas V. Morris, *The Logic of God Incarnate* (Ithaca, NY: Cornell University Press, 1986), 48–49.

Eleonore Stump disagrees with Morris and offers an argument, based on Aquinas's metaphysics, that seeks to resolve Morris's malaise. The central strategy of Stump's response is to reiterate the fact that propositions of the kind discussed must always be interpreted in terms of their respective referents. To posit something of the whole—in this case, Christ—without understanding it to refer to a particular nature of Christ, is to forget that, with respect to the person of Christ, the whole (person) consists of two (previously) incompatible natures. When speaking of Christ in this way, therefore, terms must be, as Thomas says, "placed in reduplication."[6]

> So a whole can borrow properties from its constituents. . . . Consequently, there is no reason for denying that Christ can have properties borrowed from either his human nature or his divine nature, even if the natures are not integral parts of Christ and the properties are contradictories. Because each of the incompatible properties is had in its own right by a different constituent of the whole and because they attach to the whole only derivatively, in consequence of the fact that the whole has these constituents, there is no incoherence in attributing both otherwise incompatible properties to the whole.[7]

This seems true enough. As Stump points out, there are other things, things which are complex in their essential make-up, to which we can coherently attribute otherwise incompatible properties. When we say, therefore, that Christ is infinite, we speak truly because what we say refers, not to Christ's human nature, but to his divine nature.

There are, however, as Stump admits, properties that are had by Christ "in their own right" and other properties that are borrowed from one or the other of his natures. While which properties are which is not the immediate concern of the reduplicative strategy,

---

6. Thomas Aquinas, *On the Truth of the Catholic Faith: Summa Contra Gentiles* (Garden City, N. Y.: Hanover House, 1955), 3.16.2: "in reduplicatione positus."

7. Eleonore Stump, "Aquinas' Metaphysics of the Incarnation," in *The Incarnation*, ed. Stephen T. Davis, Daniel Kendall, and Gerald O'Collins (Oxford: Oxford University Press, 2002), 217.

delineating *these* properties may be beyond the capacity of such a strategy.

For example, Stump notes the following:

> In the case of Christ, who is a composite of one person and two natures, the property of being unlimited in power is a property had by the whole only in virtue of the fact that one constituent of the whole has this property. Furthermore, if all the constituents of Christ other than the divine nature were removed, what remained would still be omnipotent.[8]

But there may be problems with this kind of assessment.

Given our understanding of essentialism with respect to God, we have already seen that God is essentially God; there is nothing in him that is in any way contingent or otherwise not necessary. This is true, as we have said, of the triune God. Thus, it is true of Father, Son, and Holy Spirit, individually and collectively, as one God. The Father's "God-ness" is his essentially, as is the Son's, as is the Spirit's.

Thus, orthodox theology has always held that, in Christ, there was not a union of two persons, but rather a union of the person of the Son of God with human nature. This union did not produce a third person, but it produced a change in the Son of God such that he became something that he was not, all the while remaining who he essentially was and is. He became the God-man, Jesus Christ.

What we have in the incarnation, therefore, is not a union of the divine and human natures *simpliciter*. Rather, it is a union of the divine nature, *which just is the person of the Son of God*, with human nature, which nature, apart from that union, does not subsist.[9]

With regard to essentialism, therefore, two truths, difficult to state precisely, obtain. The first is that the Son of God is the per-

---

8. Ibid., 215.

9. "By this, the human nature (which was destitute of proper personality and was without subsistence [*anypostatos*] because otherwise it would have been a person) was assumed into the person of the Logos (*Logou*), and either conjoined with or adjoined to him in unity of person, so that now it is substantial with the Logos (*enypostatos Logō*)." Francis Turretin, *Institutes of Elenctic Theology*, ed. James T. Dennison Jr., trans. George Musgrave Giger, 3 vols. (Phillipsburg, NJ: P&R, 1992–97), 2:311.

son who took on a contingent property (human nature) and, thus, became something that he was not previously (while remaining what he is essentially). The second is that Jesus Christ, who is (numerically) the same person as the Son of God, is composed essentially of two natures. That is, though it may be that there is a possible world in which Jesus Christ does not exist (which is not the case with respect to the Son of God), in any world in which he does exist, he exists necessarily as one person with a divine and a human nature.

Therefore, with respect to Stump's assertion above that "if all the constituents of Christ other than the divine nature were removed, what remained would still be omnipotent," we need also to understand that "if all the constituents of Christ other than the divine nature were removed, what remained would still be omnipotent," but it would not be an omnipotent Jesus Christ. This is because, if all the constituents of Christ other than the divine nature were removed, then the human nature would be removed from him, in which case he would not be Jesus Christ, since to be Jesus Christ he must be both divine and human.

Herein lies a problem. When Stump argues for the reduplicative strategy as a means of coherent articulation with respect to Christ, she argues that there is no incoherence in attributing otherwise incompatible properties to the whole, given that the attribution refers to a constituent part of that whole. As Stump notes, "On Aquinas' view, there is a distinction between a property a whole has in its own right and a property it has in virtue of having a constituent that has that property in its own right . . . , a whole can borrow a property from one of its constituents."[10] Given this, argues Stump, we have "a helpful way to analyse *qua* locutions of the form *x qua A is N*."[11] The "helpful way" is that we can attribute something of the whole that is a property of a constituent part of that whole.

The "whole" to which she refers here is the person of Christ.[12] And the person of Christ is composed of two natures, one of which,

10. Stump, "Metaphysics of Incarnation," 212.

11. Ibid.

12. Turretin makes a distinction between the masculine and neuter use of the term "whole," such that the former refers to the person and the latter to the natures. The for-

the human, would not subsist except if assumed by the person himself, and the other of which is identical with the person (given simplicity). The divine nature "part" of Christ, therefore, is not in any coherent sense a "part" of Christ. Rather, it just *is* the person who takes on the human nature. But the person of Christ is the same person as the Son of God. So what we actually have in the person of Christ is the same person, who has taken to himself contingent properties (or *a* contingent property if the unity of human nature be in view), becoming, thereby, something different while remaining the same essential person.[13]

When speaking of "the whole," therefore, with respect to Christ, we are speaking of a whole that is contingent (given that it necessarily includes a human nature). What we have in Christ, therefore, is a person whose essence is identical with him, who is essentially who he is, and who in history takes on new properties, assuming to himself a human nature, all the while remaining the same person.

Given our discussion thus far, the rejoinder to Morris, given this construal of the hypostatic union, could be somewhat different than Stump's. We will remember Morris's charge of contradiction, even given the reduplicative strategy. The following conditions (previously) laid down by Morris seem to obtain: When we say, "Christ as God is infinite," and, "Christ as man is not infinite," the subject of both conjuncts must be the same. Also, it must be the case that the reduplication predicates "being God" of Christ and "being man" of Christ. And "being infinite" is entailed by being God, and "not being infinite" is entailed by being man. So far, so good. But one other condition must obtain according to Morris for there to be contradiction, namely, that the "substituends of N are univocal across the conjunction." But is this really the case? When we say,

---

mer refers to "the whole Christ," while the latter refers to "the whole of Christ." It seems, however, that what is referenced is, on the one hand, an essential property of Christ and, on the other, that which is contingent in him. See Turretin, *Institutes*, 2:321.

13. Obviously, we are using the words "essentially" and "essential" here in different ways. The Son of God became something essentially different in that, once he takes on a human nature in this world, he cannot be who he is without that nature. It is (hypothetically) necessary that he be both human and divine. He remains who he is essentially because he is essentially and necessarily divine.

"Christ as God is infinite," and "Christ as man is not infinite," are we using the term *infinite* univocally? It wouldn't seem so.

Let us take the notion of essential and contingent properties as defined in chapter 10:

E_{df} = For any thing x and any possible world, W, in which x exists and any property P, x has P in W.

C_{df} = For any thing x and any possible world, W, in which x exists and any property P, x has P in W and x does not have P in W_1.

If we take the notion of infinite to be, as we have seen, an essential property of God's, and thus also identical to him, then when we say, "Christ as God is infinite," we are not, in the first place, predicating something of the whole in virtue of one of its constituent parts. Rather, we are predicating something of the whole that it has in its own right (since the whole is the person and the person is the Son of God *qua* Christ). Thus, infinity is not constitutive of the person, but just *is* the person. What we are saying is that there is no possible world in which Christ is not infinite; infinity is of the essence of who the person of Christ is (since he is the same person as the Son of God).[14]

This, however, is not the case with respect to "Christ as man is not infinite." In this case, "not infinite" is a contingent property of Christ's, something that is not of the essence of the person.[15] It seems, therefore, that the term *infinite* is not used univocally, since its reference in the one case is essential to (and identical to) its predicate, (the Son of) God, and in the other case is to something contingent and created, the human nature. And, as Aquinas argues,

14. There are, of course, many possible worlds in which Christ does not exist, but it does not follow that there are many possible worlds in which the same person who is Christ does not exist. There is no possible world in which the Son of God, who is Christ, does not exist.

15. It is, of course, of the essence of the person of *Christ*, but it is not of the essence of the (same) person of the *Son of God*. Thus, it is essential that Christ be infinite, but, as essentially infinite, he is only contingently not infinite. If he determined to be infinite *only*, he surely would not be Christ, but the Son of God. This is only to affirm that he would have different (or no) contingent properties.

whenever the same term is used, on the one hand, to refer to God and, on the other hand, to refer to something created, it cannot be used univocally. We must affirm, then, that the word itself is used analogically. Thus, in response to Morris and in agreement with Stump: while there is no contradiction per se between the propositions, "Christ as God is infinite," and, "Christ as man is not infinite," so that the propositions can be somewhat understood, we, nevertheless, encounter quickly our own intellectual limits when we ponder the fact that the person who took on human nature is the same, eternally, as the Son of God, though from the time of the incarnation he is different (though not essentially), and this difference obtains into eternity.

To put it another way, can the same person be both created and uncreated? With respect to the person of Jesus Christ, the answer is a qualified yes. First, the qualifications.

It must first be said that the existence of Jesus Christ is itself a contingent existence. In that sense, his existence as the God-man is not something that is the case in every possible world. He did not have to exist. Thus, his existence is "creaturely."[16]

Second, we can affirm that the person of Jesus Christ is both created and uncreated only if we remember that such ascriptions are not applied in exactly the same way. We are not affirming something that is blatantly contradictory, therefore, but we are affirming something that is ultimately mysterious and beyond the pale of understanding for our finite (and sinful) minds.

Third, the notion of haecceity might help us to categorize the person of Christ.[17] If we avoid some of the confusions surrounding

16. John Owen makes this point as he compares the union of persons in the Trinity with the union of natures in the one person of Christ. See John Owen, *The Works of John Owen*, ed. W. H. Gould (Edinburgh: Banner of Truth, 1977), 1:228.

17. Haecceity is not a concept that is used uniformly in philosophy. We are thinking here primarily of its use in medieval philosophy, wherein it refers to a principle of individuation of a concrete existent. To what extent the developments of Leibniz and others apply to this use, we need not elaborate here.

In keeping with our discussion of essentialism, it may be that what we can affirm with regard to the person of Christ, given this notion of haecceity, is *mereological* essentialism, which affirms (in this case) that the two natures of Christ are essential to his being the person that he is, and without which he would not, and could not, be that person.

that notion and think of haecceity as an individual essence, then the individual, Jesus Christ, can rightly be seen as a haecceity. With that in mind, we can affirm that there is a hypothetical necessity that attaches to Jesus Christ in that he must have both a divine and a human nature. Apart from the possession of those two natures he would not be who he is. His haecceity is a unique combination and illustration of the way in which God can and does interact with that which is created.

The matter becomes complex (as we might expect in a discussion of the incarnation) when we consider that the necessary components of this haecceity are, first, that which is necessarily and essentially what it (he) is and, second, that which is contingent; and further that these two combine to constitute one individual who is both God and man. Because there are two *natures* (rather than simply various kinds of essentially differing properties) involved in this one person, it is not the case that Christ is part God and part man. Rather, *as* a particular essential person (i.e., the Son of God who is God), he has taken on a different particular, contingent nature (a human nature), which, having taken it on, constitutes a different *kind* of essential individual—an individual who is both fully God and fully man.

Or, to put it another way, the person of the Son of God assumed a contingent nature (without thereby altering his essential nature) with the result that he became the God-man Jesus Christ. As this individual—Jesus Christ—he is both created and uncreated (there are essential properties, necessary to him and without which he would not *be*, and also contingent properties, not necessary to him for *being*, but necessary to him for *being Jesus Christ*).

We are forced, therefore, to say that the haecceity who is the individual Jesus Christ is both an eternal and a temporal haecceity. He is an eternal haecceity in that he is the person of the Son of God, a particular individual of the Trinity, who is essentially identical with God. He is a temporal haecceity in that, once the human nature is assumed in history, it is essential for him that, from that time forward, he be both (essentially) divine and (contingently) human.

This way of describing the incarnation might serve to help us formulate a reduplicative strategy that would apply, climactically, to Christ, but would also apply to other propositions ascribed to God and his relationship to his creation.

In discussing the relationship of Christ's divinity to his humanity, Turretin uses the analogy of the body and the soul.

> As the body and soul form one person, so the divinity and humanity; and as the soul operates through the body (as the organ substantially united to itself) *so also the divinity through the humanity.* . . . But the divinity is properly neither a part nor an incomplete nature. Finally, from the soul and the body a certain third nature arises; but not from the divinity and humanity.[18]

What, therefore, does it mean that Christ's divinity operates *through* his humanity? In part, it means that Christ's divinity is manifested through the human nature that he assumed (Col. 1:15). But it means more than that. For example, when Christ says, concerning the day of his second coming, "But concerning that day or that hour, no one knows, not even the angels in heaven, nor the Son, but only the Father" (Mark 13:32), we should not read this as an admission on the part of Christ of total ignorance. On the contrary, we should read this as an expression of Christ's humanity, which humanity is the vehicle through which his divinity is displayed. Hence, Calvin:

> For we know that in Christ the two natures were united into one person in such a manner that each retained its own properties; and more especially the Divine nature was in a state of repose, and did not at all exert itself, whenever it was necessary that the human nature should act separately, according to what was peculiar to itself, in discharging the office of Mediator. There would be no impropriety, therefore in saying that Christ, who knew all things, was ignorant of something in respect of his perception as a man; for otherwise he could not have been liable to grief and anxiety, and could not have been *like us.* Again, the objection

18. Turretin, *Institutes*, 2:321.

urged by some that ignorance cannot apply to Christ, because it is the punishment of sin is beyond measure ridiculous. For, first, it is prodigious folly to assert that the ignorance which is ascribed to angels proceeds from sin; but they discover themselves to be equally foolish on another ground, by not perceiving that Christ clothed himself with our flesh, for the purpose of enduring the punishment due to our sins. And if Christ, as man, did not know the last day, that does not any more derogate from his Divine nature than to have been mortal. I have no doubt that he refers to the office appointed to him by the Father as in a former instance, when he said that it *did not belong to him* to place this or that person at his right or left hand. For . . . he did not absolutely say that this was not in his power, but the meaning was, that he had not been sent by the Father with this commission, so long as he lived among mortals. So now I understand that, so far as he had come down to us to be Mediator, until he had fully discharged his office that information was not given to him which he received after his resurrection; for then he expressly declared that power over all things had been given to him.[19]

With respect to reduplicative predication, therefore, perhaps we could attribute those passages which serve to highlight Christ's humanity as referring to his covenantal properties, and those which highlight his essential divinity as referring to his essential properties. Thus, we could say,

(1) Christ, with respect to his covenantal properties, did not know when the last day would be,

and

(2) Christ, with respect to his essential properties, knew when the last day would be.

However, as Turretin notes, because his divinity operates *through* his humanity (and not vice versa), we should not be surprised

19. Calvin's commentary on Mark 13:32 in John Calvin, *The Comprehensive John Calvin Collection*, CD-ROM (The Ages Digital Library System, 2002).

when such statements of humanity are given to us. Neither should we think that such statements deny who Christ essentially is, that is, the Son of God.

Not only so, but statements in Scripture that seem to confuse, that seem to be in stark contrast to other statements, should be interpreted in the context of God's condescension such that his divinity operates through his covenant properties. When Scripture says, therefore, "And the LORD relented from the disaster that he had spoken of bringing on his people" (Ex. 32:14), and "For I the LORD do not change" (Mal. 3:6), we should be aware that, while both statements are true, and while both show us something of God's essential character *through* his contingent properties, the first verse should be seen in the context of God's covenant, in which he takes on contingent properties in order to fulfill his promises to his people, while the second verse refers us to God's immutable character (and the application of that essential property in the context of God's covenant). It should not surprise us, therefore, that we will see in Scripture both "sides" of God's activity with his creation, even as it does not surprise us when we see Christ both forgive sins (according to his essential character) and become tired (according to his covenantal character).

Necessary Freedom

What this means for our understanding of compatibility generally, as well as for our understanding of the way(s) in which God is able to interact with the world, is both deep and rich. Discussions of the relationship of God's essential attributes to created reality seem to be oblivious to the ways in which God actually *has* related himself to the world. Discussions, for example, of the essential character of God's knowledge relative to our choices (usually assumed by philosophers to be libertarian choices) almost invariably conclude by "combining the natures" of God and man such that the former becomes an expression of the latter; God, it is thought, gives up (at least some of) his own essential character in order actually to become like one of us.[20] One further example should suffice here.

One attempt to formulate the relationship of God, specifically God's knowledge (or beliefs), to our human choices is developed by John Martin Fischer.[21] Problems with this discussion abound, not the least of which is the supposition that God is essentially constrained by time. It might help us, however, to see one example of an attempt to come to grips with the relationship of our choices to God's own character.

In order to get straight what is being argued, we need two notions proffered by Fischer; we need the central thesis of Fischer's argument, which is a thesis concerning the fixity of the past, FP:

(FP) For any agent A, time t, action X, and property P, if it is true that if A were to perform X at t, then some individual who actually possessed P at some time prior to t would *not* have possessed P at this prior time, then A cannot do X at t.

We also need Fischer's understanding of immutability (what he calls immutability I). Fischer considers immutability to inhere in an object just in case all its intrinsic properties, if possessed at some time t_1, cannot be such that an agent can act so that they are not possessed by that object at t_2. What Fischer is seeking in his article is the possibility of holding to a compatibilism that is consistent with FP and that includes this notion of immutability (immutability I).

At one point, Fischer introduces us to a notion he calls world-indexed compatibilism, or "WI compatibilism" (WIC).[22] In WIC, one holds that God's past beliefs are world-indexed beliefs and thus would be consistent with events that occur in the future. For

20. Though not a new position to hold, it is one that will invariably bode ill for the holders. See Israel's plight when falling prey to such notions in Ps. 50, especially v. 21.

21. John Martin Fischer, "Freedom and Actuality," in *Divine and Human Action: Essays in the Metaphysics of Theism*, ed. Thomas V. Morris (Ithaca, NY: Cornell University Press, 1988), 236–54.

22. We should be clear here that WIC is not Fischer's own position. While not summarizing the entirety of Fischer's article, we will be heavily dependent on relevant parts of it in this discussion.

example, suppose that the actual world is W_1, and suppose that, in W_1, Jane goes to the movies on Tuesday. It is true in W_1, therefore, that God believed on Monday that Jane would go to the movies on Tuesday. But suppose that W_2 is a world in which Jane refrains from going to the movies. WIC holds that, if Jane had not gone to the movies on Tuesday in W_2, then God would have held the true belief that Jane refrains from going to the movies on Tuesday in W_2. Part of the appeal of this approach is that God has a complete set of all true beliefs at every possible world. Since all of God's beliefs are world-indexed properties of God, what he believes neither alters the past nor requires a change in God's properties.

WIC is consistent with FP and with immutability I. With regard to FP, since all of God's beliefs (at least all of God's beliefs of *this kind*) are such that they are indexed to a possible world, and since God has a complete set of beliefs at every world, Jane can do whatever she pleases without in any way altering God's world-indexed beliefs. God believes that Jane will go to the movies at W_1 and that she will refrain from going at W_2. "Apparently, in virtue of the world-indexation of the contents of God's beliefs, the catalogue of God's beliefs would not change if Jane were to refrain from going to the movies on Tuesday."[23] So WIC is compatible with FP. But it is also compatible with immutability I. Since God's world-indexed beliefs do not change according to the action of an agent (in this case Jane), God's properties do not change, so that immutability I is not denied either.

But Fischer objects to WIC. His objections have to do both with FP and with immutability I, as defined above. With regard to FP, while it may be the case that God's beliefs about Jane are world-indexed, it is also the case that God's belief about which world is actual is a property of God's. If God believes on Monday that Jane will go to the movies on Tuesday in W_1, and Jane goes to the movies on Tuesday, then God believes that W_1 is the actual world. But suppose Jane refrains from going to the movies on Tuesday in W_2. In such a case, then God would believe on Monday that W_2 is the

23. Fischer, "Freedom and Actuality," 244–45.

actual world. Thus, FP is denied with respect to a property of God's, that property of God's belief as to which world is actual.

The same problem is in effect with respect to immutability I. If it is the case that God believes that W_1 is the actual world on Sunday, and if Jane can refrain from going to the movies on Tuesday, then Jane has the power on Tuesday to ensure that God would not hold a belief that W_1 is the actual world on Monday.

One further problem noted by Fischer is that God's belief that Jane will go to the movies on Tuesday is closed under known entailment. That is, if it is the case that Jane will go to the movies on Tuesday, God believes on Monday that Jane will go to the movies on Tuesday in W_1, and he also believes on Monday that W_1 is actual. But God's belief on Monday that W_1 is actual, together with his belief on Monday that Jane will go to the movies on Tuesday in W_1 entail the belief that Jane will go to the movies on Tuesday. And this latter belief is "index-free." It is a belief that is not indexed to a world at all.[24] Since the index-free belief is, thereby, contingent, then we cannot hold to immutability I; nor can we affirm FP.

Fischer attempts to extricate himself from the problems he outlines with WIC by way of a combination of WIC with "indexical possibilism." Indexical possibilism views each possible world as ontologically on a par with every other possible world, including the actual world. If indexical possibilism is correct, then any belief that God has will necessarily be a world-indexed belief, since that's the only kinds of beliefs that can be had. In this case, it could not be argued that "Jane will go to the movies on Tuesday" is an index-free belief; it is a belief relative to W_1. Index-free beliefs, if there are any, are not such that God, or anyone else, can have them. Omniscience with respect to God, therefore, must be defined thus:

24. Fischer notes that the belief that "Jane will go to the movies on Tuesday in W_1" cannot be the same as the "index-free" belief that "Jane will go to the movies," since the former is a necessary truth whereas the latter is contingent. See ibid., 247.

It is necessarily true that, if God exists, then for any time t and *world-indexed* proposition P, God knows (and thus believes) at t that P if and only if P is true at t.[25]

But, as Fischer notes, indexical possibilism is a shaky theory at best. If compatibilism's merit is measured by the plausibility of indexical possibilism, then compatibilism is in deep trouble. According to Fischer, if it is the case that the theological tenet of creation is correct, then indexical possibilism is false. If it is the case, in other words, that God created *this* world, then there is a significant difference between W_1 as the actual world and W_2, W_3, and so forth, as possible worlds.

In response to Fischer, first, a couple of minor points of clarification. Though Fischer wants to posit the possibility of some kind of compatibilism, his notion of FP seems to deny any cogent understanding of compatibility with respect to God's knowledge and human choices. Any typical understanding of compatibilism, in this context, affirms that all events are known and caused[26] by God. If that is the case, then Fischer would need to affirm that no matter what Jane decides to do on Tuesday, her decision is caused by God (and if caused, then also known). This would leave no room for a discussion of the possibility of a change in past events. God causes (and knows) each and every event, and Jane's choices cannot in any way change God's causing (and knowing) them.[27] Not only is FP implausible on a compatibilist basis, but immutability I suffers from the same malady. If it is the case that God causes all that happens, then his knowledge does not change with respect to those things at any point in time. Perhaps the lure of incompatibilism and the assumed all-pervasive character of time were, like the

25. Ibid., 250. Fischer goes on to suggest that since God believes all the world-indexed truths that there are, it is not clear just what information, on this scheme, has been denied God.

26. The notion of cause here we'll take to mean simply that, for any event x, God's action was necessary, though perhaps not sufficient, for x to take place.

27. This is the case with compatibilism. With regard to incompatibilism, this is not the case. Hence, Owen on Arminianism: "It maketh all the decrees of God, whose execution dependeth on human actions, to be altogether uncertain, and his foreknowledge of such things to be fallible and easily to be deceived." Owen, *Works*, 10:59.

Sirens of old, too compelling for Fischer to steer even a possible course through them.

Fischer mentions, but readily dismisses, a rejoinder to all of this that deserves more consideration than he is willing to give it. A possible response to objections to WIC, he says, might begin "by assuming that God is not situated within possible worlds." But, since "it is not obvious that God is not situated in possible worlds, . . . this response is unappealing."[28] The question ready at hand, however, is, "Unappealing or not obvious to whom?" Surely the (orthodox) Christian church from its inception to the present has held that God fundamentally transcends the properties and limitations of anything external to his own being.

The problems that Fischer poses are problems, in the end, of his own devising. The god of Fischer's discussions is a god made in the image of creation.[29] There seems to be no question in Fischer's mind that the notion of possibility, as well as the constraints of time, are themselves necessary aspects of the one grand scheme of reality, and are such that God, in order really and effectively to interact with his human creatures, is himself subject to them.

This is perhaps the most telling aspect of Fischer's discussion. If God is himself subject to possibility, then he is, *ipso facto*, decidedly *not* the one who determines what is and what is not possible. Just what *does* determine the range and limits of possibility is (as in virtually all philosophical discussions of possibility) not altogether clear. What is clear is that, whatever determines it, determines as well what is possible for God.

This understanding, however, wreaks havoc on a Christian understanding of God. On this construal, God is subject to all kinds of contingencies over which he has no (or little) control. This seems to get things backward. It tends to make possibility equal to (if not above) God himself. In a thoughtful rebuke of this kind of reasoning, James Ross questions the standard notion of possibility (and related concepts of essence, haecceity, etc.).

28. Fischer, "Freedom and Actuality," 250.
29. See Rom. 1:23–25.

Problem: Does God create from a universal domain the divine exemplars? That's so familiar that it seems unimaginable for a theist to disagree. Yet it is inconsistent to say that God works from a domain of kinds and individuals (or exemplars, such as natures, haecceities, individual essences, or complete concepts) *lying outside his will, determined by his nature*.[30]

The emphasis here is all-important. In part, Ross's concern, (a concern the depth of which has perhaps not always been understood), is that some suppose that the possibilities and necessities that are meant to designate the "core" modality of possible worlds are possibilities and necessities that are assumed to be intrinsic to God's own self-knowledge. "For Neoplatonists, God's prismatic self-knowledge 'refracts' a universal domain, the divine ideas of all the kinds of things there might be and of all the things of those kinds there might be."[31]

In other words, it is thought by some (and Ross mentions them) that possibility, necessity, and so on are products of the self-knowledge of God; they reside in God's understanding of himself. Ross, rightly, denies this. It cannot be the case, he argues, that possibility and necessity are products of divine ideas.

Ross does not deny the "received tradition" because he rejects the notions of possibility and necessity. Rather, those notions must be delimited within the context of God's willing certain things to be so. Hence,

Every individual of a material nature, regardless of its nature, is apt TO HAVE BEEN OTHERWISE, no matter what temporal state you choose for it or whether we regard its whole actual being as one state. At the extreme, it might not have been at all; trivially, it might have coexisted with more things than there are; more significantly, it might have done something else.[32]

30. James F. Ross, "God, Creator of Kinds and Possibilities: Requiescant Universalia Ante Res," in *Rationality, Religious Belief, and Moral Commitment*, ed. Robert Audi, William J. Wainwright (Ithaca, NY: Cornell University Press, 1986), 315, my emphasis.

31. Ibid.

32. Ibid., 324.

While Ross is concerned to oppose other aspects of possible-worlds semantics that need not be debated here (e.g., that there are no merely possible individuals), his affirmation that it is God's *will*, and not his *essential properties* (assuming his self-knowledge to be a component of his essence) that determines the possible is fundamentally correct. This is in keeping with our previous distinction between God's essential properties and those which are covenantal. Whenever God determines to act *ad extra*, that is, whenever his actions are directed toward something outside of himself, he must thereby condescend; his actions are covenantal and are thus contingent properties accruing to God just in case he determines to will (or act) *ad extra*. His actions, in this case, are not essential to his own character. Possibility, therefore, is something that pertains to God's activity *ad extra*, and not to his being *ad intra*. So, says Ross:

> What is possible *ad extra* is a result of what God does. God's power has no exemplar objects, only a perimeter (that is, finite being) plus a limit (that of internal consistency, compatibility with the divine being). God creates the kinds, the natures of things, along with things. And he settles what-might-have-been insofar as it is a consequence of what exists. . . . Thus, there is no *mere* possibility with content . . . there are only descriptions, actual and potential, that might, for all we know so far, have been satisfied. . . . In sum, God creates the possibility, impossibility, and counter-factuality that has content (real situations) involving being other than God.[33]

In other words, possibility has its foundation in actuality, and not in someone's abstract notions of what God thinks he might or might not have done. And note, most importantly, that, according to Ross, "God creates the possibility, impossibility, and counter-factuality that has content." There can be no real content to, because no referent for, abstract possibility; only possibility as a consequence of God's creative activity has any real content.

33. Ibid., 318–19.

What Ross is saying here has precedence in Reformed thought. Richard Muller, elaborating specifically on a Reformed view of counterfactuals notes:

> . . . a so-called future conditional—"if David will stay the night"— when posed as pure possibility, prior to God's decree, is literally "nothing" (or nothing more than a logical hypothesis). It cannot be known or foreknown as actual. Indeed, insofar as it is noth-ing, it cannot be known at all. Nor does it detract from God's omniscience to state that it is unknowable, because it is not an unknowable something, but simply nothing at all. In other words, contrary propositions standing prior to the decree of God to ac-tualize one or the other are "not entities," and thus are neither true nor false, nor, indeed, knowable—such propositions "are indifferent to truth and falsehood."[34]

Considered apart from God's all-encompassing decree, therefore, the "possible" is, as a matter of fact, *nothing*. It is not possible, therefore, that possibility is something that surrounds God; it is even incoherent to think that possibility is something *identical* to God, or something that is a necessary part of his essential nature. Possibility is related to the covenantal character of God in which, in his determination to create all that is, he also determined *not* to create other things that might have been.[35] And it relates to God's actual determinations, his decree(s), such that it presup-poses that which is actual. The triune God is in no way subject to possibility.[36]

---

34. Richard A. Muller, *Post-Reformation Reformed Dogmatics: The Rise and Develop-ment of Reformed Orthodoxy, Ca. 1520 to Ca. 1725: The Divine Essence and Attributes*, 2nd ed. (Grand Rapids, MI: Baker, 2002), 431. Muller is, in this discussion, referencing Baxter's *Catholike Theologie* and Rutherford's *Exercitationes apologeticae*.

35. We should remember here that, as in Christ, the two aspects of God's nature, the essential and the covenantal, are compatible and in no way work against each other. That which is possible, by virtue of God's covenantal nature, is not in any way in conflict with God's essential nature, which includes his immutability.

36. This does not mean, however, that the notions of possibility and necessity do not in any way apply to God, any more than our saying that God is not subject to goodness means that goodness does not apply to him. It only means that any such notions, just in case they apply to God, are themselves equal to him and are therefore not of the created

Nor is God essentially subject to time or the created order. Here again is where our Christology is absolutely central to our discussion. As God created, he condescended to relate himself to his creation, and thus his creation to himself. He has done that, as we have seen, by taking on attributes, or properties, or characteristics, that are not essential to him, and that in no way change or otherwise affect his essential character *ad intra*.

As we saw above, this is what God has done preeminently and supremely in Christ. In Christ, God the Son took on human flesh, without in any way ceasing to be fully and completely what he already was and is as God. So, to the question "Is God subject to time?" we can answer reduplicatively. We can say, "God as essentially God is not subject to time," and, "God as covenantal is subject to time." So, the answer given must be something like, "Essentially, no, but covenantally, yes." And because he is subject to time only covenantally, there is no situation in which his essential character is compromised, undermined, or otherwise altered. *That* character is not confused, mixed, divided, or separated with respect to his covenantal properties, though those properties are fully a part of who he is, as a person, to and for us.

How does this change our understanding of compatibility? It should instigate a radical change in how we think about compatibility itself. Specifically, just what two (or more) seemingly incompatible things can be cogently and coherently brought together must initially be determined by *God* and what *he* has done, rather than by us and our notions of what we deem to be possible and what we deem to be impossible.

For example, with respect to God's relationship to the world, the two propositions

(1) At time t_1, the incarnated second person of the Trinity, as the person Jesus Christ, was fully *a se*, immutable, infinite, and so forth

---

order. Necessity, for example, as a mode of God's existence, applies to God, but it applies to him by way of his essential attributes; the same is true for the impossibility of God's nonexistence.

and

> (2) At time t_1, the incarnated second person of the Trinity, as the person Jesus Christ, was fully dependent, subject to change, limited, and so forth

would, by any human reckoning, appear to be incompatible, for a number of reasons. With regard to (1), how could a person be fully God and yet *be* in relation to time at all? Or how could a person *be* Jesus Christ, and at the same time be *fully* God, who himself is fully personal? With regard to (2), how could this person, Jesus Christ, at the same time that he is fully God (and in the same person), be fully dependent? How could the full deity of God be so compatible to the full humanity of man such that both could fully reside in one haecceity, one individual essence, one person?

Yet this is just what a *Christian* compatibility teaches us. The muddle of many philosophers (and theologians) concerning how God can accommodate himself to his creation without giving up on (at least aspects of) his essential character is clearly (though, ultimately, mysteriously) revealed to us in the coming in the flesh of the second person of the Trinity. The person of Jesus Christ shows God and creation (humanity) to be compatible without sacrificing the essential character of each.

16

Reformed Freedom

Since, therefore, the essential structure of freedom is not placed in indifference, it cannot be sought elsewhere than in rational willingness, by which man does what he pleases by a previous judgment of reason. —TURRETIN

As we have seen, it is revelation from God (preeminently in Christ) that gives us a paradigm of Christian compatibility, a paradigm that might help us understand how we should frame the relationship of the existence of God to the existence of evil. Properties that are otherwise incompatible are brought together by God under one unifying entity.

Freedom from Necessity

We need to respond further to Fischer. We need, finally, to note how we might begin to think of the nature of necessity with respect to our human decisions. We have already seen, in chapter 14, that

326

God's decree, itself eternal and necessary, is unified with our human decisions by way of God's providence. God's providence both carries out the details of that decree and establishes the contingency and freedom, as secondary causes, that take place in this world according to that decree. But isn't the necessity of God's decree opposed to freedom? Isn't that why the FWD denies *any* necessity to God's decree in the first place?[1]

We have already seen that, in Plantinga's ingenious response to the problem of evil, libertarian freedom, together with its concomitant notion of incompatibilism, is a rock-bottom and necessary assumption. Without it, it might just be the case that God *could* actualize any possible world, and it might be the case that no one could possibly suffer from transworld depravity. Without a notion of libertarian freedom at its disposal, the FWD is paralyzed.

How might a RFWD articulate the relationship of the necessity of God's decree to the freedom and responsibility of our choices? Is there a better response to the problem of evil from a Calvinistic, Reformed perspective?[2] Is there a way ahead for those to whom a limited and dependent God is not an option? Perhaps there is.

It should be noted, first, that the notion of free will itself is denied by no orthodox theology.[3] The central question concerning free will is what is meant by freedom, and to what extent freedom

1. Again, as in Molinism (see next note) so also in the FWD, since whatever God decrees with respect to human choices is determined by those choices, there is no necessity in God's decree with respect to those choices.

2. We should state here explicitly what has been implicit in our discussion of the FWD: its philosophical principles with respect to libertarian freedom and God's dependence on that freedom are consistent with the theology of Molinism specifically and Arminianism generally. And as Muller notes, Molinism consistently applied leads to Socinianism. See Richard A. Muller, *Post-Reformation Reformed Dogmatics: The Rise and Development of Reformed Orthodoxy, Ca. 1520 to Ca. 1725: The Divine Essence and Attributes*, 2nd ed. (Grand Rapids, MI: Baker, 2002), 425. On Molinism, see, for example, Robert Merrihew Adams, "Middle Knowledge and the Problem of Evil," *American Philosophical Quarterly* 14 (1977); and "Plantinga on the Problem of Evil," in James E. Tomberlin and Peter van Inwagen, eds., *Alvin Plantinga* (Dordrecht: D. Reidel, 1985), esp. 230–32.

3. Note, for example, John Owen, *The Works of John Owen*, ed. W. H. Gould (Edinburgh: Banner of Truth, 1977), 10:145: "Yet here observe that we do not absolutely oppose free-will, as if it were 'nomen inane,' a mere figment, when there is no such thing in the world, but only in that sense the Pelagians and Arminians do assert it. About words we will not contend."

obtains in human beings. Turretin has arguably the best and most succinct discussion of a Reformed understanding of free will. He first makes clear that not every notion of necessity is, *ipso facto*, opposed to liberty.[4] He then goes on to delimit what kind of necessity is agreeable to liberty. While an extrinsic necessity of coaction is incompatible with liberty, "hypothetical necessity, arising either from a decree of God or from the existence of the thing, conspires with it."[5] The liberty that Adam enjoyed, therefore, before the fall was a freedom from coaction and from physical necessity, but a liberty that "conspires with" the decree of God. It was a liberty that flowed from the hypothetical necessity of God's own determination.

For Turretin and many of the orthodox Reformed, hypothetical necessity was a necessity that obtained by virtue of a previous decision, in this case, on the part of God. Thus, while creation itself was never absolutely necessary, it *became* necessary once God (covenantally) determined to create. The necessity of creation has its foundation in a free and contingent decision by God so to create.

The Consequence of Freedom

So, initially, what Turretin means when he speaks of a hypothetical necessity is a necessity of something that did not *have to* be, but that, once decided, necessarily *was*. And he notes that this hypothetical necessity, which arises from God's decree, in some way

4. Muller makes this point as well. Commenting on Stephen Strehle's article, "Calvinism, Augustinianism, and the Will of God," Muller notes, "What Strehle does not understand is that necessity and freedom are neither contraries nor contradictories: the contrary of necessity is impossibility; the contrary of freedom is coercion." Muller, *The Divine Essence and Attributes*, 434, n. 360.

Note also, "For the freedom of our will does not consist in this, that it is driven by no necessity to sinning, but in this, that it is free from all coercion." And further, "Therefore free choice in man always remains free, namely from coercion, although not from necessity in whatever state." Girolamo Zanchi, "Always Free, but Not Always Good: Girolamo Zanchi (1516–1590) on Free Will," in Willem J. van Asselt, J. M. Bac, and R. T. te Velde, *Reformed Thought on Freedom: The Concept of Free Choice in the History of Early-Modern Reformed Theology* (Utrecht: Research Group Classic Reformed Theology, forthcoming), 60–61.

5. Francis Turretin, *Institutes of Elenctic Theology*, ed. James T. Dennison Jr., trans. George Musgrave Giger, 3 vols. (Phillipsburg, NJ: P&R, 1992–97), 1:570.

works together with liberty. "The freedom of the will," he says, "is indeed overthrown by a physical and coactive necessity . . . , but not by a hypothetical necessity and of the infallibility of the event, for the same thing in this respect can be both free and necessary."[6]

In order to see how the same thing can be both free and necessary, Turretin employs a distinction that was used also by John Calvin[7] (and by Thomas Aquinas), a distinction between the *necessity of the consequent* and the *necessity of the consequence*. Generally, the necessity of the consequent affirms,

If God knows x, then necessarily x,

while the necessity of the consequence affirms,

Necessarily, if God knows x, then x.[8]

We need to have Turretin's distinction more clearly before us before we can relate it to Fischer's problem above, and to the problem of evil specifically.

> The infallibility and certainty of the event does not take away the nature of the contingency of things because things can happen necessarily as to the event and yet contingently as to the mode of production. If there is granted a prescience of future contingent things, all things would take place necessarily by necessity of consequence, by the necessity of infallibility; not by necessity of the consequent and absolute. Therefore, there remains always this distinction between necessary and contingent things. The former have an intrinsic necessity because they arise from necessary proximate causes and are such in themselves; while the contingent,

6. Ibid., 1:211.

7. See John Calvin, *Institutes of the Christian Religion*, ed. John T. McNeill, trans. Ford Lewis Battles, Library of Christian Classics (London: SCM, 1960), 1.16.9 and 3.23.8. See also Paul Helm, *John Calvin's Ideas* (Oxford: Oxford University Press, 2004), 117, 323f.

8. There are other distinctions to be made here between modality *de dicto*, in which modality attaches to a proposition, and modality *de re*, in which modality attaches to a thing. These distinctions, though they can be helpful in discussions of this sort, will not occupy us here.

although having an extrinsic necessity by reason of the event, yet in their nature take place by contingent causes.[9]

Given Turretin's rock-ribbed Calvinism, there are certain assumptions in the quotation above, assumptions that Turretin makes explicit elsewhere. First, for Turretin (as indeed for the vast majority of orthodox theologians for over two thousand years), God is both simple and eternal. This means, as we have seen, that there are no "parts" of which God is essentially composed (including "parts" of his knowledge), and that God is not in any way essentially limited by or subject to the constraints of time. God's duration is not past, present, or future.

As we have argued, God, in bringing creation about (i.e., actualizing it), takes on properties that are covenantal, properties that are distinct from his essential being. But what we must continue to remember and to stress is that, in taking on these covenantal properties, God in no way violates, repudiates, or negates his essential character. When God, as God, knows all that there is to know about creation, he does not depend on creation and its process in order to know those things. If he did so depend, he would violate his essential character; he would be schizophrenic. He would be one who, on the one hand, thought himself independent and, on the other hand, depended on creation before he could act. But he is not one who must wait on things to occur in order to know *that* they are, *when* they are, and *what* they are.

Thus, what God knows "prior to" creation *about* creation, is in no way subject to or dependent on that creation in order for him to know it. He knows all that there is to know, and he knows all eternally. His knowledge in no way depends on something *ad extra*, something of which he is the author, and over which he is sovereign; nor does it depend on the temporal, created event or thing in order to be known.

It is because God knows in this way that Turretin recognizes the tension between God's knowledge of an event that is brought about by human decision and the human freedom (hypothetically)

9. Turretin, *Institutes*, 1:217.

necessary for bringing that event about. Concerning any event that God knows, therefore, Turretin affirms the necessity of the consequence (and we should remember that we are within the realm of a hypothetical necessity, given that God did not have to create, and, once he determined to, he did not have to order things in the way that he did). That is, it is (hypothetically) necessarily the case that "if God knows S will do x, then S will do x."

This understanding of God, however, does not entail that God's knowledge cannot be referenced to temporal propositions. God knows, for example, and knows essentially, eternally, as well as covenantally, that I will be typing these words at this time. Because God's knowledge provides the foundation for any and every thing that occurs, it can have reference to a temporal sequence, without at the same time being essentially subject to that sequence. This, in part, because God took on covenantal properties in which he relates himself to his creation without violating his essential character. So his knowledge of what I am actually doing now is covenantal knowledge in that he can know "now" *as* "now." But that knowledge in no way compromises the fact that God, in eternity, prior to his act to create, knew (knows) what I am typing now. This latter knowledge, however, could not have been anything but essentially God (who is altogether simple), since, prior to his act to create, there was nothing but God, and thus any and every "now" was referenced to that knowledge alone.

Turretin's point above is that the temporal event, S will do x, because known prior to creation, eternally, by God, will necessarily take place; thus, the necessity of the consequence. Tied to God's decree as it is, there is no possible world in which it cannot happen. It is also the case, however, that the temporal event, S will do x, is a contingent event in that it does not take place by the necessity of the consequent. The reason the necessity of the consequent does not come into play here, as Turretin notes, is that we can make a distinction between the necessity of the event and the "mode of production."

Given that God knows (and decrees) that S will do x, S will do x can only obtain just in case S exists (which is itself a contingency), and just in case S does x (which is a contingent event, depending on S for its "production"). Therefore,

Necessarily, if God knows S will do x, S will do x

is true. The event itself, given God's knowledge of it, will necessarily happen. But its "mode of production" does not partake of that necessity.[10] Therefore, says Turretin,

> The foreknowledge of God implies indeed the infallibility of futurition and of the event and the necessity of the consequence, and yet does not imply coaction or violence, nor take away from the will its intrinsic liberty.[11]

Because of the "mode of production," therefore, there is in the event no necessity of the consequent. It is not the case that

if God knows S will do x, necessarily S will do x,

since the production of the consequent is a contingency. This allows for the certainty of the consequence—there is no possible world at which, if God knows S will do x, S will not do x. But it also allows for the fact that the actual production of the event, the *doing* of x, is a contingent event, requiring a free decision by S in order to happen.[12]

10. In this distinction, we can see a grain of truth in libertarian views of the will. While it is not the case that God is dependent on his human creatures to act in order to know what they will do (or in order to decree what they will do, as in the case of middle knowledge), it is the case that, given the creation of creatures in God's image, certain things cannot be done unless those creatures decide and act to do them. So, for example, God could never, of himself, bring anything evil to pass; for that to happen, creatures made in his image must be the "mode of production" (in Turretin's words).

11. Turretin, *Institutes*, 1:211.

12. It is interesting in this context that some among the Reformed argued that it is Molinism, not Calvinism, that results in the necessity of the consequent. "The attempt to gain freedom at the expense of the divine causality results, therefore, in a new fatalism, a replacement of the conception of overarching divine purpose with a model of blind natural necessity." There is a necessity of the consequent introduced, that is an absolute necessity, and is independent of the divine decree. Muller, *The Divine Essence and Attributes*, 425.

What this means for RFWD is this: the event of the sin of Adam, for example, was an event that happened by way of the necessity of the consequence. God knows eternally that Adam will go wrong with respect to the forbidden fruit. His knowledge of Adam's action is infallible; the event itself is (hypothetically) necessary. Necessarily, once God decrees that it will happen, it will happen.

But that does not change the fact that Adam's decision to eat from the forbidden tree is a decision done "by a previous judgment of the reason and spontaneously."[13] It is not coerced (in that there is nothing extrinsically forcing Adam's hand), and it is not against Adam's will (in that there is nothing intrinsically violating Adam's ability to choose for or against eating the forbidden fruit). Thus, the predetermination of God (by virtue of the necessity of the consequence) and the freedom of man (by virtue of Adam's ability to choose among the options given) are not in competition with each other, nor does the one violate the other. Rather, both are executed according to the providence of God, in which the application of God's decree includes the free decision of Adam to eat the forbidden fruit. Just as with the person of Christ, now with God's knowledge and human decision, God brings together both the divine (decree) and the human (free decision) under one unifying entity, providence, such that the two seemingly incompatible properties are made compatible by his sovereign design and plan.

How might we delineate a defense in this context? If we were to use Plantinga's structure of defense,[14] we could perhaps say that

(1) God ordains whatsoever comes to pass

and

(3) There is evil

can be shown to be compatible with the addition of

---

13. Turretin, *Institutes*, 1:570.
14. Recall the basic structure of a defense: $(\Diamond(P\&R) \ \& \ ((P\&R)\rightarrow Q)\rightarrow\Diamond(P\&Q))$.

(2) It is possible that God's covenantal providence, which is carried out in the world, *W*, that God actualizes, includes the compatibility of (a) the eternal decree of God and (b) the free (and responsible) response of Adam to bring it about that there is evil.

Or another way to say it is that, since there is a possible world in which the otherwise incompatible properties of God and of human nature are, by God, brought together in one person, so also is there a possible world in which the otherwise incompatible properties of the divine decree and human responsibility are brought together by God by way of his one covenantal providence.

Since all that is needed for a defense is that (2) be plausible (which it is, since it is true), be compatible with (1) (which it is), and together with (1) entail (3) (which it does), this too could be offered as a RFWD, a FWD that is Reformed in its theological content.

The RFWD may not, we should admit, release the tension between God's existence and the existence of evil in the way that the FWD does. This is because it is easier to see how a god who is not sovereign could be caught by the surprise of evil. As we saw above, in order to show (1) and (3) to be compatible, the FWD had to assume, first, that God was dependent on human choices such that there was no intellectual tension between God's own character and the decisions of human beings. To put it more directly, God had to be made compatible with our free choices first, in order, second, to show the compatibility of his existence with the existence of evil in the world. But this option is not open to Reformed theology.

What *is* open to Reformed theology (and any other theology that sees the person of Christ as the paradigm through which we understand God's relationship to the world generally) is to define compatibility in such a way that two mutually and essentially different states of affairs—in this case the decree of God and the free and responsible decision of Adam—can compatibly coexist because that which Adam "produced" or "caused" by his decision to eat the forbidden fruit in no way violates, undermines, or eliminates God's sovereign, independent control and knowledge of that act, which control and knowledge is, nevertheless, not the responsible agent of the act. The act itself remains contingent (since there are possible worlds in which it did not happen), while at the same time being providentially guided (since decreed by God).

There is one more point to make with this notion of compatibility. We can better understand what is taking place if we remember that, with respect to the notion of cause, that which applies to God is essentially different from that which applies to us. Perhaps, in order to illustrate this point, an example in another context might help. One of God's covenantal attributes is his omnipresence (like others of his covenantal attributes, it is an implication of his aseity). By omnipresent we mean that there is no place where God is not. He is everywhere. And he is not everywhere in the sense that he is spread over his creation like a blanket. Rather he is everywhere in that, wherever there is anything at all, God is there, fully there, as well.

Yet, by human reckoning, as I sit here in my chair, it seems obvious and without controversy that no one else is occupying the space that I am occupying. There is no space left to occupy except the space that I now fully take up. As a matter of fact, however, it is also the case that, at every point in space, and in space *in toto*, God is fully and completely at each and every point. *He* is fully where *I* am fully. And, unlike me, he is fully everywhere else as well, no matter what other thing might be fully occupying that same space.

Now what kind of "presence" is it that can occupy space that is already fully occupied by something else? We simply don't know. What we do know is that my presence, fully and completely, in this chair and God's full and complete presence here are fully compatible one with the other. God's presence is infinitely different from mine. But he is able to bring together two otherwise incompatible entities, just by virtue of the fact that he does not exist in the same way that we do.

So also with God's "causal" activity.[15] While it is proper to speak of God as primary cause and (in the case of responsible decisions) our-

15. Though foreknowledge per se does not necessarily entail causality, there is no question that for the magisterial Reformers and the orthodox Reformed, including Turretin, embedded in God's foreknowledge is, as well, his sovereign control. For an interpretation of Augustine in which foreknowledge may not entail causality, see David P. Hunt, "On Augustine's Way Out," *Faith and Philosophy* 16, no. 1 (January 1999): 3–26. Hunt's

selves as secondary causes, or of God as remote cause and ourselves as proximate causes, we should not think thereby that the notion of causality is the same when applied to God as it is when applied to us.[16] His causality is, though essentially different, nevertheless compatible with ours. Not only so, but he is the one who defines the who, what, when, and where of responsibility with respect to this compatibility. As in God's-presence-with-ours, we should not think that compatibility means a fifty-fifty split, as if God occupies part of a space and I the other part. It means (again we can think of the person of Christ) that within one unifying entity, the context of the *Eimi/eikon*, we are fully involved and freely responsible creatures, even while God himself is fully involved and receives all the glory for what takes place. This christological—Christian—notion of compatibility creates a context for our thinking about the existence of God together with the existence of evil. To put it another way, a way that incorporates explicitly our previous discussion, since it is the case that we have a dual metaphysic, one in which there are two *kinds* of being, it is also the case that there are two *kinds* of presence (God's and ours), two *kinds* of causality, and so forth.

It might just be that adherents of the FWD will likely not view the RFWD as a persuasive response. After all, part of the pressure embedded in the problem of evil is, if possible, to relinquish God from (our notion of) responsibility for the evil that predominates. Plantinga's version attempts to do that by setting forth the possibility that there are worlds that God cannot actualize (and implicit in this is that this world happens to be one of them). But, as was said above, this only pushes the problem one step back. For surely since God did not have to create, and since (as is assumed in the FWD) in creating creatures with libertarian freedom he runs the risk of unprecedented evil, one who is thought to be infinitely wise

---

article interacts with another possible "way out" of the tension between foreknowledge and human freedom in Alvin Plantinga, "On Ockham's Way Out," in *The Analytic Theist: A Collection of Alvin Plantinga's Work in Philosophy of Religion*, ed. Alvin Plantinga and James F. Sennett (Grand Rapids, MI: Eerdmans, 1998), 258–92.

16. It is worth noting here that this view of compatibility with respect to the problem of evil accommodates the notion of *concursus divinus*, and not the notion of occasionalism or of conservationism. Thus, a Reformed view of providence is maintained as well.

would refrain from taking such risks, given the massive amount of suffering and pain that could be actualized if he chose to create. To say that God determined to actualize such a world because he thought so highly of libertarian freedom strains the limits of credibility (and, it should be said, seems altogether absent from God's revelation).[17]

A notion of compatibility that takes seriously the reality of the person of Christ as the *Eimi/eikon*, can take seriously as well the reality of other states of affairs that don't seem to come naturally together in our own minds, but which God brings together in his creation and providence over all things. If this too strains the limits of credibility, at least it has the support of God's own revelation (climactically in Christ), as well as (with respect to Christology) the history of orthodox Christianity since its inception.

Conclusion

One of the problems that plagues the FWD plagues the RFWD as well. The question remains in the RFWD as to why God would create just this world. An answer to that question moves us inexorably toward the only real solution to the problem of evil. It should not go unnoticed that, in this case, the logical problem of evil intersects with the personal, or pastoral, problem of evil. That is as it should be.

How might Reformed Christianity respond to the question posed by Leibniz: Is this the best of all possible worlds? Certainly such a question presupposes a number of ideas and concepts that need clarification. Just what do we mean by "the best"? How do we determine what is possible? Are we able to determine, in some satisfactory way, enough about what is possible to extrapolate to every possibility?

17. Interesting in this regard is Hugh LaFollette's argument that, in part, asserts that since being significantly free obtains in God, who cannot commit evil, there seems to be no reason to claim that such freedom requires that evil be possible. It is not possible for or in God, who is free; why must it be in humans? See Hugh LaFollette, "Plantinga on the Free Will Defense," in *The Impossibility of God*, ed. Michael Martin (Amherst, NY: Prometheus, 2003), 97–105.

As we have seen, some of these questions move us into quag-mires and labyrinths that may, in the end, serve to confuse rather than clarify. The first question, however, needs some attention. Just what *do* we mean by "the best."

Whenever this concept is discussed, what can be meant is "the best for us." And what is sometimes assumed in "the best for us" is a world without any suffering, pain, or other anomalies that seem only to provide misery and discomfort.

But how do we know that a world without evil really is the best? In one sense, we think such things because God himself is without evil, and surely he is the best *in excelsus*. Whenever we ponder perfection, we turn immediately to God's own character and rightly conclude that a world that was in conformity to that character would be, thereby, better than one that was not. That seems true enough.

So, there must be more to this world than simply a possible exemplification of "the best." God must have had more in mind when he determined that he would create this world, knowing full well that men (and angels) would go wrong and thus attempt to move this world away from his character and control.

Just what might this "more" be? The only way to answer that question is by way of God's own revelation to us. And while we don't have any specifics given to us in that revelation as to the thoughts of God in making this world rather than another, we do have unavoid-ably strong indications of some elements of this world that are important to God's own plan, important enough that he determined, freely, to set that plan into motion. Two will be mentioned.

First, it certainly seems true that a manifestation of evil shows us something, if only by contrast, of the character of God himself. Here we must face the question as to why it was that the Serpent's temptation of Eve in the garden was something that actually per-suaded her (cf. 2 Cor. 11:2). Surely it was not that what the Serpent proposed to Eve was fundamentally irrational, insane, or out of touch with *everything* that Eve knew to be the case.[18] At least part

---

18. This is one reason why we are given the information that the Serpent was the most subtle, the most crafty, of beasts.

of the persuasion lay in the fact that, while God certainly knew both good and evil (because God knows all things), Eve did not. She was deceived into thinking that she could know evil, and thus be more like God, without at the same time falling from her relationship to him. She was deceived, but deception carries with it a persuasive grain of truth. Eve wanted to know as God knows. The introduction of evil on the earth shows us, in part, that to desire to be like God, except in those ways in which God has already created us (and re-created us) to be like him, is not a lofty goal at all, but is a sin. With sin's entrance into the world, we see by contrast what we might only have seen by comparison.

Second, and most importantly, God determined to create a world in which he himself would choose to subject himself to the very evil that was and is in no way an aspect of his character—not of his essential character, and not of his covenantal character. God, in Christ, determined that it would be "best" if he created a world in which he himself would condescend to come, to live, to *suffer, and to die*. And he determined that the death that he would die, as horrendous as it was, would not simply be a horrendous death, but would be worse than horrendous; it would be a death in which he would take on himself the curse of his own people in order that those who are not worthy of living at all should live for eternity with him.

The One who is all wise and who knows all things, the One who does all things well and in whom is no shadow of turning, determined to create a world in which he himself would have to take on limits and sufferings and pains and even death, in order to bring to consummation all things, to his glory. God is not a spectator when it comes to evil. He does not determine to create a world with evil and then simply watch to see how his pitiful creatures will manage in it. Rather, he determines to create a world in which he will involve himself, personally and painfully, in the resolution to the problem for which we ourselves are responsible. He comes, as the *Eimi/eikon*, as the God-man, in the person of Jesus Christ, and he comes to die. Surely no greater evil has ever been perpetrated in the universe than the putting to death of the One who alone was such that he deserved only heavenly bliss. Not only so, but in

339

that death (and this is even worse than the death itself) he takes on the rebellion that is not his, and he makes it his, so that those whose rebellion it is will not suffer eternally because of it, but will be counted as righteous before him (2 Cor. 5:21).

There can be no question that this demonstration of sacrificial love—of a love that is not conditioned by or dependent on those to whom it is given—shows us something of the character of this God that was not a part of the perfection of Eden.

Is this a good reason for creating a world in which evil would be so exhaustively present? There is no indication that God is torn as to which world to actualize. He chooses to create, and to create this world. Embedded in that choice is that he himself, in the second person of the Trinity, would stoop to our level in order to suffer and die.

Perhaps Ross is right. Perhaps possibility is subject to God's prior actualization. Perhaps there is no possibility *in abstraction*. So if it seemed to the One who is all-wise and immutably good that it was wise and good to create this world, then we who follow him must admit that this world, with the abundance of evil and sin present in it, is nevertheless the best of all possible worlds, because it is the best of all actualized worlds.

What, then, shall we say to all of this? What's a Christian theologian, or philosopher of religion, or philosopher to do with all that has preceded?

Perhaps Turretin sums it up best for us. Speaking of "the orthodox," Turretin says:

> They do not confound theology with sound philosophy as the parts of a whole; nor do they set them against each other as contraries, but subordinate and compound them as subordinates which are not at variance with, but mutually assist each other. . . . Theology rules over philosophy, and this latter acts as a handmaid to and subserves the former.[19]

The primary point to be made in all of this is that "theology rules over philosophy." This is especially the case when we are involved

19. Turretin, *Institutes*, 1:44.

340

in discussions of natural theology, philosophy of religion, or philosophical theology.

If it is true that theology rules over philosophy, then it is also true that the foundational and fundamental content of our philosophical investigations must come from the teaching of Scripture. For what else is theology but a reflection on that teaching?

We affirm, then, a revelational epistemology, in which the basic truths of our theory of knowledge, derived as they are from the nature of the world, are taken initially from the teaching of God's special revelation and from the reality of God's general revelation.

We affirm as well a covenantal metaphysic, in which our understanding of God is derived from his revelation. We know God only inasmuch as he has revealed himself to us. Given that revelation, we know something of his character as he stoops to interact with his creation.

Theology, therefore, provides the parameters in which philosophy must work. It does not define all of philosophy's content; it does not define the specific method(s) that philosophy must use; it does not define the specific details of a philosophical system. But it does provide the ground, as well as the boundaries, from and within which philosophy must do its work.

This is, as we said in the beginning, philosophical good news for the Christian. This means that Christians who wish to engage in the philosophical task are free to do so, and to do so within the context of a rich and deep theological heritage.

It also means, appropriately, that even and perhaps especially when engaged in the philosophical task, when we reach our intellectual limits, when we come to a place where we can say only so much and nothing more, we do not thereby jump from our secure place, break through our boundaries, and move into areas that are in conflict with our theology. Rather, we are content, even constrained, in such cases gladly and expectantly to exclaim with the apostle Paul:

Oh, the depth of the riches and wisdom and knowledge of God! How unsearchable are his judgments and how inscrutable his ways!

"For who has known the mind of the Lord,
   or who has been his counselor?"
"Or who has given a gift to him
   that he might be repaid?"

For from him and through him and to him are all things. To him be glory forever. Amen. (Rom. 11:33–36)

Bibliography

Adams, Robert Merrihew. "Middle Knowledge and the Problem of Evil." *American Philosophical Quarterly* 14 (1977): 109–17.

———. "Plantinga on the Problem of Evil." In *Alvin Plantinga*, edited by James E. Tomberlin and Peter van Inwagen, 225–55. Dordrecht: D. Reidel, 1985.

Alston, William P. "Aquinas on Theological Predication." In *Reasoned Faith*, edited by Eleanore Stump, 145–78. Ithaca, NY: Cornell University Press, 1993.

Aquinas, Thomas. *Commentary on the Posterior Analytics of Aristotle*. Translated by F. R. Larcher. Albany, NY: Magi Books, 1970.

———. "On Being and Essence." In *Selected Writings of St. Thomas Aquinas*, translated by Robert P. Goodwin, 162. New York: Bobbs, 1965.

———. *On the Truth of the Catholic Faith: Summa Contra Gentiles*. Garden City, NY: Hanover House, 1955.

———. *Summa Contra Gentiles*. Translated by Anton C. Pegis. Notre Dame, IN: Notre Dame University Press, 1957.

———. *Summa Theologiae: Latin Text, English Translation, Introduction, Notes, Appendices and Glossary*. Edited by Thomas Gilby. London and New York: Eyre & Spottiswoode and McGraw-Hill, 1964.

Aristotle. *The Basic Works of Aristotle*. Edited by Richard McKeon. New York: Random House, 1968.

Audi, Robert. *The Cambridge Dictionary of Philosophy*. Cambridge: Cambridge University Press, 1995.

————. "Self-Deception, Rationalization, and Reasons for Acting." In *Perspectives on Self-Deception*, edited by Brian P. McLaughlin and Amelie Oksenberg Rorty, 92–122. Berkeley: University of California Press, 1988.

Bateson, Gregory, and Mary Catherine Bateson. *Angels Fear: Towards an Epistemology of the Sacred*. New York: Macmillan, 1987.

Bavinck, Herman. *Gereformeerde Dogmatiek*. Kampen: J. H. Kok, 1967.

————. *Reformed Dogmatics: God and Creation*. Edited by John Bolt. Translated by John Vriend. Grand Rapids, MI: Baker, 2004.

Bergmann, Michael. "Might-Counterfactuals, Transworld Untrustworthiness and Plantinga's Free Will Defense." *Faith and Philosophy* 16, no. 3 (1999): 336–51.

Biderman, Shlomo. *Scripture and Knowledge: An Essay on Religious Epistemology*. Studies in the History of Religions, 69. New York: E. J. Brill, 1995.

Borland, James A. *Christ in the Old Testament*. Chicago: Moody Press, 1978.

Boyd, Gregory A. *God of the Possible: A Biblical Introduction to the Open View of God*. Grand Rapids, MI: Baker, 2000.

Caird, John. *An Introduction to the Philosophy of Religion*. The Croall Lectures; 1878–79. Glasgow: J. Maclehose, 1880.

Calvin, John. *Commentaries on the Epistle of Paul, the Apostle, to the Romans*. Edinburgh: Calvin Translation Society, 1849.

————. *The Comprehensive John Calvin Collection*. CD-ROM. The Ages Digital Library System, 2002.

————. *Institutes of the Christian Religion*. Edited by John T. McNeill. Translated by Ford Lewis Battles. Library of Christian Classics. London: SCM, 1960.

Clark, Gordon Haddon. *The Incarnation*. Jefferson, MD: The Trinity Foundation, 1988.

Clarke, W. Norris. "Charles Hartshorne's Philosophy of God: A Thomistic Critique." In *Charles Hartshorne's Concept of God: Philosophical and Theological Responses*, edited by Santiago Sia, 103–23. Boston: Kluwer Academic, 1990.

Clayton, Philip. *The Problem of God in Modern Thought*. Grand Rapids, MI: Eerdmans, 2000.

Craig, William Lane. *Time and Eternity: Exploring God's Relationship to Time*. Wheaton, IL: Crossway, 2001.

Creel, Richard E. *Divine Impassibility: An Essay in Philosophical Theology*. Cambridge: Cambridge University Press, 1986.

Cupitt, Don. *Taking Leave of God*. New York: Crossroad, 1981.

Davis, Stephen T. "Temporal Eternity." In *Philosophy of Religion: An Anthology*, 4th ed., edited by Louis P. Pojman, 209–16. Belmont, CA: Wadsworth, 2003.

Dole, Andrew. "Cognitive Faculties, Cognitive Processes, and the Holy Spirit in Plantinga's Warrant Series." *Faith and Philosophy* 19, no. 1 (2002): 32–46.

Dooyeweerd, Herman. *A New Critique of Theoretical Thought*. Edited by William S. Young. Translated by David H. Freeman. Nutley, NJ: Presbyterian and Reformed, 1969.

Dowey, Edward A. *The Knowledge of God in Calvin's Theology*. Expanded edition. Grand Rapids, MI: Eerdmans, 1994.

Drange, Theodore M. "Incompatible-Properties Arguments: A Survey." In *The Impossibility of God*, edited by Michael Martin, 185–97. Amherst, NY: Prometheus, 2003.

Eckhart, Meister. *Meister Eckhart*. Translated by C. de B. Evans. London: John M. Watkins, 1924.

Feinberg, John S. " 'And the Atheist Shall Lie Down with the Calvinist': Atheism, Calvinism, and the Free Will Defense." *Trinity Journal* 1, no. 2 (Fall 1980): 142–52.

Fischer, John Martin. "Freedom and Actuality." In *Divine and Human Action: Essays in the Metaphysics of Theism*, edited by Thomas V. Morris, 236–54. Ithaca, NY and London: Cornell University Press, 1988.

Ganssle, Gregory E., and David M. Woodruff. *God and Time: Essays on the Divine Nature*. Oxford: Oxford University Press, 2002.

Gaskin, J. C. A. *Dialogues and Natural History of Religion*. Oxford: Oxford University Press, 1993.

Gettier, Edmund. "Is Justified True Belief Knowledge." *Analysis* 23 (1963): 121–23.

Gilson, Etienne. *The Christian Philosophy of St. Thomas Aquinas. With a Catalog of St. Thomas's Works*. New York: Random House, 1956.

Gutenson, Charles. "Can Belief in the Christian God Be Properly Basic? A Pannenbergian Perspective on Plantinga and Basic Beliefs." *Christian Scholar's Review* 29, no. 1 (1999): 49–72.

Helm, Paul. *Faith and Reason*. Oxford Readers. Oxford: Oxford University Press, 1999.

————. *John Calvin's Ideas*. Oxford: Oxford University Press, 2004.

Hodge, Charles. *Commentary on the Epistle to the Romans*. Grand Rapids, MI: Eerdmans, 1994.

Hughes, Christopher. *Kripke: Names, Necessity and Identity*. Oxford: Clarendon Press, 2004.

Hume, David. *Enquiries Concerning the Human Understanding and Concerning the Principles of Morals*. 2nd ed. Oxford: Clarendon Press, 1902.

Hunt, David P. "On Augustine's Way Out." *Faith and Philosophy* 16, no. 1 (January 1999): 3–26.

Israel, Jonathan Irvine. *Radical Enlightenment: Philosophy and the Making of Modernity, 1650–1750*. Oxford: Oxford University Press, 2001.

Kant, Immanuel. *Critique of Pure Reason*. Translated by Norman Kemp Smith. New York: St. Martin's, 1958.

Kenny, Anthony John Patrick. "Omniscience, Eternity, and Time." In *The Impossibility of God*, edited by Michael Martin, 210–19. Amherst, NY: Prometheus, 2003.

Klement, Kevin C. *Gottlob Frege (1848–1925)*. The Internet Encyclopedia of Philosophy. www.iep.utm.edu.

Kooi, Cornelis van der. "The Assurance of Faith. A Theme in Reformed Dogmatics in Light of Alvin Plantinga's Epistemology." *Neue Zeitschrift Für Systematische Theologie und Religionsphilosophie* 40, no. 1 (1998): 91–106.

Kretzmann, Norman. "Omniscience and Immutability." In *The Impossibility of God*, edited by Michael Martin, 198–209. Amherst, NY: Prometheus, 2003.

Kripke, Saul. *Naming and Necessity*. Cambridge, MA: Harvard University Press, 1982.

Kvanvig, Jonathan L. *Warrant and Contemporary Epistemology: Essays in Honor of Plantinga's Theory of Knowledge*. Lanham, MD: Rowman & Littlefield, 1996.

LaFollette, Hugh. "Plantinga on the Free Will Defense." In *The Impossibility of God*, edited by Michael Martin, 97–105. Amherst, NY: Prometheus, 2003.

Le Morvan, Pierre, and Dana Radcliffe. "Plantinga on Warranted Christian Belief." *Heythrop* 44, no. 3 (2003): 345–51.

Leftow, Brian. "A Timeless God Incarnate." In *The Incarnation*, edited by Stephen T. Davis, Daniel Kendall, and Gerald O'Collins, 273–99. Oxford: Oxford University Press, 2002.

Leibniz, Gottfried Wilhelm, and Austin Marsden Farrer. *Theodicy: Essays on the Goodness of God, the Freedom of Man, and the Origin of Evil*. London: Routledge & K. Paul, 1952.

Lévinas, Emmanuel, and Seán Hand. *The Levinas Reader*. New York: B.Blackwell, 1989.

Loux, Michael J. "Essentialism." In *The Cambridge Dictionary of Philosophy*, edited by Robert Audi, 241–43. Cambridge: Cambridge University Press, 1995.

MacDonald, Scott. "Theory of Knowledge." In *The Cambridge Companion to Aquinas*, edited by Norman Kretzmann and Eleanor Stump, 160–95. Cambridge: Cambridge University Press, 1993.

Malcolm, Norman. "The Groundlessness of Belief." In *Philosophy of Religion: An Anthology*, 4th ed., edited by Louis P. Pojman, 391–99. Belmont, CA: Wadsworth, 2003.

Mann, William E. "God's Freedom, Human Freedom, and God's Responsibility for Sin." In *Divine and Human Action: Essays in the Metaphysics of Theism*, edited by Thomas V. Morris, 182–210. Ithaca, NY: Cornell University Press, 1988.

Marion, Jean-Luc. *God without Being: Hors-Texte*. Translated by Thomas A. Carlson. Chicago: University of Chicago Press, 1991.

———. "Is the Ontological Argument Ontological: The Argument according to Anselm and Its Metaphysical Interpretation according to Kant." *Journal of the History of Philosophy* 30, no. 2 (April 1992): 201–18.

———. "Metaphysics and Phenomenology: A Theological Reader." In *The Postmodern God*, edited by Graham Ward, 279–96. Malden, MA: Blackwell, 1997.

Marsden, George. "The Collapse of American Evangelical Academia." In *Faith and Rationality*, edited by Alvin Plantinga and Nicholas Wolterstorff, 219–64. Notre Dame, IN: University of Notre Dame Press, 1983.

Mavrodes, George I. "How Does God Know the Things He Knows?" In *Divine and Human Action: Essays in the Metaphysics of Theism*, edited by Thomas V. Morris, 345–61. Ithaca, NY: Cornell University Press, 1988.

———. "Self-Referential Incoherence." *American Philosophical Quarterly* 22, no. 1 (January 1985): 65–72.

McLaughlin, Brian P. "Exploring the Possibility of Self-Deception in Belief." In *Perspectives on Self-Deception*, edited by Brian P. McLaughlin and Amelie Oksenberg Rorty, 29–62. Berkeley: University of California Press, 1988.

McLeod, Mark S. "The Analogy Argument for the Proper Basicality of Belief in God." *International Journal for Philosophy of Religion* 21 (1987): 3–20.

Meek, Esther L. *Longing to Know*. Grand Rapids, MI: Brazos, 2003.

Morris, Thomas V. *The Logic of God Incarnate*. Ithaca, NY: Cornell University Press, 1986.

Muller, Richard A. *Post-Reformation Reformed Dogmatics: Prolegomena to Theology*. Grand Rapids, MI: Baker, 1987.

———. *Post-Reformation Reformed Dogmatics: The Rise and Development of Reformed Orthodoxy, Ca. 1520 to Ca. 1725: The Divine Essence and Attributes*. 2nd ed. Grand Rapids, MI: Baker, 2002.

———. *Post-Reformation Reformed Dogmatics: The Rise and Development of Reformed Orthodoxy, Ca. 1520 to Ca. 1725: The Triunity of God*. Grand Rapids, MI: Baker, 2003.

Oliphint, K. Scott. *The Battle Belongs to the Lord: The Power of Scripture for Defending Our Faith*. Phillipsburg, NJ: P&R, 2003.

———. "The Consistency of Van Til's Methodology." *Westminster Theological Journal* 52, no. 2 (Spring 1990): 27–49.

———. "Epistemology and Christian Belief." *Westminster Theological Journal* 63, no. 1 (Spring 2001): 151–82.

———. "The Irrationality of Unbelief." In *Revelation and Reason: New Essays in Reformed Apologetics*, edited by K. Scott Oliphint and Lane G. Tipton. Phillipsburg, NJ: P&R, forthcoming.

———. "Most Moved Mediator." *Themelios* 30, no. 1 (Autumn 2004): 39–51.

———. "Plantinga on Warrant." *Westminster Theological Journal* 57, no. 1 (Spring 1995): 81–102.

———. "Review of God and Time." *Westminster Theological Journal* 63, no. 2 (Fall 2001): 439–45.

Oliphint, K. Scott, and Lane G. Tipton, eds. *Revelation and Reason: New Essays in Reformed Apologetics.* Phillipsburg, NJ: P&R, forthcoming.

Owen, John. *The Works of John Owen.* Edited by W. H. Gould. Edinburgh: Banner of Truth, 1977.

Pinnock, Clark H. *Most Moved Mover: A Theology of God's Openness.* Grand Rapids, MI: Baker, 2001.

Pinnock, Clark H., et al. *The Openness of God: A Biblical Challenge to the Traditional Understanding of God.* Downers Grove, IL: InterVarsity, 1994.

Plantinga, Alvin. "Actualism and Possible Worlds." *Theoria* 42 (1976): 139–60.

———. "Advice to Christian Philosophers." *Faith and Philosophy* 1, no. 3 (1984): 253–71.

———. *The Analytic Theist: A Collection of Alvin Plantinga's Work in Philosophy of Religion.* Edited by James F. Sennett. Grand Rapids, MI: Eerdmans, 1998.

———. "Divine Knowledge." In *Christian Perspectives on Religious Knowledge*, edited by C. Stephen Evans, Merold Westphal, 40–65. Grand Rapids, MI: Eerdmans, 1993.

———. "Does God Have a Nature?" In *The Analytic Theist: An Alvin Plantinga Reader*, edited by James F. Sennett, 225–57. Grand Rapids, MI: Eerdmans, 1998.

———. *God and Other Minds: A Study of the Rational Justification of Belief in God.* Ithaca, NY: Cornell University Press, 1972.

———. *God, Freedom, and Evil.* New York: Harper & Row, 1974.

———. *The Nature of Necessity.* Clarendon Library of Logic and Philosophy. Oxford: Clarendon Press, 1974.

———. "On Ockham's Way Out." In *The Analytic Theist: A Collection of Alvin Plantinga's Work in Philosophy of Religion*, edited by James F. Sennett, 258–92. Grand Rapids, MI: Eerdmans, 1998.

———. "Rationality and Religious Belief." In *Contemporary Philosophy of Religion*, edited by Stephen M. Cahn and David Shatz, 255–77. New York: Oxford University Press, 1982.

————. "Reason and Belief in God." In *Faith and Rationality*, edited by Alvin Plantinga and Nicholas Wolterstorff, 16–93. Notre Dame, IN: University of Notre Dame Press, 1983.

————. "Supralapsarianism, or 'O Felix Culpa.' " In *Christian Faith and the Problem of Evil*, edited by Peter van Inwagen, 1–25. Grand Rapids, MI: Eerdmans, 2004.

————. *Warrant and Proper Function*. Oxford: Oxford University Press, 1993.

————. *Warranted Christian Belief*. Oxford: Oxford University Press, 2000.

Plato. *Euthyphro, Apology, Crito, Phaedo, Phaedrus*. The Loeb Classical Library. Translated by H. N. Fowler. New York: Macmillan, 1913.

Reid, Thomas, Ronald E. Beanblossom, and Keith Lehrer. *Thomas Reid's Inquiry and Essays*. Indianapolis: Hackett, 1983.

Reiter, David. "Calvin's 'Sense of Divinity' and Externalist Knowledge of God." *Faith and Philosophy* 15, no. 3 (1998): 253–70.

Ritschl, Albrecht, H. R. Mackintosh, and A. B. Macaulay. *The Christian Doctrine of Justification and Reconciliation: The Positive Development of the Doctrine*. Edinburgh: T.&T. Clark, 1900.

Ross, James F. "God, Creator of Kinds and Possibilities: Requiescant Universalia Ante Res." In *Rationality, Religious Belief, and Moral Commitment*, edited by Robert Audi, William J. Wainwright, 315–34. Ithaca, NY: Cornell University Press, 1986.

Runzo, Joseph, and Graig K. Ihara, eds. *Religious Experience and Religious Belief: Essays in the Epistemology of Religion*. Lanham, MD: University Press of America, 1986.

Russell, Bertrand. *Logic and Knowledge: Essays, 1901–1950*. New York: Macmillan, 1956.

————. *Mysticism and Logic and Other Essays*. London: George Allen & Unwin, 1917.

Schleiermacher, Friedrich, and Frederica Rowan. *The Life of Schleiermacher as Unfolded in His Autobiography and Letters*. London: Smith Elder and Co., 1860.

Schrag, Calvin O. *God Otherwise than Being*. Evanston, IL: Northwestern University Press, 2002.

Sennett, James F. *Modality, Probability, and Rationality: A Critical Examination of Alvin Plantinga's Philosophy*. New York: Peter Lang, 1992.

———. "Why Think There Are Any True Counterfactuals of Freedom?" *Philosophy of Religion* 32 (1992): 105–16.

Sobel, Jordan Howard. *Logic and Theism: Arguments for and against Beliefs in God.* Cambridge: Cambridge University Press, 2004.

Sosa, Ernest. "The Raft and the Pyramid: Coherence versus Foundations in the Theory of Knowledge." In *Knowledge in Perspective: Selected Essays in Epistemology*, edited by Ernest Sosa, 165–91. Cambridge: Cambridge University Press, 1991.

Stoker, Hendrik G. *Oorsprong en Rigting.* Kaapstad: Tafelberg-Uitgewers, 1970.

———. "Reconnoitering the Theory of Knowledge of Professor Dr. Cornelius Van Til." In *Jerusalem and Athens: Critical Discussions on the Theology and Apologetics of Cornelius Van Til*, edited by E. R. Geehan, 25–71. Nutley, NJ: Presbyterian and Reformed, 1971.

Stump, Eleonore. *Aquinas.* New York: Routledge, 2003.

———. "Aquinas' Metaphysics of the Incarnation." In *The Incarnation*, edited by Stephen T. Davis, Daniel Kendall, and Gerald O'Collins, 197–218. Oxford: Oxford University Press, 2002.

———. "Revelation and Biblical Exegesis." In *Reason and the Christian Religion: Essays in Honour of Richard Swinburne*, ed. Alan G. Padgett and Richard Swinburne, 161–98. Oxford: Clarendon Press; Oxford University Press, 1994.

Sudduth, Michael C. "Can Religious Unbelief Be Proper Function Rational?" *Faith and Philosophy* 16, no. 3 (July 1999): 297–314.

Swinburne, Richard. *The Coherence of Theism.* Rev. ed. Oxford: Clarendon Press; Oxford University Press, 1993.

Tomberlin, James E., and Peter van Inwagen, eds. *Alvin Plantinga.* Dordrecht: D. Reidel, 1985.

Turretin, Francis. *Institutes of Elenctic Theology.* Edited by James T. Dennison Jr. Translated by George Musgrave Giger. 3 vols. Phillipsburg, NJ: P&R, 1992–97.

van Asselt, Willem J. "The Fundamental Meaning of Theology: Archetypal and Ectypal Theology in Seventeenth-Century Reformed Thought." *Westminster Theological Journal* 64, no. 2 (Fall 2002): 319–36.

van Asselt, Willem J., J. M. Bac, and R. T. te Velde. *Reformed Thought on Freedom: The Concept of Free Choice in the History of Early-Modern Reformed Theology.* Utrecht: Research Group Classic Reformed Theology, forthcoming.

van Inwagen, Peter. *Metaphysics*. 2nd ed. Dimensions of Philosophy Series. Boulder, CO: Westview, 2002.

———. *Ontology, Identity, and Modality: Essays in Metaphysics*. Cambridge: Cambridge University Press, 2001.

Van Til, Cornelius. "Nature and Scripture." In *The Infallible Word: A Symposium by the Members of the Faculty of Westminster Theological Seminary*, 2nd edition, edited by N. B. Stonehouse and Paul Woolley, 263–301. Philadelphia: Presbyterian and Reformed, 1967.

———. *The Works of Cornelius Van Til*. CD-ROM. New York: Labels Army Co., 1997.

Weinandy, Thomas G. *Does God Suffer?* Notre Dame, IN: University of Notre Dame Press, 2000.

Westphal, Merold. "Taking St. Paul Seriously: Sin as an Epistemological Category." In *Christian Philosophy*, edited by Thomas P. Flint, 200–26. Notre Dame, IN: Notre Dame Press, 1990.

Willard, Julian. "Plantinga's Epistemology of Religious Belief and the Problem of Religious Diversity." *Heythrop* 44, no. 3 (2003): 275–93.

Williams, Michael. *Groundless Belief: An Essay on the Possibility of Epistemology*. 2nd ed. Princeton, NJ: Princeton University Press, 1999.

Wolterstorff, Nicholas. "God Everlasting." In *God and the Good: Essays in Honor of Henry Stob*, edited by Henry Stob, Clifton Henry, and Lewis B. Smedes, 181–203. Grand Rapids, MI: Eerdmans, 1975.

———. "In Defense of Guanilo's Defense of the Fool." In *Christian Perspectives on Religious Knowledge*, edited by C. Stephen Evans and Merold Westphal, 87–111. Grand Rapids, MI: Eerdmans, 1993.

Wright, N. T. "Jesus' Self-Understanding." In *The Incarnation*, edited by Stephen T. Davis, Daniel Kendall, and Gerald O'Collins, 47–63. Oxford: Oxford University Press, 2002.

Index of Subjects and Names

K. Scott Oliphint (M.A.R., Th.M., Ph.D., Westminster Theological Seminary) is professor of apologetics and systematic theology at Westminster Seminary, Philadelphia. He has written numerous journal articles in the field of apologetics, is the author of *The Battle Belongs to the Lord: The Power of Scripture for Defending Our Faith*, and is coeditor of *Revelation and Reason: New Essays in Reformed Apologetics*.